CROSS
SOL

CROSSWORD SOLVER

Compiled by Elaine Henderson

This is a Parragon Book
This edition published in 2004

Parragon
Queen Street House
4 Queen Street
Bath BA1 1HE
UK

Produced by Magpie Books, an imprint of
Constable & Robinson Ltd, London

Cover courtesy of Simon Levy

ISBN 1-40541-989-X

A copy of the British Library Cataloguing-in-Publication Data
is available from the British Library

Printed and bound in the EU

Contents

Contents

Introduction

Crossword Solver is very simple to use and is guaranteed to help you increase your success rate fast. We've arranged the words to help you find what you need within seconds. If you want to find words simply by word length, turn to Section 1. If you want to find them according to subject, then Section 2 includes a wide range of topics to help you out. If you need an anagram, Section 3 is the quick and easy way to get one.

As a quick and easy reference, here are the three sections and what they include:

- Section 1 lists words alphabetically and according to the number of letters they contain, to help you to fill in the blanks on a crossword grid.
- Section 2 lists words alphabetically and by word length, under a range of subject headings such as Film, Theatre, TV and Radio, Planets and their Satellites and Rulers of the UK.
- Section 3 is a list of anagrams arranged according to word length.

Section 1

2

aa
ad
ai
as
ba
bo
do
el
em
en
fa
gu
ha
id
la
li
ma
me
mi
mu
no
or
os
ox
oz
pa
pi
ra
re
si
so
ta
ti
us
ut
va
we
ya
ye
za
zo

3

aam
aba
abb
ace
act
add
ads
adz
aft
aga
age
ago
air
aka
alb
ale
alp
alt
amp
ant
ape
arc
are
ark
arm
art
ash
asp
ass
auk
ave
awl
awn
axe
ayn
bac
bag
bap
bar
bat
bay
bed
bee
bel
ben
bet
bey
bib
bid
bin
bis
bit
boa
bob
bog
bok
bom
bop
bot
bow
box
bra
bub
bud
bug
bun
bus
buy
bye
cab
cad
cam
can
cap
car
cat
cay
cha
cid
cob
cod
cog
col
com
con
cor
cos
cot
cow
cox
cub
cud
cue
cup
cur
cut
cwm
cwt
dab
dad
dag
dai
dam
dan
dar
daw
day
deb
die
dig
doc
doe
dog
doh
don
dop
dor
dry
dub
dud
dun
duo
dzo
ear
ebb
ecu
eel
eft
egg
ego
elf
elk
ell
elm
emu
end
eon
era
erg
ewe
eye
fag
fah
fan
far
fat
fax
fay
fee
fen
feu
fez
fid
fig
fin
fir
fit
flu
fly
foe
fog
fop
fou
fox
fry
fum
fun
fur
gab
gad
gag
gap
gar
gas
ged
gel
gem
gib
gig
gin
gnu
goa
gue
gum
gun
gut
guy
gym
gyp
hag
haj
ham
hat
haw
hay
hem
hen
hep
hin
hip
hit
hob
hod
hoe
hog
hop
hoy
hub
hue
hum
hut
ice
icy
ide
imp
ink
inn
ion
ita
ivy
jam
jar
jaw
jay
jet
jib
jig
jim
job
jog
jug
kaa
kae
kaf
kat
kea
keg
ket
kex
key
kha
kia
kid
kin
kip
kir
kit
kob
kor

lab
lac
lad
lag
lah
lam
lap
lat
law
lay
lea
lee
lei
leu
lev
lid
lie
lip
lob
log
lot
low
lox
loy
lug
lux
lym
mac
mag
man
map
mat
may
men
mev
mew
mig
mil
mim
mix
mna
moa
mob
mog
moo
mop
mow
mud
mug
mum
mya
nag
nan
net
nib
nip
nit
niu
nog
now
nun
nut
oaf
oak
oar
oat
oca
ode
oft
ohm
oil
oka
oke
olm
oof
opt
orb
ore
out
ova
owe
owl
oxo
pad
pal
pan
pap
par
pas
pay
pea
ped
peg
pen
pet
pew
pic
pie
pig
pin
pip
pit
piu
ply
pod
poe
poi
pop
pot
pro
pub
pug
pun
pup
put
puy
pyx
qaf
rad
rag
rai
ram
rat
ray
red
ree
rei
rem
rep
ret
rev
ria
rib
rig
rim
rob
roc
rod
roe
roo
rub
ruc
rue
rug
rum
run
rye
sad
sag
sai
sal
sap
sar
saw
sax
sea
see
sei
sen
set
sex
she
sho
sin
sir
sit
ski
soh
sol
son
sot
sou
sow
soy
spa
spy
sty
sub
sue
sum
sun
tab
tag
tai
tam
tan
tap
tar
tau
taw
tax
tea
ted
tee
teg
tha
tie
tin
tip
tit
tod
tog
tom
ton
top
tor
tot
tow
toy
try
tub
tug
tui
tun
tup
tux
ure
urn
use
uva
vag
van
vat
vei
vet
vin
voe
vow
vox
wad
wag
wah
war
wat
waw
way
web
wet
wey
wig
win
wit
wok
won
yak
yam
yaw
yen
yew
yin
yob
you
zac
zax
zay
zea
zel
zho
zip
zuz

4
abba
abbé
aber
abet
acer
ache
acid
acne
acre
adit
adze
aeon
ages
agon
ahoy
aide
airy
akee
alca
alfa
alif
alla
ally
alma
alms
aloe
alto
alum
ambo
amen
amia
amla
amm
a
ammo
anal
anas
anna
anoa
anta
anus
apex
apod
apse
arak
arar
arch
arco
area
aria
arid
aril
arms
army
arna
arts
arum
atap
atoc
atok
atom
aunt
auto
avel
aves
axes
axis
axle
axon
ayah
ayes
ayre
babe
baby
back
bael
baht
bait
bake
bale
ball
balm
band
bang
bank
barb
bard
bark
barn
bars
base
bass
bath
bawn
baya
bead
beam
bean
bear
beat
beau
beck
beef
beer
beet
beka
bell
belt
bend
bent
bere
berm
bhel
bias
biga
bike
bile
bill
bind
bird
bite
bito
bixa
blay
bley
blue
boar
boat
bock
body
boil
bold
bole
boll
bolt
bomb
bond
bone
book
boom
boon
boor
boot
bore
bort
boss
boud
bowl
bows
brag
bran
bret
brie
brig
brim
brio
bris
brit
brut
bubo
buck
bulb
bulk
bull
bump
bunk
bunt
buoy
burn
burr
burt
bush
busk
buss
bust
butt
buzz
byre
byte
cade
cadi
café
cage
cake
cale
calf
calk
call
calm
calx
camp
cane
cant
cape
caps
carp
cart
case
cash
cask
cast
cate
cauk
caul
cave
cavy
cell
celt
cent
cess
chad
chap
char
chat
chef
chic
chip
chop
chou
chow
chub
chum
cist
city
clam
clan
clap
claw
clay
clef
cleg
clio
clip
clog
club
coal
coat
cock
coda
code
coed
coho
coif
coil
coin
coir
coke
cole
colt
comb
comp
cone
cony
cook
cool
coon
coot
cope
copy
cord
cork
corm
corn
cosh
coss
cost
cosy
cote
cott
coue
coup
cove
cowl
crab
crag
cran
crax
crew
crib
crop
crow
croy
cube
cuff
culm
cult
curb
curd
curé
cusk
cusp
cyan
cyst
czar
dace
dada
dado
dais
dale

dali
dame
damp
daps
dare
darg
dari
dart
dash
data
date
daub
daum
dawm
dawn
deal
dean
dear
debt
deck
deed
deer
dell
demy
desk
dhai
dhak
dhow
dial
dice
dieb
digs
dike
dill
dime
dirk
disc
dish
disk
diss
diva
dive
dock
dodo
doer
doge
dogo
dogy
dohl
doit
dole
doll
dolt
dome
doob
door
dopa
dorn
dory
douc
dove
down
doxy
drag
drah
dram
draw
dray
drey
drip
drop
drum
dual
duan
duce
duck
dude
duds
duel
dues
duet
duke
dull
dump
dune
dung
dupe
dura
duro
dust
duty
dyer
dyke
dyne
earl
earn
east
easy
echo
eddy
edge
edit
ekka
elva
emir
emys
enty
epée
epha
epic
epos
erne
eruv
esox
etch
etui
euro
even
ever
evet
evil
ewer
exam
exit
eyas
eyot
eyra
face
fair
fall
fare
farm
faro
fash
fast
fawn
feed
fees
feet
felt
fend
fern
fess
fife
file
film
fine
fino
fire
firm
fisc
fish
fizz
flag
flak
flan
flap
flat
flaw
flea
flip
flop
flow
flue
flux
foal
foam
foci
foil
fold
folk
font
food
fool
foot
ford
fore
fork
form
fort
foul
four
fowl
fray
free
fret
frit
frog
frow
fuel
fund
fung
funk
furl
fuse
gaff
gage
gain
gait
gala
gale
gall
galt
game
gang
gaol
gape
garb
gate
gaud
gaur
gawk
gear
gene
germ
gest
ghee
gier
gild
gill
gilt
girl
giro
girt
glee
glen
glue
glut
gnat
goad
goal
goat
goby
gods
goer
gold
golf
gong
good
gown
grab
gram
grid
grig
grip
grit
grog
grot
grub
guan
gulf
gull
guni
gust
gyal
hack
hadj
haha
hail
hair
haji
hake
half
hall
halo
halt
hand
hank
hard
hare
harl
harp
hart
hash
hasp
hath
haul
haum
hawk
haze
hazy
head
heap
heat
heel
heir
hell
helm
heml
hemp
herb
herd
hern
hero
hick
hide
hi-fi
high
hill
hind

hink
hire
hobo
hock
hold
holm
holt
holy
home
hood
hoof
hook
hoot
hops
horn
hose
host
hour
hove
huck
huia
hula
hulk
hull
huma
hunt
hura
husk
huso
hymn
iamb
ibex
ibis
icon
idle
idol
idyl
ikon
ilex
imam
inch
iris
iron
isle
iunx
ixia
jack
jade
jail
jamb
jazz
jeep
jill
jilt
jive
joey
joke
jomo
jota
jowl
judo
juke
junk
jury
jute
kaka
kaki
kale
kali
kame
kara
keel
keep
kela
kelt
kent
kepi
kesh
keta
keto
khan
kick
kill
kiln
kilo
kilt
kina
kine
king
kiri
kirk
kite
kith
kiwi
knar
knot
knur
koel
koff
kola
kora
koss
koto
kran
kris
kudu
kufi
kuku
kyat
lace
lady
lake
lakh
lama
lamb
lamé
lamp
lana
land
lane
lard
lark
lass
last
late
lath
lava
lawn
lead
leaf
lean
leek
left
lema
lend
lens
levy
liar
lice
lien
life
lift
lilt
lily
lima
limb
lime
limn
limo
limp
line
ling
link
lion
lipp
lira
lire
list
live
load
loaf
loam
loan
loch
loci
lock
loco
lode
loft
logo
loin
lomp
long
loof
loom
loon
loop
loot
lord
lory
loss
lote
lout
love
luce
ludo
luff
luge
lung
lush
lute
lyme
lynx
lyre
mace
mach
maid
mail
main
mako
male
mall
malm
malt
mam
a
mara
mare
mark
marl
mart
mash
mask
mass
mast
masu
mate
maté
math
maul
mawk
mawl
maze
mead
meal
mean
meat
meet
menu
mere
merk
mesa
mesh
mess
meta
mews
mica
mice
mico
mida
mild
mile
milk
mill
mime
mina
mine
mini
mink
mint
minx
miss
mist
mite
mitt
moat
mode
mohr
moio
moke
moki
mole
moly
mome
mona
monk
mood
moon
moor
mora
morn
mort
moss
moth
move
mowa
mudd
muff
muid
mule
mull
mush
musk
mute
mutt
myna
myth
naan
naff
naga
naia
nail
nard
nave
navy
naze
neap
neat
neck
neep

nene
neon
ness
nett
neum
news
newt
nias
nide
nipa
node
noes
nook
noon
nose
note
noun
nout
nova
nowt
nude
nyas
oars
oast
oath
oats
oboe
obol
odal
odds
oder
ogee
ogre
oils
oily
okia
okra
omer
once
onyx
onza
oont
opah
opal
open
opus
orca
orfe
orle
oryx
otis
ouch
ouzo
oven
ovum
owed
oxen
paal
paca
pace
pack
paco
pact
page
paid
pail
pain
pair
pale
pall
palm
paly
pama
pane
papa
pard
pare
park
parr
part
paso
pass
past
pâté
path
pauw
pave
pavo
pawl
pawn
peag
peak
peal
pean
pear
peas
peat
peba
peck
peel
peer
pelt
peon
perl
pern
peso
pest
phon
phot
pica
pice
pick
pier
piet
pika
pike
pile
pimp
pine
ping
pink
pint
pipa
pipe
pipi
pith
pium
plan
play
plea
plot
plow
plug
plum
plus
poco
poem
poet
pogo
poke
pole
polk
poll
polo
polt
poly
pome
pond
pone
pony
pood
pool
poop
pope
pore
pork
port
pose
post
pour
pout
prad
pram
pray
prig
prop
prow
puff
puja
puli
pull
puma
pump
pund
punk
punt
pupa
push
puss
puxi
quab
quad
quay
quey
quip
quit
quiz
rabi
race
rack
raft
raid
raik
rail
rain
rake
raki
ramp
rana
rand
rank
rape
rare
rash
rasp
rata
rate
raun
rays
raze
real
ream
rear
reed
reef
reel
reid
rent
resp
rest
rhea
rial
rice
ride
riel
rill
rime
rimu
ring
rink
riot
risk
rite
rixy
road
roan
robe
roch
rock
role
roll
rood
roof
rook
room
root
rope
rose
rôti
rotl
roué
roup
rout
roux
rove
rube
ruby
rudd
ruff
ruin
rukh
rule
rump
rune
rung
runn
runt
rusa
ruse
rush
rusk
rust
ryal
ryot
rype
sack
safe
saga
sage
sago
saic
sail
sake
saki
sale
salt
sand
sang
sapo
sari
sash
sauk
save
sawm
scab
scad
scan
scar
scot
scud

scup
seah
seal
seam
sear
seat
sect
seed
seer
sego
self
sell
semé
semi
seps
sere
serf
sewn
sext
shad
shag
shah
shaw
shed
shin
ship
shoe
shop
shot
show
sial
sice
side
sift
sign
silk
sill
silo
sima
sine
sing
sink
sire
site
skeg
skep
skid
skin
skip
skis
skit
skua
skug
slag
slam
slat
slay
sled
slip
slit
slob
sloe
slow
slue
slug
slur
slut
smee
smew
smog
snap
snig
snob
snow
snub
soak
soap
sock
soda
sofa
soil
sold
sole
solo
sone
song
soon
sora
sorb
sord
sore
sort
soul
soup
soya
spam
span
spar
spat
spin
spit
spot
spud
spur
stag
star
stay
stem
step
stet
stew
stoa
stop
stot
stud
stum
stye
suet
suit
sump
surf
swab
swan
swig
swim
swot
tace
tack
tael
taha
tahr
tail
taka
take
talc
tamp
tank
tant
tape
taps
tare
tarn
taro
tart
taut
taxi
teak
teal
team
teff
tegg
tehr
teil
temp
tend
term
tern
test
text
thea
them
then
thug
tick
tide
tige
tike
tile
till
tilt
time
tint
tire
titi
toad
tody
toff
toft
toga
togs
tola
toll
tomb
tone
tool
tope
topi
torc
tore
torr
tort
tory
toss
tote
tour
tout
town
tram
trap
tray
tree
tret
trey
trim
trio
trip
trot
troy
trug
tsar
tuba
tube
tufa
tuff
tump
tuna
tune
turf
turn
turr
tusk
tutu
twig
twin
twit
tyke
type
tyre
tyro
udal
ugli
ulex
ulna
unau
unik
unio
unit
ural
urdé
urea
urus
urva
user
utas
vair
vale
vamp
vane
vara
vase
veal
veer
vega
veil
vein
vend
vent
verb
vert
vest
veto
vice
vill
vina
vine
vint
viol
vira
vivo
voce
void
vola
vole
volt
vote
vows
vyse
wadi
waft
wage
waif
wain
wair
wake
wald
walk
wall
wapp
ward
warm
warp
wash
wasp
watt
wave
wavy
weak
wean
wear
weed

week
weft
weir
weld
west
when
whey
whig
whim
whip
wick
wide
wife
will
wilt
wind
wine
wing
wino
wire
woad
wold
wolf
wood
woof
wool
word
work
worm
wort
wrap
wren
writ
wynd
xema
xyst
yale
yang
yard
yarn
yaup
yawl
yean
year
yite
yoga
yogi
yolk
yomp
yore
york
yo-yo
yuan
yunx
zack
zant
zati
zebu
zend
zero
zimb
zinc
zobo
zone
zoom

5

aback
abaft
abbey
abbot
abeam
abele
ablen
ablet
abode
aboma
A-bomb
abort
abyss
acera
acorn
actor
acuta
acute
adapt
adays
addax
adder
adept
ad-lib
ad-man
aegis
affix
afore
afoul
after
again
agama
agami
agape
agate
agave
agent
agila
aglet
agora
aguti
ahead
ahull
aider
aioli
airer
aisle
ajuru
akita
albin
album
alder
aldol
alert
algae
alias
alibi
alien
alkyl
alley
allis
alloy
almud
aloes
aloft
altar
alway
amber
ameer
amend
amice
amide
amine
amino
ammon
amsel
amuse
amzel
angel
angle
anion
anise
anker
annex
anode
anole
anona
anura
anvil
aorta
apeak
aphid
aphis
apode
aport
apple
apron
araba
arack
arbor
ardea
ardeb
areca
arena
arête
argil
argon
ariel
armed
armor
arnot
arras
array
arris
arrow
arsis
arson
artic
aside
aspen
asper
aspic
assai
asset
aster
atlas
atoll
atone
at par
atrip
attic
audit
auger
aunty
aurei
auxin
avast
aviso
award
ayala
azote
azure
backs
bacon
badge
bahar
baign
bails
bairn

baize
bajra
bajri
baker
baler
baloo
balsa
balti
bandy
banjo
banns
banny
barca
barge
baria
baril
baron
barre
barry
basic
basil
basin
basso
basta
basto
batch
batel
batik
baton
bayed
bayou
beach
beads
beans
beard
beast
bebop
bedel
beech
beele
begum
beige
being
belay
belee
belga
belle
bells
below
bench
bendy
beret
beroe
berry
berth
beryl
beset
besom
betel
betso
betty
bevel
bezel
bhang
bibbs
biddy
bidet
bidon
bid up
bigha
bight
bigot
bijou
bilbo
bilge
bilts
bingo
binny
biome
biped
birch
birth
bison
bitch
biter
bitts
black
blade
blain
blare
blast
bleak
bleck
bleed
bless
blimp
blind
blini
blirt
blitz
block
blood
bloom
blues
bluff
blurb
board
bodhi
bogey
bogie
bogue
bohea
bolas
bombe
bonds
bones
bongo
bonus
booby
books
boole
boops
booth
boots
booty
borax
borer
boron
borsh
bosky
bosun
botel
bothy
boule
bower
bowet
bowle
bowls
bowse
boxer
boyar
boyer
brace
brach
bract
braid
brail
brain
brait
brake
brand
brant
brass
brawn
braxy
braze
bread
break
bream
brest
brett
breve
briar
bribe
brick
bride
brill
briny
briza
brize
broad
brock
broil
brook
broom
brose
broth
bruin
brush
brute
bucco
buggy
bugle
build
built
bulla
bully
bumbo
bunny
bunya
burin
burro
busby
butea
butte
buyer
buy in
buy up
bylaw
byrrh
cabin
cable
cacao
cache
caddy
cadet
cadre
cairn
cakes
calla
calve
calyx
camel
cameo
canal
candy
caneh
canis
canna
canoe
canon
canto
caper
caple
capoc
capon
capot
capul
carat
cards
caret
cargo
carob
carol
carse
carve
casal
casco
cased
catty
caulk
cause
cavie
cawny
cedar
cello
cells
cento
chads
chaff

chain
chair
chalk
chama
chang
chank
chant
chaps
chard
charr
chase
chasm
cheap
cheat
check
cheer
chela
cheng
chert
chess
chest
chiao
chica
chick
chief
child
chili
chill
chime
china
chine
chino
chips
chirm
chive
chock
choir
choke
choli
chord
chuck
chuff
chump
churl
churn
cider
cigar
cilia
cimex
cisco
civet
civil
claik
clamp
clams
clang
clank
clary
clasp
class
clean
clear
cleat
clerk
clevy
click
cliff
cline
cloak
clock
cloff
clogs
clone
close
closh
cloth
cloud
clout
clove
clown
clubs
clump
coach
coast
coati
cobia
coble
cobra
cocoa
codex
cohoe
coign
colin
colon
colza
combe
comet
comic
comma
compo
conch
coney
conga
congo
conic
conto
coomb
copec
coppy
copse
coral
corgi
corno
corps
cosec
costa
costs
cotan
cotta
couch
count
coupe
coupé
court
cover
coypu
craft
crake
cramp
crane
crank
crape
craps
crash
crate
creak
cream
credo
creed
creek
creel
creep
crêpe
cress
crest
crier
crime
crock
croft
croma
crone
crony
crook
croom
croon
crops
crore
cross
croup
crowd
crown
croze
cruet
cruse
crust
crypt
cubeb
cubic
cubit
cuddy
cudle
cueca
culex
culpa
cumin
cupel
cuppa
curds
curer
curia
curie
curio
curry
curve
cusec
cutin
cut in
cycad
cycle
cynic
daily
dairy
daisy
daker
daman
dance
danda
dandy
danio
dansa
daric
darts
dated
davit
death
debit
debug
debut
décor
decoy
deist
deity
delta
demob
demon
denim
depot
depth
deuce
devil
dhole
dicer
didus
digit
dilly
dinar
dingo
diode
diota
dirge
disco
ditch
ditty
divan
diver
dogie
dogma
doily
dolce
dolly
domed
donax
donna
donor
doree
dormy
dorny
dorse
doser
doter

dough
douse
dowel
downs
dowse
doyen
dozer
draco
draft
drain
drake
drama
drawn
dress
drier
drift
drill
drive
droll
drone
drove
drupe
druse
dry up
dsomo
ducat
duchy
dulse
dummy
dunce
dunny
duper
duple
durum
duvet
dwarf
eagle
early
earth
easel
eater
eaves
ebola
ebony
edict
egret
eider
eight
eland
elaps
elbow
elder
elect
elegy
elide
elops
elver
email
emery
emmer
emmet
enact
enemy
enrol
ensis
enter
entry
envoy
epact
ephah
ephod
epoch
epode
equal
equip
equus
erbia
erect
ergot
erica
erode
error
eruca
ervum
esker
essay
ester
ether
ethyl
etude
exalt
exile
exode
expel
extra
fable
fagus
faith
fakir
false
farad
farce
farcy
fault
fauna
feast
feint
felis
felly
felon
femur
fence
fermi
ferry
fesse
fibre
fichu
field
fiend
fifer
fifie
fight
filer
filet
filly
finch
fiord
firer
first
firth
fitch
fives
fjord
flail
flake
flame
flang
flank
flaps
flare
flash
flask
flats
fleam
fleck
fleet
flier
flies
fling
flint
flirt
float
flock
flong
flood
floor
flora
floss
flour
flows
fluid
fluke
flume
fluor
flush
flute
focal
focus
fogey
foggy
folio
foray
force
forge
forte
forum
fossa
fount
fovea
foyer
frame
franc
fraud
freak
freon
friar
frill
frock
front
frost
fruit
fudge
fugal
fugue
fundi
funds
fungi
furze
fusée
fusil
fusus
gable
gadus
galah
galea
galon
galop
gamba
gamin
gamut
ganza
gaper
garne
gauge
gauze
gavel
gayal
gazer
gebur
gecko
geese
genet
genre
genus
gerah
geste
get-up
ghayn
giant
gibel
gigot
gigue
gilet
gilts
gipsy
giver
glade
gland
glass
glaze
glede
glide
globe
glory
gloss
glove
gluer
glume
godly
gonad

goods
goose
goral
gorge
gorse
gouge
goura
gourd
gowan
grace
graft
grain
grant
grape
graph
grass
grate
grave
gravy
graze
grebe
green
grice
grill
gripe
grist
groat
groom
gross
group
grout
grove
gruel
guana
guano
guard
guava
guest
guide
guilt
gules
gully
gumbo
gummy
guppy
gusty
gutta
gypsy
gyron
habit
hafiz
haiku
halal
haler
halfa
halma
hands
haoma
hards
harem
harpy
harry
hatch
hater
haugh
haulm
haven
hawse
hazel
heart
heath
heavy
hedge
heels
hejab
helix
henna
henry
herbs
heron
hewer
hexad
hider
hijab
hiker
hilsa
hilum
hinge
hinny
hippo
hippy
hirer
hitch
hiver
hobby
hobit
hogan
hogen
hoist
hokum
holly
homer
honey
hooch
hoove
horal
horse
horst
hotel
hound
house
hovel
human
humor
humus
hurst
husky
hussy
hutia
hydra
hydro
hyena
hymen
hyrax
hyson
icing
ictus
idiom
idiot
idler
idyll
igloo
ileum
iliac
iliad
ilium
image
imago
incus
index
indri
infix
ingot
in-law
inlay
inlet
input
invar
ionic
irony
irroy
islet
issue
ivory
izard
jacks
jalap
japan
jeans
jelly
jemmy
jenny
jerid
jesse
jetty
jewel
jiboa
jiffy
jihad
jocko
joint
joist
joker
joram
jorum
joule
joust
judge
juice
julep
julis
julus
jumbo
junco
junta
juror
jutty
kaama
kaneh
kapok
karri
katti
kauri
kayak
kayle
kebab
kedge
kefir
kendo
ketch
kevel
keyed
key in
khaki
kilah
kiosk
kitty
knave
knead
knell
knife
knock
knoll
koala
koban
kopek
kraal
krait
krona
krone
kukri
kulak
kulan
kunai
kvass
kyloe
kyrie
label
ladle
lager
laird
laity
laker
lance
lande
lapel
larch
largo
larus
larva
laser
lasso
latch
later
latex
lathe
lathi
lauds
laver
lay-by

lay-to
lay up
l-dopa
leach
leads
leaky
lease
leash
leave
ledge
leech
legal
legua
lemma
lemon
lemur
lento
leper
levee
level
lever
liana
liang
liard
libel
libra
liege
ligan
light
ligne
lilac
limax
limbo
limey
limit
linen
liner
lines
links
lipid
lippy
lists
litas
litho
litre
liver
livre
llama
llano
loach
lobby
local
loche
locho
locum
locus
lodge
loess
logic
log in
log on
logos
lolly
loris
lorry
loser
lotto
lotus
lough
louis
loure
louse
lover
lowan
lucky
lumen
lumia
lunar
lunch
lungi
lupin
lupus
lurch
lymph
lyric
lyrie
lysol
macaw
macle
macro
madam
madge
magma
mahdi
maize
major
maker
mamba
mambo
mamma
maneh
mango
manis
manna
manse
manul
maple
maray
march
marsh
maser
masha
mason
match
mater
maths
matin
matzo
maund
mavis
maxim
mayor
mease
medal
medic
medio
melba
melee
melon
melts
mercy
merle
merry
meson
metal
metre
mezzo
mhoor
micro
midge
mimer
mimic
minah
mince
miner
minim
minor
minus
miser
misty
mitre
mitts
mixed
mixer
mobby
mocha
model
modem
mohar
mohel
mohur
moiré
molar
molto
monad
monal
money
monte
month
mooli
moose
moped
morat
moray
morel
moron
morse
mosso
motet
motif
motor
motto
mould
mound
mount
mouse
mouth
mover
movie
mower
mucus
mufti
muggy
mugil
mummy
mumps
mural
muray
murex
murre
murry
musca
muser
music
myall
mynah
myrrh
mysis
myxon
nabob
nacre
nadir
nagor
naiad
naker
nandu
nanny
nantz
nappe
nasal
nasty
naval
navvy
nawab
nebel
negus
neper
nerve
neume
never
newel
niche
niece
night
ninny
nitre
noble
nodal
noddy
nomad
nones
nonet
north
notes
novel
noyau
nurse
nyala
nylon
nymph

nyssa
oaken
oakum
oasis
obang
obolo
ocean
ochre
octal
octet
offer
often
ogive
ogler
oiler
okapi
okiya
olive
ombre
oncer
oncia
on cue
onion
onset
on tow
opera
opium
opt-in
orbit
order
organ
oribi
oriel
orient
orlop
ormer
ornis
ortyx
osier
otary
otter
ounce
ousel
ouzel
ovary
ovine
ovule
owing
owler
owlet
owner
ox-eye
ox-fly
oxide
oxlip
ozone
pacer
pacha
paddy
padre
paean
pagan
pahul
paint
palas
pally
panch
panda
paned
panel
panga
panic
pansy
pants
paolo
papal
papaw
paper
parer
parka
parry
parse
party
pasha
pasta
paste
pasty
paten
pater
patin
patio
patsy
patty
pause
pavan
payee
payer
peace
peach
pearl
pease
peavy
pecan
pecul
pedal
pekan
pekoe
penal
pence
pengo
penis
penny
peony
perai
perca
perch
perry
petal
peuce
pewee
pewit
phage
phase
pheon
phlox
phoca
photo
phula
piano
picea
picul
picus
pi-dog
piece
piede
pieno
piety
pilaf
pilau
pilaw
piler
piles
pilot
pinna
pinon
pinta
pin-up
pious
piper
pipit
pique
piqué
piste
pitch
pitta
pivot
pixel
pizza
plack
plaid
plain
plane
plank
plant
plate
plead
pleat
plonk
plumb
plume
plush
plyer
poach
poaka
poesy
pogge
point
poise
poker
polar
polio
polka
polyp
pongo
pooch
poppy
porer
porgy
poser
posse
potto
pouch
poulp
poult
pound
powan
power
prahu
prawn
preen
press
price
prick
prime
primo
print
prion
prior
prise
prism
prize
probe
prong
proof
props
prore
prose
prove
proxy
prude
prune
pryer
psalm
psoas
pubic
pubis
pugil
puker
pulex
pulka
pulse
pumps
punch
pupil
puppy
purée
purge
purre
purse
pussy
putty
pygmy
pylon
qirat
quack
quail
quart
quash
quass
queen

queer
quern
query
queue
quick
quill
quilt
quina
quire
quits
quoif
quoin
quoll
quota
quote
rabbi
racer
radar
radge
radii
radio
radix
radon
rails
rainy
rajah
raker
rally
ramus
ranch
range
ranks
ratch
ratel
rater
rates
ratha
ratio
raven
raver
rayon
razee
razor
rebec
rebel
rebus
recce
recto
redox
reeds
reeve
refit
regal
reign
reiki
reins
relay
relic
remit
renal
repay
repel
reset
resin
reuse
rev up
revel
revue
rheum
rhino
rhumb
rhyme
ribes
rider
ridge
rifle
right
rigid
rival
river
rivet
roach
roast
robin
roble
rodeo
rodge
rogue
roker
roman
rondo
roots
ropes
roque
rotor
rough
round
route
rover
rowan
rower
royal
rubia
ruble
rubus
ruffe
rugby
ruler
rules
rumba
rumbo
rumen
rummy
runic
run-on
rupee
rusty
sable
sabot
sabre
sacre
sahib
saiga
saint
saiok
saith
sajou
saker
salad
salal
salat
salep
sally
salmi
salmo
salon
salve
salvo
samba
sands
sanko
sansa
sapan
sargo
sarse
sasia
sasin
satin
satyr
sauba
sauce
saury
sauté
saver
savoy
scald
scale
scamp
scape
scarf
scarp
scaup
sceat
scena
scene
scion
scoff
scold
scone
scoop
scops
score
scout
scray
screw
scrip
scrod
scudi
scudo
scull
scurf
sedan
sedge
segno
segue
seize
selah
semen
semis
senex
senna
sense
senza
sepal
sepia
sepoy
serge
serif
serin
serow
sewel
sewer
sewin
shade
shaft
shake
shako
shaku
shale
shalm
shama
shape
share
shark
sharp
shawn
sheep
sheer
sheet
sheik
shelf
shell
sheth
shift
shine
shire
shoal
shoat
shock
shoer
shoot
shore
short
shout
shrew
shrub
shuck
shunt
sicca
siege
sieve
sight
sigla
silex
silly
sinus
siren
sirop
sisal
sitar

sit-in
sitta
sixth
skate
skeel
skeet
skein
skier
skiff
skink
skite
skull
skunk
slack
slang
slate
slatt
slave
sleet
slice
slide
sling
sloop
slope
slosh
sloth
slots
slump
smack
smart
smash
smear
smell
smelt
smith
smoke
smolt
smout
smowt
snack
snail
snake
snare
sneak
snipe
snook
snort
snowy
soave
socle
solan
solar
soldi
soldo
solen
sol-fa
solid
sonar
sonic
soree
sorex
sorry
sorts
sound
south
sower
space
spade
spado
spalt
spark
spars
spasm
spear
speed
spell
spelt
sperm
spice
spike
spile
spill
spine
spink
spire
spitz
splex
split
spoke
spool
spoon
spore
sport
spout
sprag
sprat
sprit
sprod
spuds
spurt
squab
squad
squaw
squid
stack
staff
stage
staig
stair
stake
stalk
stall
stamp
stand
stare
stars
start
state
stave
staws
stead
steak
steal
steam
steed
steel
steer
steps
stern
stica
stich
stick
stile
still
stilt
stint
stipa
stirk
stoat
stock
stoic
stole
stoma
stomp
stone
stool
store
stork
storm
story
stoup
stout
stove
strad
strap
straw
stray
strix
strop
strum
strut
study
stuff
stump
stunt
styca
style
sucre
sudak
suede
sugar
suite
sulky
sumac
sunny
surge
sushi
swage
swain
swamp
sward
swarm
swats
sweat
swede
sweep
sweet
swell
swift
swill
swine
swing
sword
sycee
sylva
synod
syrup
tabby
table
taboo
tabor
tacet
tache
taffy
tafia
taiga
taker
takin
talon
talpa
talus
tamer
tango
tansy
taper
tapir
tapis
tardo
targe
tarin
tarot
taste
tatoo
tawse
taxes
taxus
tayra
teddy
teens
telly
tempo
temse
tench
tenor
tense
terce
terek
teres
terry
tesla
tewel
thane
theme
therm
thief
thigh
third
thole
thong
thorn

thorp
throw
thrum
thyme
tiara
tibia
tical
ticcy
tidal
tiger
tight
tigon
tilde
tiled
tiler
tilia
tilth
timer
times
tinea
tinge
tithe
title
tiver
tizzy
toado
toady
toast
today
toddy
togue
toise
tokay
token
toman
tommy
toner
tonga
tongs
tonic
tonne
ton-up
tonus
tools
tooth
topau
topaz
topee
toper
topet
torch
torse
torsk
torso
tosto
touch
tourn
towel
tower
toxic
trace
track
tract
trade
train
tramp
traps
trash
tread
trend
trews
triad
trial
trice
trier
trike
trill
tripe
trite
troll
tromp
trone
troop
trope
trout
truce
truck
trump
trunk
truss
trust
tsubo
tsuga
tuber
tucan
tulip
tulle
tuner
tunic
tunny
turde
turps
tutor
tutti
twait
twang
tweed
twill
twine
twins
twist
twite
typha
uhlan
ulcer
ulnar
umber
umbra
umbre
uncia
uncle
union
unite
until
urena
urger
urial
urine
urson
urubu
usher
usury
u-turn
vagus
valet
valid
valse
value
valve
vamps
varan
vault
vedic
vedro
veery
vegan
veldt
veney
venus
verse
verso
verst
vespa
vesta
vetch
vexer
viand
vibes
vicar
vicia
video
vigil
villa
villi
vimen
vinyl
viola
viper
virgo
virtu
virus
vison
visor
vitis
vives
vixen
v-neck
vocal
vodka
voice
voile
volta
volti
vomer
voter
vowel
wader
wafer
wagel
wager
wages
wagon
waist
waits
walan
waler
waltz
waral
waste
watch
water
wazir
weald
weber
wedge
weeds
weigh
welly
wench
whale
wharf
whaup
wheat
wheel
whelk
whelp
whiff
while
whisk
whist
whore
whorl
widow
wight
winch
windy
wings
winox
wiper
witch
withe
withy
women
wonga
wooer
works
worms
worth
wound
wrack
wreck
wrest
wrist
xebec
xerox
x-rays
xylem
yacht
yahoo
yapok

yeast
yeode
yerba
yield
yobbo
yodel
yokel
youth
yucca
yulan
yupon
zakat
zamia
zazen
zebra
zibet
zinke
zizel
zloty
zoril
zorra
zorro

6
abacus
abaser
abbacy
abbess
aboard
abuser
acacia
acaena
acarid
acarus
accent
accept
access
accrue
acetal
acetic
acetyl
achene
acidic
ack-ack
acorus
action
active
adagio
adduct
adjust
adonic
adored
adorer
adrift
adverb
advice
aerate
aerato
aerial
aerobe
affirm
afghan
afloat
agamid
agency
agenda
agouti
aiglet
aigret
aikido
air bag
air bed
airbus

air dam
airgun
airman
airway
albert
albino
alburn
alcaic
alcedo
alcove
alcyon
alegar
alette
A-level
alevin
aliped
alkali
alkane
alkene
alkyne
allele
allice
allies
all out
almond
alpaca
alpine
alsike
alumna
amania
amatol
amazon
ambler
ambush
ammine
amnion
amomum
amount
ampere
amrita
amulet
anabas
analog
anchor
ancona
angina
angler
angora
animal
animus

anklet
annals
anneal
annexe
annual
anoint
anolis
anorak
ant cow
anthem
anther
aorist
apozem
appeal
appear
applet
aptera
aptote
arabis
arable
aralia
arbour
arbute
arcade
archer
archie
archin
arctic
argala
argali
argent
argosy
arioso
arista
arkose
armada
armlet
armory
armour
arnica
arpent
arrack
arrest
arroba
arroyo
arshin
artery
artist
ascend
ascent

ash bin
ash can
ash-fly
ashlar
ashore
ash pan
ashram
assail
assent
assets
assign
assize
astern
asthma
astral
asylum
atabal
at cost
at ease
at gaze
atomic
atonal
atrium
attack
attorn
attune
aubade
augury
auklet
auntie
au pair
aureus
aurist
auroch
aurora
auster
author
autumn
avails
aviary
avocet
aweigh
awning
aye-aye
azalea
baboon
backer
backup
back up
badger

bagman
bailee
bailer
bailey
bailie
bailor
bakery
balata
balboa
balker
ballad
ballet
ballot
balsam
bamboo
banana
bandar
bandit
bandle
bandog
banger
bangle
banker
banner
bantam
banyan
baobab
barbel
barber
barbet
barfly
bargee
barium
barker
barley
barman
barque
barrel
barrow
barter
baryon
basalt
basket
basnet
basque
basset
baston
batata
bathos
batman
batten
batter
battle
battue
baubee
bauble
bawbee
bawley
bayard
beacon
beadle
beagle
beaker
beakie
bearer
beater
beauty
beaver
becket
bedaub
bedbug
bee-fly
beemol
beetle
beeves
before
beldam
belfry
bellis
belone
beluga
bender
bennet
berlin
betime
betony
better
bewits
bezant
bharal
bibber
biceps
bicker
bidder
biffin
bigamy
big end
big top
bigwig
bikini
billet
billow
binary
binder
biotic
bireme
bishop
bit-end
bitmap
bitter
blanch
blatta
blazer
blazon
bleach
blenny
blintz
blonde
blouse
blower
blow up
boards
boater
bob wig
bobbin
bobcat
bob wig
bodice
bodkin
bodley
bodole
bog oak
boiler
bolero
bomber
bonbon
bonito
bonnet
bonsai
bonxie
boogie
bookie
boomer
boot up
boozer
borage
borane
borate
borcer
border
borrow
borsch
borzoi
bosket
boston
botany
bot fly
bo-tree
bottle
boucle
bought
bounce
bounty
bourne
bourse
bovine
bowess
bowfin
bowler
bowman
bow-saw
bowser
bow tie
boxing
braces
brains
braise
branch
brandy
brayer
brazil
breach
breech
breese
breeze
brewer
briard
bricks
bridge
bridie
briefs
bright
broach
brogue
broker
brolga
bronco
bronze
brooch
bruise
brumal
brumby
brunch
bryony
bubble
bubbly
buccal
bucket
buckie
buckle
budget
budgie
buffel
buffer
bug-eye
bugler
bulbul
bullet
bumkin
bumper
bundle
bunker
burbot
burden
bureau
burger
burhel
burial
buriti
burlap
burner
burnet
bursar
burton
bushel
busker
buskin
buster
bustle
butane
butler
butter
button
buying
buy out
buzzer
by-laws
bypass
cabbie
cablet

cabman
cabrie
cactus
caddie
caddis
cadent
cadger
caecum
caesar
caftan
cagmag
caiman
caique
calash
calico
caliph
calker
caller
calory
camass
camber
camera
camion
camper
canapé
canary
cancan
cancer
candie
candle
canine
canner
cannon
canopy
cantar
canton
cantor
canvas
canyon
capers
caplin
capote
caprid
capsid
captor
carafe
caranx
carapa
carboy
careen

caries
carina
carney
carpal
carpel
carper
carpet
carpus
carrot
car tax
cartel
carter
carvel
carver
casein
cashew
casing
casino
casket
cassia
cassis
caster
castle
castor
casual
catalo
cat bed
catgut
catkin
catnip
catsup
cattle
caucus
caudal
caudex
caudle
caviar
cayman
cayuse
cedrat
celery
cellar
cement
censer
censor
cental
centre
cepola
cereal
ceriph

cerium
cerris
cerrus
cha-cha
chacma
chador
chafer
chaise
chalet
change
chanty
chapel
charge
chaser
chasse
chatak
chaunt
checky
cheese
cheque
chequy
cherry
cherub
cheval
cheven
chevet
chevin
chewet
chicha
chigoe
chigre
childe
chilli
chilly
chimes
chinch
chinos
chintz
chisel
chitin
chiton
chives
choice
choker
chopin
choral
choric
chorus
chough
chrism

chrome
chukar
chunam
church
cicada
cicala
cicely
cilery
cimbex
cimiss
cinema
cinque
cintre
circle
circus
cirque
cirrus
cissus
cistus
citole
citril
citron
citrus
claque
claret
clause
clergy
cleric
cliche
client
climax
clique
cloaca
cloche
closet
cloudy
clough
clover
cloves
clumps
clupea
clutch
coaita
coated
coatee
coaxer
cobalt
cobnut
coccus
coccyx

cockal
cocker
cockle
cock-up
cocoon
codger
codist
coelom
coffee
coffer
cohort
coigne
coiner
colder
coleus
collar
collet
collie
collop
colony
colour
colter
colugo
column
combat
comber
comedy
commit
common
concha
condor
congee
conger
congou
conics
conium
conner
conoid
con rod
consol
consul
contra
convex
convoy
cooker
cookie
coolie
cooper
copang
copeck

copier
coping
copper
corant
corbel
corbie
cordon
cornea
cornel
corner
cornet
corona
corral
corrie
corset
cortex
corvus
cosine
cosmos
cosset
co-star
cottah
cotter
cotton
coucal
cougar
county
couped
couple
coupon
course
cousin
couter
coving
cowage
coward
cowboy
cowman
cowpea
cowrie
coyote
crabro
cradle
crambo
cratch
crater
cratts
cravat
craven
crayer
crayon
crease
creche
credit
creole
cretin
crevet
crisis
critic
crocus
crooks
crotch
croton
crowdy
cruise
crumbs
cruset
crusta
cuarta
cubism
cuboid
cuckoo
cudgel
cuisse
cultch
culver
cupful
cupola
cup tie
curacy
curate
curfew
curlew
cursor
cuscus
cushat
cutler
cutlet
cut-out
cutter
cuttle
cygnet
cygnus
cymbal
cynips
daboia
da capo
dactyl
dagger
dagoba
dahlia
dainty
damask
damper
damsel
damson
dancer
daphne
darnel
darner
darter
dassie
dative
dauber
davina
day bed
day boy
day-fly
day off
dazzle
deacon
deadly
dealer
deal in
deaner
debark
debris
debtor
decade
decamp
decani
decare
deceit
decime
decker
decode
decree
defeat
defect
defend
defier
defile
define
defray
degree
de-icer
de jure
delete
deluge
de luxe
delver
demand
dengue
denier
dennet
dentex
deodar
depict
deploy
deputy
derail
derive
dermis
desert
design
desman
despot
detach
detail
detour
device
devout
dexter
dharma
dhurra
diadem
diaper
diapir
dibber
dibble
dicker
dickey
diesis
digger
digram
dik-dik
dimmer
dimwit
dinghy
dingle
dinner
diodon
dioxin
dipody
dipole
dipper
dipsas
dipyre
direct
dirham
dirhem
dirndl
disarm
disbar
disbud
discus
dishes
ditone
diurna
divert
divide
divine
diving
divoto
djerib
dobbin
doblon
docker
docket
doctor
dodder
dodgem
dodger
dodman
doffer
dog bed
dog-bee
dog-fly
doggar
dogger
dog tag
dolium
dollar
domain
domify
domino
donjon
donkey
doodle
doolie
dorado
do-si-do
dossal
dossel
dotard
dot.com
double
dowser
drachm
dragon

drains
draper
drapet
drawee
drawer
dredge
driver
droger
dromon
drones
drongo
drosky
drover
drudge
dry ice
dubbed
ducker
duenna
duetto
duffer
dugong
dugout
duiker
dulcet
dumdum
dun-cow
dunlin
duplex
durain
duress
durian
duster
dyeing
dynamo
dynast
dzeren
eaglet
ear cap
earing
earwig
eatage
ecarte
éclair
ecurie
eczema
eddoes
edging
editor
effect
eggbox
eggcup
eggnog
egoist
eighth
eights
einack
elanet
elater
elegit
elevon
elixir
elk nut
ellops
embark
emblem
emblic
embody
embryo
enamel
encore
endaze
ending
endive
energy
engage
engild
engine
enlist
enmity
enosis
ensign
enspan
entire
entrée
envier
enzyme
epeira
epodic
epopee
equals
equine
equity
erased
eraser
erbium
ermine
eryngo
escape
escarp
escort
escrow
escudo
espada
estate
etcher
ethane
euchre
eunuch
euphon
eupoda
evania
excise
exedra
expend
expert
export
fabler
facade
facial
facies
factor
fading
faeces
faggot
falcon
fallow
family
fanega
fanner
farina
farmer
fascia
faster
fat hen
father
fathom
faucet
fawner
fecial
feddan
fedora
feeler
feline
feller
fellow
felony
female
fencer
fender
fennec
fennel
feriae
ferial
ferret
ferric
ferula
fescue
fiacre
fiancé
fibber
fibril
fibrin
fibula
fiddle
fiesta
figure
filler
fillet
filter
finale
finder
finial
finish
finite
finnan
firing
firkin
firlot
firrow
fiscal
fisher
fitter
flagon
flambé
flanch
flange
flares
flayer
fleece
fleury
flight
flimsy
flitch
floats
floral
flower
fluker
fluter
flying
flyman
fly net
fo'c'sle
fodder
foetus
foiler
folder
follia
fondue
for'ard
forage
forcer
forces
forest
forfex
forger
forint
format
fornix
forted
fother
foussa
fowler
fox bat
framer
freeze
fresco
fretty
friary
fridge
friend
frieze
frosty
fugato
fuller
fulmar
fumado
fungia
fungus
funnel
fuorte
furled
furrow
fusain
fusion
fustet
fustic
future
fylfot
gabbro
gabion

gablet
gadfly
gadoid
gaffer
gagger
gainer
gaiter
galago
galaxy
galeas
galeen
galena
galiot
galium
galley
gallon
gallop
gambet
gambit
gamble
gamete
gammon
gander
ganger
gangue
gannet
ganoid
gaoler
garage
gardon
gargol
garlic
garnet
garran
garret
garron
garrot
garter
gasbag
gas jet
gasket
gâteau
gaucho
gauger
gavial
gazebo
geezer
geisha
gelada
gelato
gemmae
gender
geneva
genius
genome
gentoo
gentry
gerbil
gerund
getter
gewgaw
geyser
gharry
gibbon
gigolo
gilder
gillie
gimlet
gimmer
ginger
gingle
ginkgo
ginkin
girder
girdle
giusto
glacis
glance
glazed
glazer
glider
gloria
glover
gluten
gneiss
gneous
gnomic
gnomon
gobang
goblet
go-cart
godown
godson
godurt
godwit
goglet
go-kart
golfer
gomuti
googly
gooney
gopher
goramy
gorget
gorhen
goslet
gossip
gothic
gourde
govern
graben
graces
gradin
grains
grakle
gramme
grange
granny
grappa
grater
graven
graver
grazer
grease
greave
greens
grille
grilse
grison
grivet
grocer
gromet
gromil
groper
grotto
grouch
ground
grouse
grower
growth
guards
guenon
guider
guidon
guilty
guimpe
guinea
guitar
gulden
gullet
gully
gulper
gundog
gunman
gunnel
gunner
gurami
gurnet
gusher
gusset
gutter
gymnic
gypsum
hacker
hacket
hackle
hagden
haggis
halide
hallow
hallux
halser
halter
hamlet
hammer
hamper
handle
hangar
hanger
hankie
hansom
harass
hareld
harlot
harper
harrow
hassar
hat box
hatter
hawhaw
hawker
hawser
haybox
hazard
header
healer
hearer
hearse
hearth
heater
heaven
heaver
heckle
hector
hedger
heifer
height
heller
helmet
helper
henbit
herald
herdic
heresy
hermit
hernia
heroic
heroin
herpes
hervea
heyday
hiatus
hiemal
hijack
hiking
hilsah
hinged
hinney
hinter
hippie
hitman
hoaxer
hoazin
hockey
hodman
hogget
hog pen
hogsty
holder
homily
homing
hominy
honour
hookah
hooker
hooper
hoopla
hoopoe
hoopoo
hootch

hooter
hop-fly
hopper
hoppet
horner
hornet
hosier
hostel
hot dog
hotpot
hot rod
hotter
hounds
hourly
hove-to
howler
howlet
hoyden
hubcap
hubris
huffer
huller
humbug
hummer
hummus
humour
hunter
hurdle
hurler
hussar
hussif
hybrid
hybris
hydrus
hymnal
hymner
hyphae
hyphen
hyssop
iambic
iambus
iberis
icebox
iceman
idling
iguana
illipe
impact
impala
impale
import
impost
in cash
incept
incest
incise
income
incult
in debt
indent
indigo
indium
infant
infuse
injury
inkpot
inland
inlier
inmate
inning
inroad
inship
in situ
insole
inspan
insult
insure
intake
intern
intine
intone
invade
invest
inwall
inyala
iodide
iodine
iodite
iodize
ironer
isatis
island
isobar
isomer
isopod
issuer
italic
jabiru
jacana
jacare
jackal
jacket
jaeger
jagger
jaguar
jailer
jalopy
jampan
jargon
jarrah
jeerer
jennet
jerboa
jerker
jerkin
jersey
jester
jetlag
jetsam
jet set
jetton
jezail
jigger
jigsaw
jilter
jingle
jitney
job lot
jobber
jockey
jogger
joiner
joints
jolter
jugful
juicer
jujube
jumble
jument
jumper
jungle
junior
junker
junket
junkie
junora
jurist
kabuki
kachha
kaftan
kaiser
kakapo
kakkar
kalmia
kalong
kangha
kantar
kaolin
karate
kedger
keeler
keeper
keep up
kelkel
keltie
kelvin
kennel
kennet
kentle
kephir
kermit
kernel
kettle
khurta
kibble
kicker
kidder
kiddow
kidney
kiekie
killed
killer
kimono
kipper
kirpan
kirsch
kirtle
kisser
kitbag
kitten
kittul
klaxon
klippe
knight
knower
kobang
kochia
koodoo
kopeck
kosher
kumbuk
kummel
kumpit
kung-fu
kunkur
kurkee
labial
labium
labour
labret
lacing
lacker
lackey
lacuna
ladder
lading
lagger
lagoon
lamina
lanary
lancer
lancet
landau
lander
langur
lanner
lap dog
lapper
lappet
laptop
larder
lariat
larvae
larynx
lascar
lasher
lassie
lassoo
lateen
latria
latten
launce
launch
laurel
lavabo
lavolt
lawyer
layman
lay-off
layout

leader
league
lean-to
leaper
leaser
leaven
leaver
leaves
lecher
lechwe
lector
ledger
leeway
legacy
legate
legato
leg-bye
legend
legion
leipoa
lender
lentil
lepton
lessee
lesson
lessor
letter
liable
libbra
lichen
lierne
lifter
lights
lignin
lignum
ligure
limber
limmer
limpet
linage
linden
linhay
lining
linnet
lintel
liquid
liquor
lisper
lister
litany
litmus
litter
living
lizard
llanos
loader
loafer
lobber
locals
locker
locket
lock up
locust
lodger
log bin
loggia
log hut
logman
log off
log out
loligo
lolium
loofah
looker
loonie
looter
loquat
lorica
loriot
lotion
louver
louvre
lovage
lowboy
lugger
lumper
lunary
lupine
lurker
lutist
lyceum
lychee
lydian
lyrist
macoma
macoya
macron
madcap
madder
madman
maggot
magnet
magpie
maguey
maidan
maiden
maigre
mailed
makeup
malice
malkin
mallee
mallet
mallow
malmag
mammal
manege
manger
mangle
maniac
manioc
manned
mantel
mantis
mantle
mantra
manual
manure
maquis
marble
margay
margin
margot
marina
marine
marked
marker
market
markka
mark-up
marmot
maroon
marque
marram
marrot
marrow
marten
martin
martyr
mascle
mascot
masher
mashie
masked
masker
masque
masted
master
mastic
masula
matins
matrix
matron
mature
mawkin
maxima
maybug
mayday
mayfly
maying
meadow
meagre
mealie
median
medico
medium
medlar
medley
medusa
megger
megohm
megrim
melody
melter
member
memoir
memory
mender
menial
mensal
mentor
menura
mercer
merger
merino
merlin
merops
merula
meslin
mesole
messan
meteor
method
methyl
metric
micron
midday
midget
mid-sea
mihrab
mikado
milage
milium
milker
milled
miller
millet
milsey
milter
mimosa
mincer
minima
mining
minion
minnow
minter
minuet
minute
mirror
misfit
missal
missel
missis
missus
mister
mitred
mitten
mizzen
mizzle
mob cap
mobile
mocker
mock-up
modius
module
modulo
moggie
mohair
moiety
moloch

moment
monaul
monger
monkey
monody
moored
mopoke
moppet
morass
morgay
morgen
morgue
morisk
morkin
morris
morrow
mortal
mortar
mosaic
mosque
mother
motion
motive
motley
mot-mot
motuca
mouser
mousse
movies
mowing
mucous
mud-eel
mud hut
muesli
muffin
mugger
mulier
mullah
muller
mullet
mummer
mundic
murder
murphy
muscat
muscle
museum
musket
musk ox
muslin
mussel
muster
mutant
mutiny
mutton
mutual
mutuca
mutule
muumuu
muzzle
mygale
myrtle
myself
mystic
nagger
naiant
nailer
nandow
napalm
napery
napkin
nappal
natica
nation
native
nausea
nautch
nautic
neaped
nebula
nebule
nectar
needer
needle
nenne
nephew
nerite
nestor
nettle
neural
neuron
neuter
newbie
newton
niched
nickel
nilgai
nilgau
nimbus
nipper
nipple
nitwit
no-ball
nobile
nobody
nocake
nodder
noggin
noodle
normal
nosean
notary
notice
not-out
nougat
novena
novice
noyeau
nozzle
nubbin
nudist
nuggar
nugger
nullah
numbat
number
nuncio
nutmeg
nut oil
nylons
object
oblate
oblong
oboist
obolus
obtuse
occult
occupy
ocelot
o'clock
octane
octant
octave
octavo
octile
office
offing
off-key
offset
ogress
ogygia
oilcan
oil gas
oilman
oil nut
old boy
old lag
old man
olefin
olenus
O-level
oliver
olivet
omelet
onager
on call
on cost
on deck
one act
one-off
one-way
online
on tour
oocyte
oogamy
oolith
oolong
oomiak
oorial
opaque
opener
oppose
optics
optime
option
opulus
orache
oracle
orange
orator
orchid
ordain
orders
oriole
orison
ormolu
orphan
orpine
orrery
osprey
ostler
ostrea
otaria
otitis
oulong
ourebi
outbid
outfit
outing
outlaw
outlay
outlet
output
outrun
ovibos
oxalis
oxbird
oxcart
oxgang
oxtail
oyster
ozalid
pacing
packer
packet
paddle
paella
pagoda
pagode
palace
palate
paling
pallah
pallet
palmer
pampas
panada
panama
pandit
pan-fry
panter
pantry
papacy
papaya
papist
parade
pardon
parent
parget
pariah

ON THE TRAIL OF THE TUMBLING TOMATOES

RAISING THE STANDARDS: Grow your popular crops in baskets

WHEN you don't have a greenhouse or enough room on the patio for a few tubs, you can still grow yourself a few tasty home-grown tomatoes in hanging baskets and window boxes or a trough on the conservatory windowsill if you stick to dwarf varieties.

I've even heard of these being grown by canal-boat owners on their cabin roof, since they're short enough to fit under the bridges.

You might have trouble finding suitable plants later but there's still time to raise your own from seed if you start straight away.

Look for compact "tumbling" varieties such as Totem, Gartenperle, Balconi Red or Maskotka; there are also yellow-fruited forms of Balconi and Tumbling Tom if you prefer something a bit different.

And if you're expecting another miserable summer or you live in a naturally chilly area, it's worth looking out for a unique variety called Sub-Arctic Plenty, which has a similar size and habit but performs better than most in cooler climates.

All of these will make short, rather floppy, bushy plants, ideal for pots; they can be stood anywhere with confined space or limited headroom, as long as it's sheltered and sunny.

What's more, tumbling tomatoes are very easy to grow because they don't need to have any side shoots removed and neither do they need more than a few short, twiggy sticks for support.

They'll "spill" gently down over the edges of their containers. Simply water, feed and pick.

Since the fruits are fairly small they will ripen a lot faster than conventional varieties. But if you're growing your own, buy some seeds and get going.

For more information on gardening and other subjects go to Alan Titchmarsh's website: **www.alantitchmarsh.com**

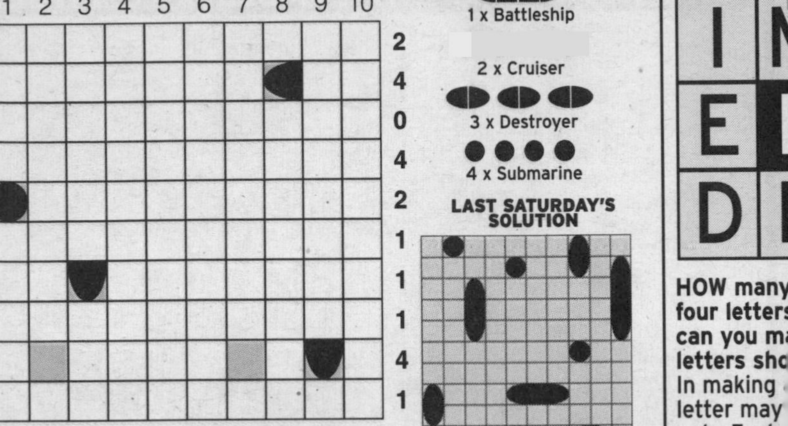

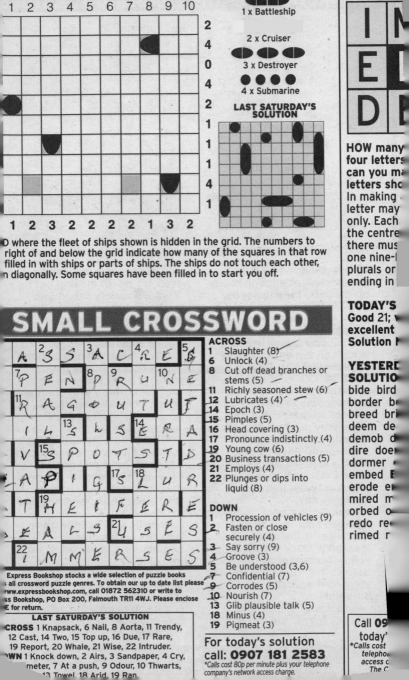

D where the fleet of ships shown is hidden in the grid. The numbers to right of and below the grid indicate how many of the squares in that row filled in with ships or parts of ships. The ships do not touch each other, n diagonally. Some squares have been filled in to start you off.

SMALL CROSSWORD

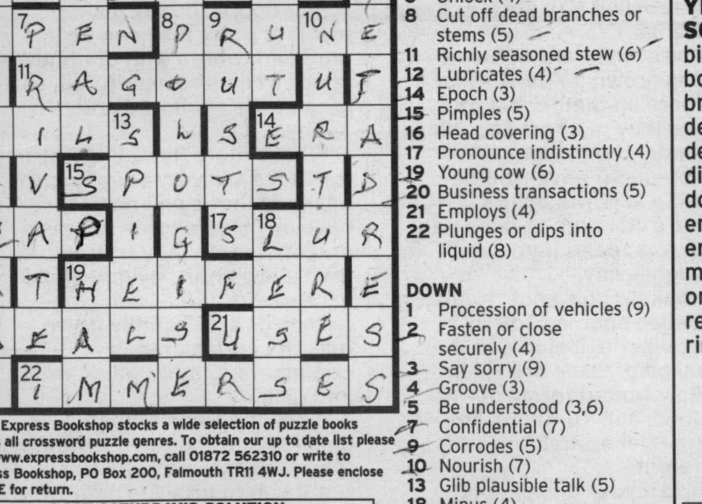

ACROSS

1 Slaughter (8)
6 Unlock (4)
8 Cut off dead branches or stems (5)
11 Richly seasoned stew (6)
12 Lubricates (4)
14 Epoch (3)
15 Pimples (5)
16 Head covering (3)
17 Pronounce indistinctly (4)
19 Young cow (6)
20 Business transactions (5)
21 Employs (4)
22 Plunges or dips into liquid (8)

DOWN

1 Procession of vehicles (9)
2 Fasten or close securely (4)
3 Say sorry (9)
4 Groove (3)
5 Be understood (3,6)
7 Confidential (7)
9 Corrodes (5)
10 Nourish (7)
13 Glib plausible talk (5)
18 Minus (4)
19 Pigmeat (3)

LAST SATURDAY'S SOLUTION

CROSS 1 Knapsack, 6 Nail, 8 Aorta, 11 Trendy, 12 Cast, 14 Two, 15 Top up, 16 Due, 17 Rare, 19 Report, 20 Whale, 21 Wise, 22 Intruder.
WN 1 Knock down, 2 Airs, 3 Sandpaper, 4 Cry, meter, 7 At a push, 9 Odour, 10 Thwarts, 13 Towel, 18 Arid, 19 Ran.

For today's solution
call: 0907 181 2583
Calls cost 80p per minute plus your telephone company's network access charge.

I N
E
D

HOW many four letters can you ma letters sho
In making letter may only. Each the centre there mus one nine- plurals or ending in

TODAY'S
Good 21; excellent Solution

YESTERD SOLUTIO
bide bird
border b
breed bri
deem de
demob d
dire doe
dormer
embed
erode e
mired m
orbed o
redo re
rimed r

Call 09 today'
*Calls cost telepho access c The C

parish
parity
parkin
parley
parody
parole
parrot
parsec
parson
partan
parter
pascal
pastel
paster
pastis
pastor
pastry
patera
pathos
patina
patine
patrol
patron
patter
paunch
pauper
pavane
pavier
paving
pavone
pawner
pawpaw
payday
paying
pay-off
pay out
peahen
peanut
pearls
pecker
pecten
pectin
pedalo
pedant
pedlar
peeler
peeper
peewee
peewit
pellet
pelmet
pelota
pelter
pelvic
pelvis
pencil
penman
pennon
penpal
pepper
period
permit
pernis
perron
person
peseta
pestle
petard
petrea
petrel
petrol
pewter
pharos
phenol
phenyl
phlegm
pholas
photon
phrase
phylum
piazza
picker
picket
pickle
pidgin
piecer
pieman
pigeon
piggin
piglet
pignut
pigpen
pigsty
pilaff
pile-up
pillar
pillau
pillow
pimint
pineal
pinery
pinion
pinner
pintle
pippin
piquer
piquet
piracy
pirate
pistil
pistol
piston
pitman
pitsaw
placer
plagal
plague
plaice
planer
planet
plaque
plasma
plater
player
pleats
pledge
pliers
plinth
plotly
plough
plover
plunge
plural
pochay
pocket
podium
podsol
podzol
poetic
poetry
poison
polder
poleyn
police
policy
poling
polish
pollan
pollen
poller
polony
pomade
pomelo
pompon
poncho
pontac
pontee
poodle
pooler
pooped
pop art
popery
poplar
poplin
poppet
porgie
porker
porret
portal
porter
poseur
posnet
posset
possum
poster
potage
potash
potato
potboy
poteen
potion
pot lid
potter
pottle
pouffe
poulet
poulpe
pourer
pouter
powder
powter
praise
prater
prayer
preach
prefix
presto
pretor
preyer
priest
primer
primus
prince
priory
prison
privet
profit
prompt
proper
protea
proton
prover
prozac
pruner
psalms
ptisan
public
puffer
puffin
pug dog
puisne
pulkha
puller
pullet
pulley
pulpit
pulque
pulsar
pulwar
pumice
pumper
pundit
punica
punkah
punner
punnet
punter
puppet
purger
purine
purism
purist
purser
pursue
pusher
puteli
putlog
putsch
puttee
putter

puzzle
pye-dog
pygarg
pyrame
pyrope
python
quagga
quahog
quaker
quango
quanta
quarry
quartz
quasar
quaver
queest
quelea
querry
quiche
quince
quinoa
quiver
quoits
quokka
quorum
quoter
quotes
rabbit
rabble
rabies
racama
raceme
rachis
racing
racist
racket
racoon
radial
radian
radish
radium
radius
raffia
raffle
rafter
raggee
raglan
ragman
ragout
ragtag
raguly
raider
railer
raisin
raking
ramjet
rammer
ramrod
rancho
randan
randem
random
ranger
ranker
ransom
ranter
rapids
rapier
rapine
rapist
rappel
rarefy
rascal
rasher
rasper
rating
ration
ratite
ratlin
rattan
ratter
rattle
ravage
ravine
ray gun
reader
realty
reamer
reaper
reaver
rebate
rebeck
reboot
rebuff
recess
recipe
recite
recoil
record
recoup
rector
rectum
rectus
redbud
redcap
red-cod
redeem
red-eye
red fir
red fox
red gum
red ink
redowa
redtop
reduce
reebok
reefed
reefer
reeler
refine
reform
refuel
refuge
refund
regent
region
reigen
relais
relief
relish
remand
remedy
remora
renard
render
rennet
rental
renter
repair
repeal
repeat
repent
report
resale
resist
retail
retake
retard
retina
retire
retort
return
reveal
revert
review
revise
revoke
rhebok
rhesus
rhumba
rhymer
rhythm
riband
ribbon
ribose
rickey
riddle
ridgil
riding
rigged
rigger
ringer
ring up
rinser
rioter
ripper
ripsaw
risker
ritual
roamer
roarer
robalo
robber
roberd
rochet
rocker
rocket
rococo
rodent
roller
romero
rondel
rondle
roofer
rookie
rooter
ropery
rosary
rosery
rosser

roster
rotary
rotche
rotolo
rotter
rouble
roughy
rouncy
rounds
rouser
router
rowing
rubato
rubber
rubble
rubric
rudder
ruddoc
ruffin
ruffle
rugger
ruling
rundle
runnel
runner
run-off
runrig
runway
rupiah
rusher
rushes
russet
rustic
rustre
rutile
sabalo
sabine
sacbut
sacker
sacred
sacrum
saddle
sadina
sadist
sagoin
sailor
saique
saithe
sajene
salami
salary
sallow
salmon
saloon
saloop
salter
saluki
salute
salver
salvia
salvor
samara
sambar
samfoo
samite
samlet
samosa
sampan
sample
sancho
sandal
sander
santon
sapota
sappan
sapper
sardel
sargus
sarong
sateen
satire
satrap
saucer
sauger
saurel
savage
savant
savate
saving
savory
saw-fly
saw-pit
saw set
sawyer
saynay
sbirro
scalar
scaler
scales
scamel
scampi
scarab
scarus
sceatt
scheme
schism
schist
school
schorl
scilla
sclera
scobby
sconce
scorer
scoria
scotch
scoter
scouse
scovel
scrape
screen
scribe
scrimp
script
scroll
sculls
sculpt
scurvy
scutch
scythe
sea-ape
sea-bar
sea-bat
Seacat
sea-cob
seacow
sea-dog
sea-ear
sea-eel
sea-egg
sea-fox
sea-hog
sealer
seaman
sea-mat
sea-mew
sea-oak
sea-owl
sea-pad
sea-pie
sea-pig
season
seaway
secant
secede
second
sector
seeker
see-saw
segger
seizer
seizor
sejant
seller
sell in
sell up
selves
senate
sender
senior
sennet
sensor
sentry
sephen
septet
sequin
serape
seraph
serial
series
sermon
serval
server
sesame
sestet
set-off
settee
setter
settle
sextet
sexton
sexual
shadow
shaker
shaman
shandy
shanny
shanty
sharer
shares

sharia
sharon
shaver
shears
sheath
sheave
sheets
sheikh
sheila
shekel
she oak
sherry
shield
shimmy
shiner
shinny
shinty
shoddy
shofar
shogun
shorts
shovel
shover
shower
shrike
shrimp
shrine
shrite
shrive
shroud
shtoff
sickle
sicsac
siding
sierra
sifter
sigher
sights
signal
signer
signet
sign on
sign up
silage
silica
silver
simian
simile
simkin
simmer
simnel
simony
simoom
simoon
simurg
sinful
singer
single
sinker
sinner
sinnet
sinter
siphon
sipper
sirdar
siskin
sissoo
sister
sitcom
sitter
skater
skerry
sketch
skewer
skibob
Skidoo
skiing
skivvy
slacks
slalom
slater
slaver
slayer
sledge
sleeve
sleigh
sleuth
slicer
slider
slogan
sloven
sluice
smalls
smeath
smilax
smiler
smiter
smithy
smoker
snacol
snarer
sniper
snorer
snow in
soaker
socage
soccer
socket
socman
soffit
soiree
solder
soleus
solute
solver
sonata
sonnet
soosoo
sop sax
sorbet
sorrel
sorter
sortie
souran
source
souter
sowans
sow-bug
sowens
sowing
sparer
sparid
spayad
specie
speech
speiss
spence
sphene
sphere
sphinx
spicer
spider
spigot
spiked
spinal
spinel
spinet
spingo
spinny
spiral
spirit
splash
spleen
splice
spoils
spokes
sponge
spouse
sprain
sprawl
spread
spring
sprout
spruce
spruit
spurge
squall
square
squash
squill
squire
stable
stadda
stager
stairs
stalls
stamen
stanza
stapes
staple
starch
starer
staten
stater
static
statue
stayer
steppe
sterol
stiddy
stigma
stingo
stithy
stiver
stocks
stoker
stolon
stooge
storer
stores

stormy
stover
strafe
strain
strait
strake
strand
strath
stream
street
stress
striae
strich
strick
strife
strike
string
stripe
stroke
stroll
strong
strunt
stucco
studio
stumps
stylet
subdue
subito
subnet
subset
subway
sucker
suffix
suitor
sultan
sultry
summer
summit
summon
sundae
sundew
sun-dog
sun hat
sunset
supper
supply
surety
surrey
surtax
suslik
suttee
suttle
sweets
swerve
swipes
switch
swivel
sylvan
symbol
syntax
syphon
system
syzygy
tabard
tabler
tablet
tabour
tabret
tacker
tackle
tactic
taguan
tai chi
tailor
taipan
takahe
talari
talent
talker
talkie
tallow
tamper
tam-tam
tandem
tanist
tanker
tanner
tannin
tapeti
tappet
tarand
target
tariff
tarots
tarpan
tarpon
tarpum
tarsal
tarsel
tarsia
tarsus
tartan
tartar
tasker
tasset
taster
tatler
tattoo
tauric
tautog
tavern
tawtog
taxman
teacup
te deum
teapot
tearer
teasel
teaser
tea set
tea urn
teepol
teflon
teledu
telesm
teller
tellin
telnet
telome
temper
temple
tenant
tender
tendon
tennis
tenrec
tenter
tenuto
tercel
tercet
teredo
termes
termly
tester
testes
testis
teston
thaler
thatch
theave
theist
thesis
thongs
thorax
thoria
thorpe
thrave
thread
thrift
throne
throng
thrush
thrust
thwart
thymol
thymus
tibial
tiburo
ticket
tickey
tie bar
tiepin
tierce
tie rod
tiffin
tights
tilery
tiling
tiller
tilter
timbal
timber
timbre
timing
tin box
tinder
tinker
tinned
tinner
tinsel
tip-cat
tippet
tipple
tipula
tirade
tirwit
tisane
tissue
titbit
tizzie

toffee
toggle
toiler
toilet
toller
tolsey
tomand
tomato
tomaun
tomboy
tomcat
tomcod
tomtit
tom-tom
tongue
tooter
top hat
top-set
torque
torrid
torsel
tosher
tosser
toss-up
toucan
toupee
tourer
touter
towage
towbar
towhee
toy box
toy dog
tracer
trader
trades
tragus
trance
travel
travis
treaty
treble
trench
trepan
trevet
trifle
trigon
trilby
tringa
triode
tripod
tripos
triton
triune
trivet
trivia
trocar
trogon
troika
troops
trophy
tropic
trough
troupe
trowel
truant
trunks
trygon
tsetse
t-shirt
tubber
tubing
tubman
tucket
tulipa
tundra
tune up
tuning
tunnel
tupaia
tupelo
turaco
turban
turbit
turbot
tureen
turkey
turkis
turner
turnip
turrel
turret
turtle
turves
tusker
tutrix
tuxedo
twaite
tweeds
tycoon
tymbal
typhus
typist
tyrant
tzetze
ulican
ultimo
umbril
umlaut
umpire
unbend
unbitt
uncoil
undock
undoer
unfair
unfurl
unholy
unhurt
unison
uniter
unlade
unload
unmoor
unpaid
unroof
unship
untile
up-beat
upland
upload
uraeus
urchin
ureter
urtica
usance
usenet
usurer
uterus
vacher
vacuum
vagina
valeta
valise
valley
vallum
valour
valuer
valuta
vamper
vandal
varlet
vassal
vastus
vector
veloce
velour
velure
velvet
vendee
vendis
vendor
vendue
veneer
venery
venial
ventil
verbal
verger
vermin
vernal
verser
vertex
vervet
vesper
vessel
vestal
vested
vestry
viands
victim
victor
vicuna
vielle
viewer
vigaro
vihara
vinery
vintry
violet
violin
vipera
virago
virgin
viscum
visham
vision
visits
vivace
vivary

vizier
voided
volant
volata
volley
volume
volute
vorant
votary
votive
voyage
voyeur
waders
waffle
wafter
waggel
waggon
waiter
walker
walk-on
walled
waller
wallet
wallop
walnut
walrus
wampan
wampum
wanton
wapiti
wapper
warble
war cry
warden
warder
warmer
warm-up
warner
warper
warren
washer
waster
wattle
watusi
wealth
weapon
wearer
weasel
weaver
weeder
weekly
weeper
weever
weevil
weight
welded
welder
wether
whaler
wheels
wherry
whidah
whilom
whilst
whiner
whisky
whites
whydah
wicker
wicket
wigeon
wigwam
willet
willow
wimble
wimple
wincer
wincey
winder
window
winker
winkle
winner
winter
wintry
wirrah
wisher
wisket
witwal
wivern
wizard
wombat
woolly
woosel
worker
worral
worrel
worthy
woubit
wow-
wow
wrasse
wrench
wretch
wright
writer
wyvern
xystos
xystus
yaffle
yampon
yapper
yarrow
yawing
yearly
yeoman
ynambu
yogurt
yojana
yonker
yorker
zaccho
zambra
zander
zapote
zealot
zechin
zeidae
zenana
zenith
zephyr
zeugma
zigzag
zincke
zingel
zinnia
zip bag
zipgun
zircon
zither
zivola
zodiac
zombie
zoozoo
zygote

7

abacist
abalone
abb wool
abdomen
abetter
abraxas
abscess
absinth
abyssal
academy
acaleph
acceder
account
accused
accuser
acerans
acetate
acetone
acidity
acolyte
aconite
acouchy
acreage
acrobat
acronym
acroter
acrylic
actaeon
actinia
actress
actuary
adapter
adaptor
adenine
adjourn
adjunct
admiral
admirer
adorsed
adossed
adrenal
advance
adviser
aeolian
aeolist
aerator
aerobic
aerosol
agitato

agonism
agonist
agrilus
aground
aileron
air base
airboat
aircrew
airdrop
air duct
air flow
air flue
airfoil
air hose
air lane
airlift
airline
airlock
air mass
airmiss
air pipe
airport
air pump
air raid
airship
airsick
air trap
air tube
albumen
alcaide
alcazar
alchemy
alcohol
al dente
alepine
ale-wife
alfalfa
algebra
aliment
alimony
allegro
allergy
all-good
all-heal
allonge
allstar
almadie
almanac
almirah
almoner
almonry
alms bag
aloysia
also-ran
althaea
alt horn
alumina
alumnus
alyssum
amalgam
amateur
ambatch
ambitus
ambs-ace
amianth
ammeter
ammonal
ammonia
amorosa
amoroso
amphora
ampulla
anaemia
anagram
analogy
analyse
analyst
anapest
anarchy
anatomy
anchovy
ancient
ancones
andante
andiron
anemone
aneroid
angelic
angelot
angelus
angling
aniline
animato
aniseed
annelid
annuity
annulet
annulus
anodize
antacid
ant bear
antbird
antenna
anthill
anthrax
anticum
antigen
antique
antlion
antonym
anybody
aphides
aplysia
apocope
apogean
apology
apostle
apotome
apotomy
apparel
apricot
apteryx
aquatic
aquifer
arbiter
arblast
arbutus
arcaded
archaic
archery
archive
archway
arcuate
arghool
arietta
ariette
armilla
armoire
armorer
armoury
arrears
arsenal
arsenic
ars nova
art deco
artemis
art form
article
artisan
artiste
art silk
artwork
ascetic
ascidia
asexual
ashtray
ash tree
aspirin
assault
assayer
assegai
assizer
assizes
assumer
assurer
astarte
asteria
asterid
ataghan
atavism
atelier
athalia
atheist
athlete
athwart
at sight
attaché
attagas
attagen
attired
attuned
auction
auditor
aureole
auricle
aurochs
aurorae
autobus
autocar
avenage
avenger
average
averter
aviator
avocado
awarder
awlbird
axle box
axolotl
azimuth

babbler
backing
bad debt
baggage
bagpipe
bailiff
balance
balanus
balcony
baldric
bale out
ballade
ballast
ballboy
ballium
balloon
bandana
bandeau
bandman
bandore
bandsaw
banking
bank run
banksia
bannock
banquet
bantung
baptism
baptist
baptize
barchan
bargain
barilla
barmaid
barn owl
baronet
baroque
barrack
barrage
bar-shot
barytes
baryton
basenji
basinet
bassist
bassoon
bastard
bastion
batfish
bathing

bath mat
bathtub
bathyal
batiste
batsman
battery
batting
bauxite
bayonet
bay tree
bay yarn
bazooka
beached
beagles
beanbag
bean-fly
bearcat
beardie
bearing
beatify
beating
beatnik
bedding
bedmate
bedouin
bedrock
bedroom
bedtime
bee-bird
beef tea
beehive
bee moth
beeswax
begonia
beguine
beldame
believe
bellboy
bellhop
bellman
bellows
beloved
belting
bencher
bendlet
benefit
benzene
bequest
bergylt
berhyme

besagew
besiege
best man
beta ray
betimes
bezique
bicycle
bidding
big bang
big guns
bighorn
bigotry
bigshot
bilboes
biltong
binding
binocle
biology
biomass
biotime
biotope
biplane
bipolar
bird dog
birdman
biretta
biscuit
bismuth
bistort
bitonal
bit part
bittern
bitters
bitumen
bivalve
bivouac
blabber
bladder
blanket
blaster
bled off
blender
blesbok
blessed
blinker
blister
bloater
blossom
blotter
blowfly

blowing
blowout
blucher
bluebag
blue-cap
blue-eye
blue gum
bluetit
boarder
boaster
boat-fly
boating
boatman
bobstay
bocking
bodhran
body bag
bogbean
boggler
bogland
boiling
bolivar
bollard
bolster
bombard
bomb bay
bombing
bomblet
bonanza
bonasus
bonding
bone ace
bone bed
bonetta
booking
bookman
boomkin
booster
booting
bordure
borough
borscht
boscage
boshbok
bossage
bosvark
botargo
bottler
boudoir
bouilli

bouncer
bounder
bouquet
bourbon
bowline
bowling
bow wave
box-fish
boxhaul
boxwood
boycott
braccio
bracing
bracken
bracket
bradawl
bramble
bran-pie
brasier
brasset
brassie
bravura
brazier
breaker
breaths
breccia
breeder
brevier
brewery
bribery
brigade
brigand
brisket
britzka
brocade
brocket
brogans
broiler
bromate
bromide
bronchi
brother
brownie
browser
bruchus
bruiser
bubbler
buceros
buckeye
buckler
buckram
bucolic
budding
budgero
buffalo
buffoon
buff tip
bugloss
builder
build-up
bulchin
bulimia
bullace
bullbat
bull-bee
bulldog
bull fly
bullion
bullock
bulrush
bulwark
bumboat
bummalo
bumping
bumpkin
bungler
bunkage
buntine
bunting
buoyage
buphaga
burdock
burgess
burgher
burnous
bur-reed
bursary
bush cat
bushman
bushpig
bushtit
bus lane
bus stop
bustard
bustler
butcher
butlery
butment
buttery
buy back
buydown
buzzard
by and by
byssine
cabaret
cabbage
cabinet
caboose
cacique
cackler
cacolet
cadence
cadency
cadenza
cadmium
caesura
cafenet
cagoule
caisson
caitiff
cake tin
calamar
calamus
calando
calcium
caldera
caldron
calibre
caliche
calipee
calking
callboy
calomel
calorie
calotte
caltrop
calving
calypso
camaieu
cambist
cambium
cambrel
cambric
camphor
campion
can buoy
canasta
candela
canella
cantata
canteen
cantoon
canvass
canzona
canzone
capelin
capital
capitol
caponet
caprice
cap rock
capsize
capstan
capsule
captain
caption
captive
capuche
carabus
caracal
caramel
caravan
caravel
caraway
carbide
carbine
car bomb
cardiac
cardoon
cariama
caribou
carioca
cariole
carline
carling
caroche
carolus
carotid
carpark
carport
carrack
carrier
cartoon
carving
car tyre
carvist
cascara
case law
caseman
cashier

cassada
cassava
cassino
cassock
casting
castlet
cast off
casuals
casuist
catalpa
catawba
catbird
catboat
cat bowl
catcall
catchup
caterer
catfall
cat-fish
catflap
cat flea
cat food
cathead
cathode
cat hole
catling
catmint
catodon
cat's eye
cat's paw
cattalo
catwalk
caudate
caulker
cautery
caution
cavalry
caveman
caviare
cayenne
cedilla
cedrate
ceilidh
ceiling
celesta
cellist
cell sap
cellule
cembalo
censure
centava
centavo
centime
centner
century
cepheid
ceramic
certify
cesspit
cestoid
chalaza
chalder
chalice
challis
chamade
chamber
chamfer
chamois
chancel
changer
channel
chanson
chanter
chantry
chapeau
chaplet
chapman
chapter
charade
charger
chariot
charity
charmer
charter
chasing
chassis
chateau
cheater
checker
cheeper
cheetah
chelone
chemise
chemist
chervil
cheslip
cheston
chevron
chewink
chianti
chiasma
chicane
chicken
chicory
chiffon
chikara
chiliad
chimera
chimere
chimney
chip-axe
chip set
chittak
chlamys
chloral
chloric
choking
cholera
choltry
chopine
chopper
chorale
choreus
chorine
chowder
chrisom
chutney
cichlid
ciconia
cidaris
circlet
circuit
cissoid
cistern
citadel
cithara
cithern
citizen
civvies
clacker
clapper
clarify
clarion
clarkia
classic
clavier
claw off
cleaner
cleanup
cleaver
clicker
climate
climber
clinker
clip art
clipper
clippie
clobber
cloister
close-up
closure
clot-bur
clubman
clumber
cluster
coal bin
coal box
coaling
coalman
coal tit
coaming
coaster
cobbler
cobiron
cob loaf
cobswan
cob wall
cocaine
cochlea
cockade
cockler
cockney
cockpit
coconut
codeine
cod-fish
codicil
codille
codling
cognate
coir mat
cold war
colibri
colitis
collage
collate
collect
colleen
college
collier

colobus
colonel
colours
coluber
columba
column
combine
comfrey
command
commère
commode
commune
compact
company
compass
compere
compile
complex
comport
compost
compote
comrade
con brio
concave
concert
conchie
conduct
conduit
confect
confirm
conical
conifer
conning
conquer
consent
console
consols
consort
contact
content
contest
context
contour
control
convent
convert
convict
cookery
cooking
cooling
cooncan
copepod
co-pilot
copland
copycat
copyist
coquito
coracle
cordage
cordial
cordite
cordoba
corella
corinth
co-rival
cork oak
cornage
corncob
cornett
cornice
corn law
corolla
coroner
coronet
corrode
corrupt
corsage
corsair
cortile
costrel
costume
cotinga
cottage
couloir
coulomb
coulter
council
counsel
counter
country
couplet
courage
courant
courier
courlan
courser
courter
couteau
cowbane
cowbird
cow-fish
cowherd
cowhide
cow-itch
cowling
cowpoke
cowshed
cowslip
cowtree
cow weed
coxcomb
crabber
crabite
cracker
crambus
crammer
crampon
cranial
cranium
crawler
creator
creeper
cremona
cresset
cricket
cringer
cringle
crinoid
cripple
crisper
croaker
crochet
crocket
crofter
crooner
cropper
croquet
crosier
croslet
crossed
crotalo
crowbar
crowdie
crozier
crucian
crucify
cruelty
cruiser
crumble
crumpet
crusade
crusado
crusher
crusien
cry baby
crystal
cubicle
cuckold
cudbear
cudweed
cue rack
cuffing
cuirass
cuisine
culicid
culprit
culture
culvert
cumulus
cup moss
cup rose
curaçao
curator
curling
currach
currant
current
currier
curtain
curtana
curtein
cushion
custard
custody
customs
cut-away
cuticle
cutlass
cutlery
cut-rate
cutting
cuvette
cyanate
cyanide
cyclica
cycling
cyclist
cycloid
cyclone
cymbals

cypress
cyprine
czardas
czarina
dabbler
daddock
dallier
damages
damping
dancing
dangali
dangler
danseur
daphnia
dariole
darling
dashing
dastard
dasypod
dasyure
daubing
dauphin
dawdler
dawning
day book
day lily
daytime
deadeye
deadpan
dealing
deal nut
deanery
debaser
debater
debouch
decagon
decanal
deciare
decibel
decider
deckboy
declare
decline
deep-fry
deep-sea
deer-dog
deer-fly
defacer
de facto
defamer
default
defence
defiant
deficit
defiler
deflate
defrock
defunct
degauss
degrade
degrees
delaine
deltaic
deltoid
deluder
demesne
denarii
denizen
density
dentist
deposit
derider
derrick
dervish
descant
descend
descent
desirer
desmine
dessert
destroy
détente
deutzia
develop
devisee
deviser
devotee
diabolo
diagram
diamond
diarist
dibbler
dice-box
diceras
dichord
diction
diehard
dietist
digging
digital
digraph
diocese
diopsis
diopter
dioxide
diploid
diploma
dipping
diptera
diptych
disband
discard
discoid
discord
dishmat
dishmop
dismast
dismiss
display
dissent
distich
distune
ditcher
dittany
dittied
diurnal
divider
diviner
divisor
divorce
djerrid
djibbah
dockage
docking
doddart
doeskin
dogbane
dog belt
dog bowl
dog cart
dog days
dog-fish
dog flap
dog food
dog rose
dog's rue
dog vane
dogwood
dollman
dolphin
domical
dominie
dooring
doorman
doormat
doorway
dorhawk
dorking
dormant
dornock
dottard
dottrel
doubler
doubles
doublet
doubter
douceur
doucher
doucine
dovecot
dovekie
dovelet
dowager
down bed
doxepin
drabbet
drabler
drachma
draftee
draft ox
dragman
dragoon
drainer
drapery
drapier
draught
drawbar
drawboy
drawers
drawing
draw out
drayman
dreader
dreamer
dredger
dresser
dress up
dribble
drifter
driller

drinker
drive-in
driving
drizzle
drogher
drogman
dromond
droshky
drought
droving
drowner
drudger
drugget
drumlin
drummer
dry cell
dry dock
dry-foot
dry pile
dualine
dualist
dubbing
duchess
duck-ant
dudgeon
dueller
dullard
dum-bird
dumping
dun-fish
dungeon
dunnage
dunnock
duopoly
dupatta
duramen
durmast
dustbin
dustman
dustpan
dweller
dynamic
eanling
earache
earcuff
eardrop
eardrum
earring
ear stud
ear-wort
ease off
eastern
ebb tide
ebonite
ecdysis
echelon
echidna
echinus
eclipse
eclogue
ecology
economy
edifice
edifier
edition
eel-fare
eelpout
eel punt
egg-bird
egg flip
egghead
egotist
egrette
ejector
elastic
elastin
elatine
elector
elegiac
elegist
element
elf-bolt
elision
elk wood
ellipse
ellwand
elm tree
embargo
embassy
emerald
emetine
emperor
empress
emptier
emulate
emu-wren
enactor
endorse
endower
endurer
engager
engrail
engrave
engross
enjoyer
entasis
enteron
enticer
entrant
entropy
entrust
envelop
epacris
epaulet
epeirid
epergne
epicede
epicene
epicure
epigeal
epigene
epigram
epistle
epitaph
epizoon
epochal
equator
equerry
equinox
erecter
eremite
ermelin
ermines
erosion
escapee
escaper
eschara
eschera
escolar
espadon
esparto
espinel
esquire
estival
estoile
estuary
etching
eternal
etesian
etheria
euclase
eugenia
euphony
eustyle
eutonia
evacuee
evening
evolute
exactor
exalter
ex bonus
exciter
exclude
execute
exegete
exhaust
ex parte
expense
exploit
exports
exposer
extinct
ex works
eyebolt
eyelash
façonne
factory
faculty
faggots
fagotto
faience
failure
fairing
fair sex
fairway
falafel
fallals
fall due
fall guy
fallout
falsies
fanatic
fanbelt
fancier
fan club
fanfare
fan palm
fantail
fantasy
farceur

farmery
farming
farrier
farruca
fascism
fascist
fast day
fast dye
fasting
fathead
fatigue
fatling
faulter
feaster
feature
federal
fee-tail
felafel
felspar
felting
felt tip
felucca
felwort
femoral
fencing
fend off
fen duck
fermata
ferment
fermium
fernery
fern owl
ferrate
ferrous
ferrule
festoon
festuca
fete day
fiancée
ficaria
fiction
fidalgo
fiddler
fielder
fig-bird
fig cake
fig gnat
fighter
fig tree
figwort
filbert
filcher
film set
finance
finback
fin-fish
finfoot
fin keel
finnock
fir cone
firearm
firebox
firefly
fireman
fire-pot
fir tree
fishery
fish-fly
fishing
fish owl
fish pie
fission
fissure
fistuca
fistula
fitchet
fitchew
fixture
flacket
flanche
flanker
flannel
flapper
flasher
flasket
flatten
fleecer
flesher
flicker
floater
florist
flotsam
flotson
flounce
flouter
fluking
flunkey
flusher
flutina
fluting
flutist
flutter
flyboat
flyover
flypast
fly rail
foaling
fogbank
foghorn
foister
foldage
foliage
folk art
fondler
footboy
footing
footman
foot rot
forager
forceps
forcing
foreman
fore-set
foretop
forgery
forging
formate
fortify
fortlet
forward
foulard
foumart
founder
foundry
fourgon
four-oar
fowling
foxhole
fox hunt
foxtail
fox trap
foxtrot
freeman
freesia
freezer
freight
freshen
fresher
freshet
fretsaw
fretted
frigate
frijole
friseur
frisker
fritter
frogbit
frog-fly
frogman
frontal
frowner
fruggin
fuchsia
fuguist
fulcrum
fulgora
fullery
full out
fumaria
fumbler
funaria
funding
funeral
fungite
fur coat
furioso
furlong
furnace
furrier
fur seal
fuscite
fusebox
fustian
futtock
futures
gabbler
gadsman
gadwall
gaiters
galette
gallant
galla ox
galleon
gallery
gall-fly
galliot
gallium
gambler
game pie
gangway

garbler
gardant
garfish
garment
garnish
garpike
garvock
gaseous
gas fire
gas mask
gas ring
gas trap
gastric
gateman
gateway
gaudete
gavilan
gavotte
gazelle
gearbox
gearing
gelatin
gelding
gemsbok
general
genette
genipap
genista
genital
gentian
gentile
geodesy
geoduck
geogony
geology
gerbera
gerenuk
germ war
gestalt
gharial
ghavial
gherkin
giardia
gibbous
giblets
giggler
gilbert
gilding
gimbals
gin fizz
gingham
ginseng
gin sour
giraffe
girdler
gironny
girrock
gittern
give way
gizzard
glacial
glacier
gladdon
gladius
glasses
glaucus
glazier
glazing
gleaner
gleeman
gliding
globard
glorify
glosser
glucina
glucose
gluteus
glutton
gnocchi
go about
gobbler
go below
goddess
godhead
godless
godlike
goggles
golding
goldney
golf bag
gondola
good man
gorcock
gorcrow
gorilla
goshawk
gosling
go to war
gouache
goulash
gourami
gourmet
gournet
grackle
gradine
grafter
grainer
grallae
grammar
grampus
granary
grandam
grandee
grandma
granger
granite
grantee
granter
grantor
grapery
graphic
grapnel
grasper
grating
graving
gravita
gravity
gravure
gray-fly
grazier
grazing
greaves
greisen
grenade
greyhen
greylag
griddle
griffin
griffon
griller
grinder
gripper
gristle
gritter
groined
grommet
grounds
grouper
groupie
grouser
growler
grown-up
grub axe
grudger
grundel
grunter
gruyere
grysbok
G-string
guanaco
guarana
gudgeon
guereza
guesser
guilder
guipure
gumboil
gumnura
gum tree
gunboat
gun deck
gunfire
gunnage
gunnery
gunning
gun port
gunroom
gunship
gunshot
gunwale
gurnard
gutwort
guy rope
guzzler
gwiniad
gwyniad
gymnast
gymslip
gyrocar
gyronny
habitat
habitué
hackery
hackler
hackney
hacksaw
haddock
hagbolt
haggard
haggler

hailing
haireel
hair oil
halberd
halcyon
half-aum
half-day
half pay
half-ton
half-wit
halibut
hallier
hallway
halogen
halyard
hammock
hamster
handbag
handgun
handler
handsaw
hanging
hangman
haploid
harbour
hardpan
hardtop
harfang
haricot
harming
harmony
harness
harnmer
harpist
harpoon
harrier
harvest
has-been
haslets
hassock
hat-band
hatchel
hatcher
hatchet
haulage
haulier
haul off
haunter
hautboy
hawking
hawk owl
hay cart
hay fork
hay loft
hay rick
haywain
head boy
headman
head off
head see
headway
hearing
hearsay
heathen
heather
heave to
heckler
hectare
hedging
heiress
helibus
hellhag
hellion
helotry
helvine
hemlock
henbane
hen-harm
heparin
hepatic
herbage
herbary
herbist
herding
herdman
heretic
heritor
herling
heroine
herring
hessian
hexagon
hexapla
hexapod
hicatee
hickory
hickway
hidalgo
high art
high day
highway
hillock
hilltop
hine-bee
hip bath
hip bone
hip roof
hipster
hircine
hirudin
history
hitcher
hoarder
hoatzin
hobbler
hock day
hoedown
hog boat
hogcote
hoggers
hogherd
hog-plum
hogskin
holdall
holding
holiday
holland
holm oak
holster
holy day
holy war
homburg
homelyn
homonym
honesty
honours
hoodlum
hoot owl
hop bind
hoplite
hop pole
hopsack
hop vine
horizon
hormone
horn-bug
horn cup
horn-fly
horn owl
hosanna
hosiery
hospice
hostage
hostess
hostile
hostler
hothead
hot line
hotspur
hot tone
hot wall
hot-wire
hot zone
houmous
houting
huanaco
huddler
humbler
humerus
hummock
humulus
hunkers
hunting
hurling
hurrier
husband
hustler
hyacine
hydrant
hydrate
hydride
hydroid
hygiene
hymnary
hymnist
hymnody
hyperon
iceberg
ice-bird
ice boat
ice-floe
ice spar
icy cold
idyllic
iliacus
illegal
imagery
imaging
imagism
imagist

imbiber
impaled
impasto
impeach
impeder
impeyan
impiety
impious
implant
imports
imposer
imprest
imprint
impulse
imputer
inboard
incense
incisor
inciter
indexer
indices
indorse
inducer
inertia
infanta
infante
infidel
infield
inflate
inflect
in funds
infuser
ingenue
ingrate
injurer
ink horn
inlayer
innings
inquest
inshore
install
instant
insular
insulin
insured
insurer
integer
interim
introit
invader
invalid
inverse
inviter
invoice
invoker
ipomaea
iridium
ironist
ischium
isogamy
isotope
isthmus
itching
jacamar
jacchus
jacinth
jackass
jackdaw
jacksaw
jack tar
jacobin
jacobus
jamming
jam roll
jam tart
jangler
janitor
janizar
jankers
jargoon
jashawk
jasmine
javelin
jawbone
jedcock
jejunum
jemadar
jet pipe
jewelry
jewfish
jib boom
jib door
jibstay
jobbers
jobbing
jogging
joinery
jointer
jonquil
jostler
journal
joyride
jubilee
juggler
jugular
jujitsu
jukebox
jumbler
jumbuck
jumping
jump jet
juniper
junkman
juryman
justice
justify
kamichi
karaoke
karatas
katydid
keelage
keeling
keelman
keelson
keep fit
keitloa
kennels
kenosis
keratin
kestrel
ketchup
keyhole
keynote
khalifa
kibitka
kidling
killdee
killing
killjoy
kilobit
kindler
kindred
kingcup
king gum
kinglet
kingpin
kinsman
kitchen
klipdas
knacker
kneader
kneecap
kneeler
knees-up
knitter
knocker
know-all
koonkee
kremlin
kumquat
labarri
laceman
lacerta
lacquer
lacteal
lady-cow
laggard
lagging
lagopus
lakelet
lambada
lambing
lambkin
lamento
lampern
lampfly
lamping
lampoon
lamprey
lancers
landing
land tax
land use
langaha
laniary
lantana
lantern
lanyard
lapilli
lapwing
larceny
lasagne
lashing
last lap
lastage
latches
latchet
lattice
laugher
laundry

la volta
lavrock
lawless
lawsuit
lay days
layette
layland
lazaret
L driver
leading
leaguer
leaking
leaping
learner
leasing
leasowe
leather
lectern
lecture
lee-gage
lee side
lee tide
leeward
legatee
leghorn
leg show
lemming
lempira
lending
lentner
leonine
leopard
leotard
leprosy
lettuce
lexicon
libbard
liberal
library
licence
lich-owl
lift-off
lighter
limeade
limited
limiter
limpkin
linaria
linkage
linkboy
linkman
lino-cut
linsang
lion dog
lioness
liqueur
listing
literal
lithium
litoral
litotes
liturgy
llorona
loading
loafers
loather
lobcock
lobelia
lobster
lobworm
lockage
lockjaw
locknut
lock out
lockram
locrian
logbook
loggats
logging
logline
logreel
logwood
lombard
longbow
longdog
long run
long-tom
lookout
looting
lorilet
lottery
love all
love set
low bell
lowbrow
lowland
low wine
lozenge
lozengy
L plates
lucerne
luffing
luggage
lugsail
lugworm
lullaby
lumbago
lump sum
lunatic
lunette
lupinus
lurcher
lustrum
lycaena
lychnis
lyddite
lyrical
macaque
mace ale
machete
machine
macrame
madonna
madoqua
madzoon
maestro
magnate
magneto
mahatma
mahjong
mahonica
mahseer
mailbox
mail car
mailman
mail-van
maintop
maizena
majesty
malaria
mallard
malleus
malmsey
maltman
mammary
mammoth
manager
manakin
manatee
manchet
mandala
mandate
mandrel
mangler
manhole
manikin
manilla
maniple
mankind
man-o'-war
mansard
mansion
mantlet
map-case
mapping
marabou
maracan
marbler
marbles
marcher
march on
maribou
marimba
mariner
marines
markhor
marline
marling
marlite
marmose
marplot
marquis
marshal
martial
martlet
marybud
masking
masonry
massage
masseur
mastaba
mastiff
mastoid
matador
matches
matelot
matinee
matting
mattins
mattock

matweed
matzoon
mawworm
maxilla
maximum
maxwell
mayduke
may lily
maypole
mazurka
mealman
meander
measles
measure
meat pie
meddler
mediant
medulla
meerkat
megabit
megaerg
megamys
megaron
megaton
meiosis
melisma
melissa
melodic
menacer
menorah
menthol
menu bar
mercury
merling
messman
mestizo
methane
mew gull
mezuzah
microbe
mid-term
midweek
midwife
migrant
mileage
milfoil
militia
milk can
milking
milk jug
milkman
milksop
mill cog
mill dam
millier
milling
milreis
mimesis
mimicry
minaret
mineola
mineral
mingler
minibus
minicab
minicar
minikin
minimum
minimus
minisub
miniver
minivet
minster
mint par
minutes
miracle
misdeal
misdoer
misfire
missile
missing
mission
mistune
misyoke
mitosis
mixture
mobster
mock sun
modicum
modiste
modulus
modwall
moellon
mogadon
moidore
molasse
mole rat
mollusc
monarch
mongrel
monitor
monocle
monocot
monodon
monsoon
montage
montane
montant
monthly
moon-eye
moorage
moorhen
mooring
moraine
mordant
morello
morisco
morling
mormops
morning
mortice
morwong
mosaics
motacil
moth-owl
mouflon
moulded
moulder
mounter
mourner
mouther
mud-fish
mud hole
mudhook
mudlark
mud sill
mud wall
muezzin
muffler
muggent
mugwort
mugwump
mulatto
muletta
mullein
mullion
multure
mumbler
mummery
munnion
muntjak
muraena
murexes
murices
murrain
murrion
muscite
musette
musical
musimon
musk rat
mustang
mustard
mustela
mustine
mycetes
mycosis
mylodon
myology
myotome
mystery
mytilis
nacelle
nailery
name day
narthex
narwhal
natural
nauplii
nebulae
nebular
necktie
nectary
neglect
nemesis
neptune
neritic
nest egg
netball
net gain
net sale
netsuke
nettler
network
neutral
neutron
new moon
newsboy
new town
new wave

ngusang
nibbler
niblick
nigella
niggard
niggler
nightie
nightly
nippers
nirvana
nitrate
nitride
nitrite
noctule
nocturn
no entry
no funds
nogging
nombril
nomimal
nominee
non-skid
nonsuch
non suit
nonzero
noonday
nose-cap
nosegay
nostril
notable
novalia
novella
nuclear
nucleon
nucleus
nuclide
numeral
nunnery
nursery
nut hook
nut pine
nylghau
oak tree
oar-fish
oarsman
oarsmen
oatcake
oatmeal
obelisk
obesity
obligee
obliger
oblique
ocarina
oceanic
octagon
octette
octopod
octopus
oculist
oddball
offbeat
offence
offerer
officer
offline
off-ramp
off-side
offward
oilbird
oil bomb
oil-feed
oil fuel
oil lamp
oil palm
oil pump
oilskin
old fogy
old girl
old maid
old salt
old-wife
olivine
oloroso
olycook
omnibus
on board
one-step
on guard
on offer
on order
on stage
oogonia
opening
ophidia
ophitic
opossum
opposer
optical
opuntia
oratory
orbital
orchard
orderer
orderly
ordinal
oregano
organic
organum
organza
origami
orology
orphrey
ortolan
oscines
osmosis
osmotic
osseter
ossuary
ostrich
otology
ottoman
outcast
outdoor
out gate
outlier
outline
outport
outpost
outride
outsize
outvote
outwork
oven tit
overact
overall
overrun
oversea
overset
oviduct
ovulite
oxidant
oxidize
pabular
package
packman
paddler
paddock
padlock
pageant
pageboy
pailful
painter
pairing
pair-oar
paisley
paladin
pale ale
palette
palfrey
pallone
palmist
palmyra
pancake
pandect
pandion
pandora
pandore
panicum
panikin
pannage
pannier
panoply
pan pipe
panther
panties
pantile
papaver
papilio
papmeat
papoose
paprika
papyrus
parados
paradox
paragon
paralic
parapet
parasol
parboil
parelle
parking
parlour
parotid
parsing
parsley
parsnip
partlet
partner
parvenu

paschal
passage
passant
passion
passive
pass out
pastime
pasture
pat ball
patcher
patella
path-fly
patient
patriot
pattern
payable
pay cash
payload
payment
payroll
pay slip
pea bean
pea coat
peacock
peafowl
peanism
pearler
peasant
peccary
peddler
pedicab
pedrail
pegasus
pelican
penalty
penance
pendant
pen-fish
penguin
pennant
pension
pentice
pentile
pentium
peonage
peppers
peptide
percent
percher
perfect
perform
pergola
peridot
perigee
periwig
perjury
permagy
persona
peruser
pervert
peterel
petiole
petunia
pfennig
phaeton
phalanx
pharaoh
pharynx
pH meter
phoenix
phone-in
phoneme
phonica
phonics
physics
pianino
pianist
pianola
piastre
pibroch
picador
piccolo
pickaxe
pickles
picquet
picture
piddock
piebald
pie dish
piercer
piffero
pig-fish
piggery
pig iron
pigment
pigskin
pikeman
pilgrim
pillbox
pillion
pimento
pi-meson
pincers
pincher
pinetum
pinfold
pinhole
pink gin
pinking
pinnace
pinnate
pinnock
pintado
pintail
pioneer
piragua
pirogue
piscina
pismire
pistole
pitcher
plaiter
planner
planter
planxty
plaster
plastic
plastid
plateau
platoon
platter
playboy
play day
players
playing
playlet
play off
playpen
pleader
pleaser
plodder
plotter
plottie
plucker
plumber
plum jam
plummet
plum pie
plumule
plunger
poacher
pochard
poe-bird
poetics
pointer
polacca
polacre
polders
poleaxe
polecat
polemic
polenta
politic
pollack
pollard
pollock
poll tax
polygon
polymer
polypus
polyzoa
pomatum
pomfret
pomposo
poniard
pontiff
pontoon
pool cue
pooping
poor law
popcorn
pop star
port-bar
portico
portray
posaune
postboy
post bus
post-doc
postern
postman
potager
potargo
potenty
pot hook
potoroo
pottage
pottery
potting
poultry

poundal
pounder
pouring
poverty
praetor
prairie
praiser
praline
pranker
praties
prayers
prebend
precept
predial
pre-empt
preface
prefect
prelate
prelims
prelude
premier
premium
prepaid
present
presser
pretzel
preview
pricing
pricker
pricket
primacy
primary
primate
primero
priming
primula
prinker
printer
private
probate
problem
procast
proctor
procyon
prodigy
produce
product
profane
profile
profits

progeny
proggie
program
project
prolong
promote
pronoun
propane
prophet
propose
pro rata
prosaic
prosody
protect
protegé
protein
proverb
provine
proving
provost
prowler
proximo
pruning
psalter
publish
pub quiz
puceron
pudding
puddler
pugging
pug mill
pug moth
pulchra
pullman
pull out
pulping
pulvule
pummace
pumpkin
puncher
punster
puritan
purpura
purpure
pursuer
pursuit
pushpin
puttees
putting
puttock

puzzler
pyjamas
pyloric
pyramid
pyrites
quabird
quadrat
quaffer
quahaug
quamash
quantar
quantum
quarrel
quartan
quarter
quartet
quassia
quayage
queller
querent
querist
questor
quetzal
quillai
quinary
quinine
quinnet
quintal
quintan
quintet
quitter
rabinet
raccoon
rackets
raddock
radiant
radical
radicel
radicle
rafting
rag bolt
ragdoll
ragtime
ragwort
railbus
railcar
railing
railway
raiment
rainbow

rain hat
raining
rambler
ramekin
rampage
rampant
rampart
rampion
rancher
rantock
rarebit
ratafia
ratchet
rations
ratline
rat-tail
rattler
ravages
ravelin
ravener
ravioli
raw silk
rayonny
reacher
reactor
reading
readout
reagent
realgar
realism
realist
realize
realtor
reaping
rearing
rebirth
rebuild
rebuker
receipt
recital
reciter
recluse
recount
recover
recruit
rectory
recycle
red clay
redcoat
red deer

red-fish
redhead
redoubt
red pine
redpoll
red self
redskin
reducer
red wine
redwing
redwood
re-edify
reeding
reed rat
reef-eel
reefing
re-elect
reeming
re-enact
re-entry
referee
refiner
refract
refrain
refresh
refugee
refuser
refuter
regalia
regatta
regency
regular
reissue
rejoice
rejoint
relapse
relater
release
relievo
remodel
remover
renewal
renewer
rent day
repairs
replica
replier
reprint
reprise
repulse
requiem
reredos
rescore
rescuer
reserve
resting
restore
retable
retaker
retinue
retract
retreat
retsina
retting
returns
revenue
reverer
reverse
reversi
revival
reviver
rewrite
rhachis
rhizoid
rhizome
rhombic
rhombus
rhubarb
rhymist
rice bun
rickets
ricotta
riddler
ride out
rietbok
rigging
ringgit
ringlet
ringtaw
rinking
ripcord
ripieno
ripsack
risotto
rissole
riveter
rivière
rivulet
road bed
roadhog
roadman
road map
road tax
roadway
roaster
robbery
robinet
robinia
rock-cod
rock doe
rockery
rococco
roe buck
roe deer
rokeage
rollers
rolling
romance
romeine
rompers
ronchil
rondeau
rondino
ronquil
röntgen
roofing
rooster
root cap
rope end
rorqual
rosalia
rosebay
rose-bug
rosehip
rosella
roselle
rostrum
rotchie
rotifer
rottolo
rotunda
roulade
roundel
rowboat
rowlock
royalty
rubella
rubicel
ruddock
ruffian
ruffler
rumbler
runaway
rundale
rundlet
run down
run into
running
rupture
rush mat
rustler
sabaton
sabbath
saccule
sackbut
sacking
sacrist
saddler
sadiron
saffron
sailing
sainted
saintly
sakeret
salamis
salient
salsify
salsola
saltant
salt box
saltire
salt-pan
saluter
salvage
sambhur
sambuca
sambuke
samisen
samovar
samoyed
sampler
samshoo
samurai
sanctum
sanctus
sandbag
sandbox
sand-eel
sandfly
sangria

sanicle
sapajou
sapling
sapples
sapsago
sapwood
sarangi
sarcasm
sarcina
sardana
sardine
sardius
sarplar
sassaby
satanic
satchel
satsuma
saurian
sausage
savanna
savarin
saveloy
saviour
savoury
sawback
sawbill
sawfish
sawmill
saxhorn
scabies
scalder
scaldic
scalene
scallop
scalpel
scalper
scammel
scanner
scapula
scauper
scenery
scenist
sceptic
sceptre
schelly
schemer
scherzo
schisma
scholar
science
scincus
sciolto
sciurus
scoffer
scolder
scomber
scooper
scooter
scoring
scorner
scourer
scraper
scratch
screwer
scriber
scrooge
scruple
sculler
sculpin
scumble
scupper
scuttle
seabank
sea-bass
sea-bear
sea-calf
seacard
sea cave
sea-crow
sea-duck
sea-fish
seafolk
seafood
sea-fowl
seagull
sea haar
sea hare
sea-hawk
seakale
sea lane
sea legs
sealion
sea-lord
seamark
seamile
sea ooze
sea-pike
sea-pink
seaport
sea room
seasick
seaside
sea sled
sea-slug
sea trip
sea wall
seaward
sea-wolf
seceder
secondo
section
secular
securer
seducer
seed lop
seether
segment
seizing
seizure
selling
sell-out
seminar
semiped
senator
senecio
senegal
septole
sequoia
seriema
seringa
serinus
serpent
servant
service
servile
session
set sail
settina
setting
settino
settled
settler
seventh
sexfoil
sextain
sextans
sextant
sextile
shackle
shad-fly
shadine
shading
shahada
shallon
shallop
shallot
shalwar
shammer
shariah
shariat
sharpei
sharper
shearer
shebeen
shedder
shelter
shelves
sherbet
sheriff
shiatsu
shifter
shingle
shipman
shipper
shipway
shirley
shoaler
shoebox
shooter
shophar
shopper
shotgun
shouter
showbiz
showery
showman
show-off
shrouds
shuffle
shunter
shutter
shuttle
shyster
sibling
sickbay
sickled
side-arm
sidecar
sievert
signior

silkman
silk oak
sillock
silurus
simargh
simpler
sine die
singing
singles
singlet
sinking
sinoper
sirgang
sirloin
sirocco
sistrum
sithara
sits vac
sjambok
skating
skegger
sketchy
ski boot
skidpan
skiffle
ski jump
skillet
skimmer
skinner
skipper
skirret
skulker
skybolt
skyjack
skylark
skysail
slacker
slammer
slander
slanket
slasher
slating
sleeper
sliding
slinger
slip-ons
slipped
slipper
slipway
sloe gin
sloughi
slurred
smasher
smelter
smerlin
snap dog
snapper
snarler
sniffer
snifter
sniping
snipper
snooker
snoozer
snorter
snow-fly
snow gum
snowing
snow-owl
snubber
snuffer
soapbox
socager
society
sock-eye
soda ash
sofa bed
solanum
soldier
sold out
soloist
soluble
solvent
someone
soother
sophist
soprano
sordine
sordono
sorghum
sospiro
sotalol
soufflé
soup pan
soursop
souslik
soutane
soybean
spaddle
spadger
spammer
spancel
spangle
spaniel
spanker
spanner
sparrow
spatula
spawner
speaker
species
spectra
speeder
speller
spencer
spender
sphyrna
spicery
spignel
spiller
spinach
spindle
spinner
spinnet
spiraea
spirits
spirula
spitter
spittle
spondee
spondyl
sponger
sponsor
sporran
sporule
spotter
sprayer
springs
sprouts
spunkie
spurner
spurrer
sputnik
spy boat
squacco
squally
squalus
squeeze
stabber
stacker
stadium
stagery
staging
stainer
stamper
standby
stand-in
staniel
stannel
stanyel
stapler
stardom
starlet
starter
statant
statice
statics
station
stature
statute
stealer
steamer
steeple
stellar
stencil
stepson
sterlet
sternum
stetson
steward
stew pan
stichic
sticker
stiller
stinger
stinker
stinter
stipend
stipple
stir-fry
stirrer
stirrup
stomach
stomata
stooker
stooper
stooter
stopped
stopper
stopple

storage
storied
stowage
straits
stratus
strayer
stremma
stretto
striker
stripey
striver
strocal
stroker
strophe
strudel
stubble
stuckle
student
stumpie
sturnus
stylist
stylops
subadar
sub-aqua
sub-bass
sub-dean
subduer
subedit
subject
subsidy
subsoil
subtend
subvert
succado
succory
sucrose
suction
suicide
suiting
sultana
summary
summery
summons
sump pit
sumpter
sunbear
sunbird
sundial
sundown
sun-fish
sunrise
sun roof
sun room
sunspot
sun suit
support
supremo
suramin
surcoat
surface
surfing
surgeon
surgery
surplus
surtout
suspect
suspend
swabber
swagman
swallow
swearer
sweater
sweeper
swiller
swimmer
swindle
swinery
swinger
synapse
syncope
synodal
synonym
syringa
syringe
systole
systyle
tabasco
tableau
tabloid
taborer
taboret
taccata
tacking
tackled
tackler
tactics
tadorna
tadpole
taffeta
taffety
tail fin
take-off
takings
talkies
tallboy
tallier
tamarin
tambour
tambura
tamping
tanager
tandava
tangelo
tangent
tanghin
tankard
tannery
tanning
tantony
tantric
tapetum
tapioca
taproom
tap root
tapster
tarrier
tarrock
tarsier
tartane
tartlet
tatting
tattler
taunter
tax cart
tax disc
tax-free
taxicab
taxiing
tax year
teacake
teacher
teach-in
tea cosy
tear gas
tea rose
tea time
tea tray
teatree
tegular
tellina
tempera
tempest
templar
tempter
tenoner
tension
tent bed
tequila
termite
ternary
ternion
terrace
terrier
terrine
tertian
test bay
testing
testoon
testril
test run
testudo
tetanus
texture
thallus
theatre
the gods
theorbo
theorem
thermal
thicket
thiller
thimble
thinker
thinner
thistle
thorium
threave
thriver
thrower
thrymsa
thumper
thunder
thwaite
thyroid
tibicen
ticking
tickler
tiddler
tie beam
tierced

tiercel
tiercet
tigress
tilbury
tillage
tilling
tilting
timbrel
time gun
timeous
timothy
timpani
timpano
tinamou
tinamus
tin case
tinchel
tin mine
tinning
tintara
tin-worm
tipcart
tipping
tippler
tipster
titlark
titling
titmice
titrate
toaster
tobacco
toccata
toddler
toheroa
toluene
tombola
tomfool
tone row
tonight
tonkong
tonnage
tonneau
tonsure
toolbar
toolkit
top coat
top deck
top gear
topknot
top mast
topping
toppler
topsail
topside
top spin
torgoch
tornado
torpedo
torpids
torrent
torsion
tortynx
toryism
tosspot
touch up
touraco
touring
tourist
tourney
tow boat
towline
towpath
towrope
tracery
trachea
tracing
tracker
tractor
trade in
trading
traffic
tragedy
trailer
trained
trainee
trainer
traitor
tramcar
trammel
tramway
transit
transom
trapeze
trapper
trawler
treacle
treader
treadle
treason
treater
tree tit
trefoil
trekker
trellis
tremolo
trepang
trestle
triblet
tribune
triceps
tricker
triduan
trifler
trigger
trilogy
trimmer
trimtab
trinity
trinket
triolet
triplet
tripper
trireme
trishaw
tritium
triumph
trivium
trochee
trochil
trolley
trollop
trooper
tropics
tropism
trotter
trouper
trucker
truckle
trudger
truffle
trumpet
trundle
trustee
truster
trysail
tsarina
T-square
tsunami
tuatara
tub-fish
tubicen
tugboat
tuition
tumbler
tumbrel
tumbril
tun dish
tuneful
turakoo
turbine
turncap
turning
turnkey
turnout
turn-ups
TV guide
twibill
twinjet
twinset
twinter
twirler
twister
two-step
tylocin
typeset
typhoon
tyranny
udaller
ukelele
ulichon
umbrine
unarmed
unbuilt
uncaria
unction
undated
unicorn
uniform
unitary
unladen
unpaved
unscrew
unsling
unslung
untiled
upright
upstage
upstart
up-tempo
upthrow

uranium
urethra
urinant
urodela
urology
ursinia
usurper
utility
utopian
utricle
utterer
vacancy
vachery
vacuist
vacuole
vagrant
valance
valence
valency
valiant
vampire
vamplet
vanfoss
vanilla
vaquero
varanus
variety
varnish
vaulted
vaulter
vaunter
vedette
veering
vehicle
vendace
vending
venison
ventail
venture
veranda
verbena
verdict
vernier
veronal
vertigo
vervain
vesicle
vespers
veteran
vetiver
viaduct
vibrato
viceroy
victory
vicuana
viewing
vihuela
village
villain
villein
vinegar
vintner
violist
violone
virelay
virgate
vis-à-vis
viscera
visitor
vitamin
vitrain
vitriol
vitular
viverra
voiture
volcano
voltage
voltaic
voluted
vouchee
voucher
voyager
vulture
vulturn
waddler
waftage
wagerer
wage war
wagoner
wagtail
walking
wallaba
wallaby
waltzer
want-wit
wapacut
waratah
war baby
warbler
war bond
wardian
ward off
warfare
war game
warhead
warlike
war loan
warlock
warlord
warmish
warning
warpath
warping
warrant
warrior
warship
war song
warthog
wartime
warworn
washtub
wasp-fly
wastrel
watcher
waterer
wavelet
waverer
waveson
waxbill
wax palm
wax tree
waxwing
way bill
weaving
webbing
web page
website
webster
weebill
wee free
weekday
weekend
weigher
weights
welcher
welding
wellies
wencher
western
wet bulb
wet dock
wetland
wetsuit
whatnot
wheeler
whetter
whilere
whipper
whippet
whip saw
whip top
whisker
whisket
whiskey
whistle
whiting
whittle
whooper
widgeon
widower
wielder
wiggery
wild ass
wildcat
wild dog
wilding
wimbrel
windage
windbag
wind gap
wind gun
windows
windrow
windsor
wine bag
winglet
wingnut
wingtip
winning
wintery
wireman
wise guy
wistiti
witling
witloof
witness
witwall
wolf cub
wolf dog
wolfram

wood ant
woodcut
woodman
wood owl
woolder
woollen
woolman
work bag
work box
workday
workman
worm-eel
worrier
worship
worsted
wounded
wounder
wrapper
wrecked
wrecker
wrester
wrestle
wringer
writing
wrought
wrybill
wryneck
xippias
yardarm
yardman
yashmak
year end
yeldrin
yestern
yielder
yoghurt
yttrium
yule log
yu-stone
zamouse
zea mays
zedoary
ziganka
zithern
zizania
zonurus
zoolite
zoology
zootomy
zuffolo

8

aardvark
aardwolf
aasvogel
abat-jour
abattoir
abdicant
abductor
ablative
ablution
above par
abrasion
abscisin
abscissa
absentee
absinthe
absolute
absonant
absonous
abstract
abutilon
abutment
academic
acalepha
acanthus
acaridan
accentor
accepter
acceptor
accounts
accoutre
a-centric
achiever
acid rain
acontias
acrosome
acrostic
actinide
activate
act of God
act of law
Adam's ale
adder-fly
addition
addorsed
adductor
adherent
adhesion
adiantum
adjutant
adscript
adularia
adulator
advanced
advocate
aeration
aerodyne
aerofoil
aerolite
aerolith
aerology
aeronaut
aerostat
aesthete
aestival
afferent
affinity
affluent
after tax
ageratum
agiotage
agitator
agnostic
agnus dei
agrimony
agronomy
aigrette
airborne
air brake
air brick
aircraft
air drain
airfield
air force
airframe
air inlet
airliner
airplane
air plant
air route
airscrew
airspace
airspeed
airstrip
airtight
air valve
alarmist
albacore
albicore
alburnum
alcatras
alcyonic
aldehyde
alderman
ale bench
algerine
alkaline
alkaloid
alkermes
alleluia
all-fours
alliance
allogamy
allosaur
allottee
allotter
allspice
allusion
alluvial
almagest
almighty
alphabet
alqueire
altar boy
alter ego
altitude
alto clef
altruist
alveolus
amadavat
amaranth
ambrosia
ambrosin
amethyst
ammodyte
ammonite
ammonium
amoebean
amoeboid
amortize
amphibia
amphigen
amusette
anableps
anaconda
anaerobe
anaglyph
analyser
analysis
analyzer

anapaest
anaphora
anathema
ancestor
anchored
anconeus
angel bed
angelica
angstrom
anguilla
anhedral
anisette
annealed
anodonta
anointed
anorexia
antabuse
anteater
antecede
antedate
antelope
antennae
anteport
anterior
anteroom
anthemis
anthozoa
antibody
antihero
anti-icer
antimony
antinode
antiphon
antipope
antiques
aperitif
aphelion
aphorist
apiarist
aplustre
apodosis
apophyge
apostasy
apostate
appeaser
appellee
appellor
appendix
applause
apple jam
apple pie
appliqué
appraise
approach
approver
apron-man
aquarium
aquatics
aquatint
aqueduct
arachnid
arapauma
arapunga
arbalest
arborist
arboured
archaism
archduke
arch lute
argonaut
armalite
armament
armature
armchair
armillet
armorial
armorist
armoured
armourer
arms race
aromatic
arpeggio
arquebus
arranger
arrestor
arrow key
arsonist
art board
art class
arterial
artistic
artistry
art paper
arum lily
asbestos
ascender
ash grove
asphodel
aspirant
asp viper
assassin
assemble
assembly
assertor
assessor
assignee
assigner
assignor
assonant
assuager
asterias
asterisk
asterism
asteroid
astragal
at anchor
atheneum
atmology
atom bomb
atropine
attacker
attaghan
attercop
attestor
attitude
attorney
audience
auditing
audition
auditory
au gratin
auricula
autarchy
autocrat
auto-da-fé
autogamy
autogiro
autoharp
autumnal
avadavat
ave maria
aviation
aviatrix
aweather
axletree
babirusa
baby bath
baccarat
bacchius
bachelor
backache
back bond
backbone
back door
backdrop
backfire
backroom
back seat
backstay
backward
backwash
bacteria
baghalak
bagpiper
bagpipes
bailment
balancer
balanite
baldrick
balister
balladry
ball cock
ballgirl
ballista
ballonet
ballroom
baluster
band-fish
bandsman
banewort
banister
bank bill
bankbook
bank giro
bank loan
banknote
bank rate
bankrupt
banterer
barbecue
barberry
barbette
barbican
barbital
bargeman
baritone
bark mill
barnacle
barology
baroness

barostat
barouche
barracks
barratry
bar shear
bartizan
barytone
bascinet
baseball
baseline
basement
basic pay
basilica
basilisk
bass clef
bass drum
bassetto
bassinet
bass horn
bass note
bass oboe
bass viol
bass wood
bateleur
bathrobe
bathroom
bath wrap
baud rate
bawdrick
bayberry
beachnut
beakiron
beam-bird
beam ends
beam tree
beanpole
bear's ear
bearbind
bearherd
bearings
bearskin
beatific
beat note
beat time
becafico
becalmed
bed cover
bedesman
bed linen
bedmaker
bed quilt
bedsocks
bedstead
bedstraw
beechnut
bee-eater
beetroot
beginner
beguiler
behemoth
believer
bell-bird
bell harp
bellower
bellwort
below par
bench peg
bendibus
benifice
berberis
berberry
berceuse
bergamot
beri-beri
berretta
berthage
berthing
bestower
betatron
betelnut
betrayer
bevelled
beverage
biathlon
biblical
biennial
bifocals
bigamist
big noise
bignonia
bilander
bilberry
bile duct
bill fish
bill hook
bimensal
bindweed
binnacle
binomial
bio-assay
biograph
biometry
biomorph
bioscope
birching
bird bath
birdbolt
birdcage
birthday
biscotin
bisector
biserial
bisexual
bistoury
bit-maker
black ant
black box
black cap
black-fly
black fox
black gum
black ice
blackleg
black rat
blast off
blastula
blazoner
blazonry
bleacher
bleeding
blessing
bless you
blighter
blizzard
blockade
block tea
bloomary
bloomers
blowhole
blowlamp
blowpipe
bludgeon
bluebell
bluebill
bluebird
blue chip
bluecoat
blue fish
blue John
blue-wren
boarfish
boat-bill
boat deck
boathook
boat-neck
boat race
boatsman
boat-tail
bobolink
bobwhite
bockelet
bockeret
body belt
body shop
bodywork
bogberry
bogwhort
bohemian
boldface
bolt rope
bomb site
bondmaid
bondsman
bonelace
bontebok
boob tube
boogaloo
bookcase
book debt
bookends
bookmark
bookworm
boot disk
bootjack
boot last
boot tree
borderer
borecole
borrower
botanist
bottomry
botulism
bouillon
boundary
bowdrill
bowmaker
bowsprit
box elder
boxmaker
boxthorn

boxwagon
boy scout
bracelet
brachial
braconid
braggart
brakerod
brakevan
brancher
branding
brant fox
brassica
brawling
bread bin
breadnut
breeches
breeding
brethren
breviary
brevipen
brewster
brick tea
bridging
britzska
broacher
broach to
broad-axe
broccoli
brooklet
brougham
brownian
brown rat
bruising
brunette
bryology
buccinum
buckling
buckmast
buckskin
buddleia
building
bulkhead
bull frog
bullhead
bull nose
bull's eye
bullweed
bulwarks
bungalow
buntline
buoyancy
burgamot
burganet
burglary
burgonet
burgrave
burletta
burnoose
bush chat
bush lark
bush wren
bushbaby
bushbuck
business
bus mouse
busybody
butteris
buttress
buying in
buzz bomb
cabalist
cabin boy
cablecar
caboched
caboshed
cabriole
cachalot
cackerel
caesural
caffeine
cake walk
calabash
calamary
calamine
calandra
calandre
calangay
calc-spar
calculus
calendar
calender
caliduct
calipers
callgirl
calomela
camellia
camisole
camomile
campaign
camp bath
camshaft
cam wheel
caneroma
canister
cannabis
cannibal
canoeing
canoeist
canonize
canon law
canthook
canticle
canzonet
capacity
capsicum
caps lock
capstone
capuchin
capucine
capybara
carabine
caracara
carapace
carbolic
carbonic
carbonyl
carcajou
carcanet
cardamom
cardamon
card case
cardiace
cardigan
cardinal
car ferry
cargoose
cariacou
carillon
carnival
carolina
caroteel
carotene
carouser
carriage
carriole
carryall
carrycot
caryatid
casemate
casement
case moth
case shot
case-worm
cashbook
cash down
cash flow
cashmere
cash sale
cassette
castanet
castaway
castings
cast iron
castrato
casualty
catacomb
catalyst
catapult
cataract
catchfly
cathedra
cat's eyes
cat's head
cat snake
cat's tail
caudillo
cauldron
caulking
causeuse
causeway
cavalier
cavatina
cavation
cave bear
cavicorn
caviller
celeriac
celibacy
celibate
cellarer
cellaret
cellular
cell wall
cemetery
cenobite
cenotaph
centaury
centiare
centibar
centre bit

centroid
cephalic
cerambyx
ceramics
ceramist
cerastes
ceratite
cerealia
cerebral
cerebrum
ceremony
cesspool
chaconne
chair bed
chairman
chaldron
champers
champion
chancery
chandler
chapatti
chaperon
chaplain
chaptrel
charades
charcoal
charlock
chastity
chasuble
chatelet
chat room
chat show
chattels
chaudron
chauffer
chausses
chayroot
cheating
cheewink
chelifer
chelonia
chemical
chenille
cherubic
cherubim
chessmen
chestnut
chetvert
cheville
chiasmus

chickpea
children
chimaera
chipmunk
chivalry
chlorate
chloride
choanite
choirboy
choliamb
chopness
chop suey
chordate
choriamb
choroids
chow-chow
chow mein
chrismal
christen
chromate
chromism
chromite
chromium
chuckler
ciborium
cicerone
cider cup
ciderkin
cinchona
cincture
cinnabar
cinnamon
circular
civet cat
civilian
civil law
civil war
claddagh
claimant
clansman
clapdish
clappers
clapping
claqueur
clarence
clarinet
clarsach
clavecin
claviary
clavicle

claw away
claymore
clay pipe
clearing
clearway
cleavage
cleavers
clematis
clerical
clerihew
climbing
clipping
clitoris
cloister
clot-bird
cloth cap
clothier
clowning
club-haul
clubmoss
clubroom
coachdog
coachman
coalfish
coal hole
coal shed
coalship
coasting
coat hook
cocculus
cockatoo
cockboat
cockerel
cockloft
cockspur
cocktail
cockweed
coco palm
coco tree
codifier
codomain
codpiece
coenzyme
coercion
cofferer
cognizee
cognizor
cog wheel
cohesion
coiffure

colander
colcynth
cold boot
cold snap
cold sore
coleseed
coleslaw
coliseum
colistin
collagen
collapse
collator
cololite
colonial
colonist
colophon
combiner
comedian
commando
commerce
commoner
commuter
compiler
complier
compline
composer
composto
compound
comptoir
computer
con amore
con anima
concerto
conchite
conclave
concrete
confetti
conflict
confusco
congo eel
conjurer
conjusto
conquest
conserve
consommé
constant
consumer
contango
continuo
contract

contrast
convener
converge
converse
conveyer
conveyor
coolabah
cool tone
coquette
coquilla
coquimbo
cordovan
corduroy
cordwain
co-regent
cork tree
corkwing
corn bird
cornflag
corn laws
corn loft
corn mill
corn moth
cornrose
corocole
corporal
corridor
corselet
corundum
corvette
coryphee
corystes
cosecant
costmary
costumer
cotillon
cottager
couchant
coulisse
counters
coupling
courante
couranto
coursing
courtier
couscous
covalent
covenant
covercle
coverlet

cowberry
cowgrass
cow house
cow-leech
co-worker
cow-wheat
coxswain
crab tree
cracknel
crackpot
cradling
crane fly
crankpin
crawfish
crayfish
cream bun
cream jug
cream nut
creation
credence
credenza
creditor
credit to
creodont
crescent
cretonne
crevasse
cribbage
cricetus
criminal
critique
crockery
cromlech
cromorna
cropping
crossbow
cross bun
crossing
cross tie
crotchet
croupier
crowfoot
crow mill
crow silk
crucible
crucifer
crucifix
cruising
crusader
cryolite

cryotron
cube root
cubic ton
cuboidal
cucumber
cul-de-sac
culettes
culottes
cum bonus
cunjevoi
cupboard
cup final
curassow
curb roof
currency
curricle
cursores
curtains
cuspidor
customer
cutchery
cut flush
cut-price
cutpurse
cutwater
cyanogen
cyclamen
cycle car
cyclonic
cylinder
cystitis
cytology
czarevna
dabchick
dactylic
daffodil
dahabeah
dahabiya
dainties
dairying
dairyman
daker-hen
dalesman
dalmatic
damaskin
dancetty
dandy-hen
danewort
danseuse
dapedium

dapedius
darkroom
databank
database
databits
dateline
date palm
date plum
date roll
daughter
Davy lamp
daybreak
day by day
deaconry
dead heat
dead lift
deadline
deadlock
dead slow
dead wall
deadwood
deaf-mute
dealfish
dealings
debutant
decagram
decalage
decanter
decapoda
deceased
deceiver
decigram
decimate
decisive
deck golf
deckhand
declutch
decorate
deed poll
deep tone
deerskin
defector
defender
deferrer
definite
defrayed
delegate
delicacy
delivery
dementia

demijohn
demilune
demi-tone
demi-wolf
democrat
denarius
dendrite
dentures
depicter
depriver
Derby dog
derelict
deserter
deserver
designer
despatch
despiser
detached
detainee
detainer
detector
detonate
devilish
devotion
devourer
dewberry
diabetes
diaconal
diagonal
diagraph
diallage
dialogue
diamanté
diameter
diandria
dianthus
diapason
diatomic
diatonic
diazcpam
diborane
dictator
didapper
didrachm
didymium
dieresis
dies irae
die stock
diffuser
digester
dihedral
diminish
diner-out
ding-dong
dinornis
dinosaur
diocesan
diopside
dipchick
diplomat
dipstick
dipthong
director
dirty dog
disarray
disburse
disciple
discount
discrete
disembay
disgrace
disguise
dish rack
disilane
diskette
disorder
dispatch
disponee
disponer
disposer
disputer
dissolve
distance
distress
district
ditching
ditheist
ditty-bag
ditty box
dive-bomb
diverter
dividend
divinity
division
divorcee
divulger
dockyard
doctoral
doctrine
document
dogberry
dog briar
dog chain
dogfight
doggerel
dog grass
doghouse
dog-leech
dog-louse
do-gooder
dog's bane
dogsbody
dog's meat
dog's nose
dogwatch
dog whelk
doldrums
dolichos
dolomite
doloroso
domestic
domicile
dominant
dominion
dominoes
doomsday
doorbell
door case
doorknob
door nail
doorpost
doorsill
doorstep
dormouse
dorr-hawk
dosology
dotterel
douanier
doublets
doubling
doubloon
doughboy
doughnut
dovecote
dovetail
dowel bit
dowel pin
down beat
downhaul
downland
download
downpour
downweed
doxology
draconic
drafting
drag-hunt
dragoman
dragonet
dragster
drainage
drake-fly
dramatic
draughts
draughty
draw gear
drawings
draw link
drencher
dress tie
dribbler
drifting
driftway
drill bow
drilling
drip-flap
dripping
driveway
drone-bee
drone-fly
drop-tank
dropwort
druggist
drumbeat
drumfire
drum-fish
drumhead
drunkard
dry goods
dry store
dry stove
dry wines
ducatoon
duckbill
duck-hawk
duckling
duckmeat
duckweed
ductless
duelling

duellist
duettist
dukeling
dulcimer
dumb cane
dumb show
dumpling
dun-diver
dungaree
duodenum
duo-diode
duologue
duration
dustcart
dust hole
dwelling
dybiscus
dynamics
dynamite
dyslexic
eagle-owl
eagle-ray
earmuffs
earnings
earshell
earth bag
earthhog
earthnut
earth pea
easterly
eastward
east wind
eau-de-vie
ecclesia
echinite
ecliptic
ectoderm
edge rail
edge tool
educator
eel spear
effector
efferent
effluent
egestion
eggplant
eggshell
egg slice
egg spoon
egg timer
egg whisk
eglatere
eight-oar
election
elective
electric
electron
elegiast
elephant
elevator
eleventh
elf arrow
elkhound
ellipsis
elliptic
embalmer
embattle
embezzle
emblazon
embodied
embolism
embracer
emeritus
emigrant
emissary
emission
employee
employer
emporium
emulator
emulsion
enceinte
enclitic
endirons
endoderm
endorsee
endorser
endpaper
energico
enfilade
enforcer
engineer
enginery
engraver
enhancer
enjoiner
enlarger
enquirer
enricher
enroller
ensemble
ensilage
enslaver
ensnarer
entailed
entellus
enthalpy
enthrone
entr'acte
entrance
entrench
entrepot
entresol
envelope
environs
ephemera
epic poem
epicycle
epigraph
epilepsy
epilogue
epiornis
epiphany
epiphyte
episcopy
epistyle
epitrite
equation
equipage
equities
erection
erigeron
erisimum
erminois
erotylus
errantes
erycinia
escalate
escallop
escalope
eschalot
eschewer
espalier
espouser
espresso
essayist
esteemer
estimate
estivate
estoppel
estridge
eternity
ethereal
ethernet
ethology
ethotoin
ethylene
etiology
ettercap
eucalypt
eucharis
eugenics
eulachon
eulogist
euonymus
euphonic
euphonon
euphuism
eurythme
evacuate
evaluate
even keel
evensong
eventide
eventing
evermore
everyday
everyman
everyone
eviction
evidence
evildoer
evocator
examinee
examiner
excavate
exceeder
exceptor
exchange
excuse-me
executor
exegesis
exegetic
exequies
exercise
ex gratia
exit line
exocetus
exocrine
exorcism

exorcist
exorcize
expenses
expiator
expirant
exploder
explorer
exponent
exporter
exposure
ex rights
extender
exterior
extoller
extranet
eyeglass
eyes left
face card
factotum
fair copy
fair play
faithful
falchion
falconer
falconet
falconry
falsetto
faltboat
fan blast
fan dance
fandango
fanlight
fantasia
fantasie
farceuse
farmhand
farmyard
farthing
fastback
fast lane
fatalist
fauteuil
fauvette
favosite
favourer
fax modem
feedback
feed pipe
feed pump
feldspar
felo de se
felstone
feminine
feminism
feminist
fencible
ferreter
ferryman
festival
feverfew
fidelity
field bed
field day
field gun
fielding
fife rail
figapple
fig-eater
fighting
figurant
figurine
filatory
file-fish
file type
filigree
film crew
filmgoer
film star
film unit
finalist
finances
fine arts
finisher
finnikin
finochio
fin-scale
firearms
fireball
fireboat
firebomb
fireclay
fire-fish
fire kiln
firelock
fireplug
fireship
firetail
firewall
fireweed
firewood
firmware
first act
fish fork
fish-hawk
fish meal
fish weir
fixative
flagella
flagpole
flagpost
flag rank
flagship
flagtail
flame gun
flamenco
flamingo
flanched
flannels
flan ring
flapjack
flash ram
flatboat
flat file
flatfish
flathead
flat-iron
flat race
flat rate
flat spin
flatting
flat tyre
flatworm
flaunter
flautist
flax comb
flaxweed
fleabane
fleshfly
fletcher
flincher
flixweed
floating
flock bed
flooring
florence
flotilla
flounder
flummery
fluoride
fly coach
fly paper
flywheel
foalfoot
fodderer
fogbound
foglight
foliated
folk hero
folk song
folk tale
follicle
follower
fomenter
foolscap
football
footbath
footnote
footpump
foot race
foot rope
footrule
footwear
forefoot
foregoer
foreland
foremast
forenoon
forensic
forepeak
foresail
foreseer
foreship
forestay
forester
forestry
forewind
forfeits
forgeman
forgiver
forktail
formalin
fortress
forzando
fossores
fox chase
foxglove
fox grape
foxhound
fox-shark
fox snake

fracture
franklin
fraxinus
free fall
freedman
freehand
freehold
free port
free vote
freezing
freshman
fretwork
friction
frog-fish
frontage
frontier
frontlet
front man
frosting
fructose
fruit fly
fruit pie
frumenty
frustrum
fudge box
fuel pipe
fuel tank
fugelman
fugitive
fugleman
full back
full moon
full stop
fumarole
fumitory
function
funny man
furlough
fusarole
fuse clip
fuselage
fuse wire
fusilier
futurist
futurity
gabarage
gadabout
gadlings
gaffsail
gaiement
gairfowl
galangal
galerite
galleass
gall-gnat
galliard
galliass
gallipot
gallivat
galloper
gall-wasp
galoshes
galvanic
gambling
gamecock
game laws
game port
gamester
gammarus
gang-gang
ganglion
gangrene
gangster
ganister
gaolbird
garaging
garcinia
gardener
gardenia
garefowl
garganey
gargoyle
garrison
garroter
garrotte
gasalier
gas gauge
gas mains
gas meter
gasoline
gas shell
gas stove
gas works
gatherer
gauntlet
gavelman
gavelock
gee cramp
gemshorn
generate
genetics
genitals
genitive
genotype
geodesic
geometer
geometry
geranium
germ cell
giantess
giant gum
gigabyte
gillaroo
gilt-head
gin horse
gin rummy
gin sling
girasole
gisarme
gladiola
glad rags
gland nut
glass-eel
glassman
glass pot
glaucoma
gleaning
gloaming
gloriosa
glossary
glow worm
gloxinia
glucagon
glucinum
glumales
glumella
glyceria
glycerol
glyptics
go aboard
goal line
go ashore
goatfish
goatherd
goat moth
godchild
God's acre
go-getter
gold fish
gold lace
gold lamé
gold wire
golf ball
golfcart
golf club
gonfalon
goods van
goodwife
goodwill
gossamer
gourmand
goutweed
governor
gradient
graduate
graffiti
grafting
graining
grand mal
grandson
granular
graphics
graphite
gratiola
gratuity
graviton
grayling
grazioso
great tit
green eel
greenfly
greenlet
green tea
grey teal
grey wolf
gridiron
gridlock
grillage
gromwell
grosbeak
groschen
grounded
grouping
grouting
grub-fish
grumbler
guachero
guaiacum
guardian
guerilla

guernsey
guidance
guide dog
guide-rod
guimbard
gull wing
gumboots
gunsight
gunsmith
gurdwara
guttural
gymkhana
gymnotus
gymshoes
gyrodyne
gyrostat
habanera
habitant
hackbolt
hairline
hair seal
hair-tail
half-deck
half-hose
half hour
half inch
half-life
half mile
half-note
half-past
half-pike
half term
half time
halftone
half year
halicore
halliard
hallmark
hallowed
ham actor
hamburgh
hammered
hammerer
handball
handbell
handcart
handcuff
handfast
hand-fish
handicap
hand jive
handling
handloom
handmaid
handmill
hand-pike
handpump
handrail
hand vice
handyman
hang fire
hanger-on
hangings
haquebut
harasser
hardback
hardbake
hardbeam
hard cash
hard disc
hard disk
hardener
hardline
hard sell
hardware
harebell
hare's ear
harmonic
harp lute
harp seal
harridan
harriers
harrower
hartbees
hartwort
hastener
hat brush
hatching
hatchway
hatmaker
hatstand
hatteria
hauriant
havildar
hawfinch
hawk bell
hawk moth
hawk's-eye
hawkweed
hawthorn
hayfield
hay knife
haymaker
haystack
haywagon
hazarder
hazel-hen
hazelnut
headache
headband
headfast
head girl
head into
headland
headline
headsail
headsman
headwind
heat haze
heatwave
heavenly
heavy gun
hecatomb
hectorer
hedgehog
hedgepig
hedonist
heel bone
heirloom
helicoid
heliport
hell fire
helmless
helmsman
helpmate
helpmeet
hematite
hemipode
henchman
hen house
hepatica
heptagon
heraldic
herb beer
herdsman
hernshaw
hibernal
hibiscus
hiccatee
hickwall
hierarch
hieratic
highball
highbrow
high jump
highland
highness
high noon
high note
high seas
high tide
hijacker
hill fort
hillside
hinayana
hinderer
hipflask
hipsters
hireling
histrion
hoarding
hockclip
hoggerel
hog's bean
hogshead
hoistway
holdfast
hold fire
holidays
holiness
holly oak
holy city
holy name
homebody
home farm
home help
home page
home rule
homespun
homework
homicide
homodont
honey-bee
honeydew
honourer
hoogarts
hooligan
hopfield
horation
horn-beak

hornbeam
hornbill
horn-fish
hornpipe
horn toad
horologe
horology
horse-bot
horsefly
horse hoe
horseman
hospital
hostelry
hot blast
hotchpot
hotelier
hothouse
hot metal
hotplate
hot press
hotspots
hound dog
house dog
houseboy
housefly
hoveller
howitzer
huckster
hula-bird
hula-hula
hull-down
humanist
humorist
humpback
hung beef
hunt ball
huntsman
hurdling
hustings
hyacinth
hydrated
hydromel
hydroxyl
hylobate
hymn book
hyoscine
hypogeal
icebound
ice cream
iced cake
icefield
ice house
ice plant
ice sheet
ice yacht
ideal gas
idealism
idealist
identity
idolater
idolizer
ignition
image map
imaginer
imbecile
imitator
immortal
impairer
imparter
impeller
imperial
impetigo
implorer
importer
impostor
improver
impugner
in camera
inceptor
increase
indebted
indecent
indented
indicter
indigene
inductee
inductor
indulger
industry
inert gas
infantry
inferior
infernal
infinito
infinity
inflamer
in-flight
informer
infra-red
initiate
injector
ink maker
inkstand
ink stone
inlet cam
inner ear
innocent
inquirer
inscribe
insignia
insister
inspirer
insulate
insulter
intaglio
integers
integral
intended
intender
interest
interior
internet
internic
interval
in the red
intimate
intonate
intrados
intranet
intruder
invasion
invected
inventor
investor
involute
iodoform
iriscope
ironbark
ironclad
iron-sick
ironwood
ironwork
irrigate
islander
isogonic
isotonic
isthmian
itchmite
ivory nut
jabberer
jackaroo
jackboot
jack tree
jack wood
jackstay
jacquard
jailbird
jalousie
janizary
janthina
japanner
japonica
jararaca
jasponyx
jaundice
jazerant
jeffison
jentling
jerrycan
jet-boat
jetliner
jet pilot
jet plane
Jew's harp
jeweller
jingoism
jingoist
jiujitsu
johannes
johnboat
joint box
jongleur
jousting
joyrider
joystick
judgment
judicial
juggling
jugulars
julienne
jumbo jet
jump lead
jump seat
jump suit
junk ring
jury mast
juvenile
kamikaze
kangaroo
kassabah

kedgeree
keel arch
keelback
keelboat
keelhaul
keel over
keeshond
kelp-fish
kerchief
kerosene
keskidee
keyboard
key bugle
key stage
keystone
kickshaw
killdeer
kilobyte
kilodyne
kilogram
kilowatt
kincatty
kinetics
kingbird
king crab
king-fish
kingling
kingpost
kingwood
kinkajou
kinsfolk
kiwikiwi
klystron
knackers
knapsack
knapweed
knickers
knitting
knitwear
knocking
kohlrabi
komondor
korfball
kreutzer
labourer
laburnum
lacebark
laceleaf
lace-leap
lachesis
lacrosse
ladybird
lady-fish
lady love
ladyship
laetrile
lamantin
lamb chop
lambskin
lame duck
lamellae
lamenter
laminate
lampwick
lancelet
land ahoy
land crab
landfall
landfill
landgirl
landlady
landlord
landmark
land mass
land mine
landrail
land roll
landslip
landsman
landward
land wind
langshan
language
lanneret
lanthorn
lapidary
lapstone
larboard
larcener
larderer
larkspur
last post
latchkey
lathwork
latinist
latitude
launcher
laureate
lavatera
lavatory
lavender
laverock
law agent
lawgiver
law lords
lawmaker
layabout
lay clerk
lay elder
layer-out
lay siege
lay waste
laywoman
lead line
lead mill
leadsman
leapfrog
leap year
learning
lecanium
lecturer
leeboard
lee shore
left-wing
legal aid
legalist
legation
leggings
lemonade
lemon top
lent lily
lentando
lenticel
levanter
leveller
leverage
levodopa
Lewis gun
libation
libellee
libeller
libretto
licensee
licenser
lichgate
liegeman
lifebelt
lifeboat
lifebuoy
lifeline
life peer
life span
lift well
ligament
ligature
likeness
lima bean
lima wood
limekiln
limerick
limewash
linchpin
Lindy hop
linesman
lingerer
lingerie
linguist
linoleum
linotype
lipstick
listener
literacy
literati
litharge
litigant
littoral
live show
livewire
load line
loblolly
local bus
location
lock gate
lock sill
lock weir
lodgment
logboard
log cabin
loghouse
logician
logogram
loiterer
lollipop
longboat
longeron
long haul
longhorn
long jack
long jump
longship

long stop
loophole
loop line
loosebox
loo table
lopolith
lordling
Lord's day
lordship
lorikeet
louis d'or
love-bird
love game
love seat
lowlands
low water
loyalist
lucky dip
lumberer
luminary
luminist
lump-fish
luncheon
lung-fish
lungwort
lustwort
lutanist
lutenist
lych gate
lyrebird
lyricism
lyricist
macaroni
macaroon
mackerel
madhouse
madisona
madrigal
maestoso
maganese
magazine
magician
magister
magnesia
magnetic
magneton
magnolia
maharaja
mahogany
mailboat
mail cart
mainboom
main deck
mainland
main line
mainmast
mainsail
mainstay
mainyard
majolica
majority
major key
make sail
malarmat
male fern
male lead
malemute
maligner
maltster
manciple
mandamus
mandarin
mandible
mandolin
mandrake
mandrill
mangabey
manganin
mangcorn
mangelia
mangrove
man-hater
manifest
manifold
manna-ash
mannikin
mannitol
man-of-war
manostat
mantelet
mantilla
mantling
marabout
marathon
marauder
maravedi
marching
margrave
marigold
marinade
marinate
maritime
marjoram
mark down
markings
marksman
mark time
marmoset
marquess
marquise
marsh gas
marsh tit
martello
martenot
martinet
marzipan
massacre
Mass book
masseter
masseuse
massicot
mast cell
masthead
mastitis
mastless
mastodon
masurium
matamata
matchbox
mat grass
matrices
mattress
maturing
maturity
maxillae
Maxim gun
may apple
may bloom
may games
mayoress
mea culpa
mealtime
mealy-bug
measurer
meatball
meatloaf
meatsafe
mechanic
mediator
medicine
meditate
megabuck
megabyte
megapode
melanure
melodeon
melodics
melodist
melodize
membrane
memorial
menhaden
menopome
menswear
mercator
merchant
merengue
meridian
meringue
merryman
mesoderm
mesotype
messmate
metal-man
metaphor
meteoric
methanol
metrical
midbrain
midnight
midships
migraine
militant
military
milkcart
milkmaid
milk tree
milkweed
mill pond
mill race
milleped
millhand
milliner
mimicker
mina bird
mince pie
minister
ministry
minneola
minorite

minority
minor key
minstrel
mire crow
mire drum
mirliton
miserere
mishmash
mislayer
mispoint
mistress
mitre box
mobilize
moccasin
mock epic
modalist
modeller
moderato
modifier
modulate
molasses
molecule
molegrip
moleskin
molester
momentum
monachal
monastic
monetary
monetize
mongoose
monkfish
monocarp
monohull
monolith
monopoly
monorail
monotone
monotony
monotype
monsieur
montilla
monument
moon calf
moon-fish
moonling
moonseed
moonshot
moonwalk
moorcock
moorfowl
moorgame
moorings
moorland
moquette
moralist
morality
moray eel
morillon
mormyrus
morpheme
morphine
mortgage
mortuary
mosquito
moss rose
motorbus
motorcar
motoring
motorist
motorman
motorway
moulding
moulinet
moulting
mountain
mounting
moussaka
movement
mozzetta
mucivora
muck-rake
mudguard
mudpuppy
mud valve
mudstone
muffneer
mujtahid
mulberry
muleteer
multiped
multiply
mung bean
muralist
murciana
murderer
muricite
murmurer
muscatel
muscular
mushroom
musicale
musician
musk deer
musk duck
musketry
musk pear
musk rose
musk wood
musquash
mutation
mutchkin
mute swan
mutineer
mutinous
mutterer
mycelium
mycology
mynabird
myosotis
myriapod
mytilite
nailfile
naissant
namesake
nannygai
napoleon
naproxen
narrator
narrower
natal day
natantes
natation
national
nativity
naturist
nauscopy
nautical
nautilus
naval gun
navigate
neap tide
near beer
near miss
nearside
neckband
necklace
negative
negatron
negligee
neomycin
neophyte
nepotist
nerve net
nestling
netlayer
net price
neuritis
neurosis
neurotic
neutrino
new broom
newcomer
new maths
newsreel
newsroom
nichrome
nicotine
nightcap
night-fly
nightjar
nihilist
ninepins
nobility
noble gas
nobleman
noctilio
nocturna
nocturne
noisette
nonesuch
non-metal
non-rigid
nonsense
noontide
noon time
northern
nose-cone
nosedive
nose down
nose ring
nose stud
nosology
notation
notebook
notornis
notturno
novation
novelist
nowadays

nucellus
nuisance
numberer
numbfish
numeracy
numskull
nundinal
nursling
nut grass
nuthatch
nut screw
nymphaea
oak chest
obituary
objector
oblation
obligato
obscurer
observer
obtainer
obtruder
occident
occulted
occupant
occupier
octoroon
odometer
offender
offering
official
offshore
offstage
oft-times
ohm meter
oilcloth
oil gauge
oil paint
oil spill
oilstone
oil store
oil stove
old crock
oldsquaw
old-timer
old woman
oleander
oleaster
oligarch
olive oil
olympiad
olympics
omelette
oncology
oncoming
on credit
on demand
onion-man
onlooker
on parade
on strike
ontogeny
ontology
oopak tea
open fire
open road
openwork
opera hat
operatic
operator
operetta
ophidian
ophidion
opinicus
opponens
opponent
optative
optician
optimist
orangery
oratorio
orchitis
ordainer
ordinand
ordinary
ordinate
ordnance
organdie
organist
oriental
origanum
original
ornament
orthodox
osculate
ossicles
ostinato
ostracea
otoscope
outboard
out-field
outflank
outguard
outhouse
outrider
outsider
overalls
overcast
overcoat
overcome
overhang
overhaul
overhead
overkill
overlord
overpass
overrake
overseas
overseer
overshoe
overtake
overtime
overtone
overture
overturn
oxazepam
oxpecker
oxymoron
ozonizer
pacarana
pachanga
pacifier
pacifist
packmule
padra tea
paginate
pagurian
painting
paint pad
paitrick
palatine
paleface
palestra
palisade
pall-mall
palmetto
palm tree
palomino
palstaff
pamperer
pancreas
pandanus
panderer
panelled
panel saw
pangolin
panorama
pan pipes
pantheon
papillae
papillon
parabola
paradigm
paradrop
parakeet
parallax
parallel
paramour
paranoia
parasang
parasite
paravane
pardoner
pargeter
parhelia
parmesan
parodist
paropsis
paroquet
partaker
parterre
particle
partisan
part song
par value
passbook
passer-by
password
pastiche
pastoral
pastrami
patentee
patience
patty pan
pauldron
pavement
pavilion
pay corps
peachick
pearmain
pear tree

pea stone
peat moss
pectoral
pedestal
pedigree
pediment
pedipalp
pedireme
peep show
pekoe tea
pemmican
pendulum
penitent
penknife
penmaker
pennydog
penology
penstock
pentagon
pentroof
penumbra
peperoni
percolin
perfumer
perianth
pericope
perigean
perineum
periodic
periplus
perjurer
perjuror
peroneus
peroxide
personal
pesterer
petanque
petchary
peterman
petition
petit mal
petronel
pewterer
phacetia
phantasy
pharisee
pharmacy
pheasant
phinnock
phonetic
phormium
phosgene
photoset
phrasing
phyllite
phyllium
physalia
physeter
pianette
picaroon
picayune
pickerel
picklock
pictures
pierhead
pigmy-eel
pig swill
pilaster
pilchard
pile shoe
pilewort
pilferer
pillager
pilotage
pimozide
pinacoid
pinafore
pinaster
pinchers
pine cone
pine tree
ping-pong
pink root
pinmaker
pinnacle
pinochle
pinscher
pipe bomb
pipe-fish
pipe rack
piraruck
pisolith
pistacia
pistolet
pitching
pit stall
pit viper
placeman
placenta
plankton
plantain
plantlet
plantule
plashing
plastron
platanna
plateful
platform
platinum
platypus
platysma
playbill
playgoer
playmate
playsuit
pleading
plebeian
plectrum
pleurisy
plimsoll
pliosaur
plougher
plucking
plumbago
plumb bob
plumbing
plungeon
pockwood
podargus
poetical
pointing
poisoner
polarity
polaroid
pole jump
polisher
politics
polluter
pollywog
polo-neck
polo pony
poltroon
polygala
polyneme
polypary
polysome
pomology
ponderer
pond lily
pond weed
pontifex
pony race
poop deck
popinjay
poppadum
populace
porifera
porosity
porphyry
porpoise
porridge
portague
porthole
portrait
portress
portside
positive
positron
posology
post boat
postcard
post horn
postiler
postpone
postural
pothouse
potmaker
pot-roast
pottager
pouchong
poundage
pour down
power saw
prasites
pratique
prattler
preacher
preamble
predella
prefacer
pregnant
premiere
preparer
presager
presbyte
preserve
press bed
pressman
pressure
presumer

price cut
price war
prie-dieu
priestly
primrose
princess
printing
print out
print run
prioress
prisoner
probator
proceeds
procurer
prodigal
producer
profaner
prologue
promisee
promiser
promoter
prompter
prong hoe
property
prophecy
prophesy
proposer
prop root
propylon
prorogue
prostate
protasis
protegée
protocol
protozoa
proverbs
provider
provisor
provoker
prowl car
prunella
prunello
psalmist
psalmody
psaltery
publican
puffball
puff-bird
pugilism
pugilist

pullover
pump gear
pump hood
pump room
puncheon
punctual
puncture
punisher
pupipara
purchase
purifier
purslane
purveyor
pushcart
puss moth
put about
putchock
pygmy owl
pyramids
pyroxene
pyroxyle
quad bike
quadrans
quadrant
quadrate
quadriga
quadroon
quaestor
quagmire
quandong
quantity
quarrier
quarters
quartile
quatorze
quatrain
quaverer
queen ant
queen bee
quencher
quetzale
quibbler
quietism
quietist
quillaia
quillpen
quintile
quisling
quiz show
quotient

rabbinic
racahout
racquets
radiator
radio fix
raft-fish
raftsman
ragstone
rag wheel
railhead
railroad
raincoat
raindrop
rainfall
raintree
raisinee
rally car
rambling
ramboose
rambutan
ramequin
ramparts
ram's horn
ranchero
ransomer
rapperee
ratifier
rational
rat snake
rattling
ravisher
reactant
reaction
real time
reap hook
rear axle
rear lamp
rear line
rearward
reasoner
rebutter
recaptor
receipts
receiver
receptor
recharge
reckoner
recoiler
recorder
recovery

recreant
red algae
redbelly
red biddy
red brick
red-brick
red cedar
red coral
red earth
redeemer
red giant
red maple
red panda
red perch
redshank
red snake
redstart
red wines
reedbuck
reedling
reed pipe
reef knot
re-embark
refinery
refining
reformer
refunder
regicide
regiment
register
registry
rehearse
reindeer
reinvest
rejecter
rejoicer
relapser
relation
relative
releasee
releaser
relessor
reliever
religion
remarker
remedial
reminder
remitter
renderer
renegade

repairer
repealer
repeater
repeller
reporter
repousse
reprieve
reprisal
reprover
republic
repulser
research
resenter
reserver
reserves
resetter
resident
resigner
resister
resolver
resonant
resorter
response
rest mass
restorer
retailer
retainer
retarder
reticule
retinite
retorter
returner
revealed
revealer
reveille
reveller
revenger
reverend
reverent
reviewer
revolter
revolver
rewarder
rhapsody
rheology
rheostat
rhetoric
rhizopod
rhomboid
rib grass
ribosome
ricebird
rice cake
rickshaw
ricochet
ride easy
ride hard
riffraff
rifleman
rifle pit
rigadoon
right now
rigidity
ring bolt
ring dove
ring down
ring dyke
ringhals
ringmail
ring road
ringtail
ringworm
risaldar
riverhog
road book
road rage
roadside
road sign
roadster
road test
roccella
rockaway
rock-bass
rock cale
rock cork
rock dove
rock-fish
rockling
rock rose
rock ruby
rock salt
rock soap
rock wood
rock wool
rockwork
roentgen
rogation
rollback
roll call
rollmops
roly-poly
romancer
romantic
roncador
rood loft
roof rack
roof tree
root beer
rootcrop
root hair
ropewalk
ropy lava
rosebush
rosemary
rosewood
rotarian
rotation
rotifera
roulette
rounders
royalist
royal oak
ruby port
rugmaker
ruminant
rumourer
rum punch
rum shrub
runabout
ruralist
rush hour
rye bread
rye grass
ryotwari
sabotage
saboteur
sack race
sacristy
saddlery
safe seat
sagecock
sago palm
sailboat
sailfish
sail loft
sail room
sail yard
sainfoin
salad oil
sale room
salesman
salivary
salpicon
saltbush
salt-fish
salt junk
salt lake
salt pork
saltwort
saluting
salvable
salvager
samphire
sanctify
sanctity
sandbank
sand-fish
sand flea
sandpeep
sandshoe
sand toad
sand wasp
sandwich
sangaree
sanguine
sapphire
saraband
sardelle
sardonyx
sarsenet
satanist
satirist
saturate
saucepan
sawbones
saw-shark
saw wrest
scabbard
scabious
scaffold
scalable
scalenus
scallion
scanning
scansion
scaphite
scaphoid
scapular
scarcity
scarf pin

scenario
schedule
schimmel
schnapps
schooner
sciatica
scimitar
scirocco
scissors
sclereid
scolytus
scopelus
scorpion
scout car
scrag end
scramble
scrawler
screamer
scrofula
scrub oak
scrub tit
scudding
scuffler
sculling
scullion
sculptor
se'nnight
sea-acorn
seaboard
seaborne
sea chest
sea-devil
sea eagle
seafarer
seagoing
seahorse
sea lemon
sea level
sea-louse
sealskin
seamster
sea otter
sea-perch
seaplane
searcher
sea-robin
seascape
seashell
seashore
sea snail
sea snake
sea-snipe
seasonal
sea-squirt
seconder
security
sediment
sedition
seedcake
seed corn
seedling
seedsman
seed time
seigneur
selector
semester
seminary
semitone
semolina
sempster
send down
sengreen
sentence
sentinel
sentry-go
septette
septfoil
sequence
seraglio
seraphic
seraphim
serenade
serenata
sergeant
serjeant
serology
serotine
serplath
serratus
servitor
sesterce
sestetto
set aside
set piece
sewellel
sewer rat
sextette
sforzato
shabrack
shaddock
shagreen
shalloon
shallows
shamisen
shamrock
shantung
shark net
shearing
shearman
sheep dip
sheepdog
sheer off
sheeting
shelduck
shelling
shepherd
sherwani
shift key
shingles
ship ahoy
ship-load
shipmate
shipment
ship oars
shipping
ship's boy
shipworm
shirring
shirting
shirt pin
shoebill
shoehorn
shoelace
shooting
shopgirl
shore eel
shortcut
short ton
shot hole
shot silk
shoulder
shoveler
showbill
showboat
showcase
showgirl
showroom
shrapnel
shrieker
shrimper
shrinker
shuffler
shutdown
sickness
side drum
sidekick
sideline
sidereal
side road
side show
sideslip
sidesman
siege gun
sika deer
silencer
silicane
silicate
silk mill
silky oak
sillabub
simperer
sinecure
sing-song
singular
sinister
sink unit
sinology
sirenian
siskiwit
sitology
sittella
sitz bath
skean-dhu
skeletal
skeleton
sketcher
skew arch
skewbald
ski boots
skid mark
skidding
ski pants
skipjack
skipping
skirmish
skirting
skittles
skullcap
skylight
skyscape

slapjack
slate axe
slattern
sledding
slipcase
slippers
slip road
slop bowl
slop pail
slop shop
slow down
slow lane
slowpoke
slow time
slow-worm
slugabed
sluggard
slyboots
small ale
small fry
smallpox
smaltine
smash hit
smeltery
smelting
smocking
smorzato
smuggler
snake eel
snatcher
sneakers
snowbird
snowdrop
snowfall
snowline
snowshoe
snowy owl
snuffbox
snuffers
snuffler
soapdish
soapwort
sociable
soda cake
sodomite
soft iron
softball
software
soil pipe
solarium
soldiery
solecism
solenite
solenoid
solitary
solstice
solution
solvency
sombrero
somebody
somerset
sometime
sonatina
songbird
songlark
songster
son-in-law
sorcerer
souchong
sounding
sourdock
sour milk
southern
sow bread
soyabean
space bar
spaceman
spadille
spadroon
spanroof
spare rib
sparkler
sparling
sparring
spearman
spectrum
speed cop
speed gun
speedily
speeding
spelding
speldrin
speldron
spending
spherics
spheroid
spiccato
spinelle
spinette
spinnery
spinster
spiracle
spirifer
spirling
spittoon
split pin
splitter
spontoon
spooling
spoonful
sporting
spot cash
spreader
springer
sprinter
spritzer
spurling
spurrier
spyglass
squab pie
squad car
squadron
squaller
squasher
squatter
squeaker
squealer
squeezer
squinter
squireen
squirrel
squirter
stabling
staccato
stagebox
staggard
stair rod
stalking
stalwart
stampede
stamping
stancher
standard
standish
stand off
stanhope
stanzaic
stapelia
stapella
starcher
starfish
star fort
starless
starling
star ruby
star turn
starwort
statuary
statutes
stave off
staysail
steak pie
stealing
steambok
steam car
steam gun
steam tug
steel pen
steerage
sterling
sternage
sternway
sticcado
stickler
stiletto
stingray
stinkard
stitcher
stockade
stock car
stocking
stockman
stockpot
stonefly
stone pit
stopcock
stopover
stoppage
storeman
storming
stotinka
stowaway
straddle
strafing
straight
strainer
stranded
stranger
strategy
straw hat

streamer
strength
strickle
stripper
stroller
strombus
struggle
strummer
struthio
strutter
stuccoed
stuffing
stumbler
stumping
stunsail
stuntman
sturgeon
submerge
suborner
suboxide
subpoena
sub-polar
subsonic
subtilin
subtitle
subtonic
subtract
suckling
sudatory
sufferer
suffrage
sugar gum
sui juris
suilline
suitcase
sulphate
sulphide
sulphite
summoner
sunblind
sun-bream
sun dress
sun plant
sunproof
sunshade
sunshine
sunstone
superior
superman
supertax
supplier
supplies
supposer
surfboat
surf-fish
suricate
surmiser
surplice
surprise
surround
surveyor
survivor
suspense
suzerain
swamphen
swamp oak
swan song
swapfile
swastika
sweet bay
sweet gum
sweeting
sweet pea
sweetsop
swimming
swimsuit
swindler
sword arm
sybarite
sycamore
syllabub
symmetry
symphony
syncarpy
syncline
syntaxis
syntonic
syphilis
systemic
systolic
table mat
tabourer
tabouret
tachisme
tackling
tacksman
tactical
tafferel
taffrail
tailband
tailcoat
tail gate
tail pipe
tail race
tail skid
tail unit
tailwind
takeover
talapoin
tallyman
tamandua
tamanoir
tamarack
tamarind
tamarisk
tamboura
tanagers
tantalus
tap dance
tape line
tapering
tapestry
tapeworm
taphouse
tara fern
tarantas
tarragon
tartuffe
tarwhine
taverner
tawny owl
taxation
tax dodge
tax haven
taxi rank
taxonomy
taxpayer
tayberry
tea board
tea caddy
tea chest
tea cloth
tea dance
teamster
teamwork
tea plant
tea plate
teaspoon
tea table
tectonic
teddy boy
teenager
teetotum
tegument
telecast
telltale
telotype
tempered
template
temporal
tenebrio
tenement
tenon saw
tenoroon
tentacle
terabyte
teraglin
teredine
terminal
terminus
terntero
terrapin
terzetto
testacea
testacel
testator
test tube
tetrapod
textbook
Thai silk
thalamus
thallium
thatched
thatcher
theodicy
theogony
theology
theorist
thespian
third act
third man
thole pin
thoracic
thornbut
thrasher
threader
threnody
thresher
thriller
throstle

throttle
throwing
thruster
thundery
thurible
thurifer
thwarter
tibialis
tickweed
tide mill
tidology
tightwad
tile kiln
tilt boat
time ball
timed out
time fuse
timeless
timoneer
timoroso
tin miner
tin stone
tincture
tinnitus
tinplate
tinsmith
tiny golf
tire pump
titanium
titmouse
toad-fish
toadflax
toboggan
tocology
toll dish
tollgate
tomahawk
Tommy gun
tomnoddy
tomorrow
tonalist
tonality
tone down
tonelada
tone poem
toon wood
tooth key
top brass
topazine
topology
tortilla
tortoise
torturer
total war
town hall
townsman
toxaemia
toxicity
toymaker
tracheid
trachoma
trachyte
track rod
tractile
traction
tractive
trade gap
traducer
tragical
tragopan
trainers
training
train oil
tram rail
trampler
transept
transfer
tranship
trapdoor
trap drum
traverse
travesty
tray-trip
trecento
tree frog
tremando
trembler
tremella
trencher
trenches
trespass
tressure
trevally
trial run
triangle
tribrach
tribunal
trichord
tricycle
tridacna
triglyph
trigonal
trimaran
trimeter
trimming
triphane
triplane
triplets
trippant
triptote
triptych
triumvir
trochite
trombone
tropical
trotting
trousers
troutlet
truckler
truckman
true bill
truelove
truetype
truncate
tsarevna
tube-nose
tuberose
tubipore
tuck shop
tumbling
tungsten
tung-tung
tunicary
tunshell
turbofan
turbojet
turf club
turf roof
turk's cap
turmeric
turncoat
turncock
turnover
turnpike
turnsole
turnspit
tusk-fish
tutoress
tutorial
twaddler
tweezers
twilight
twin-tail
twist bit
twitcher
two-piece
two-speed
two-timer
tympanon
tympanum
type area
typecast
typeface
typhlops
typology
tyre pump
udometer
umbrella
umbrette
umpiring
unallied
unbelief
unbuoyed
uncoiled
undercut
underdog
underpin
underset
under way
unfurled
ungulata
unharmed
unicycle
unionism
unionist
unit cell
universe
unlawful
unpoetic
unquoted
unsolder
unstable
untimely
upholder
uprising
up to date
upstairs
urethane
vacation
vagabond

valerian
validity
valuator
vambrace
vamplate
vanguard
vanquish
vapourer
variable
vascular
vaulting
vauntlay
velocity
venerate
venturer
veratrum
verbatim
verifier
verjuice
vermouth
veronica
versicle
vertebra
vestiary
vestment
vestuary
vesuvian
viaticum
viburnum
vicarage
victoria
victuals
vigilant
vignette
vigoroso
vilifier
villager
vin blanc
vineyard
vintager
violator
viomycin
virginal
virology
virtuosi
virtuoso
viscacha
viscaria
viscount
visitant

vitiligo
viva voce
vocalion
vocalist
vocation
vocative
voce colo
volcanic
volplane
volulite
vomiting
wage rate
wagon-lit
wainscot
wait-a-bit
waitress
walkover
wallaroo
wall-game
wall knot
wallmoss
wallower
wall safe
wall-wort
waltzing
wanderer
wanderoo
warbling
war bride
war crime
war dance
wardress
wardrobe
wardroom
warfarin
war grave
warhorse
warm boot
warm tone
warplane
warranty
warrener
warrigal
wartwort
watchdog
watch key
watchman
waterbug
waterbus
water can

water-dog
water-fly
water-fox
water gas
waterhen
water-hog
watering
water jug
waterman
water-poa
water pot
water ram
water-rat
water rot
water tap
waterway
waveworm
wax cloth
wax light
waxworks
wayfarer
waylayer
waymaker
waywiser
weakener
weanling
weaponry
weedfish
weed hook
welcomer
well boat
well deck
well done
well hole
well room
west wind
westerly
westward
wet nurse
whaleman
wheatear
wheat-fly
wheedler
wheezing
whenever
whiggery
whimbrel
whinchat
whip-bird
whipcord

whirlwig
whistler
white ant
white ash
white-ear
white-eye
white fir
whitefly
white gum
whitener
white oak
whitepot
whitsour
whiz-bang
whizz-kid
whodunit
wigmaker
wild boar
wildcard
wildfowl
wild goat
wildlife
wild oats
wild rose
winchman
wind cone
windfall
wind farm
windlass
windmill
windowed
wind pump
wind-rode
windsail
wind seed
windsock
windward
wineskin
wing flap
winnower
wire-draw
wireless
wireworm
wiseacre
wish-wash
wisteria
witch elm
with-wine
wolf-fish
wonderer

woodbine
woodchat
woodcock
wood duck
woodland
woodlark
woodlice
wood mill
woodmite
wood moth
wood opal
woodpulp
wood rock
woodruff
woodsage
wood shed
woodskin
woodwind
woodwork
woolding
woollens
woolsack
word play
word wrap
workable
workroom
workshop
world war
wormwood
wrangler
wreckage
wrestler
wriggler
wristlet
write-off
xanthium
xanthura
xenolith
yachting
yardland
yardwand
yarmulka
yarmulke
yearling
yeldring
yeldrock
yeomanry
yodeller
yoghourt
yokemate
yoldring
yourself
zambomba
zemindar
zero hour
ziggurat
zikkurat
zingiber
zip drive
zirconia
zodiacal
zolotnik
zoom lens
zoophyte
zoospore
zootrope
zopilote
zorrillo
zucchini
zymology

9

Aaron's rod
abatement
abduction
ablutions
aborigine
about ship
abrotanum
absconder
abstainer
academist
acalephae
accessory
accidence
accipiter
acclaimer
accordion
acephalan
acetylene
acipenser
ack-ack gun
acoumeter
acoustics
acquittal
acropolis
acroteria
actuarial
acylation
addiction
addressee
addresser
ademption
adiabatic
adjective
admiralty
adoration
adrenalin
adulterer
ad valorem
advantage
adventure
adversary
aeolipile
aepiornis
aepyornis
aerodrome
aerolitic
aerometer
aerometry
aerophyte
aerostyle
aesthetic
aetiology
affirmant
affreight
afterdeck
afternoon
afterward
aggregate
aggressor
agonistes
agonistic
agreement
agrimotor
agriology
agroville
ailanthus
air attack
air engine
air filter
air funnel
air gunner
air strike
air vessel
aitiology
alabaster
alarm bell
alarm post
alasmodon
albatross
alchemist
alcoholic
alcyoneae
alcyonite
algarroba
Alice band
alignment
aliphatic
all aboard
allantois
alleluiah
allemande
alligator
allopathy
allophane
allotment
allotropy
allowance
alluminor
almandine

almshouse
aloes wood
alongside
aloxiprin
alpine fir
altar rail
altimeter
altimetry
altitude
altometer
alto viola
alum shale
alum slate
aluminate
aluminium
amaryllis
Amazon ant
ambulance
ambulator
amendment
amianthus
amidships
amiloride
amino acid
amorphous
ampersand
amphibian
amphibole
amphipoda
amplifier
amplitude
amusement
amygdales
anabolism
anaerobic
anapestic
anarchism
anarchist
anatomist
anchorage
anchoring
anchorite
ancillary
andamento
andantino
andorinha
andrology
anemology
angelfish
angophora
anhedral
anhydrous
animation
anisogamy
anklebone
ankle boot
annealing
annotator
announcer
annuitant
annulment
anointing
anonymous
anopheles
antarctic
antedated
antelucan
antennule
anthology
anticline
anti-glare
antimeson
antimeter
antiphony
antipodal
antipodes
antiquity
antispast
anti-trust
ant-thrush
apartheid
apartment
apex stone
aphid pest
apocopate
apologist
apostolic
apparatus
appellant
appendage
appetizer
applauder
applecart
applejack
apple john
applicant
appraisal
appraiser
aqua regia
aquarelle
aquatinta
aquilegia
arabesque
arachnida
araucaria
arbitrage
arborator
arbor-vine
arc-en-ciel
archangel
arch brick
archdruid
archenemy
archeress
archetype
archfiend
archilute
architect
archivist
archivolt
archstone
arcograph
arctic fox
areometer
areometry
armadillo
armistice
army corps
arquebuse
arquifoux
arrearage
arriviste
arrowhead
arrowroot
art critic
art dealer
art editor
artemisia
arteriole
arthritis
artichoke
artificer
artillery
art master
art school
ascendant
ascension
ascidians
asclepias
ashlaring
asparagus
asphaltum
assailant
associate
assonance
assurance
asteroida
astrakhan
astrolabe
astrology
astronaut
astronomy
asymmetry
asymptote
athenaeum
athletics
atmometer
atomic war
atonality
atonement
attainder
attendant
attention
attrition
aubergine
audiology
augmenter
au gratin
auriscalp
authoress
authority
autocracy
automatic
automaton
autonomic
autophagi
autoroute
auxiliary
auxometer
avalanche
aventaile
averaging
awapetine
ayurvedic
babacoote
babirussa
baby buggy
babyhouse
baby linen
backbiter

backcloth
backpiece
back plane
backspace
backstaff
backstage
back stays
back wheel
badger dog
badminton
bagatelle
bain-marie
bakehouse
balaclava
balalaika
balas ruby
balladeer
ballerina
ball games
ballistic
ballot box
ballpoint
ball-valve
balsam fir
balsamine
baltimore
bamboo rat
bandalore
banderole
bandicoot
bandolier
bandstand
bandwagon
bandwidth
baneberry
banjoline
bank agent
bank stock
banqueter
banquette
baptismal
baptistry
barbarian
barbastel
barbecue
barbitone
barcarole
bargainer
bargepole
barley pop
barnacles
barn dance
barnstorm
barograph
barometer
barometry
baroscope
barracuda
barricade
barrister
barrow boy
basal body
basaltine
baseplate
basil weed
bas-relief
bass flute
bastinado
batch file
bath chair
batholith
bath towel
bathybius
batrachia
battalion
batteries
battleaxe
battle cry
bay window
beachhead
beachwear
beaconage
bean caper
bean goose
bear's foot
bearberry
beatitude
beccafico
beclamide
bede house
bedfellow
bedjacket
bedlamite
bed settee
bedspread
beechmast
beefeater
beef steak
beekeeper
beggarman
beleaguer
belemnite
bel esprit
bell gable
bellicose
bell metal
bellminah
bell tower
below deck
belt punch
belvedere
bench hook
bench mark
bent grass
benzhexol
bergander
berserker
bevel gear
biblicist
bicameral
bicycling
bicyclist
bilateral
bilboquet
bilge keel
bilge pump
bilharzia
billiards
billycock
bimonthly
binturong
biography
biologist
biosphere
biperiden
birch wine
bird organ
bird's foot
birgander
birthsong
bisacodyl
bisegment
bishopric
bismillah
bisulphan
bit player
bitter ale
bivaulted
black bear
black beer
blackbird
black body
black box
black buck
black cock
black duck
blackfish
black hole
blackjack
blackmail
black onyx
black opal
black sole
black swan
blacktail
black tern
blackware
blackwood
blank bill
blasphemy
blast off
blazoning
bleaching
blind spot
blindworm
blockhead
block lava
blond lace
bloodroot
bloodshed
blue algae
bluebeard
blueberry
blue crane
blue jeans
blue krait
blue light
blue nurse
blue peter
blue-point
blueprint
blue shark
blue sprat
blue whale
blunderer
blusterer
boardable
boarhound
boar spear
boat drill

boathouse
boatswain
boat train
bob cherry
bobsleigh
body count
bodyguard
Bofors gun
boilerman
boliviano
bolometer
bolsterer
bolt auger
bomb aimer
bombardon
bombazine
bomb chest
bombed-out
bomb ketch
bombproof
bombs away
bombshell
bombsight
bomb squad
bona fides
bondslave
bondwoman
bon vivant
bony bream
booby trap
book louse
bookmaker
bookplate
bookshelf
book stand
book value
boomerang
boomslang
boot brush
boot crimp
bootmaker
bordereau
born-again
borrowing
bossa nova
bottletit
bourgeois
bower-bird
bowler hat
bow string

bow window
box number
box turtle
boyfriend
brakedrum
brakepipe
brakeshoe
brambling
branchial
branching
brandling
brass band
brassiere
brazil nut
breakdown
breakfast
breast pin
breeze-fly
briar root
bric-a-brac
brick-clay
brick dust
brick kiln
bride cake
brigadier
brillante
brilliant
brimstone
broad bean
broadbill
broadcast
broad jump
broadside
brokerage
brood mare
brooklime
brookmint
brookweed
broomcorn
broomrape
brown bear
brown coal
brown hawk
brown pine
brown-spur
brushwork
brut wines
bubble car
bubblegum
buccaneer

buccinite
bucentaur
buckboard
buckhound
buck's fizz
buck's horn
buckthorn
buckwheat
bugle call
bugle horn
bull board
bulldozer
bull fight
bullfinch
bull snake
bulltrout
bumblebee
bummaloti
bump-start
bumper car
bunkering
buphenine
burlesque
burnisher
burrelfly
bus driver
bush shirt
butterbur
buttercup
butterfly
butternut
buzzardet
by-product
bystander
cab driver
cabin crew
cable ship
cabriolet
cacophony
caddis-fly
caelilian
cafe owner
cake stand
calabrese
calamanco
calcancus
calendula
call money
call price
camelhair

camelling
cameraman
camouflet
campanero
campanile
campanula
camp chair
camp stool
canal boat
cancerite
candidate
candytuft
canebrake
cane chair
canker bit
canker-fly
cannipers
cannonade
cannoneer
canonical
can opener
cantabile
cantharus
canvasser
capacitor
capillary
capriccio
captaincy
carbachol
carbonado
carbonate
carbonium
carbon tax
carbromal
carbuncle
cardamine
car driver
card sharp
card table
careenage
careerist
caretaker
cargo boat
carmelite
carnation
carnelian
carnivore
carob tree
carpenter
carpet bag

carpeting
carpolite
carrageen
carry over
carthorse
cartilage
cartology
cartouche
cartridge
caryopsis
casebound
case knife
casemaker
cashiered
casholong
cassareep
casserole
cassimere
cassonade
cassowary
castanets
castellan
castor oil
cast steel
catalysis
catamaran
catamount
cat basket
catchpole
catechism
catechist
catechize
catharsis
cathedral
cat-silver
cattle car
cavalcade
ceasefire
cedar moth
ceilinged
celandine
celebrant
celebrate
celebrity
celestial
celestina
cellarage
cellarist
cellarman
cellulose
centenary
centipede
centrebit
centriole
centurion
ceratodus
cerecloth
cereopsis
cerograph
certified
cestui que
cha-cha-cha
chaetodon
chaffinch
chain belt
chain gang
chain-link
chain mail
chain pump
challenge
chameleon
chamomile
champagne
champerty
chanteuse
chantilly
chantress
chaparral
charabanc
character
charivari
charlatan
chartered
charterer
chartroom
charwoman
chatterer
chauffeur
chaya root
cheapjack
checkmate
cheekbone
cheese-fly
chelonian
chemistry
cheongsam
cherimoya
cherry bay
cherry pie
cherry pit
chevalier
chiasmata
chicanery
chickaree
chickling
chickweed
chieftain
chihuahua
china bowl
china root
China rose
china tree
chinaware
chipolata
chiropody
chiseller
chi-square
chlamydia
chocolate
chokedamp
choke weed
chop house
chorister
chorology
chorus boy
chromatic
chromatid
chromatin
chrysalis
chump chop
churching
churchman
church owl
churrworm
cicindela
cigarette
cinematic
cineraria
cirrhosis
cityscape
civil year
clack dish
claret cup
clarifier
clarionet
clary sage
clasp lock
classical
classroom
clatterer

clausilia
claustral
clavicorn
claviharp
clay slate
clay stone
clearance
clearwing
clemizole
clepsydra
clergyman
clientele
cling-fish
clinician
clinodome
clipboard
clip joint
cloakroom
clock golf
clockwork
clog dance
clogmaker
cloisonne
cloisters
clonidine
clopamide
close haul
close time
cloudless
clove pink
club chair
club grass
clubhouse
clump boot
coach horn
coachwork
coadjutor
coalhouse
coalition
coalminer
coalmouse
coalowner
coal plant
coal store
coastline
coastwise
cobaltine
cochineal
cockatiel
cocked hat
cockfight
cockmatch
cockroach
cockscomb
cock's head
cocoonery
code of law
co-edition
coenobite
coffeebug
coffee cup
coffee pot
coffer dam
coherence
colchicum
cold steel
colemouse
coleopter
cole-perch
collating
colleague
collector
collegian
collusion
colocynth
colonelcy
colonnade
colosseum
colourful
colourist
coltsfoot
columbine
columnist
combatant
combative
comb brush
comb-jelly
comfiture
comforter
commander
commensal
commissar
committee
commodity
commodore
common law
communion
communism
communist
community
companion
compasses
composite
comprador
concierge
concourse
concubine
condenser
condiment
conductor
cone sheet
confessor
confidant
confiture
conformer
conger eel
conjugate
conjuring
conqueror
conscript
consenter
conserver
consignee
consignor
consonant
consonate
constable
construct
consulate
container
contemner
contender
continent
contralto
contriver
conularia
converted
converter
cook's mate
cooperage
co-patriot
copestone
copralite
copypaper
copyright
coral fish
corallite
coral reef
coral tree
coral wort

cordelier
coreopsis
coriander
corkscrew
cormorant
corn aphis
corn borer
corn bread
corncrake
cornelian
cornfield
cornmeter
cornopean
corn poppy
corn salad
corn snake
corn stone
corollary
corozo nut
corposant
corpuscle
corrasion
corrector
corrosion
corrupter
cortisone
coryphene
cosmogony
cosmolabe
cosmology
cosmonaut
cost clerk
cost price
costumier
cotangent
cotillion
cotter pin
cotton gin
cotyledon
coulisses
courgette
court card
courtesan
court fool
courtyard
couturier
cover-clip
cover girl
cowfeeder
cowkeeper
crab apple
crab-louse
crack shot
crackling
cracksman
craftsman
cramp bark
cramp iron
cranberry
crank axle
crankcase
crayonist
crazy golf
cream cake
cremation
crescendo
cricketer
crinoline
criticism
crocodile
crookback
croquette
cross beam
crossbill
crossfire
crosshead
crossjack
crossroad
crosstree
crosswind
crossword
crowberry
crown post
crow's foot
crow's nest
crow stone
crumb tray
crustacea
cuartilla
cuartillo
Cuban heel
cubic foot
cubic inch
cubic yard
cuckoo bud
cufflinks
cullender
culver key
cum rights
cup winner
cupbearer
curly kale
currawong
curry comb
cushionet
custodian
cutter bar
cut-throat
cutting in
cyclizine
cyclorama
cyclotron
cymbalist
cymbidium
cynipides
cytoplasm
dachshund
daily help
dairy farm
dairymaid
Dales pony
dalmatica
damascene
damnation
dandelion
dandy-cock
daredevil
dark horse
dartboard
dart snake
dashboard
dashlight
datum-line
davenport
day school
deaconess
dead level
deadly sin
dead march
dead water
death bell
death seat
deathtrap
debauchee
debenture
debit card
debit note
debutante
decachord
decagynia

decalitre
decametre
decandria
decastich
decathlon
decennary
decennial
deciduous
decilitre
decimetre
decistere
deck cargo
deckchair
deck games
declarant
decorated
decorator
decoy duck
dedicated
deduction
deep-toned
deerhound
deermouse
defaulter
defeatist
defection
defendant
defensive
deflation
defoliant
defrauder
defroster
deinornis
dekalitre
dekametre
deliverer
delundung
demagogue
demandant
demi-lance
demi-monde
demitasse
democracy
demurrage
dentalium
dent fault
dentistry
departure
dependant
depletion
depositor
depot ship
depressor
dermestes
descender
desecrate
desertion
desert rat
desert rod
desk clerk
de son tort
desperado
despoiler
destroyer
detective
detention
deterrent
detonator
detractor
devastate
deviation
devil fish
devonport
devotions
diaconate
diaeresis
dialog box
diaphragm
diarrhoea
diazonium
dicynodon
didelphid
didrachma
dietetics
dietitian
digestion
digitalin
digitalis
digitaria
digitoxin
dignitary
diligence
dimension
dimyarian
dining car
diplomacy
dipswitch
dipterans
directory
directrix
dirt track
disanchor
disburser
disc brake
disc drill
discerner
discharge
discloser
discovery
disembark
disengage
disgracer
disguiser
dishcloth
dish clout
dish cover
dishonour
disk brake
disk cache
disk drive
dismissal
dispeller
dispenser
disperser
displayed
displayer
disprover
disputant
dissector
dissenter
dissident
dissonant
distemper
distiller
distraint
disturber
dithranol
dithyramb
ditrochee
dittander
diurnally
diuturnal
diversion
divinator
dizziness
dockcress
doctorate
doctrinal
dodecagon
dodgem car

doggerman
dogmatist
dogshores
dog basket
dog clutch
dog collar
dog kennel
dog racing
dog violet
dolabella
dolly bird
dominance
dominator
donkeyman
do-nothing
doob grass
doodlebug
doorplate
doorstead
doorstone
dorbeetle
dormitory
dormobile
dot matrix
double act
dove's foot
dowelling
dowitcher
downstage
downthrow
draconian
draftsman
dragonfly
drain trap
dramatics
dramatist
dramatize
draught ox
draw knife
drawlatch
drawn game
draw-plate
dray horse
dress coat
dress ship
dress suit
drift sail
drift wind
driftwood
drip-flap
dripstone
driveller
driver-ant
drizzling
dromedary
drone pipe
drop scene
drop scone
drop-tank
drum brake
drum major
drum maker
drumstick
dry season
dry valley
drysalter
duck's foot
duck's meat
duffle bag
dulcamara
dulcitone
dumbbells
dumbledor
dune buggy
dungarees
dupondius
duralumin
dura mater
dust brush
dust devil
dust sheet
dust stove
Dutch oven
DVD player
Dyer's weed
dynameter
dynamical
dynometer
dysentery
dyspeptic
dysploidy
dziggetai
eagle-hawk
eared seal
early bird
earth flax
earthbank
earthling
earthwork
earthworm
easy chair
easy money
easy terms
ecardines
eccentric
echinidan
ecologist
e-commerce
economics
economies
economist
economize
ecosphere
ecossaise
ecosystem
ectoplasm
edelweiss
editorial
egg beater
egg boiler
eglantine
eiderdown
eider duck
eidograph
eightsome
elbow pipe
elder wine
electoral
electress
electrify
electrode
elegiacal
elevation
elevator
ellipsoid
embalming
embattled
emblemata
embossing
embracery
embrasure
embrocado
emendator
emetology
emolument
emoticons
emphysema
enameller
enchanter
enchilada

enclitics
encomiast
encompass
encounter
encrinite
encyclical
endocrine
endolymph
endoplasm
endowment
enemy camp
enemy fire
energizer
energumen
enfeebler
engineman
engiscope
engrailed
engraulis
engraving
engrosser
enlivener
enrolment
entangler
enteritis
entertain
entourage
entreater
entrechat
entremets
epaulette
ephemeris
epicentre
epicyclic
epidermis
epileptic
episcopal
episenium
epistoler
equalizer
equipment
equisetum
equitable
equitancy
eremitage
eriometer
erminites
errand boy
erythrine
escalator
espionage
esplanade
estafette
estaminet
estate car
estimator
ethnology
etoglucid
etymology
eucharist
eumenidae
euphemism
euphonism
euphonium
euphonize
euphorbia
euphrasia
evacuator
evaporite
evergreen
everybody
evolution
evolvulus
examinant
excavator
excerptor
exchanger
exchequer
exciseman
excitator
exclusion
exclusive
excretion
excretory
execution
executive
executory
executrix
exhibiter
exhibitor
exodermis
ex-officer
expansion
exploiter
expositor
expounder
expulsion
exquisite
extempore
extortion
extractor
extravert
extremist
extrovert
extrusion
eyebright
eye doctor
eyed skink
eyeleteer
eyes front
eyes right
fabricant
face towel
face value
facsimile
factorize
fair price
fair trade
fairy tale
faldstool
fallochat
false keel
falsifier
family man
fancy ball
fan mussel
farandole
farmhouse
fashioner
fat client
favourite
feast days
fee simple
felt maker
female die
fenugreek
ferestral
ferreting
ferryboat
fertility
fertilize
fetishist
fever root
feverwort
fiat money
fiddle-bow
fiduciary
field army
field-duck
fieldfare

field rank
field wren
fig parrot
figpecker
fig-psylla
figurante
filler cap
fillister
film actor
film extra
film house
film maker
filmstrip
financial
financier
fine paper
fining pot
finny-scad
fire alarm
fire board
firebrick
fire brush
firecrest
fire drill
fire eater
fire float
fire-flair
fire grate
fire guard
fire irons
fireplace
firepower
firestone
firewater
fir-framed
firmament
firm offer
firm price
first-born
first call
first cost
first lead
first lord
fish curer
fisherman
fishgarth
fish-louse
fish joint
fish knife
fishroyal
fish slice
fish spear
flageolet
flag maker
flagstaff
flagstone
flame tree
flash burn
flashback
flashings
flat spin
flatterer
flintlock
flip-flops
flood tide
floodgate
floodmark
floorshow
floptical
floriated
floss silk
flotation
flowchart
flowerpot
flow meter
flue brush
fluorspar
flute stop
flying ant
flying fox
flying jib
fog signal
folk dance
folk music
food mixer
foot board
footbrake
foothills
foot-pound
footstool
foot valve
forage cap
forcemeat
force pump
forebears
forebrain
foreigner
foreshore
forest-fly
forest oak
forfeiter
forficula
forgetter
fork chuck
formalist
formation
formative
forsythia
fortalice
fortesque
fortifier
fort major
fortnight
forwarder
fossicker
foster son
foundling
foxhunter
framework
franchise
francolin
free agent
freelance
free-liver
freemason
freestone
free trade
free verse
free-wheel
freighter
frequency
friar-bird
fricassee
fried eggs
fried fish
frigatoon
fringilla
frivolity
frock coat
frogmouth
front axle
front door
front line
front room
front seat
frost-fish
fruit cake
fruit tart
fruiterer
fruit time

fruit tree
frusemide
frying pan
fucoid bed
fuel gauge
fulfiller
full dress
full house
full skirt
fully paid
fungicide
funicular
funny boat
funny bone
furbisher
fur collar
furibondo
furnisher
furniture
furtherer
fusillade
gaberdine
gainsayer
gala night
galantine
gallamine
gallantry
gallinazo
gallinule
galliwasp
gall-midge
gallopade
gallstone
galvanism
galvanist
galvanize
gamma rays
gangboard
gangplank
garavance
garde-bras
gardening
garnishee
garnisher
garoscope
garreting
garrotter
gas attack
gas burner
gas cooker
gas engine
gas fitter
gas geyser
gas holder
gasometer
gas pliers
gas retort
gastropod
gatehouse
gate money
gathering
gather way
gauntlets
gazetteer
gear lever
gearshift
gearwheel
gelanthus
gelignite
gem cutter
generator
gentleman
genuflect
geography
geologist
geometric
georgette
gerfalcon
germander
germinate
gerundive
gestation
ghost moth
giant clam
giant frog
giant toad
giblet pie
gier-eagle
gilt-edged
ginger ale
ginger pop
ginger tom
gin palace
girandole
girl guide
girl scout
gladiator
gladiolus
glassware
glasswort
glaucopis
glengarry
glissando
globalism
globe-fish
gluemaker
glymidine
gnomonics
goal posts
go-between
godfather
godliness
godmother
going rate
gold broad
goldcrest
golden cup
golden-eye
goldenrod
goldfinch
gold noble
gold penny
goldsinny
goldsmith
goldspink
gold tooth
gold watch
golf clubs
golomynka
gondolier
good faith
goosander
goose corn
goosedown
goosefoot
gospeller
governess
grace note
gradation
graduator
grammatic
grand duke
grandioso
grand jury
grandpapa
grandsire
grand slam
grapeshot
grapevine
grapewort

grassbird
grassland
grasspoly
grass wren
gratifier
gravel pit
graveyard
gravy boat
gravy soup
graystone
grease box
grease gun
great-aunt
greatcoat
great hall
great skua
greengage
greenhorn
green peas
greensand
green toad
greenwash
greenweed
greenwood
grenadier
grenadine
greybeard
grey heron
greyhound
greystone
grey water
grey whale
grid north
grimalkin
grisaille
grossbeak
grotesque
ground ash
groundage
groundhog
ground ivy
groundnut
ground oak
groundsel
groupware
groveller
guarantee
guarantor
guard boat
guardroom
guard ship
guard's van
guerrilla
guestroom
guest star
guildhall
guillemot
guinea-hen
guinea pig
guitarist
gull wing
gullyhole
gun battle
guncotton
gunpowder
gun turret
gustation
gymnasium
gymnastic
gynaecium
gyrfalcon
gyroscope
hackberry
haematite
haemocoel
hagiology
hailstorm
hairbrush
haircloth
hair grass
hairpiece
hair tonic
hairy frog
half-angle
half-caste
half-hitch
half ounce
half pound
half shift
half-track
halitosis
hall table
halophyte
hamadryad
hamburger
hammer axe
hammerkop
handbrace
handbrake
hand organ
handscrew
handspike
hand-staff
hand towel
hansom cab
happy hour
haranguer
harbinger
harbourer
hard aport
hard-belly
hard drive
hard frost
hard money
hard sauce
hard times
hardyhead
harlequin
harmonica
harmonics
harmonist
harmonium
harmonize
harnesser
harpooner
harrowing
harvester
hatchback
hatchment
hatha yoga
haversack
haymaking
headdress
headlight
headpiece
headscarf
headstone
headwind
hearkener
heartburn
heathbird
heathcock
heathland
heavy beer
heavy cake
heavy fire
heavy spar
hectogram
heelpiece
heliostat

hellebore
hellhound
hemiptera
hemistich
hendiadys
hepatitis
herbalism
herbalist
herbarian
herbivore
herborist
hercynian
hereafter
hermitage
heronshaw
herringer
heterodox
hexachord
hexagonal
hexameter
hexastich
hexastyle
hierogram
hierology
high altar
high chair
high court
highflier
high heels
highlands
highlight
high-pitch
hightoned
high water
hillbilly
hindberry
hindbrain
hippodame
hippurite
hired hand
hired help
histamine
histology
historian
hit-and-run
hoarfrost
hoarhound
hodiernal
hodmandod
hodometer
hoist sail
holing axe
holly blue
holly fern
hollyhock
holometer
holystone
holy table
holy water
home front
homeopath
homestall
homestead
homolysis
homophony
honey bear
honeycomb
honeymoon
honeywort
hoop skirt
hop picker
hopscotch
horehound
horned asp
horned owl
hornet-fly
horn slate
hornstone
horometry
horsebean
horse boat
horsefoot
horsehair
horse mill
horseplay
horserace
horserake
horsetail
hosteller
hostility
hot colour
houndfish
hour angle
hourglass
houseboat
housecoat
house flag
household
houseline
housemaid
housewife
humblebee
hummeller
hunchback
hurricane
husbandry
hybodonts
hydrangea
hydration
hydraulic
hydrofoil
hydrology
hydrostat
hydroxide
hygienist
hygrology
hylaesaur
hymnodist
hymnology
hyoid bone
hypallage
hyperbola
hyperbole
hypericum
hyperlink
hypertext
hypnotist
hypocaust
hypocrite
iced water
ice hockey
ice skates
ichneumon
ichnology
identical
idiomatic
idiot tape
idle wheel
ignoramus
iguanodon
iliopsoas
imaginary
imbroglio
immigrant
immolator
immusical
impatiens
impeacher
impedance
imperfect

implement
import tax
impotence
impromptu
improvise
inamorata
inamorato
in arrears
incentive
income tax
increaser
increment
incubator
incumbent
incurable
incursion
indelible
indemnify
indemnity
indenture
indian ink
indicator
indiction
induction
inductive
indweller
inebriate
inertness
infirmary
inflation
inflexion
inflicter
in-flight
influenza
informant
infractor
infringer
ingestion
ingle nook
ingrafter
in harmony
inheritor
inhibitor
initiator
injection
ink bottle
ink holder
inner tube
innkeeper
innocence
innovator
inorganic
in-patient
inscriber
insequent
insertion
insoluble
insolvent
inspector
instiller
insulated
insulator
insurance
insurgent
intendant
interaxal
interaxis
intercept
interdict
interface
interlude
interment
internode
intersect
intestacy
intestate
intestine
intriguer
introvert
invalided
inveigher
inveigler
inventory
inversion
iprindole
iridology
ironsmith
ironstone
ironworks
irregular
isoclinal
isoclinic
isomerism
isometric
isoniazid
isosceles
isostatic
isotropic
itinerant
ivory palm
jacaranda
jack block
jackboots
jackknife
jackplane
jackscrew
jack-smith
jack staff
jack stays
jack towel
jaculator
jadestone
janissary
japanning
jay-walker
jazz music
jellyfish
jerfalcon
jessamine
jet engine
jettyhead
jewel case
jewellery
jitterbug
job hunter
job seeker
jobsworth
jockey cap
joint heir
jollyboat
jollytail
joss stick
journeyer
joyriding
joystick
judiciary
jumbo jet
jungle cat
justified
justifier
jut window
kanamycin
kennel man
kentledge
kerbstone
kid gloves
kidnapper
kilocycle
kilohertz
kilolitre

kilometre
king apple
king cobra
king snake
kingstone
kinswoman
kitchener
kite's foot
kittiwake
knee holly
knee socks
knife edge
knot grass
know-it-all
kokrawood
labyrinth
laccolith
lace frame
lacemaker
lac-insect
lackbrain
lacquerer
ladies' man
lady's maid
lady's muck
lager beer
lagomorph
lagrimoso
lambswool
laminated
lampadist
lampooner
lampshade
lampshell
lampstand
lance rest
lance wood
land agent
land ahead
landaulet
land court
land force
landowner
landreeve
landscape
landslide
languente
larcenist
lardy cake
large blue
large sack
larghetto
lark's heel
last rites
laudation
launch pad
launderer
laundress
lavalière
lawmonger
lawnmower
lay figure
layperson
lay reader
lazaretto
lazybones
lazy Susan
leaflouse
lean years
leasehold
leger-line
legionary
legislate
leitmotif
leitmotiv
lemon balm
lemon curd
letterbox
leukaemia
leviathan
liability
libellant
liberator
libertine
librarian
licensing
life cycle
life forms
lifeguard
lift shaft
lightbulb
lightning
lightship
light year
lilang-eni
lime juice
limelight
limestone
limewater
limousine
lineblock
linen mesh
linenfold
line space
linotyper
lint-white
lionceaux
lioncelle
lionheart
lion tamer
lip-reader
liquidate
liquidity
liquorice
list price
lithocarp
lithodome
lithology
lithophyl
lithotint
lithotome
litigious
liturgist
liverwort
liveryman
livestock
loaf sugar
loan agent
loan shark
lob bowler
lobscouse
locksmith
lodestone
logarithm
logistics
logometer
log roller
log-runner
loincloth
loitering
lollshrob
long-dated
long dozen
long dress
longeron
long-haul
longicorn
longitude
long-range
long skirt

long socks
loopholed
lorazepam
lord mayor
lost sheep
lotus lily
loudmouth
love apple
love scene
loving cup
low comedy
lower case
lower deck
low-impact
lowlander
low-loader
low relief
lubricant
lubricate
lucimeter
lumberman
lump sugar
lunar year
lunch time
lyric poem
macartney
maçedoine
machinery
machinist
macintosh
macrodome
madeleine
mad moment
madrepore
maelstrom
magnesium
magnetism
magnetist
magnetite
magnetize
magnetron
magnifico
magnifier
magnitude
maharajah
mail coach
mail merge
mail order
mail train
mainbrace
mainframe
mainsheet
majordomo
major role
make merry
makepeace
make ready
malachite
mala fides
male model
male screw
mallemuck
mammalogy
mammonist
man-at-arms
mandatory
mandolute
man engine
manganese
mangetout
mango bird
mango fish
mangroves
mannequin
mannerism
mannerist
manoeuvre
manometer
march-past
margarine
marigraph
marinade
marinate
market day
marketing
marl slate
marmalade
marooning
marquetry
marrowfat
marshbird
marsh frog
marshland
marsupite
martyrdom
masculine
masochist
master key
matchlock
matriarch
matricide
matutinal
maulstick
mausoleum
maxillary
maxi skirt
mayflower
meadow rue
meanderer
mechanics
mechanism
mechanist
mechanize
meclozine
medallion
medallist
megacycle
megadeath
megahertz
megaphone
megascope
megaspore
megestrol
meibomian
melaphyre
melodious
melodrama
melphalan
meltwater
membracid
memoirist
menominee
menstrual
mepacrine
mercenary
merganser
merrimake
merriment
merriness
merulidan
mesmerist
messenger
messieurs
mestranol
metalling
metallist
metalloid
metaplasm
meteorite
meteoroid

metformin
methadone
metheglin
metrician
metric ton
metronome
mezzanine
mezzotint
mezzo-voce
mianserin
mica slate
microchip
micrology
micropyle
microtome
microtron
middle ear
middleman
middlings
midi skirt
midstream
midsummer
midwinter
migration
mild steel
milestone
miliolite
militancy
milk float
milk punch
milkshake
milk snake
milk stout
milk train
milk vetch
mill owner
milligram
millinery
millipede
millstone
mincemeat
minefield
minelayer
mine shaft
miniature
mini skirt
minor poet
minor role
mint julep
mint sauce
minute gun
mirabelle
miresnipe
miscreant
mispickel
mistletoe
mitigator
mixed-race
mizenmast
mizzentop
mock-Tudor
modelling
moderator
modern art
modernism
modernist
modillion
modulator
moiré silk
molecular
mollymauk
monastery
monatomic
monkey nut
monkshood
monoceros
monochord
monocoque
monocycle
monodrama
monologue
monometer
monophony
monorhyme
monotonic
monotreme
moon daisy
moonraker
moonshine
moonshot
moon snail
moonstone
moralizer
mortal sin
mortgagee
mortgagor
mortician
moschatel
moss agate
motorbike
motorboat
motorcade
motor show
mouse deer
mouse-hawk
mousetail
mousetrap
mouth harp
movie buff
movie-goer
movie star
moving van
mud sluice
mud-sucker
muffineer
mujahedin
muletrain
mulled ale
multihull
multitude
munitions
murderous
murray cod
muscadine
muscalite
muscicapa
muscleman
muscovite
music book
music hall
music room
musk apple
musketeer
musketoon
musk melon
mutagenic
mutilator
mutton ham
mutton pie
mycomycin
mylohyoid
myologist
mysticism
mythmaker
nadrolone
nail brush
nail punch
nanometre
narcissus
nasal bone

natatores
naumachia
nautilite
navel ring
navel stud
navicular
navigable
navigator
near miss
near money
neckcloth
necrology
nectarine
needle gun
needletin
neglecter
negotiate
neighbour
neologian
neologism
neologist
nepenthes
nepheline
nephridia
nephritis
neptunian
nerve cell
net income
net weight
neurology
newmarket
newsagent
news group
newspaper
newsprint
next of kin
nialamide
nicotinyl
nifuratel
night club
nightfall
nightgown
night hawk
night-time
nightwear
nilometer
nine holes
nipperkin
nipple key
nitration
nodal line
nominator
nonentity
nonostich
nonpareil
non-rigid
non-smoker
northeast
northerly
northward
northwest
north wind
nose flute
nose piece
notepaper
not guilty
notochord
not proven
nourisher
novelette
novitiate
nucleolus
nullifier
numbskull
numerator
numerical
nummulite
nursemaid
nutriment
nut wrench
nux vomica
obbligato
obedience
obeisance
objective
objet d'art
obsequies
obturator
occultist
ocean lane
octachord
octagonal
octastyle
octennial
octostyle
odd job man
oestrogen
offensive
offertory
office boy
officiant
officiate
offspring
off-the-peg
oil colour
oil engine
oil filter
oil geyser
oil tanker
old growth
old master
oleograph
oleometer
olfactory
oligarchy
oligopoly
ombudsman
onslaught
oogenesis
oolong tea
operation
operative
operculum
ophiology
ophiosaur
oppressor
optic lobe
optigraph
optometer
orangeade
orange-bug
orange gin
orange tip
orangutan
orchestra
order book
ordinator
organelle
organizer
organzine
orlop deck
ornaments
orography
orphanage
orthodoxy
orthotics
ossifrage
osteology
osteopath
ostracian

ostracite
other half
otography
otologist
oubliette
ourselves
outer door
outer gate
outfitter
outgoings
outrigger
overboard
overdraft
overdrawn
overdress
overdrive
overheads
overmatch
overnight
overpower
overprint
overrider
overshoes
overthrow
overwhelm
overwrite
oxacillin
oxbow lake
oxidation
oxycoccus
ozone hole
pacemaker
pachyderm
packaging
packdrill
packhorse
pademelon
pageantry
pageproof
paillasse
paillette
painterly
palanquin
palaverer
palestric
palladian
palladium
palliasse
palm civet
palmacite
palmistry
panama hat
panel game
panellist
pantaloon
pantomime
papal bull
paperback
paper bark
paperclip
paper rack
papillion
parabolic
parachute
paradisea
paragraph
paralegal
paralysis
paralytic
paramedic
parameter
paraquito
parataxis
parbuckle
parcheesi
parchment
pardalote
pargeting
parhelian
parquetry
parrakeet
parricide
parroquet
parsonage
part music
parthenon
partition
partitive
part-owner
partridge
party line
party wall
pas de deux
paso doble
passenger
passepied
passerine
past tense
pastorale
pasturage
patchouli
patchwork
patellite
pathology
patriarch
patrician
patricide
patriotic
patrol car
patroness
paymaster
pay office
peacetime
pea jacket
peaked cap
pearl rice
pearl spar
peasantry
peculator
pecuniary
pedagogue
pedalling
pedometer
pellitory
peneplain
penfriend
peninsula
pen-pusher
pensioner
penthouse
pepperpot
perceiver
perdonium
peregrine
perennial
perfecter
perforate
performer
periclase
pericline
pericycle
perilymph
perimeter
periscope
peristyle
permalloy
permitter
persimmon
personage
personnel

persuader
perturber
perverter
pessimist
peter boat
pethidine
petrol can
petroleum
petrology
petticoat
petty cash
pewter pot
phacolith
phagocyte
phalanges
phalarope
phellogen
phenazone
phenetoin
philately
phillipic
philology
phonetics
phoney war
phonology
phosphate
phosphide
photocopy
photoplay
photostat
phylogeny
physician
physicist
phytogeny
phytology
phytotomy
pianolist
picalilli
pictorial
piecework
pied-goose
pier glass
pier table
pigeon pie
piggybank
pig trough
pilgarlic
pillarbox
pilot boat
pilot fish
pilot ship
pimpernel
pina cloth
pinchfist
pine-aphis
pineapple
pinefinch
pine snake
pink coral
PIN number
pin-up girl
pipe major
pipistrel
pirouette
pistachio
pistareen
piston rod
pitchfork
pitching
pitchpipe
pitsawyer
pit-stalls
pituitary
pixie hood
pizzicato
plainsong
plaintiff
plane iron
planetary
planetoid
plane tree
planigale
planisher
plant-lice
plasterer
plate rack
platitude
platonist
play-actor
playgroup
playhouse
plaything
pleasance
pleonaste
pleoptics
plimsolls
ploughboy
ploughing
ploughman
plumbline
plumbrule
plunderer
pluralist
plus-fours
plutocrat
plutonist
plutonium
pneumatic
pneumonia
poetaster
point duty
point lace
pointsman
poison gas
poison ivy
poison oak
polar bear
polar bond
polarizer
pole vault
police car
police dog
policeman
politburo
pollutant
pollution
polonaise
polychord
polyester
polygonal
polygonum
polygraph
polyhedra
polymixin
polyphony
polyscope
polythene
polytonal
polyvinyl
pond snail
pontifice
pool table
poorhouse
pop artist
popliteus
porbeagle
porcupine
porous pot
porringer
portfolio

port glass
portioner
portrayal
portrayer
portreeve
possessor
post chaise
post-dated
postilion
postponed
postponer
postulant
postwoman
pot barley
pot boiler
pot hanger
potassium
potato pie
potentate
potential
potholing
pot-hunter
pot-pourri
pot-roast
poulterer
pound cake
pourpoint
poussette
powder box
powder boy
powder keg
powerboat
power loom
prayer mat
prayer rug
preaching
precatory
precedent
precentor
preceptor
precipice
precursor
predicant
predictor
preferred
preferrer
prelatist
prelector
premature
presbyter
presentee
presenter
preserver
president
press stud
press-gang
pressroom
pretender
preterite
preventer
price list
price rise
pricksong
priestess
prime cost
primidone
primitive
principal
prison van
privateer
privative
privatize
privilege
prize crew
prize ring
prize ship
probation
proboscis
procedure
proceeder
processor
proconsul
profanity
professor
profferer
profilist
profiteer
programme
projector
prolonger
promazine
promenade
promissor
promotion
prompt-box
promulger
prongbuck
pronghorn
propeller
proquanil
proselyte
prose poem
prosodian
prosodist
protector
protester
prothesis
prototype
protruder
provedore
provelone
provender
psalm book
pseudonym
psoriasis
psychosis
ptarmigan
pteropods
pterosaur
publicist
publicity
publisher
puff adder
puff paste
pulmonary
pulpiteer
pump break
pump spear
pump stock
punchbowl
punch-line
puppeteer
purchaser
purgatory
purloiner
put option
puy lentil
pyllopodo
pyocyanin
pyracanth
pyralidae
pyrethrum
pyrometer
pyrophane
quachilto
quadratic
quadratus
quadrille
quadruman
quadruped

quadruple
quailpipe
quaker gun
qualifier
quarryman
quarterly
quartette
quickbeam
quicklime
quicksand
quickstep
quick time
quinidine
quintette
quintuple
quittance
quoiffure
quotation
quotidian
rabbinist
racehorse
racestand
racing car
racketeer
raconteur
radiation
radiogram
radiology
radio wave
rafflesia
rail fence
railmaker
rain cloud
rain gauge
rainmaker
rainproof
raintight
raised pie
rambostan
ransacker
rapturist
rare gases
raspberry
ratepayer
razorbill
razor fish
ready cash
ready made
real image
rearguard
rear light
rearmouse
rebellion
recension
reception
recession
recessive
recharter
recipient
reckoning
reconquer
recording
recoverer
recruiter
rectangle
rectifier
recurrent
recycling
redbreast
red clover
reddition
red ensign
red grouse
red guards
red mullet
red pepper
redresser
red setter
redstreak
reductant
reduction
redundant
reed organ
reef point
reermouse
refectory
refitment
reflation
reflector
reflexive
reformist
refractor
refresher
regardant
registrar
regulator
rehearsal
rehearser
reimburse
reinforce
reinsurer
relay race
religious
reliquary
reliquiae
remainder
remission
rencontre
rendering
renewable
renouncer
renovator
repairing
reparable
repasture
repayable
repayment
repentant
represent
represser
reprobate
requester
reservoir
residence
residency
resonance
resources
respecter
rest house
restraint
resultant
reticulum
retractor
retriever
return day
revelment
revel rout
reverence
reversion
revetment
revictual
revving up
rheometer
rheomotor
rheoscope
rheotrope
rhinology
rhombspar
rhumb line
rhymester

rhynchops
rhythmics
ribbonman
rice field
ricercare
ridiculer
rifamycin
rifle-bird
righteous
right-wing
rillettes
rimiterol
ring fence
ring ousel
ring ouzel
ring snake
ritualist
river boat
river crab
river trip
rixdollar
road metal
roadmaker
road sense
roadstead
road works
rocambole
rock cress
rock hyrax
rock-borer
rockbound
rocket car
rock 'n' roll
roisterer
ropemaker
rosefinch
rose-noble
rosmarine
rossignol
rotameter
rotor ship
roughcast
rough copy
roughneck
roundelay
roundhead
round-neck
roundsman
routinist
rowan tree
royal mast
royalties
rubrician
rudaceous
rugweevil
ruminator
rump steak
rum-runner
rural dean
rushlight
saccarium
sackcloth
sack dress
sacrament
sacrarium
sacrifice
sacrilege
sacristan
safe haven
safe house
safemaker
safety pin
safflower
sailboard
sailcloth
sailmaker
sailor cap
sailor hat
salamander
salangale
sallyport
salt marsh
saloon car
saltation
saltpetre
salvation
sanctions
sanctuary
sandbanks
sand-lance
sandpaper
sandpiper
sandstone
sand yacht
sans serif
sapodilla
sartorius
sassafras
satellite
satinette
satin spar
satinwood
satisfier
saunterer
saury-pike
saxifrage
saxophone
scale post
scantling
scapegoat
scaphopod
scarecrow
scarifier
scaur-cock
scavenger
scenarist
schilling
schipperke
schnapper
schnauzer
schnitzel
scholarly
scholiast
schoolboy
school cap
schoolman
scientist
sclerosis
sclerotic
scoop-neck
scorching
scorecard
scotch egg
scoundrel
scrambler
scrapbook
scratcher
screening
screwjack
screw pine
scribbler
scribe awl
scrimshaw
scripture
scrivener
scrub-bird
scrub-fowl
scrub-wren
sculpture
scumbling

scutcheon
scytheman
sea battle
sea breeze
sea chanty
seafaring
sea fennel
sea lawyer
sea league
sea letter
sealpoint
sea-mullet
sea-needle
seaparrot
seasoning
sea-spirit
seat earth
sea-urchin
seaworthy
sebaceous
second act
secretary
secretion
secretory
sectarian
sectional
seed grain
seed pearl
selection
sell short
semantics
semaphore
semibreve
semicolon
semi-metal
semitonic
semivowel
sentry box
separates
separator
septimole
sepulchre
seraphine
serenader
sermonist
serpulite
serviette
servitude
sestertii
set-square
sevillana
sexennial
sforzando
shade tree
shakedown
shareware
shark skin
shaveling
shearbill
shearlegs
sheat-fish
sheep hook
sheep lice
sheepskin
sheep tick
sheer-hulk
sheething
sheldrake
shell bark
shellfire
shellfish
shell suit
shift key
shift work
ship's cook
shipboard
ship owner
ship's cook
shipshape
ship's mate
shipwreck
shire-moot
shitepoke
shockwave
shoeblack
shoe brush
shoemaker
shop board
shoreline
shoreward
short bill
shortcake
shortener
shortfall
shorthorn
short time
shot gauge
shovel hat
shoveller
shower cap
showplace
show trial
shrew mole
shrike-tit
shrimping
shunt coil
siciliana
siciliano
sick berth
sideboard
sidelight
side table
sieve cell
sieve tube
sight bill
sight land
sightseer
sightsman
signaller
signalman
signature
silk serge
siltstone
silver-eel
silver-eye
silver fir
silver fox
simpleton
single-sex
sinologue
sitatunga
sitiology
sketching
sketch pad
skimobile
skindiver
skinflint
ski runner
skunk-bird
skylarker
slanderer
slapstick
slaughter
slave dhow
sleighing
slide rule
slingshot
slobberer
slop basin
slope arms

sloppy joe
slouch hat
slowcoach
slow march
slow waltz
slumberer
slush fund
smack mill
small arms
small beer
small blue
small bore
small pica
smartweed
smatterer
smock race
smoke bomb
snail mail
snake-bird
snakebite
snakeroot
snakeweed
snake wood
snare drum
sniveller
snowberry
snowbound
snow goose
snowstorm
soapmaker
soap opera
soap plant
soapstone
soareagle
socialism
socialist
socialite
sociology
socotrine
soda water
soft drink
soft-pedal
sojourner
solar wind
soldering
solemnize
solfeggio
solicitor
soliloquy
solitaire
sollecito
sonneteer
son-of-a-gun
sonometer
sooty tern
sophister
sophomore
sopranist
sorbapple
sore eagle
sostenuto
sotto voce
sou'wester
soubrette
soundcard
sound post
soupspoon
sour cream
sour dough
sour gourd
south-east
southerly
southward
south-west
south wind
sovereign
spaghetti
spare room
spare tyre
spark coil
sparklers
spatangus
spear-fish
spearmint
spearwort
spectacle
spectator
speculate
speech day
speedboat
speed trap
speedwell
sphenodon
spherical
sphincter
spider-fly
spikenard
spin-drier
spindrift
spin-dryer
spinebill
spinnaker
spiritosa
spiritual
spirogyra
split peas
spokesman
sponge bag
spoonbill
spoonwort
sporangia
sporogony
sports car
sportsman
spotlight
spot price
springbok
spring box
spring gun
springing
sprinkler
spritsail
spun rayon
spur-rowel
spur royal
spur wheel
sputterer
squabbler
squadron
square-leg
squashbug
stability
stableboy
stable lad
stableman
stack arms
staff room
stage door
stagehand
stage left
stage-name
stage play
staghound
staircase
stair rods
stalemate
stammerer
stamp case
stamp duty
stanchion

stand fast
stand fire
stanolone
star apple
starboard
stargazer
starlight
star pupil
starshell
starstone
statement
stateroom
statesman
stationer
statuette
statutory
steamboat
steam pipe
steamship
steel wool
steelyard
steersman
stegosaur
steinbock
sternfast
sternmost
sternpost
stevedore
stick-bird
stiffener
stigmatic
stilettos
still life
stillroom
stilt-bird
stingaree
sting-fish
stinkbomb
stink-fish
stippling
stir-about
stock dove
stockfish
stockinet
stockings
stock list
stock lock
stockpile
stockroom
stokehold
stoke hole
stomacher
stomapoda
stonebuck
stone cell
stonechat
stonecrop
stonehand
stone-hawk
stone lily
stone pine
stonewall
stonework
stool ball
stoplight
stopover
stopwatch
storeroom
storeship
storm-beat
storm-bird
stormsail
stormstay
storybook
straggler
strangler
strapless
strapwork
strascino
strategic
streaming
streamlet
streetcar
stretcher
striation
strigidae
string box
stripling
stroke oar
strombite
strongman
strontium
structure
struggler
stud horse
stutterer
stylobate
sub judice
sub-aerial
sub-alpine
subaltern
subeditor
subhedral
sublunary
submarine
submitter
sub-rector
subscribe
subsidize
subsonic
substrate
subverter
succeeder
succentor
successor
succotash
succourer
succulent
suctorian
suede coat
suffragan
suffrages
sugar beet
sugar bowl
sugar cane
sugar loaf
sugar mill
sugar-mite
sugar plum
suggester
sulphuric
sultaness
sulthiame
summerset
summing-up
sun bonnet
sundowner
sunflower
sunrising
sun spurge
supergene
superheat
supernova
supinator
suppliant
supporter
surcharge
surfeiter
surmullet
surrender

surveying
susceptor
suspecter
sustainer
swaggerer
swallower
swampboat
swamp-hawk
swansdown
sweatband
sweetcorn
sweet flag
sweet john
sweetlips
sweetmeat
sweet root
sweet rush
sweetwood
sweet wort
swinecote
swineherd
switch off
swine-pipe
switchman
sword cane
swordfish
sword knot
swordsman
sycophant
syllepsis
symbiosis
symbolism
symbolist
symphonic
symposiac
symposium
symptosis
synagogue
synalepha
syncopate
syncopist
syndicate
synodical
synoptics
synoptist
syntactic
synthesis
synthetic
tablature
table bell
tablegame
table hook
table lamp
tableland
tablemaid
tabletalk
tableware
tabourine
tactician
tail light
tailpiece
tail skid
tail unit
tail wheel
take a part
talegalla
tamarinds
tambourin
tangerine
tanystoma
tap dancer
tarantass
tarantula
taraxacum
tarentula
tarpaulin
tasimeter
task force
tattooing
tawny port
taxidermy
taximeter
tax return
tea kettle
tear sheet
technique
tectonics
telegraph
teleology
telephone
telephony
telescope
telestich
televisor
tellinite
tellurion
tellurium
tempering
temptress
tenebrism
tenements
tenor bass
tenor clef
tenor horn
tenor tuba
tenor viol
tentmaker
termagant
terminist
terrapeen
terrorism
terrorist
terza rima
tessitura
testament
test drive
testifier
testimony
test match
test pilot
tetraonid
text white
the boards
the morgue
theocracy
theomachy
theophany
theorbist
theorizer
therapist
theurgist
thickhead
thighbone
third gear
thorn-back
thornbill
thorn-bush
thorn tree
thrashing
threadfin
threshing
threshold
thumbring
thunderer
thylacine
thysamura
ticket day
tidal wave
tide gauge
tide table

tie dyeing
tiercelet
tiffenbat
tiger lily
tiger moth
tile drain
timberman
timepiece
times past
timetable
timpanist
tinderbox
tin lining
tin lizzie
tin mining
tin opener
tip and run
tipsy cake
title role
titration
tittlebat
T junction
toadstone
toadstool
tollbooth
tollhouse
tonka bean
toolsmith
toothpick
toothwort
tophamper
torch lily
torch race
tormentil
tormentor
touch line
touch-wood
towelling
tower room
town clerk
town crier
townhouse
townscape
townsfolk
tracksuit
trade fair
trademark
trade name
tradesman
trade wind
tragedian
tragelaph
trainband
train road
transform
transport
trapezium
trapezius
trapezoid
trap stick
traveller
traverser
treachery
treasurer
treatment
trebucket
tree hyrax
tree louse
tree shrew
tree snake
treillage
trenching
trepanner
triad axis
trial game
trial race
tribesman
tributary
trickster
triclofos
tricolour
tricuspid
triennial
trifolium
triforium
trilby hat
trillando
trilobite
trimester
trinketry
trioctile
trisagion
trochilus
troopship
troubador
trousseau
troutling
troxidone
true north
trump card
trumpeter
truncated
truncheon
trunk fish
trunk line
trunk road
try square
tsetse fly
tubophone
tugmaster
tulip tree
tumblebug
tunnel pit
tunny boat
tunny fish
turban top
turbinite
turf house
turf spade
turn bench
turnip top
turnip-fly
turnscrew
turnstile
turnstone
turntable
turquoise
turret gun
turrilite
twin cable
twin-screw
two-decker
two-seater
tympanist
tyre lever
umbilical
umbilicus
unballast
uncharted
underfelt
under fire
underling
undermine
underpass
underprop
underseal
undersell
underwear
undrained
unguarded

unharbour
uniformed
uninjured
uninstall
union pipe
unisexual
unit plane
unit trust
unlighted
unmusical
unopposed
unscathed
unscrewed
unsheathe
unsounded
untrained
untunable
unworldly
updraught
uplighter
upper case
upper deck
uranology
usherette
utilities
valentine
valuation
vanity box
vanomycin
vaporetto
variation
varnisher
vegetable
veinstone
velveteen
vendition
venerable
venerator
venial sin
ventifact
ventricle
venus clam
verbalist
verbascum
versifier
vestibule
vestments
vestryman
vetturino
vexillary
viability
vibration
victoress
victorine
video card
vigilance
vigilante
villarsia
vine snake
vingt-et-un
viola alto
violinist
virus scan
viscosity
visionary
viverrine
vodkatini
volcanist
volley gun
voltigeur
voltmeter
voluntary
volunteer
vox humana
vulcanist
vulcanite
vulcanize
wadsetter
wage claim
wagonette
waistband
waistcoat
wall clock
wall cress
wall light
wallpaper
wallplate
wandering
warble-fly
ward staff
war effort
warehouse
warmonger
warranter
wart snake
washbasin
washboard
washerman
washstand
wassailer
waste pipe
waste weir
watchword
waterbird
waterbuck
water butt
water cart
waterfall
water flag
water-flea
waterfowl
water jump
waterlath
water lily
waterline
watermark
watermill
water mole
water newt
water opal
water polo
water-rail
water sail
watershed
water tank
water vole
waterwort
wattmeter
wax candle
wax-insect
wax myrtle
wax polish
waxworker
wealth tax
webmaster
web-offset
wedgebill
wedge heel
well done
well drain
whaleback
whaleboat
wheat-bird
wheel base
wheelboat
wheel spin
whip graft
whip snake
whipper-in
whirligig

whirlwind
whirlygig
whistling
whitebait
whitebeam
white bear
whitecrop
whiteface
whitefish
white flag
white heat
white lady
white meat
white pine
white port
whitester
whitetail
whitewash
white wine
whitewood
wholemeal
wholesale
whole time
whosoever
widow-bird
widow wail
wild goose
wild honey
wild horse
willow tit
wind cone
wind gauge
windhover
winding up
windmill
windowbox
windpower
windproof
windsock
windtight
wineglass
winemaker
winepress
winevault
wing flap
winnowing
wiregauze
wire wheel
wisecrack
wobbegong
wolfhound
wolf's bane
wolf's claw
wolf snake
wolverene
womanizer
womankind
womenfolk
woodblock
woodborer
woodchuck
woodcraft
woodlouse
wood reeve
woodspite
woodstone
word break
worker ant
worker bee
work force
workhouse
work of art
work sheet
work study
work table
workwoman
worldling
wormgrass
worm wheel
woundwort
wrestling
wristband
wristbone
wrongdoer
wrong font
wyandotte
xanthocon
xanthosia
xenophobe
xerophyte
X-ray plant
xyloidine
xylophaga
xylophone
yacca wood
yacht race
yachtsman
yardstick
yellow boy
yesterday
yestereve
young lady
youngling
youngster
zebra wood
zoeotrope
zoography
zookeeper
zoologist
zoophagon
zootomist
zumbooruk

10

aberdevine
aberration
able seaman
aboard ship
aboriginal
abrotanoid
absolution
absolutist
absorption
abstinence
acacia moth
accelerate
acceptance
access fund
access road
accidental
accomplice
accomptant
accoucheur
accountant
account day
accounting
accumulate
accusative
acetic acid
acetimeter
achromatic
acidimeter
acoelomate
acolothist
acrobatics
active bond
active duty
active list
actomyosin
adaptation
adder grass
adjustment
admonisher
Adonis blue
adsorption
adulteress
adventurer
advertiser
advice boat
advice note
adzuki bean
aerobatics
aero-engine
aerography
aerologist
aeronautic
aerostatic
aesthetics
affettuoso
aficionado
after-guard
after-hatch
afterpiece
after-sails
agapanthus
agonistics
agonothete
agronomist
agrostemma
aide-de-camp
air balloon
air control
air cushion
air defence
air hostess
air machine
air marshal
air quality
air service
air steward
air support
air traffic
alabastrus
alarm clock
alarm gauge
alarm watch
alcoholism
alcoranist
algebraist
alienation
alimentary
allargando
allegorist
allegretto
allotropes
almond tree
alongshore
alprenolol
altar bread
altar cloth
altar front
altarpiece
altar steps
altar table
altazimuth
alternator
alva marina
amantadine
amanuensis
amaranthus
ambassador
amber beads
amber light
ambidexter
ammunition
amphibians
amphibious
amphibrach
amphimacer
amphineura
amphitrite
ampicillin
anaglyphic
anaglyptic
analytical
anapaestic
anarthrous
anastrophe
anastrophy
ancestress
anchorable
anchor buoy
anchor hold
androecium
anecdotist
anemograph
anemometer
anemoscope
angel shark
angioscope
angiosperm
anglemeter
angler fish
anglophile
anglophobe
anglophone
angora goat
angora wool
angwantibo
animalcule
ankle socks
annexation
annihilate

annotation
antagonism
antagonist
antazoline
ant-catcher
antecedent
antecessor
antechapel
antecursor
antemosaic
antepenult
antheridia
anthracite
anthropoid
antichrist
anticlimax
anticlinal
anti-dazzle
antifreeze
antilepton
antimatter
antiphonal
antiphonic
antiproton
aortic arch
apical cell
apiculture
apitherapy
apocalypse
apostrophe
apothecary
apparition
appearance
apple corer
apple sauce
appoggiato
apposition
appreciate
apprentice
apricot jam
aquamarine
araeostyle
Aran jumper
arbitrator
arbor vitae
arc-boutant
archbishop
archdeacon
archegonia
archerfish
archimagus
architrave
archivault
archpriest
Arctic skua
Arctic tern
arcubalist
aristocrat
arithmetic
armageddon
armed truce
art gallery
arthropods
art teacher
art therapy
asafoetida
asbestosis
aspidistra
assault gun
assemblage
assembling
assessment
assignment
assumption
astarboard
astragalus
astrologer
astrometer
astronomer
astronomic
astroscope
asymptotic
atmosphere
atomic bomb
atomic mass
attachment
attackable
attainment
attornment
attunement
auctioneer
audiometer
audiophone
audit clerk
auditorium
autecology
autogenics
automation
automatism
automobile
avant-garde
aventurine
average out
axial plane
axial ratio
azure stone
babe-in-arms
babiroussa
babysitter
backgammon
background
backstairs
ballasting
ballet shoe
ball flower
balling-gun
ballistics
ballooning
balloonist
ballplayer
balustered
balustrade
bamboozler
banana boat
bandmaster
bank credit
bank return
bankruptcy
banstickle
baptistery
Barbary ape
barbed wire
barcarolle
bargeboard
barge yacht
barkentine
bark weevil
barleycorn
barleymeal
bar mitzvah
barracoota
barrelbulk
barrel roll
base memory
base spring
basitracin
basketball
basket case
basket fish
basset horn

bassoonist
bat fowling
bathing cap
bath oliver
bathymetry
bat mitzvah
batrachian
batrachite
batten down
battery gun
battery hen
battledoor
battledore
battle flag
battle hymn
battle line
battlement
battleship
beach buggy
beadswoman
bearded tit
bearer bond
bear garden
bear market
beautician
beautifier
bedchamber
bedclothes
beefburger
beet radish
beforehand
before time
behind time
belladonna
bell flower
bell-magpie
bell ringer
bell turret
belly dance
benedicite
benefactor
benorylate
bergmaster
Berlin wool
Bermuda rig
bestseller
better half
bevel wheel
bible study
bibliopole
biennially
big brother
bilgewater
bill broker
bill of sale
billposter
bimestrial
bimetallic
binoculars
binotonous
biochemist
biodegrade
biographer
biological
biometrics
biomorphic
biophysics
birch mouse
bird cherry
bird of prey
bird spider
bird strike
biscuit box
biscuit tin
bitter beer
bitterwort
blackamoor
blackberry
blackboard
black bream
black friar
blackguard
blackheart
black mambo
black pearl
black rhino
black sheep
blacksmith
black snake
blackthorn
black whale
bladesmith
blancmange
blanketing
blank verse
blanquette
blasphemer
blastocoel
blastocyst
blastoderm
blastopore
blight-bird
blind harry
blind shark
blind shell
blisterfly
blitzkrieg
block grant
blockhouse
blockmaker
block print
bloodhound
bloodstone
bloody Mary
blue-bonnet
bluebottle
blue-breast
blue ensign
blue groper
bluejacket
blue mantle
blue puller
blue spruce
blue-throat
bobbin lace
bobbysocks
bobbysoxer
body armour
body colour
body matter
bogtrotter
boiler suit
boll weevil
bombardier
Bombay duck
bombing run
bomb vessel
bond energy
bondholder
bond length
bondswoman
bonesetter
boneshaker
bonus issue
bonus share
boobook owl
bookbinder
bookkeeper
bookseller
bootlegger

bootlicker
boot polish
borstal boy
bosh butter
boston reel
bottlefish
bottlenose
bottom gear
bowdlerize
bowie knife
box spanner
brachialis
brachiopod
brakeblock
brake light
brake pedal
brazilwood
bread board
bread crock
breadfruit
bread knife
breadstuff
break dance
breakwater
breastbone
breastfast
breastwork
brent goose
brick-built
brick earth
bricklayer
brickmaker
bridegroom
bridescake
bridesmaid
bridge deck
bridgehead
brigandine
brigantine
brightness
broad arrow
broadcloth
broad gauge
broad piece
broadsheet
broadsword
brocatelle
broken down
brome grass
bronchiole
bronchitis
brontosaur
broomstick
brown algae
brown argus
brown bread
brown hyena
brown paper
brown trout
brushmaker
buccinator
buck basket
bucket shop
buckjumper
budgerigar
budgerygah
bugle corps
bulk buying
bull fiddle
bull market
bunya-bunya
bureaucrat
burnet moth
burra-murra
burrel shot
burrow-duck
bush harrow
bush jacket
bushmaster
bush ranger
busy lizzie
butter-bird
butterbump
butterbush
butter dish
butterfish
buttermilk
butter tree
butterweed
buttonhole
by-election
cabbage fly
cabbage net
caddicefly
café au lait
calcareous
calc-sinter
calculator
caledonoid
calefactor
calliopsis
call option
call to arms
calorifier
camel corps
camelopard
camouflage
campaigner
canary bird
candelabra
candelilla
candicidin
candlewick
cankerworm
cannelloni
cannonball
cannon bone
cannon shot
canolefish
canonicals
cantaloupe
canterbury
cantilever
cantillate
cantonment
canvasback
canzonetta
capillaire
capitalism
capitalist
capitalize
capitation
capitulate
cappuccino
carabineer
caramelize
caravaneer
caravanner
carbomycin
cardiology
card player
cargo plane
cargo space
caricature
car licence
carpet moth
cartoonist
cartwright
cascarilla
caseharden

cash keeper
cast anchor
casting box
casting net
casting-off
catabolism
catafalque
cataphract
cat breeder
catch a crab
catch title
catechumen
catenation
cat hammock
cathode ray
catoptrics
catterhine
cattleboat
cattle cake
cavalryman
cavity wall
ceiling fan
cell biology
centennial
centesimal
centigrade
centilitre
centimetre
centipoise
centralist
centrosome
cephalexin
cephalopod
ceramicist
cerebellum
ceremonial
cerography
cestracion
chain cable
chain ferry
chain plate
chain store
chair maker
chalcedony
challenger
chalybeate
chancellor
chandelier
changeable
changeling

chapel cart
chapellany
charentais
chargehand
charioteer
charleston
charthouse
chatterbox
chauvinism
chauvinist
checkpoint
cheesecake
cheese flan
cheese-mite
Chelsea bun
chemically
chemisette
chemotaxis
chequebook
chessboard
chevrotain
chickenpox
chiffchaff
chiffonier
chiliastic
chimney cap
chimney pot
chimpanzee
China aster
chinchilla
chiroplast
chitlarone
chittagong
chloroform
choliambic
chopsticks
choriambic
choriambus
chorus girl
chromatics
chromosome
chronicler
chronogram
chrysomela
church bell
churchgoer
churchyard
churn staff
cinquefoil
circuiteer

circumcise
circumflex
citronella
city editor
clack valve
claim agent
clamp irons
clapper boy
clarichord
clary water
claspknife
classicism
classicist
clavichord
clawed frog
clawhammer
clementine
clerestory
clingstone
clinkstone
clinometer
clinometry
clockmaker
clock speed
clock tower
clodhopper
clofibrate
clog dancer
cloistered
cloisterer
cloistress
clonazepam
clorindole
closed shop
clothes peg
clothes pin
cloth maker
cloudberry
clouded eel
cloudscape
clypeaster
coach horse
coachhouse
coachmaker
coach screw
coadjutant
coadjutrix
coal backer
coal bucket
coal bunker

coalcellar
coalheaver
coastal tea
coastguard
coat hanger
coatimundi
coat of arms
coat of mail
coccinella
cockatrice
cockchafer
cockleboat
cock-paddle
coddy-moddy
coelacanth
coffee mill
cohabitant
colchicine
cold chisel
coleoptera
coleoptile
collarbone
collateral
collecting
collective
collegiate
collimator
collocutor
colloquial
colloquist
coloration
coloratura
colporteur
combat zone
combustion
comedienne
comedietta
comestible
cometarium
comic opera
commandant
commandeer
commercial
commission
common blue
common cold
common pleas
common riot
common room
common seal
commutator
compaction
comparison
compensate
competitor
complainer
compositor
compounder
concentric
concertina
conchifera
conchology
concordist
conduction
confection
conference
confervite
confessant
confession
confidante
confluence
coniferous
connivance
consecrate
considerer
consistory
consortium
conspiracy
con spirito
consultant
contendent
contestant
continuato
continuity
contrabass
contractor
control key
controller
conundrums
convection
conversion
conveyance
cook's knife
cool colour
co-operator
coordinate
copperhead
copulation
copyholder
copytaster
copywriter
coquelicot
coral beads
coral snake
cor anglais
cordwainer
corkjacket
corn beetle
corncockle
corned beef
cornettist
cornflakes
cornflower
corn rocket
corn violet
corn weevil
corregidor
corruption
coryphaeus
cos lettuce
cosmic rays
cottage pie
cotton rose
cottontail
cotton tree
cottonweed
cottonwood
cotylosaur
couch grass
councillor
councilman
counsellor
countryman
county town
coursework
court dress
court house
court shoes
covenanter
coverchief
covered way
cover-point
cowanyoung
cow-buntung
cow parsley
cow parsnip
Crab nebula
crackbrain
crake berry
cranesbill

craniology
crankshaft
cream fruit
credit bank
credit card
credit note
credit slip
crenulated
crêpe soles
crested tit
cricket bat
cricket cap
cringeling
cripplings
cross-aisle
crosspatch
cross-piece
crossroads
cross staff
crosstrees
crotalaria
crowd scene
crow flower
crown agent
crown glass
crown piece
crown wheel
crow-shrike
crumb brush
crumb cloth
cryophorus
ctenoidans
ctenophore
cubic metre
cuckoopint
cuirassier
cultivator
culver tail
cummerbund
cumulative
cup-and-ball
curmudgeon
currant bun
curtain rod
customs man
cut and fold
cuttlefish
cyanometer
cyclograph
cytarabine
cytologist
czarevitch
dabb lizard
daggle-tail
daisy chain
damask plum
damask rose
damp course
dance music
dandy brush
date mussel
dative bond
dauphiness
daydreamer
day release
days of yore
day-tripper
dead colour
deadlights
dead matter
dead-weight
Deal lugger
death adder
decagramme
decahedron
decampment
decigramme
deck quoits
deck tennis
declaimant
declare war
declension
declinator
decoration
decorative
decree nisi
decryption
dedication
deed of gift
deep freeze
defalcator
defamation
defendable
defensible
definition
definitive
degaussing
dehiscence
del credere
delegation
delicacies
delineator
delinquent
delphinium
demi-cannon
demiditone
demobilize
demography
demoiselle
dendrolite
dendrology
dendrophis
denouement
denudation
deployment
depositary
depository
deprecator
depreciate
depredator
depression
deputation
derailment
derby sweep
deregulate
derivation
derivative
dermatogen
descendant
despatches
dessiatine
dessyatine
detachment
detonation
devil's club
devolution
devotional
diadelphia
diagenetic
diastaltic
dickey seat
dicoumarol
didunculus
dielectric
difference
digger wasp
dilettante
dimensions
diminisher
diminuendo

dining hall
dining room
dinner time
dipenzepin
diphtheria
diphyodont
direct cost
direct fire
directress
dirty money
dirty proof
discharger
disc jockey
disclaimer
discordant
discounter
discoverer
disc wheels
dish wheels
disharmony
dishwasher
disparager
dispatcher
dispatches
dispensary
dispersion
dissembler
dissonance
dissonancy
distillery
distracter
distrainer
disulfiram
ditriglyph
dive-bomber
diving bell
diving suit
divisional
docimology
dockmaster
dog biscuit
dog blanket
dog breeder
dogmatizer
dog's fennel
dog's poison
dog's tongue
dog trainer
dog walking
dolcemente
dolichorus
dollar bird
doll's house
dolphin-fly
domain name
dome-shaped
dominicide
donkey cart
donkey pump
doorhandle
doorkeeper
Doric order
dorr-beetle
double bass
double bond
double-demy
double hung
double lock
double-post
double star
double time
Douglas fir
dowel joint
down pillow
downstream
dracontium
draft horse
dragonfish
dragonnade
dragon tree
drainpipes
drama group
dramatizer
dramaturge
dramaturgy
drawbridge
drawn bonds
dray plough
dressmaker
dress shoes
drift bolts
drillpress
drillstock
drive shaft
drop anchor
drop astern
drosometer
drosophila
drug addict
drug dealer
drug pusher
drumbledor
drummer boy
dry battery
dry cleaner
drying room
dry measure
duffle coat
dulcet tone
dumb crambo
dumbledore
dumb waiter
dunderhead
dung beetle
duplicator
dusky minah
dusky robin
Dutch tiles
Dutch uncle
duty roster
dynastidan
eagle stone
early riser
earth house
earth plate
earthquake
ear trumpet
earthshine
Easter lily
easterling
Easter term
echinoderm
economizer
ecumenical
edible frog
eel fishing
efficiency
egg poacher
elaborator
elaeometer
elaiometer
elasticity
elbow chair
elderberry
electorate
electrical
electronic
eleven-plus
elongation
elucidator

emaciation
emalangeni
embankment
embarkment
ember goose
Ember weeks
emblazoner
emblazonry
emboldener
embossment
embouchure
embroidery
embryology
emery cloth
emery paper
emery wheel
empiricist
employment
empoisoner
enamelling
enamellist
enamelware
encampment
encourager
encroacher
encryption
encumbered
endangered
endiometer
endorsement
energetics
engagement
engarrison
engenderer
engine room
engrossing
enharmonic
enigmatist
enlistment
enrockment
enthusiast
enticement
entomolite
entomology
entomotomy
entophytes
entrenched
entrochite
enumerator
enunciator
enzymology
Eolian harp
Eolian lyre
epauletted
epenthesis
epenthetic
ephemerans
ephemerist
epicranius
epicycloid
epigenetic
epiglottis
episcopacy
episcopate
epitaphist
epithelium
epitomizer
equatorial
equestrian
equitation
equivalent
ergonomics
eriocaulon
ermine moth
erythritol
escalation
escalloped
escapement
escarpment
escritoire
escutcheon
estate duty
estivation
estouffade
eternalist
ethambutol
ethinamate
ethynodiol
Eton collar
Eton jacket
eucalyptus
eudiometry
euomphalus
eupatorium
euphonicon
euphonious
eurylaimus
evacuation
evaluation
evangelism
evangelist
evangelize
evil spirit
exaltation
excavation
excellency
excise duty
ex dividend
exhibition
exhortator
Exmoor pony
exothermic
expatiator
expedition
explicator
expression
expurgator
extenuator
extinction
extirpator
extra-mural
extraneous
extra-solar
eyas-musket
eyed lizard
eye witness
fabricator
facia panel
factionist
fagot-voter
fahrenheit
fallow deer
false nails
false topaz
false viper
fan cricket
fancy dress
fantoccini
fashionist
fast bowler
fathomless
fault scarp
feather bed
feather boa
feathering
federalist
feeder dyke
fellmonger
fellowship
fence month

fen cricket
fenoprofen
fer-de-lance
fertilizer
feruginous
feuilleton
fibrinogen
fiddle-fish
fiddlehead
fiddle wood
field games
field glass
fieldmouse
field-piece
fifth wheel
fig pudding
figurehead
file cutter
file format
file server
filibuster
film critic
film editor
filmscript
fimble hemp
finance act
fingerbowl
fingerling
fire basket
fire bucket
fire engine
fire escape
fire master
fire-raiser
fire screen
fire shovel
fire worker
firing iron
firing line
first brass
first floor
first night
first offer
fir-wrought
fiscal year
fish basket
fish carver
fishing net
fishing rod
fish kettle
fishmonger
fish trowel
fisticuffs
fitch brush
fives court
fixed costs
fixed price
fixed trust
flagellant
flange rail
flat colour
flat racing
flea beetle
fledgeling
flesh broth
flesh brush
fleur-de-lis
fleur-de-lys
flick knife
flight crew
flight deck
flight path
flight plan
flint glass
floatstone
flocculate
flock paper
flooded gum
floorcloth
floor price
flop-dragon
floppy disk
florentine
flour crock
flourisher
flower bowl
flowergirl
flugelhorn
fluid drive
fluid ounce
flurazepam
flute-mouth
fluviatile
fly-by-night
flycatcher
fly-fishing
flying boat
flying bomb
flying camp
flying fish
fly swatter
folk dancer
folk singer
footballer
footbridge
footlicker
footlights
footwarmer
forcing pit
fore-and-aft
forecaster
forecastle
forefather
foreground
foreleader
foremother
forerunner
forfeiture
forge ahead
formic acid
forswearer
fortissimo
forwarding
fossil fuel
foundation
four-by-four
four colour
four-in-hand
four-master
four-poster
four-seater
fox-hunting
fox terrier
frame maker
frame relay
frangipane
frangipani
fratercula
fraternity
fratricide
fraudulent
freebooter
free chapel
free energy
freeholder
freelancer
free market
free spirit
free trader
freightage

French bean
French harp
French horn
French loaf
frequenter
freshening
freshwater
friar's cowl
fricandeau
frigid zone
fritillary
froghopper
front wheel
frostbound
fruit salad
fuddy-duddy
fuel intake
full-length
full-rigged
funded debt
fund-holder
fund-raiser
furrow weed
Furry dance
fuse holder
gaff-rigged
gaillardia
galvanized
gamekeeper
game warden
gaming acts
ganoidians
garbage can
garden city
garlic pear
garrisoned
garter fish
gas bracket
gas lighter
gastrology
gastronome
gas turbine
gatekeeper
Gatling gun
gaultheria
gay Gordons
gear casing
gear change
gear cutter
geisha girl
generation
generative
geneticist
gentamycin
gentlefolk
geographer
geophysics
geotropism
geriatrics
Gerson cure
get the bird
ghost-shark
giant panda
giant toado
giblet soup
ginger beer
ginger cake
ginger wine
gingivitis
girdle cake
girlfriend
glacialist
glaciation
glass beads
glass coach
glasshouse
glass paper
glass snake
glitterati
globe daisy
globularia
glomerulus
glossarist
glue boiler
goalkeeper
goalkicker
goatchafer
goatmilker
goatsbeard
goatsucker
goblin fish
god-fearing
gold beater
gold-digger
golden drop
goldhammer
gold stater
gold thread
gold washer
goniometer
gonorrhoea
goodfellow
goods train
goods truck
gooneybird
gooseberry
goosegrass
gorgonzola
governante
government
graduation
grainstaff
grammarian
gramophone
granadilla
grandchild
grand juror
grandmamma
grandniece
grand opera
grand piano
grandstand
grand-uncle
grapefruit
grape sugar
graphic art
grass cloth
grassfinch
grass skirt
grass snake
grass widow
grass wrack
gravimeter
greasy pole
great skate
great-uncle
Greek cross
greendrake
greenfinch
green-heart
greenhouse
green light
green mamba
green racer
greenshank
green snake
greenstone
grey falcon
grey matter
grey mullet

grey parrot
grey plover
grid system
grindstone
gross value
groundbait
ground bass
ground crew
ground dove
ground fire
ground lark
groundling
ground plan
ground rent
ground rice
ground sill
growth area
guard cells
guardhouse
guava jelly
gudgeon pin
guillotine
guinea-fowl
gun captain
gun licence
gunslinger
gymnastics
gymnocitta
gymnosperm
gypsophila
gyrocopter
gyrogonite
habitation
hackney cab
hair brooch
hair lotion
hair pencil
hair pomade
hair spring
hairstreak
halberdier
half-length
half-sister
haliotidae
hall porter
halter-neck
ham and eggs
hammerfish
hammerhead
hand barrow
handmaiden
handspring
hand-to-hand
handy-dandy
hang glider
harbourage
hard labour
harmonicon
harmonizer
harp-string
harpy eagle
harquebuse
hartebeest
harvest bug
harvesting
harvestman
hatcheller
hatchet man
haunch bone
headhunter
headlights
headmaster
head porter
head waiter
hearing aid
hearing dog
heartsease
heart wheel
heavy-laden
heavy water
hebdomadal
hectolitre
hectometre
helianthus
helicopter
heliograph
heliometer
helioscope
heliotrope
hellbender
hemisphere
hen-harrier
herald moth
herb robert
herbaceous
herds grass
hereditary
heresiarch
her indoors
hermit crab
hessian-fly
heterodoxy
heteropoda
hexametric
hierocracy
hierophant
high and dry
high comedy
highlander
high priest
high treason
highwayman
Hilary term
hipped roof
hippodrome
hippogryff
histrionic
hitch-hiker
hobbyhorse
hockey ball
hockey club
hodge-podge
hokey-cokey
hollow mast
holly berry
holothuria
holy roller
homeopathy
homocercal
homoeopath
homophonic
homorelaps
homozygous
honeyeater
honey-guide
honey mouse
honey stalk
honorarium
honourable
hooded crow
hoodie crow
horn player
hornblende
horned frog
horned toad
hornsilver
horologist
horror film
horse-emmet
horseleech

horse opera
horsepower
horse's neck
hotchpotch
hot climate
hotcockles
hour circle
house agent
house mouse
house of God
hovercraft
hucklebone
huckstress
human being
humidifier
humming-top
hunting box
hurdle race
hurdy-gurdy
husbandman
hydraulics
hydrolysis
hydrometer
hydrometry
hydropathy
hydrophore
hydroplane
hydroscope
hyetograph
hyetometer
hygrometer
hygrometry
hygrophyte
hygroscope
hylaeosaur
hyoglossus
hyoscyamus
hypaethral
hyperbaton
hyperbolic
hypermedia
hyphenated
hypophysis
hypotenuse
hypothesis
hypsometry
icebreaker
ice dancing
iced drinks
ice pudding
ice sailing
ice skating
ichthammol
iconoclasm
iconoclast
identifier
ideologist
idolatress
illegality
illiteracy
illuminate
immaculate
immortelle
immunology
impalement
impanation
impediment
impenitent
imperative
impersonal
import duty
importuner
imposition
impresario
impression
imprimatur
imprisoner
incendiary
in chambers
incidental
income bond
incubation
indefinite
indexation
Indian corn
Indian date
Indian fire
Indian reed
Indian shot
India paper
indictment
individual
inductance
indulgence
industrial
infallible
infinitive
inflatable
inflection
inflexible
inhabitant
inhibition
injunction
inlet valve
inner light
innominate
inoculator
inquisitor
insinuator
insolvency
inspection
instalment
instigator
institutor
instructor
instrument
insulating
insulation
insurgency
integument
interferer
interferon
interleave
interloper
intermezzo
interposer
intervener
inter vivos
in the black
in the round
in the wings
intonation
intramural
introducer
invalidate
invalid cab
investment
invincible
invocation
involution
ionic order
ionic style
ionization
Irish linen
iron glance
iron heater
ironmonger
ironworker
irrational
irreverent

irrigation
isochronal
isocyanide
isodynamic
isoxuprine
jackadandy
jackanapes
jackrabbit
Jamaica rum
japati palm
jardiniere
jelly mould
jerry-built
jersey silk
jersey wool
jet fighter
Jew's mallow
jigger flea
jigger mast
jingoistic
jinricksha
joint stock
Joshua tree
journalese
journalism
journalist
journeyman
judicature
jugged hare
juggernaut
jungle-fowl
junior lead
jury-rigged
jury rudder
kennelmaid
Kentish rag
ketoprofen
kettle drum
kettle pin
khaki drill
kidney bean
kidneywort
kilogramme
kinematics
kinetic art
kingfisher
king parrot
king's spear
kith and kin
kitten heel
knackerman
knapbottle
knife board
knight-fish
knighthood
knobkerrie
knockabout
knot garden
Kodiak bear
kookaburra
Krebs cycle
kunai grass
laboratory
lace making
laceration
lactic acid
lactometer
lactoscope
lady chapel
lady-killer
lady's smock
lamb cutlet
lambrequin
lamination
lampadrome
lancet arch
land breeze
landholder
landing net
landing run
landlocked
landlubber
land tenure
land worker
languisher
lansquenet
lantern-fly
lanthanide
lappet moth
laryngitis
Lassa fever
lateen sail
lateen yard
latent heat
Latin cross
laundryman
lawbreaker
lawn tennis
law officer
law sitting
lay a course
lay brother
lay siege to
lazar house
leader page
lead glance
leading man
lead pencil
leaf bridge
leaf insect
leafroller
leaf sheath
ledger line
left-winger
legislator
legitimacy
legitimate
legitimist
legwarmers
lemon thyme
lentamente
letter bomb
letter rack
letter wood
leucoplast
lexicology
liberty man
librettist
licentiate
lieutenant
lifejacket
lighterage
lighterman
light horse
lighthouse
lighting up
light opera
lilac-point
lime burner
lime squash
limitation
limited war
limpet mine
lincomycin
line of fire
linguistic
linotypist
linseed oil
liquidator
liquid core

liquidizer
liquor laws
literalist
lithograph
litigation
litrameter
living wage
lob bowling
lobsterman
lock keeper
lock paddle
locomotion
locomotive
loganberry
loggerhead
London clay
longhaired
long period
long primer
lookout man
looper moth
loose cover
loss leader
lotus-eater
lounge suit
love-parrot
lower class
lower house
low-tension
loxodromic
lubricator
lumber room
lumberjack
lumpsucker
lunar cycle
lunar month
lunar probe
lycopodium
lymphocyte
lyric verse
macadamize
machinator
machine gun
mach number
macrometer
Madeira nut
magistrate
magnetizer
magnificat
magpie-lark
magpie moth
maiden aunt
maidenhair
maiden lady
maisonette
major chord
major scale
Malay tapir
malefactor
male thread
malingerer
mallee-fowl
malted milk
Maltese dog
malt liquor
malt whisky
management
manageress
maned goose
mangosteen
manicurist
manila hemp
manoeuvrer
manoeuvres
man of straw
manor house
manservant
manuscript
maple sugar
maraschino
marguerite
marine soap
mariolatry
marionette
marked down
marker buoy
marketable
market town
marking ink
marking nut
married man
marrowbone
marshaller
martial law
martingale
maskanonge
maskinonge
masonry bit
masquerade
mass market
mass number
mastermind
masterwork
masticator
matchmaker
mayblossom
mayonnaise
mayor-elect
meadowlark
mechanical
medical man
meditation
medium-rare
meerschaum
megalosaur
meningitis
menu-driven
meperidine
mepyramine
mercantile
merrymaker
mesenteric
mess jacket
metabolism
metacarpal
metacarpus
metallurgy
metatarsal
metatarsus
metathesis
methuselah
methyldopa
metoprolol
metrograph
mezzotinto
mica schist
mickey finn
microfarad
micrometer
microphone
microscope
microscopy
middlebrow
middle deck
midget golf
midshipman
mignonette
mileometer
militarism
militarist

militiaman
milk boiler
millennium
millesimal
millimetre
millionary
millwright
minced meat
mindreader
mineralist
minestrone
Minie rifle
ministrant
minke whale
minor chord
minor scale
minstrelsy
mint-master
mirror dory
mirror site
misconduct
misericord
misogamist
misogynist
misprision
missionary
mitre block
mixolydian
mizzenmast
mizzensail
mizzenstay
mobile home
Mocha stone
mock heroic
mock orange
mock privet
mock turtle
mock velvet
modulation
molybdenum
monarchism
monarchist
monetarism
monetarist
moneyed man
money order
monkey boat
monkey suit
monochrome
monogamist
monologist
monomaniac
monopolist
monopolize
monotheist
monotonous
monsoonish
monstrance
moratorium
morphology
morris pike
Moses perch
mother cell
motherwort
motorcoach
motorcycle
motor lorry
motor mower
motor yacht
mould board
mountebank
mousseline
mouth organ
mouthpiece
movie actor
mujaheddin
mulled wine
multimedia
multimeter
multiplane
multiplier
muscardine
musica viva
musical box
music drama
musicology
music stand
music stool
musk beaver
musk beetle
mustard gas
muster book
muster roll
muttonbird
mutton chop
nail drawer
namby-pamby
nanosecond
napalm bomb
napkin ring
narrowboat
nasturtium
natalitial
natterjack
natural gas
naturalism
naturalist
nautch girl
navigating
navigation
ne'er-do-well
necropolis
needle book
needle case
needlecord
needlework
need to know
negentropy
negligence
negotiable
negotiator
nematology
nephrology
nerve agent
nerve fibre
nettle beer
neural tube
neuroptera
neuter verb
neutralist
neutralize
news agency
newscaster
news editor
newsreader
newsvendor
next friend
night adder
nightdress
night glass
night heron
nightlight
night piece
night raven
nightshade
nightshirt
nightstick
night watch
nincompoop
nipplewort

nitrazapam
nitric acid
nitrifying
nitrometer
noblewoman
noctograph
nodal point
noisy-minah
no man's land
nom-de-plume
nominalist
nominative
non-payment
no par value
Norman arch
nose gunner
nosography
nosologist
note of hand
novobiocin
nuclear sub
nuclear war
nucleotide
numeric pad
nurseryman
nutcracker
nylon shirt
obituarist
obligation
obstetrics
obstructer
occasioner
occidental
occupation
ocean-going
ocean liner
octahedron
odontolite
odontology
oesophagus
off-roading
oil colours
oil painter
old soldier
ombrometer
omega meson
omnipotent
omniscient
omnivorous
oneirology
on location
open cheque
open credit
opening bid
open market
open policy
opera buffa
opera cloak
opera glass
opera house
operameter
opera music
operations
ophicleide
ophiolatry
opinionist
opium eater
opposition
optic nerve
option rate
orange-ball
orange lily
orange musk
orange wood
orchardist
orchestral
ordination
ore carrier
organic art
organology
originator
orogenesis
orpheoreon
orthoclase
orthodromy
orthogonal
orthoptera
orthoptics
oscillator
osculation
osmiridium
osteoclast
osteopathy
other ranks
ottava rima
otterhound
outer space
out-patient
outwash fan
oval window
overcharge
overlooker
overmantel
overmatter
overrunner
overtaking
overthrust
over the top
overturner
oxalic acid
ox-eye daisy
Oxford bags
oxprenadol
oxygen mask
oxypertine
oyster crab
ozone layer
ozonometer
packet boat
paddleboat
paddymelon
paddy wagon
page layout
pagination
pagoda tree
painstaker
paintbrush
pale sherry
palestrian
palindrome
pall-bearer
palmacites
palnerworm
pancratist
pancratium
panegyrist
panel beater
panic grass
panopticon
pan scourer
pantaloons
pantograph
pantometer
papaverine
paper birch
paper cable
paper chase
paper knife
paper money
paper stand

paper tiger
paraboloid
paranthine
paraphrase
paraphrast
parasitism
paratroops
parcel bomb
parcelling
parenchyma
park keeper
park ranger
park warden
parliament
parrot coal
parrot fish
parson-bird
participle
party dress
pasquilant
passiflora
passion play
pastellist
past master
pastry cook
pathfinder
pathogenic
patio doors
patriotism
patrol boat
patrolling
patronizer
pawnbroker
peacemaker
pearl diver
pearl perch
pebbledash
pedagogics
pedestrian
pedicurist
Peeping Tom
peewee-lark
peltmonger
pelvimeter
pen and wash
pencil case
pencilling
penicillin
peninsular
pennyroyal
penologist
pensionary
pentachord
pentagraph
pentameter
pentathlon
pentstemon
pepper cake
peppermill
peppermint
pepperwort
percentage
percolator
percussion
perforator
performing
perihelion
periodical
periosteum
peripheral
periwinkle
perruquier
persecutor
Persian mat
Persian rug
persiennes
persifleur
personator
petitioner
petrol bomb
petrol pump
petrol tank
petty-chaps
pewter dish
pharisaism
pharmacist
phelloderm
phenacetin
phenomenon
philistine
philologer
philopoena
philosophy
phlebology
phonograph
phonoscope
phosphorus
photograph
photometer
photometry
photophone
phototaxis
phrenology
phylloxera
physiology
pianissimo
pianoforte
piano stool
piano tuner
picaresque
pichiciago
picket boat
pickpocket
picrosmine
pietra dura
piezometer
pigmentary
pigmy perch
pile carpet
piledriver
pilgrimage
pillowcase
pillow lace
pillow lava
pillowslip
pilot cloth
pilothouse
pilot plane
pilot whale
pincushion
pineal body
pine marten
pine needle
pine weevil
pinstripes
pipe aboard
piperazine
pipe wrench
pirate ship
piston ring
pith helmet
plagiarism
plagiarist
plain tract
plane table
planimeter
planimetry
plantation
plant-louse
plastering

plastic mac
plasticine
plasticity
plate glass
platelayer
play-acting
playground
playwright
plebiscite
plesiosaur
pleximeter
plough back
pluperfect
pneumatics
poached egg
pocketbook
poinsettia
point blank
pointed awl
poker plant
pole finder
politician
polo player
polyanthus
polygamist
polyhedral
polyhedron
polyhistor
polymerize
polymorphe
polynomial
polyphonic
polyploidy
polytheist
pome citron
pond turtle
pony engine
pony racing
population
portcrayon
portcullis
port of call
positivist
possession
post-chaise
postillion
postmaster
post mortem
post office
potamology
potentilla
pot hunting
potted fish
potted meat
powder horn
powder mill
powder room
power cable
powerhouse
power-plant
pragmatist
prairie dog
prairie hen
pratincole
prayerbook
preadamite
prebendary
precession
prednisone
pre-emption
preference
premier cru
prepayment
presbytery
prescriber
press agent
price index
prickly ash
priesthood
prima donna
print dress
prison base
prison camp
private car
private eye
prize court
prize fight
prize-money
procession
proclaimer
procreator
proctology
procurator
production
profitable
profits tax
profligate
progenitor
programmer
prohibiter
projectile
projection
prokaryote
prolocutor
promenader
prominence
promontory
prompt book
pronominal
pronouncer
propaganda
propagator
propanolol
properties
prophesier
prophetess
proportion
propounder
proprietor
propylaeum
proscenium
proscriber
prosecutor
prospector
prospectus
prosperity
prosperous
prostitute
protection
prothallus
protoplasm
protractor
provection
proveditor
provide for
provisions
psephology
psychiatry
psychology
psychopath
pudding pie
puff pastry
pullman car
pulmonaria
pulsimeter
pulverizer
pump handle
puncturist
puppet show
purchasing

pure profit
purplefish
pursuivant
put-and-take
puzzle ring
pycnodonts
pycnostyle
pygmy shrew
pyracantha
pyramidine
pyramiding
pyrochlore
pyrography
pyrologist
pyroxyline
quadrangle
quadrantal
quadriceps
quadrireme
quadrumana
quadrussis
quarantine
quarreller
quarter day
quartering
quatrefoil
queen apple
quercitron
questioner
quick march
quicksands
quizmaster
rabbinical
rabbit skin
raccoon dog
racecourse
race ginger
raceground
radial tyre
radicalism
radiometer
raffia palm
ragamuffin
railwayman
rainforest
raisin loaf
raisin wine
raking fire
ramphastos
ranunculus
rapier fish
rat catcher
rat opossum
rattan cane
rave notice
rave review
razor strop
ready money
real estate
real income
rear gunner
rear mirror
recidivist
reciprocal
recitalist
recitation
recitative
recitativo
reclaimant
recognitor
recognizer
recompense
reconciler
reconquest
recreation
recruiting
rectorship
recyclable
red admiral
red cabbage
redcurrant
redeemable
redemption
red gurnard
red morwong
red rockcod
reduce sail
redundancy
referendum
reflection
refraction
regent-bird
regimental
regression
reichsmark
reimburser
rejointing
relativity
relaxation
relinquent
rememberer
remittance
remunerate
rencounter
rendezvous
repair ship
repentance
repertoire
repetiteur
repointing
repository
reproacher
reprobater
reproducer
republican
repudiator
rescue boat
researcher
reshipment
resistance
resolution
resorcinol
respirator
respondent
rest harrow
restrainer
restricter
retributer
retrograde
rev counter
revelation
reverencer
reverse out
revivalist
revocation
revolution
rhapsodist
rhein berry
rheumatism
rhinanthus
rhinestone
Rhine wines
rhinoceros
Rhone wines
rhubarb pie
ribbon-fish
ribbon lake
ribbon worm
rice weevil
rich colour

riding pony
riding whip
rifle corps
rifle range
rift valley
right of way
right whale
ringbarker
ringleader
ringmaster
ripple tank
ritardando
ritornello
rivercraft
river horse
river snake
roadmender
roadroller
roadworthy
robber crab
robing room
robot plane
rock badger
rock bottom
rock butter
rocket ball
rock parrot
rock pigeon
rock python
rock rabbit
rock temple
rolled oats
rollicking
rolling pin
rood screen
roof garden
rope ladder
ropedancer
rose acacia
rosechafer
rose garden
rose mallow
rose quartz
rose window
rotary club
rotisserie
roughrider
roundabout
roundhouse
rounding up
roundtower
route march
rowing club
royal barge
rubber tree
rubber-wire
rubblework
rudder post
rudder-fish
rudderless
rules of war
rumble seat
runner bean
rye whiskey
sabbatical
sabretache
saccharide
saccharine
sacerdotal
sack posset
sacred ibis
sacrificer
sacrosanct
saddlebags
safe blower
safety belt
safety-lamp
sagegrouse
sailor suit
saki monkey
salamander
salbutamol
sales force
saleswoman
salicornia
salmagundi
salmagundy
salpinctes
saltarello
salt butter
salt cellar
saltigrade
Samson post
sanatorium
sanctified
sanctifier
sandalwood
sanderling
sand grouse
sandhopper
sand lizard
sand martin
sand-mullet
sandy shale
sandy sprat
sanitorium
sapphirine
saprophyte
sarcolemma
sassorolla
saturnalia
sauerkraut
scala media
scapegrace
scaraebeus
scattering
scatter rug
scent hound
schematist
schipperke
schismatic
schizogony
schooldays
schoolgirl
schoolmarm
schoolmate
schoolroom
school ship
school year
scoop-wheel
scopelidae
scoreboard
Scotch mist
Scotch pine
scratch man
scratch wig
screech-owl
screen name
screenplay
screw press
scrip issue
scriptural
scrutineer
sculptress
sea anemone
sea bathing
sea captain
sea-garfish
sea-leopard
sealing wax

seamanlike
seamanship
seamstress
sea poacher
sea serpent
sea-swallow
sea-unicorn
second-hand
second mate
secretaire
secularism
secularist
securities
sedan chair
seed weevil
seersucker
seggar clay
seguidilla
seismology
selenology
self-acting
self-binder
selling day
selling out
semeiology
semicircle
seminarist
semiquaver
sensualist
sentry duty
sentry post
separation
separatist
septennial
septic tank
septuagint
serial bond
serial port
serigraphy
sermonizer
serpentine
serviceman
serving man
sestertium
setterwort
settlement
seventh son
sexagesima
sex therapy
shallow-fry
shandygaff
share index
shave grass
shearwater
sheep louse
shellproof
shell shock
shibboleth
shillelagh
ship broker
ship holder
shipmaster
ship's baker
shipwright
Shire horse
shoe buckle
shoestring
shopfitter
shopkeeper
shoplifter
short bonds
shortbread
shortcrust
short-dated
short-range
short story
shovepenny
shower bath
shrew mouse
shuffle cap
shunt-wound
side mirror
siderolite
sidewinder
siege train
sieve plate
sighthound
signal fire
signalling
signet ring
signwriter
silent film
silentiary
silhouette
silk-cotton
silk mercer
silk screen
silk weaver
silver-bell
silver dory
silverfish
silver-gull
silverling
silverside
silver weed
similitude
simnel cake
sinecurist
sinologist
sismondine
sitting day
six-shooter
skateboard
sketchbook
skew bridge
skirmisher
ski running
skylarking
skyscraper
slack water
slaked lime
sleek stone
slingbacks
slipstream
slit trench
sloop-of-war
slop seller
slow bowler
slow cooker
small craft
small heath
smart aleck
smoke alarm
smokestack
smoking car
smooth newt
snake dance
snake stone
snapdragon
sneeze-wood
sneezewort
sniffer dog
snowmobile
snowplough
snuff taker
soap boiler
socket pipe
socket pole
soda syphon
soft drinks

solan goose
solar month
solar panel
soldier ant
soldiering
sole agency
sole thrust
solemnizer
solicitant
solid state
solo flight
solubility
somatology
somersault
son and heir
song shrike
songstress
song thrush
soothsayer
soprano sax
sore throat
sound track
sourdeline
sousaphone
sowing time
sow thistle
spacecraft
space frame
space probe
Spanish fir
Spanish nut
spare wheel
sparry iron
spasmology
speargrass
specialist
spectacles
speculator
speed limit
spermology
sperm whale
spillikins
spin doctor
spirit lamp
spirometer
splashdown
spleenwort
splenology
splenotomy
spoilsport
spokeshave
sponge cake
spoonerism
sporophyte
sports coat
spring cart
springhaas
spring tide
springtime
spruce beer
squanderer
square foot
square inch
square mile
square sail
square-tail
square yard
squeteague
stabilizer
staff nurse
stag beetle
stagecoach
stagecraft
stage fever
stage right
stalactite
stalagmite
stale bread
stamp album
stanchions
stand guard
staphyline
star-gazing
star player
star psylla
starveling
state coach
state house
state of war
stationary
stationery
statistics
stay tackle
steam gauge
steam press
steersmate
stepfather
stepladder
stepmother
stepsister
stereotype
stern-board
stern-frame
sternsheet
stewardess
stewed meat
sticky bomb
stiffening
stillatory
still wines
stimulator
stipulator
stirrup cup
stochastic
stockpiles
stock split
stock taker
stonebreak
stone borer
stone eater
stone fruit
stonemason
storehouse
stork's bill
storm beach
storm cloud
stour-royal
strandflat
strategist
strathspey
strawberry
streamline
street arab
street door
street ward
strepitoso
string band
string vest
stringendo
strip light
striptease
strokesman
stronghold
strophiole
structural
strychnine
sturionian
stylohyoid
subclavian
subjection

subjective
sublingual
submariner
submediant
submission
subroutine
subscriber
subsection
subspecies
substitute
subtractor
subversion
succession
sucker-fish
suede shoes
sugar candy
sugar daddy
sugar-maple
summer duck
summer term
summertime
sunglasses
supercargo
supergiant
superpower
super-royal
supersonic
supertonic
supervisor
supplanter
supplement
supplicant
supply ship
supporters
suppressor
suprarenal
surcharger
surf riding
surmounted
surmounter
surrounded
survey ship
suscipient
suspenders
suspension
sustenance
swamp buggy
swamp maple
swan keeper
sweatshirt
sweepstake
sweetbread
sweet briar
sweetheart
sweet wines
swine bread
swinegrass
swing wheel
switchback
swivel hook
sword dance
sword fight
swordgrass
sword stick
sworn enemy
syllogizer
symphonion
symphonist
synaeresis
synchronal
syncopated
syncopater
syncopator
syncretist
synecology
syngenetic
synonymist
synthesism
system disk
tabernacle
table bowls
tablecloth
table linen
tablespoon
tachograph
tachometer
tail gunner
tailorbird
tailor-fish
take in sail
take up arms
talc schist
tale bearer
talegallus
tale teller
tall wattle
tally clerk
tamboureen
tambourine
tanagridae
tangential
tantalizer
tap dancing
tarantella
target ship
taskmaster
tassel-fish
tauromachy
tax evasion
taxi driver
tea biscuit
tea blender
tea clipper
tea drinker
team spirit
tea planter
tearjerker
technician
technocrat
technology
teinoscope
telegraphy
telescopic
televiewer
television
temper heat
temporalis
temporizer
temptation
temse bread
tenderfoot
tenderling
tenderloin
tennis ball
tenterhook
teratology
terminator
terracotta
terreplein
terry nappy
tersanetus
tessellate
test flight
tetrachord
tetracolon
tetrameter
tetrastich
tetrastyle
textualist
textuarist

theatre box
theatrical
Theban year
themselves
theodolite
theologian
thermionic
thermopile
thermostat
thickskull
thimblerig
third-party
threatened
threatener
three-speed
threnodist
thrombosis
thrown silk
thumbscrew
thumbstall
ticker tape
tic polonga
tidal basin
tidal creek
tidal river
tiger's foot
tiger shark
tiger snake
tight money
tiller rope
tilt hammer
timber moth
timber wolf
timekeeper
timeserver
time signal
time switch
time-waster
timwhiskey
tin whistle
tinned food
tip-up lorry
tiring room
tithing-man
title verso
tit-warbler
tobacco jar
toilet roll
toilet seat
toll bridge
tomfoolery
tongue stud
tongue-sole
tonic chord
tonic major
tonic minor
tonic solfa
tonic water
toothbrush
toothpaste
topgallant
topography
torch dance
torpedoman
torque tube
torrid zone
tortellini
tortfeasor
touch-me-not
touchpaper
touring car
tourmaline
tournament
toxicology
tractarian
trade cycle
trade paper
trade price
trade union
traffic cop
traffic jam
trafficker
tragacanth
trajectory
tram driver
tramontane
tramway car
transactor
transferee
transferer
transients
transistor
transition
transitive
translator
transmuter
transplant
travelling
travelogue
travertine
trawlerman
treasuress
tree-runner
trench coat
trench foot
trepanning
trespasser
trial match
tribometer
trick track
tricycling
tripartite
trip hammer
triple time
triple-tail
tripondius
triverbial
trivia quiz
troglodyte
trolley bus
trolley car
trombonist
tron weight
tropic-bird
troubadour
troumadame
troy weight
truckle bed
trug basket
trundlebed
tubiporite
tub-thumper
Tudor style
tuft-hunter
tuning fork
tunnelling
turbulence
turf cutter
turkey cock
turkey-trot
turnbuckle
turnip flea
turnip tops
turpentine
turret-fish
turret ship
turtle dove
turtleneck
turtle soup
tussah silk

twankay tea
tweedledee
tweedledum
twelve tone
twig-psylla
two-wheeler
typesetter
typewriter
typography
ulodendron
ultra vires
unbaptized
unbeliever
undefended
undercroft
underpants
under siege
understudy
undertaker
underwrite
undulation
unemployed
unfathomed
unfordable
unicameral
university
unoccupied
unpoetical
unsheathed
unsoldered
untenanted
upholstery
upper class
upper crust
upper house
upperworks
upset price
uranoscopy
usquebaugh
utopianist
vacillator
vacuum tube
vampire bat
vanquished
vanquisher
vapour bath
variamento
variety act
varnishing
vaudeville
vegetarian
vegetation
vegetative
velocipede
velvet fish
veneer moth
veneration
venezolano
ventilator
Venus's comb
vermicelli
vernacular
vertebrate
vespertine
vestibular
vestry room
veterinary
V-formation
vibraphone
vice-consul
vice-master
vice-regent
victorious
victualler
video tapes
vignetting
Viking ship
vindicator
viscometer
visitation
vistomente
vivandiere
viviparity
vocal music
voetganger
voice coach
voice modem
voiturette
volley ball
voltaic arc
voltameter
voltaplast
voluptuary
vorticella
vulnerable
waffle iron
wage freeze
waggonette
wainwright
walkaround
walk-on part
wallflower
wall lizard
wall pepper
war chariot
war council
wardmaster
war machine
warm colour
warming pan
wash basket
wassail cup
watch chain
watchglass
watchguard
watch house
watchlight
watchmaker
watch night
watchstand
watchstrap
watchtower
water-borne
water clock
watercraft
watercrane
watercress
water gauge
water gruel
waterguard
waterlevel
watermelon
water meter
water ouzel
water pilot
water plant
water poise
water power
waterproof
waterscape
water snake
waterspout
water table
watertight
water tower
waterwheel
waterwings
waterworks
wave energy
wavelength

wave motion
way station
way thistle
weathering
weather man
weaver-bird
weaver fish
web browser
wedding day
weedkiller
weeping ash
weighing-in
welded tuff
well boring
well-wisher
Welsh corgi
Welsh hound
Welsh onion
wentletrap
whale shark
wharfinger
wheatfield
wheatmidge
wheelbrace
wheelchair
wheelhouse
whidah-bird
whirlabout
whiteboard
white brant
white bread
white capri
white cedar
white dwarf
white egret
white friar
white-limed
white paper
white poppy
white rhino
white sauce
white shark
whitesmith
white stork
whitethorn
white wines
wholesaler
whomsoever
whydah-bird
wicket gate
widescreen
widow-maker
wild cherry
wildebeest
wilderness
wild indigo
willow herb
willow moth
willow weed
willow wren
winchester
wind flower
windjammer
window sash
window seat
windscreen
windshield
windtunnel
wine-bibber
wine bottle
wine cellar
wine cooler
winegrower
wine waiter
wing collar
wing mirror
wing oyster
winter moth
winter pear
wintertime
wiped joint
wirehaired
wirepuller
wireworker
witch hazel
withdrawer
withholder
wolf's peach
wolf spider
woman-hater
wonga-wonga
woodcarver
woodcutter
woodgrouse
woodmonger
woodpecker
wood pigeon
wood-shrike
wood sorrel
woodworker
wool carder
wool comber
wool driver
wool sorter
wool trader
wool winder
word making
work basket
working day
working dog
working out
work to rule
worm lizard
worshipper
wraparound
wring-staff
wristwatch
written off
wrong fount
xanthidium
xerography
xylophagan
yaffingale
yardmaster
yellow-bird
yellowlegs
yellow-root
yellow spot
yellow-tail
yellow-wood
yellow-wort
yesteryear
yoke-fellow
young blood
yourselves
zebra finch
zebra shark
zinc worker
zoographer
zymologist

11

abandon ship
abbreviator
abecedarian
abstract art
academician
accelerando
accelerator
accessories
accompanist
accountancy
account book
accumulator
acetylation
achievement
acoustician
acquittance
actinograph
actinometer
acupressure
acupuncture
address book
adjournment
adjudicator
advance copy
advancement
advance note
adventuress
advertising
Aeolian harp
Aeolian lyre
aerodynamic
aeronautics
aerostatics
aestivation
affiliation
Afghan hound
afterburner
age of reason
agglomerate
aggradation
agonistical
agony column
agoraphobia
agriculture
aguardiente
aiguillette
air corridor
aircraftman
air fountain
airing horse
airsickness
air terminal
air umbrella
alarm clock
alarm watch
aleurometer
alexandrine
alkalimeter
alka seltzer
alla capella
allelomorph
allopathist
allopurinol
all-star cast
altar screen
alto-relievo
alto-ripieno
American elk
ametabolian
amodiaquine
amontillado
amphetamine
amphibology
amyl nitrate
anacoluthon
anchovy pear
anelectrode
anemography
animal lover
anniversary
antecedence
antechamber
antemundane
antenuptial
antepaschal
antibiotics
anticyclone
antiphonary
antiphrasis
antiquarian
antirrhinum
antispastic
antistrophe
anti-tank gun
apollinaris
apomorphine
aposiopesis
apostle-bird
apotheosize
apple brandy
apple grower
apple-sucker
appointment
approximate
aquatinting
arachnidans
arachnology
Aran sweater
arbitration
archaeology
archdiocese
archduchess
archenteron
arches court
archipelago
area bombing
arenaceaous
aristocracy
armed combat
armed forces
armoured car
army officer
arquebusier
arrangement
art director
arteriology
arteriotomy
artillerist
art mistress
asking price
aspect ratio
assay-master
assize court
association
associative
asterialite
asterolepis
astrography
athleticism
atmidometer
atomic clock
attaché case
attestation
at the double
auction ring
auction sale
audiologist
audiotypist
augen gneiss

auger beetle
auscultator
autotrophic
autotropism
auxiliaries
average bond
avoirdupois
bacchanalia
back-bencher
baked Alaska
baker's dozen
baking sheet
balance fish
ballad opera
ballad style
balletomane
ballot paper
balm-cricket
Banbury cake
banded krait
banded stilt
banded toado
band spectra
bandy player
bank account
bank balance
bank cashier
bank manager
bank of issue
barbastelle
bargemaster
barley broth
barley sugar
barley water
barn swallow
barnstormer
barquentine
barrack room
barrel-organ
bar sinister
bashi-bazook
basket chair
basketmaker
basket sword
basset hound
batti-wallah
battledress
battlefield
battlegroup
battle order
battle royal
battologist
beachcomber
beam compass
bean sprouts
bean trefoil
bear baiting
bear's breech
bear squeeze
beauty queen
bed hangings
beehawk moth
belaying pin
bell bottoms
bell-founder
bell foundry
belligerent
bellows fish
belly gunner
benediction
benedictory
beneficiary
bene-placito
benzoic acid
bersaglieri
besiegement
best clothes
beta version
bethanidine
Bible reader
bibliolater
bibliomancy
bibliophile
bicarbonate
bicentenary
bichon frisé
big business
billiard cue
billionaire
bill of entry
bill-sticker
bimetallism
bird-catcher
bird's-nester
birdwatcher
bishop's weed
bitter apple
bitter herbs
bittersweet
black and tan
black angler
black beetle
blackbonnet
black bottom
black cayman
black comedy
black falcon
blackmailer
black market
black martin
black patent
black silver
black velvet
black walnut
black wattle
black willow
blank cheque
blasphemous
blazing star
blind corner
blind flying
blockbuster
block system
blood flower
blood orange
bloodsucker
blue-eyed boy
blue-pointer
blunderbuss
blunderhead
boatbuilder
bodhisattva
body servant
boilermaker
boilersmith
bolster case
bombardment
bomber pilot
bonded goods
bondservant
bonebreaker
bonne bouche
bonus scheme
bookkeeping
book matches
boot scraper
bottle gourd
bottlebrush
boulder clay
bourgeoisie

bow and arrow
boysenberry
braising pan
brake-lining
Bramah press
brank ursine
bread grater
breadwinner
breast drill
breastplate
brewer's dray
bridled goby
brineshrimp
bristle-bird
Briton crown
broadcaster
broken chord
brotherhood
brown groper
brown lentil
brush-turkey
brush wheels
budget price
budgie's cage
built-up area
bulk carrier
bull baiting
bulletproof
bullfighter
bull mastiff
bullock cart
bull terrier
bumblepuppy
bumps-a-daisy
burgomaster
bush-creeper
businessman
butcherbird
butter knife
butter stamp
button quail
button stick
bye-election
cabbage moth
cabbage palm
cabbage rose
cable laying
cache memory
cake crusher
calceolaria
calcyanthus
calligraphy
calling crab
calorimeter
calumniator
cameo brooch
campanology
camphor tree
Canada goose
canary grass
candelabrum
candleberry
candlemaker
candlepower
candlestick
candystripe
canned music
cantharides
canvas shoes
capacitance
cap and bells
capharis bug
capillarity
capital gain
capital ship
capreomycin
capriccioso
captainship
captain's pie
caravansary
carbimazole
carbon cycle
carboxylase
carburetter
carcinology
cardiograph
carnivorous
carpet shark
carpet viper
carp-gudgeon
carriage dog
carriageway
car salesman
carrion crow
cartography
cash account
cassava cake
castellated
casting vote
catastrophe
caterpillar
cats and dogs
cattle egret
cauliflower
cave dweller
CD jewel case
cedar wattle
cementation
cementatory
cementstone
centenarian
centigramme
central bank
centreboard
centrepiece
centrifugal
centripetal
certificate
cetotolites
chaff cutter
chafing dish
chafing gear
chain blocks
chain bridge
chain wrench
chair mender
chalcedonyx
chalcia wasp
chalk cutter
chamberlain
chambermaid
chance-comer
chanda perch
change sides
chansonette
chanterelle
chanticleer
charcoalist
chariot race
chasse-marée
cheerleader
cheese board
cheesecloth
cheese parer
cheese press
cheirolepis
chess player
cheval glass
chiaroscuro
chicken farm

chief stoker
chiffon cake
chiffonnier
China orange
chinoiserie
chirologist
chiromancer
chiropodist
chlorine gas
chlorograph
chlorometer
chlorophane
chlorophyll
chloroplast
choirmaster
chokecherry
cholesterol
chondrodite
chondrology
chondrostei
chrismation
christening
chronograph
chronologer
chronometer
chronometry
chronoscope
chrysoberyl
chucklehead
church house
church music
churchwoman
cider brandy
cigar cutter
ciliary body
circle dance
circulation
circus-rider
citron water
civil wrongs
clairschach
clairvoyant
clarion note
cliff-hanger
climatology
clock setter
clog almanac
close button
closed order
close-hauled
closing time
clothes hook
clothes line
clothes moth
cloth-of-gold
cloth worker
cluster bomb
clutch pedal
coalitioner
coal measure
coal scuttle
coat of paint
cochinchina
cockleshell
cock-sparrow
coconut milk
coconut palm
codling moth
co-education
coefficient
coexistence
coffee plant
coffee table
cognoscenti
co-inheritor
coir matting
cold climate
collaborate
collenchyma
colour cycle
colour print
columbarium
combat plane
combination
comedy drama
comestibles
comic relief
commentator
commination
comminatory
commitments
commodities
common skate
common stock
common toado
communicant
commutative
comparative
compartment
compass card
compass rose
competition
competitive
complainant
composition
compression
comptometer
comptroller
computation
concealment
concertante
concert hall
conchometer
concordance
concrete art
condisciple
condonation
condottiere
conductance
conductress
confamiliar
confederate
confiscator
conge d'elire
congressman
conirostres
conjecturer
conjugation
conjunction
conjunctiva
conjunctive
connoisseur
conquerable
consecrator
consignment
conspirator
constituent
consumption
contabulate
contact mine
containment
contaminant
contemplate
continental
continuator
contra basso
contrapunto
contra-tenor
contributor
contrivance

conurbation
convergence
convertible
conveyancer
convocation
convolvulus
co-operative
coordinates
co-ordinator
coping stone
copper beech
copperplate
coppersmith
coprocessor
coprophagan
copyfitting
coral island
corbel steps
corn bunting
cornerstone
corn parsley
corporation
cosmogonist
cosmography
cosmologist
cosmosphere
cotoneaster
cotton grass
cottonmouth
cotton plant
cotton shirt
coulommiers
counterfeit
counterfort
countermine
counterpane
counterpart
countersink
countervair
countryside
county court
county match
coupling box
coupling pin
court jester
cowslip wine
crack troops
crane driver
craniometer
craniometry
crash helmet
crazing mill
cream cheese
credit title
crematorium
crest marine
crested goby
crested newt
cricket ball
criminal law
criminology
crisping pin
croquet ball
cross-bearer
crossbowman
crosscut saw
cross-fleury
crown lawyer
crown octavo
crown prince
crucifixion
crude plough
cryptophago
crystalline
crystallize
cub reporter
cuckoo's meat
cuffing room
cullen skink
cultivation
cum dividend
cupellation
curry powder
curtail step
curtain hook
curtain rail
curtain ring
customs duty
cut and paste
cybernetics
cycloidians
cycloserine
cypher clerk
cypress pine
damask steel
dame's violet
dance troupe
dark glasses
dawn redwood
day's journey
days of grace
deamination
death duties
debarkation
debtors' acts
decarbonize
deck cricket
declaration
declination
decrescendo
deerstalker
defenceless
degradation
dehydration
deification
deliberator
delivery man
delivery van
de-luxe model
demand curve
demand draft
demarcation
demi-cadence
demographer
demographic
demutualize
dendrachate
dendrometer
denominator
dental plate
denunciator
depopulator
deportation
deposit rate
deposit slip
depreciator
depth charge
depth finder
Derby winner
dermatology
dermography
descriptive
desecration
deserpidine
desmography
despatch box
dessication
determinant
devaluation
devastation

development
devotionist
diacoustics
diagnometer
diagnostics
diamagnetic
diamond bird
diamorphine
diatessaron
dicing house
diffraction
digitigrade
dilapidator
diluvialist
dimidiation
dining table
dinner dance
dinner plate
dinner table
dinotherium
diplomatist
dipsomaniac
direct input
directorate
disarmament
disbandment
discipliner
discordance
discordancy
discounting
discourager
dishonoured
dishonourer
disjunctive
dismastment
dispatch box
dispensator
display type
display unit
disportment
dissentient
dissolution
dissyllabic
dissyllable
distempered
distributor
disturbance
dithyrambic
dithyrambus
dive-bombing
dividend tax
divine light
divine right
diving board
diving stone
doch-an-doris
dock charges
doctrinaire
documentary
dog biscuits
dog's cabbage
dog's mercury
dolichosaur
domestician
door knocker
Dorking fowl
double agent
double crown
double eagle
double-entry
double-royal
douroucouli
dovetailing
down payment
doxological
doxorubicin
doxycycline
draft dodger
draftswoman
drag and drop
draggle-tail
dragon's head
Dragon's wort
dragoon-bird
drama critic
drama school
dramatic art
dram drinker
draughtsman
drawing room
dreadnought
dredging box
dress circle
dress parade
drill barrow
drill harrow
drill plough
drinker moth
dripping pan
driving band
driving belt
driving test
drug peddler
dry monopole
dune-bedding
Dutch clover
duty officer
dynamometer
eager beaver
Earl Grey tea
earl-marshal
eccaleobion
ecclesiarch
echo-sounder
eclecticism
eclipsareon
edge railway
edutainment
eigenvector
ejector seat
elaeocarpus
electioneer
electric eel
electrician
electricity
electric jar
electric ray
electrolyse
electrolyte
electronics
electrotype
elephant gun
elimination
emancipator
embarkation
embellisher
emblematist
embroiderer
Emperor moth
emplacement
enabling act
enchantress
encounterer
endeavourer
endless belt
endorsement
endothelium
endothermic
enforcement
enfranchise

engineering
engrailment
engravement
engrossment
enlargement
enlightener
enlisted man
entablature
entertainer
entomophaga
entozoology
envelopment
environment
epigenesist
epistolizer
equiangular
equibalance
equidistant
equilateral
equilibrist
equilibrium
equisonance
equivocator
erythrocyte
erythronium
escape hatch
eschatology
established
establisher
estate agent
eternal life
ethisterone
ethmoid bone
ethnography
ethnologist
etymologist
euphemerist
evangelical
everlasting
exaggerator
examination
exasperater
executioner
exeunt omnes
exfoliation
exhaust pipe
exhaust port
exoskeleton
expenditure
exponential
extemporize
extenuating
extradition
extra master
face painter
facilitator
factory hand
factory ship
facultative
fair comment
fairy martin
fairy stones
faith healer
falling body
falling star
fallow finch
fanning mill
fan vaulting
farmer's lung
fasciolaria
fast bowling
father-in-law
fatigue duty
fault-finder
feature film
feeler gauge
Fell terrier
female screw
femme fatale
fertilizing
fescue grass
fibre optics
fiddlestick
field sports
field worker
fieri facias
fifth column
fig marigold
fighting man
figured bass
figure maker
figure stone
filing clerk
film theatre
finance bill
finestiller
fingerboard
finger glass
finger grass
finger plate
finger stone
fire balloon
fire curtain
firefighter
fire insurer
firelighter
fire-starter
fire-watcher
firing party
firing squad
first aid box
first cousin
first violin
fishing boat
fishing line
five-fingers
five hundred
fixed assets
fixed charge
fixed income
flag captain
flag officer
flannelette
flared skirt
flat dweller
fleet-footed
floating rib
flock pigeon
floor polish
florid style
flour dredge
flour weevil
fluctuation
fluid drachm
fluking-iron
flying corps
flying lemur
flying mouse
flying party
flying snake
flying speed
flying squad
foam-crested
focal length
folk dancers
folk dancing
foot cushion
foot soldier
football cap
footscraper

forced march
foreclosure
forestaller
fore-topmast
fore-topsail
forget-me-not
form teacher
fortnightly
foster child
foundations
fountain pen
fourbisseur
four-wheeler
fox squirrel
frame bridge
francophile
francophobe
francophone
frankfurter
free balloon
free fishery
free on board
free radical
freethinker
freezing fog
freight note
French beans
French berry
French bread
french chalk
friend or foe
frieze panel
frigate bird
front lights
frontal bone
fruit picker
fruit pigeon
fuller's weed
funambulist
function key
functionary
future tense
Gaboon viper
gall bladder
galley foist
galley proof
galley slave
gallinipper
gallows tops
gallows-bird
games theory
gametophyte
gaming table
garden chair
garden party
gartersnake
gas governor
gatecrasher
genealogist
general post
genetic code
gentlefolks
gentlewoman
geomedicine
geometrical
george noble
geosyncline
germination
germ warfare
gerontology
get under way
ghost writer
giant cactus
giant fennel
giant planet
gila monster
gillyflower
gin and tonic
ginger group
gingerbread
glass blower
glass cutter
glass mosaic
glass worker
globeflower
globigerina
glue sniffer
gnat-snapper
go alongside
goddaughter
golden chain
golden eagle
golden perch
golden syrup
Golgi bodies
goliath frog
gongiatites
goods waggon
gopherspace
grain beetle
grallatores
grammatical
grand circle
grandfather
grand master
grandmother
grandnephew
grandparent
grand vizier
granny smith
grant of arms
graphic arts
graphometer
graphophone
grasshopper
grass skiing
gravedigger
graven image
graving dock
gravitation
greasepaint
great primer
Greek chorus
greenbottle
greendragon
greengrocer
green lizard
green pepper
green turtle
Grevy's zebra
grey wagtail
griddle cake
grizzly bear
gross income
ground floor
ground plane
ground robin
ground speed
ground state
ground swell
groundwater
grubbing hoe
guelder rose
Guido's scale
guinea piece
gull catcher
gun-carriage
gunner's mate
gurnet perch
gutter press

guttersnipe
gymnasiarch
gynaecology
haberdasher
haematology
haemocyanin
haemoglobin
haemophilia
haemorrhage
haemorrhoid
hagiography
hagiologist
hairdresser
hairstylist
hair trigger
half a league
half-brother
half holiday
half measure
hammer cloth
ham sandwich
hand-breadth
hand grenade
hand-me-downs
hang gliding
happy family
harbour dues
hard drinker
hard weather
hare wallaby
haricot bean
harmoniphon
harmonizing
harness cask
harpsichord
harrier-hawk
Harris tweed
hart's tongue
harum-scarum
harvest home
harvest time
hawk missile
headteacher
heart attack
hearth brush
hearthstone
heat barrier
heavy bomber
heavyweight
hebdomadary
hectogramme
hedge hyssop
hedge priest
helical gear
heliochrome
heliography
helping hand
helvehammer
hemistichal
herring cale
herring gull
herringbone
heteroclite
heterospory
hexadecimal
hibernation
hide-and-seek
hierography
hierologist
high finance
high jumping
highpitched
high society
highway code
hill walking
hippocampus
histologist
histrionics
hoary poplar
hobbledehoy
hockey stick
holiday task
holiday time
holoptychis
homeostatis
homoeopathy
homo sapiens
honey-flower
honey locust
honeysuckle
Honiton lace
hooded robin
horned viper
hors d'oeuvre
horse doctor
horse jockey
horse litter
horsemarten
horse racing
horseradish
horse riding
horse trader
hospitaller
hostilities
hot cross bun
hotel keeper
housekeeper
housemartin
housemaster
housemother
huckleberry
hudibrastic
hug the shore
humble plant
hummingbird
hunt counter
hunting-horn
hydraulicon
hydrocarbon
hydroglider
hydrography
hydrophobia
hydroxyurea
hydroxyzine
hyetography
hymnography
hymnologist
hyoscyamine
hyperbolist
hyperboloid
hypercharge
hypercritic
hypothecate
hypothermia
Iceland moss
Iceland spar
ice yachting
ichthyolite
ichthyology
ichthyosaur
ichthyotomy
iconography
icosahedron
idoxuridine
ignition key
illuminator
illusionism
illusionist
illustrator
imam bayaldi

imbrication
immortality
impeachment
imperial-cap
imperialist
impersonate
impregnable
imprimatura
inaugurator
incantation
incarnation
incinerator
income stock
indefensive
independent
Indian berry
indian club
Indian cobra
Indian cress
indigo plant
indigometer
indirect tax
industrials
infanticide
infantryman
infertility
inheritance
inking table
input device
inquisition
insecticide
integration
interactive
interceptor
intercessor
inter-county
internuncio
interpreter
interregnum
interrupter
interviewer
intimidator
ipecacuanha
Irish coffee
Irish setter
iron filings
iron founder
iron foundry
iron pyrites
iron rations
irreligious
irreverence
isochronism
isochronous
isomorphism
isomorphous
issue of writ
issuing bank
ivory carver
ivory turner
ivory worker
jackass fish
jagging iron
jam sandwich
Japan laurel
jaunting car
javelin fish
job analysis
joint return
joint tenant
jubilee year
jumping bean
jumping deer
kalashnikov
kangaroo rat
keelhauling
Kerry beagle
kestrel-hawk
kidney vetch
killer whale
kinesiology
king penguin
kingsnapper
king's pardon
king vulture
kirk session
kitchenmaid
kitchen-sink
kitten heels
knick-knacks
knucklehead
labour force
lace monitor
lace-up boots
lady's mantle
Lambeth walk
laminations
lammergeier
lamp chimney
landaulette
landfill tax
landing deck
landing gear
land steward
langesettle
lapis lazuli
laryngology
last quarter
latten-brass
lattice leaf
latticework
laundrymaid
laurustinus
lawn bowling
lay preacher
leaded light
leading-edge
leading lady
leading wren
leaf bag moth
league table
leaseholder
leather case
leathercoat
leatherhead
leatherskin
ledger clerk
legal tender
legerdemain
legionnaire
legislation
legislative
legislature
leisure time
lemon squash
leopard fish
leopard frog
leopard lily
leopardskin
leper wattle
lepidosiren
leptodactyl
letterpress
leucocratic
libertarian
liberty ship
lichenology
lickspittle
lifeboatman
life drawing

light comedy
light vessel
lightkeeper
lightweight
lignum vitae
lilliputian
lily-trotter
line dancing
line drawing
linen basket
linen draper
linguistics
liquidation
lithography
lithologist
litmus paper
litterateur
little tunny
living image
load-bearing
loan capital
loblolly-boy
locatograph
Lochaber axe
lock chamber
logopaedics
London pride
long hundred
long jumping
long measure
loop of Henle
loop the loop
loosestrife
lord provost
Lord's prayer
lorry driver
louvre board
love-in-a-mist
lower orders
lowering sky
low pressure
loxodromics
lubrication
luggage rack
lycanthrope
lyric poetry
machicolate
machicoulis
machine code
machine tool
mackerel sky
madreporite
madrigalist
magic carpet
magic square
Maginot line
magnetophon
magpie-goose
maidservant
mail phaeton
mailing list
maintenance
maintopmast
maintopsail
make-believe
make headway
mammalogist
mandolinist
manilla rope
manipulator
man-o'-war fish
mantelpiece
mantelshelf
manufactory
manufacture
marchioness
marine store
market cross
market overt
market price
marlinspike
marqueterie
marram grass
marrying man
marsh mallow
marshalling
masquerader
mass-produce
master baker
masterpiece
master's mate
materialist
mathematics
mathimazole
matinee idol
matriculate
maxim-monger
mayor's court
meadow brown
meadow-pipit
meadowsweet
meander belt
meat biscuit
meat chopper
meat pudding
mechlin lace
median strip
medicine man
medlar jelly
memorialist
merchandise
merchantman
merry Andrew
merrymaking
mess steward
metal worker
metaphorist
metemptosis
meteorolite
meteorology
methicillin
method actor
methodology
methoxamine
micrography
middle class
middle price
middle watch
midwife toad
milk pudding
milk thistle
milky quartz
millenarian
milleporite
millet grass
milligramme
millionaire
minesweeper
mine thrower
miniaturist
minimum wage
minnesinger
minor planet
minute glass
minute watch
miracle play
misanthrope
misbeliever
miscarriage
misinformer

mithramycin
mockingbird
Moine schist
mole cricket
money broker
money-lender
money market
money supply
monkey block
monkey bread
monoculture
monographer
monopolizer
mono-railway
moon landing
moonlighter
moon trefoil
mooring mast
Moorish idol
morning coat
morning room
morning star
morris dance
mortarboard
mosquito net
motherboard
mother-in-law
motor launch
motor plough
motor spirit
motor vessel
mountain ash
mountain cat
mountaineer
mountain gun
mountainous
moving plant
mule spinner
mulga parrot
Muller glass
muntjac deer
muschel kalk
muscle fibre
Muscovy duck
music critic
music master
myodynamics
myographist
myrtle berry
mysteriarch
mystery ship
mythologist
name-dropper
Nancy pretty
naphazoline
naphthalene
narrow gauge
nationalist
nationalize
natural note
naturopathy
naval rating
naval vessel
navel orange
necessarian
neckerchief
necrologist
necromancer
needlestone
needle valve
needle whelk
needlewoman
negotiation
nematoblast
neo-romantic
net curtains
netherlings
net interest
net receipts
nettiquette
nettlecloth
neurography
neurologist
neurotomist
neutralizer
neutron bomb
neutron star
newton-metre
nickelodeon
night editor
nightingale
night porter
night sister
night-walker
night-worker
nikethamide
nomenclator
nondescript
non-metallic
non-resident
nosey parker
nucleic acid
number plate
numismatist
nutcrackers
oarsmanship
oblique case
observatory
obstruction
occultation
odontograph
office block
office staff
oil painting
oil pressure
oil purifier
oil strainer
olla podrida
omnipotence
omnipresent
omniscience
onion seller
open account
open-air life
opera bouffe
opera singer
ophiologist
opportunist
optical lens
option price
orange pekoe
orange perch
orang-outang
orbicularis
orchestrate
oriel window
orientalist
orientation
original sin
ormolu clock
ornitholite
ornithology
ornithopter
orthocentre
orthodromic
orthopedist
oscillation
osteography
osteologist
outbuilding

outstanding
overfishing
overfreight
over-grazing
overhauling
overheating
overpayment
over-revving
overtrading
owner-driver
oyster drill
oyster patty
oyster plant
Pacific gull
pacificator
package deal
paddle wheel
paediatrics
painted lady
paint roller
paleography
pamphleteer
panchakarma
panel beater
panicmonger
pantomimist
panty girdle
papal legate
papal nuncio
paper basket
paperhanger
papersailor
paperweight
paracetamol
parachutist
paraldehyde
parathyroid
paratrooper
parenthesis
paring knife
parishioner
parlourmaid
paromomycin
participant
particulate
partnership
parturition
party leader
pas de basque
passing bell
passing note
passion play
pastureland
paternoster
pathologist
patron saint
pavement art
pay on demand
peace-broker
peacekeeper
peace treaty
peach brandy
peacock fish
peacock sole
pearl barley
pearlfisher
pearl millet
pearl oyster
pearly queen
pelargonium
pencil cedar
pennant fish
pennyweight
pepper elder
pepper grass
peppermints
percolation
perforation
performance
pericardium
peripatetic
permutation
perpetrator
personality
perspective
petrography
petrol gauge
petrologist
pettifogger
pharisaical
pharyngitis
phenomenist
philatelist
philologist
philosopher
phoenix palm
phonologist
photography
photosphere
phyllanthus
physicalist
phytography
phytologist
piano player
piano violin
picnic party
picture rail
picture show
picturesque
piledriving
pillow fight
pilot cutter
pilot engine
pilot jacket
pine girdler
pinocytosis
pipe lighter
pipistrelle
pitchblende
plain turkey
planetarium
plantascope
plasmolysis
plasterwork
plastic arts
platemaking
platoon fire
play therapy
ploughshare
plug and play
plum pudding
pluviameter
pluviometer
pocket flask
pocket knife
point of sale
pointillism
pointillist
poison sumac
poking stick
polar bodies
polar circle
polarimeter
polariscope
polar region
pole jumping
polemoscope
policewoman
pollination
polypeptide

polyphonism
polyphonist
polystyrene
polytechnic
pomegranate
pompelmoose
pontificate
poppy mallow
porphyritic
porridge pot
port admiral
port charges
portmanteau
port of entry
port officer
portraitist
portraiture
positronium
postal order
post captain
postern gate
poster paint
postscenium
potash water
pot marigold
pot marjoram
potter's clay
pouchong tea
poultry farm
pound-keeper
poverty line
powder chest
powder flask
power brakes
power factor
power supply
prawning net
prayer beads
prayer wheel
preceptress
precipitate
predecessor
prehistoric
pre-ignition
premium bond
preposition
prerogative
present arms
present time
press-of-sail
pressurized
prestissimo
prêt-à-porter
price fixing
price freeze
prickleback
prickly heat
prickly pear
priestcraft
primitivism
primus stove
prince royal
print seller
private bill
prize giving
prize vessel
prizewinner
probabilist
probability
probationer
problem play
procellaria
prodigal son
progestogen
programming
progression
proletarian
proletariat
promenading
promulgator
proofreader
property man
property tax
prophylaxis
propitiator
proportions
proposition
proprietrix
prosecution
proselytism
proselytize
protagonist
protectress
protestator
protocolist
protonotary
pruning hook
prussic acid
pseudopodia
pseudoscope
psychodrama
pterichthys
pteridology
pterodactyl
public house
public stand
pudding bowl
puisne judge
pumice stone
punchinello
punctualist
punctuality
punctuation
purchase tax
purgatorian
put to flight
quadrennial
quadricycle
quail-thrush
quarrington
quarterdeck
quarter note
quarter tone
quartz clock
quartz watch
queen mother
querguedule
questionary
questionist
quicken tree
quicksilver
quinquereme
rabbet plane
racing model
racing shell
rack railway
radiator cap
radioactive
radiography
radiologist
ragged robin
rag merchant
rainbow-bird
rainbow fish
rainy season
raised beach
raisin bread
rallentando
rambler rose
rangefinder

rank and file
rapscallion
rarefaction
ratatouille
rationalist
rat kangaroo
rattlesnake
raw material
reaction rim
reactionary
reading lamp
reading room
ready-to-wear
realization
real numbers
reaping-hook
rear admiral
reclamation
recommender
recompenser
reconnoitre
reconstruct
recruitment
rectangular
rectilinear
red bullseye
red firefish
red-hot poker
red-iron bark
red mahogany
red squirrel
reed bunting
reed sparrow
reed warbler
reflexology
refreshment
regatta card
regimentals
regular army
regular verb
regulations
reinsurance
reiterative
religionary
religionism
religionist
religiosity
renaissance
replenisher
replication
reprehender
representer
request stop
requisition
reservation
reservatory
reserve bank
residential
resistivity
respiration
restitution
restoration
restructure
resuscitant
retardation
reticulated
retractable
retro-rocket
revaluation
reverse gear
reverse turn
reversioner
revisionism
revisionist
revolutions
rhamphastos
rhetorician
rhyncholite
ribbon cable
ribbon grass
ribonucleic
rice biscuit
rice pudding
riding habit
riding horse
riding light
right-angled
rights issue
right-winger
ring network
ripple grass
risk capital
ritualistic
river course
river oyster
river sports
roadsweeper
Rob-Roy canoe
rock and roll
rock crystal
rock wallaby
rock warbler
rock whiting
rolling mill
roll-top desk
Roman cement
root of title
rosary beads
rouge-et-noir
rough collie
rough riding
rough sketch
round window
royal assent
royal family
royal python
rubber cable
rugby player
rum and black
running fire
running head
russet apple
rustication
sabbatarian
sacramental
sacred music
sacrilegist
sacring bell
saddle cloth
safebreaker
safe-conduct
safe deposit
safety catch
safety razor
safety valve
saffron cake
sago pudding
sailing date
sailing ship
sales ledger
salinometer
salmon-trout
Samson's post
sanctus bell
sand sailing
sand whiting
sandwich man
sans-culotte
sarcophagus
sardine boat

sausage roll
savings bank
sawing stool
saxophonist
scaffolding
scale armour
scaremonger
scarlet bean
scarlet ibis
scene change
scenography
scholarship
school board
school hours
schoolshark
schottische
Scilly shrew
scissor-bill
scolopendra
scorpion fly
scoutmaster
scrapdealer
screen wiper
screwdriver
scrip holder
scripturist
scrutinizer
scuba diving
scud missile
scuppernong
scurvy grass
sea cucumber
sea elephant
sea-hedgehog
sea lavender
sea-pheasant
searchlight
search party
sea-scorpion
seasickness
secret agent
section-sewn
sedimentary
seditionary
seeding time
seismograph
seismometer
seismoscope
self-starter
sell forward
sempervivum
senza rigore
sericulture
series wound
serpentaria
serpentfish
servant girl
service pipe
serving maid
sesquiplane
set designer
set the scene
settling day
sharebroker
shareholder
sharon fruit
sheep farmer
sheet anchor
shell-parrot
shepherdess
sheriff's act
shipbreaker
shipbuilder
shipping ton
ship's doctor
ship's master
ship's papers
shock troops
shoe leather
shooting box
shoot to kill
shopping bag
shop steward
shorthaired
short pastry
short weight
shoulderbag
shovel board
show jumping
showmanship
show-stopper
shrike-robin
shuttlecock
sideroscope
sightseeing
silicon chip
silk thrower
silver-belly
silver birch
silver penny
silver perch
silversmith
silver tabby
silver toado
simple Simon
singing-bird
single-edged
single-entry
single stick
singularist
sinking fund
siphonifers
siphon stand
sister-in-law
skating club
skating rink
skeletology
skeleton key
skim coulter
skittle pool
Skye terrier
slate pencil
slaughterer
slave bangle
slave trader
sleeping car
sleepwalker
sliding keel
sliding roof
sliding rule
slip-on shoes
slipped disc
slippery elm
slot machine
slotted wing
slow bowling
slumberwear
small copper
smallholder
small trader
smart system
smart weapon
sminthopsis
smokescreen
smoky quartz
smooth snake
smooth toado
snail clover
snail flower
snatchblock

snout beetle
snowballing
snow bunting
snow leopard
snow ortolan
soap bubbles
sociologist
socket joint
soda and milk
soft landing
soil profile
solar energy
solar system
sold forward
soldierbird
soldier-crab
soldier-fish
solid colour
solmization
somatic cell
song sparrow
souchong tea
sound effect
sounding rod
south-wester
space centre
space flight
space rocket
space travel
spade guinea
span-counter
spanking boom
sparrow wort
sparrowhawk
spear flower
spectacular
spectrogram
spectrology
speculation
speculatist
speechmaker
speed camera
speedometer
speed skater
Speeton clay
spelling bee
spendthrift
spermatozoa
spherograph
spherometer
spinach beet
spindle tree
spirit level
splashboard
sports model
spreadsheet
spring a leak
springboard
spring water
spring wheat
square dance
square metre
squaring rod
squirearchy
stabilizers
staddle roof
stage design
stage driver
stage effect
stage fright
stage player
stage school
stage-struck
stagflation
stagger bush
stair carpet
stakeholder
stamp duties
stand at ease
standing off
star billing
star quality
star-studded
star thistle
start thrust
statcoulomb
state landau
station bill
statry toado
statute book
steam boiler
steam hammer
steam launch
steamroller
steam vessel
steeplejack
steerage way
stepbrother
stereometer
stereometry
stereoscopy
stern chaser
sternohyoid
sternsheets
stethometer
stethoscope
stethoscopy
stewed fruit
stick insect
stickleback
stiff breeze
stiff collar
sting winkle
stipendiary
stirrup lamp
stockbroker
stockholder
stockinette
stockjobber
stock market
stockpiling
stocktaking
stomatology
stone curlew
stonecutter
stone hammer
stonelifter
stone plover
stonewaller
stool pigeon
storekeeper
storm petrel
storm signal
story-teller
stratigraphy
straw cutter
strawflower
straw pillow
stray bullet
streamlined
street child
strep throat
stretch limo
strike block
string music
stringboard
strip mining
stripteaser
strobolites
stubble rake

student loan
stuffing box
stump orator
stunt flying
sub-cellular
subcontract
subjunctive
sublimation
submersible
subordinate
subornation
subsemitone
subsistence
substantive
substituent
subtraction
subtropical
subulicorns
suckingfish
suction pipe
suction pump
suede jacket
suet pudding
suffragette
sugar dredge
suicide pact
summer cloud
summer house
summersault
summer wheat
summit level
sundriesman
superheater
superlative
supermarket
superstruct
supertanker
supply depot
suppression
surgeon fish
Surinam toad
surrenderee
surrenderer
sustainable
swallow fish
swallowtail
swallow-wort
sward cutter
sweepstakes
sweet cicely
sweet cistus
sweet potato
sweet rocket
sweet sultan
swine's cress
swing bridge
swingplough
switchboard
sword-bearer
sword player
sworn friend
symmetrical
sympathizer
symphonious
synchromesh
synchronism
synchronize
synchronous
synchrotron
syncopation
syndicalism
syndicalist
syndication
syntactical
syphon stand
systematist
system maker
table napkin
table runner
table tennis
tagliatelle
take by storm
take-home pay
takeover bid
take the veil
Talbot hound
tale telling
talent scout
talipot palm
tallegalane
tam-o'-shanter
tape measure
tappet valve
tautologist
tautomerism
tax assessor
tax gatherer
taxidermist
tea canister
teetotaller
telegrapher
teleologist
telepathist
telephonist
teleprinter
temperature
tempestuous
tennis court
tennis dress
tennis skirt
tent pegging
terabratula
terbutaline
terebrantia
terpsichore
terrestrial
tessellated
tetradrachm
tetrahedron
tetrapteran
thanatology
thanksgiver
thaumatrope
thaumaturgy
theatre-goer
theatre land
theatricals
theobromine
theosophist
thermal unit
thermal vest
thermometer
thermoscope
Thespian art
thick-bedded
thin red line
third degree
Thompson gun
thorn lizard
thorny devil
thorough wax
three-decker
three-in-hand
three-masted
three-master
through road
thrust plane
thumerstone
thunderbolt
thunderclap

thwartships
thymoxamine
thysanurans
ticket agent
tidal waters
tiger beetle
tiger cowrie
tiger flower
tiled hearth
timberborer
timber frame
time deposit
time-pleaser
time sharing
tinkar's root
tin-lined box
tissue paper
titanic iron
toastmaster
tobacco pipe
tobacconist
tobogganing
toggle joint
toilet brush
toilet cover
toilet table
tomato juice
tonquin bean
tonsillitis
tooth drawer
tooth powder
topographer
top-spinning
torch-bearer
torchon lace
torpedo boat
torpedo tube
torsiograph
totalisator
town council
town dweller
town planner
toxophilite
trachelipod
trafficator
tragedienne
tragicomedy
transaction
transcriber
transformer
translation
transmitter
transporter
transposing
transsexual
transuranic
trap-and-ball
travel agent
treecreeper
tree sparrow
tree surgeon
tree swallow
trelliswork
trencher cap
trencherman
trend setter
trespassing
trick riding
tridiapason
trimetrical
triploblast
trolmydames
trone weight
troposphere
trouser suit
trout stream
trumpet fish
trundle head
tube railway
tuition fees
turfing iron
turkey wheat
Turkish bath
Tuscan order
tussac grass
tussock moth
tussore silk
twelvemonth
twin-engined
two-foot rule
typographer
tyrannosaur
tyrothrycin
unaccordant
unballasted
unchartered
unchristian
unconquered
uncontested
underbearer
under canvas
undercharge
undercoated
underground
underletter
under-masted
undersigned
undervalued
undervaluer
underwriter
undesirable
unexercised
unformatted
unfurnished
uninhabited
uninsulated
unjustified
unnavigable
unnavigated
unprotected
unrehearsed
unrighteous
unsheltered
unsoundable
upholsterer
upper circle
uranography
vacuum brake
vacuum flask
valley tract
vapour trail
variety show
varsovienne
vasopressin
ventilation
ventriloquy
vesting deed
vestry clerk
vice admiral
victory roll
victual ship
vinaigrette
vincristine
vine dresser
vinefretter
vintage wine
viola d'amore
viol da gamba
violoncello
viper's grass

viscountess
visual basic
vivacissimo
V-neck jumper
voce-di-petto
voce-di-testa
voltaic pile
volti-subito
vulcanizing
waffle irons
waggon train
wainscoting
waistcloths
waiting maid
wallcreeper
war criminal
war memorial
warping bank
warping hook
warping post
washerwoman
washing line
washleather
wassail bowl
waste basket
waste mantle
wastethrift
watchkeeper
watchmaking
water beetle
water cannon
water cement
watercolour
watercourse
watered silk
water engine
water filter
water furrow
water hammer
water heater
watering can
watering pot
water lizard
waterlogged
water python
water radish
water rocket
water skater
water skiing
water supply
water trough
water violet
wax chandler
weathercock
weatherdeck
weather gage
weather girl
weathermost
weather roll
weather side
wedding band
wedding cake
wedding ring
weed control
weeding fork
weeding hook
weigh anchor
weighbridge
welding heat
wellingtons
Welsh mutton
Welsh rabbit
wheaten loaf
wheel animal
wheelbarrow
wheel cutter
wheel wobble
wheelwright
whipping-top
whistle fish
white clover
white darnel
white ensign
white matter
white poplar
white spruce
whitethroat
whitewashed
whitewasher
white willow
whooper swan
widow's weeds
wildebeeste
wild flowers
wild fowling
wind backing
windcheater
wind furnace
window blind
window frame
window glass
window ledge
windsurfing
wind turbine
wind veering
wine biscuit
wine measure
winning crew
winning side
winning team
winter apple
winter berry
winter bloom
winter cress
wintergreen
wire drawing
wire grading
wire grating
wishtonwish
witchdoctor
with profits
wolf herring
wood anemone
wood carving
woodcreeper
wood cutting
wooden house
woodfretter
wood-swallow
wood warbler
woolly lemur
woolstapler
word-perfect
workmanship
workstation
world record
wreckmaster
writing desk
wrought iron
xanthoxylum
xylophonist
yachting cap
yacht racing
yard measure
yellow fever
yellow robin
yeoman usher
yesternight
zoographist
zooplankton

zygophyllum
zymosimeter

12
abolitionist
above the line
academic year
accordionist
account payee
acetaldehyde
acetate rayon
acoustic bass
acoustic mine
acquaintance
active window
actor-manager
adder's tongue
Adele penguin
adhesive tape
adjudication
adjutant bird
ad valorem tax
advance guard
advance party
aerial plants
aerodynamics
aethrioscope
agent-general
agribusiness
agricultural
air commodore
aircraftsman
airfreighter
air-sea rescue
alcoholmeter
alkali metals
alkyd colours
alkyl halides
allegrissimo
alliteration
alliterative
almond willow
alphabetical
altar frontal
amalgamation
ambassadress
ambulanceman
amortization
amphibiolite
amphibiology
amphitheatre
amphotericin
anaesthetist
angstrom unit
annihilation
annunciation
antediluvial
antediluvian
ante meridiem
anteposition
anthropology
anti-aircraft
antibacchius
anticourtier
anticyclonic
anti-friction
antimacassar
antimetrical
antiparticle
antiphonical
antiphrastic
antistrophic
antoninianus
apfel strudel
appassionata
apple blossom
apple fritter
appoggiatura
appreciation
approach road
appropriator
April showers
aptitude test
Arabian camel
araeosystyle
archbuttress
archdeaconry
archesporium
archilochian
architecture
argillaceous
arithmometer
armour bearer
armour-plated
Armstrong gun
aromatherapy
arrester gear
arterial road
artesian well
artful dodger
artilleryman
artist's model
asbestos suit

assai allegro
assay balance
assembly line
assembly room
astronautics
astronomical
astrophysics
asylum seeker
asynchronous
athlete's foot
atmospherics
atomic number
atomic theory
atomic weight
auction rooms
augmentation
auncel weight
auscultation
autorickshaw
autumn crocus
averruncator
awkward squad
baby carriage
bachelor girl
back-crossing
backwoodsman
bacteriology
bagpipe maker
Bailey bridge
Bakewell tart
balance sheet
ball bearings
ballet dancer
ballet master
balletomania
bamboo shoots
banker's draft
banker's order
bantamweight
Barbary sheep
bargain price
barking irons
basking shark
bass baritone
bathing dress
battering ram
battleground
battlemented
beacon lights
bead necklace
beat a retreat
bedding plane
bedside light
bedside table
bellows maker
belly dancing
belly landing
below the line
belt adjuster
belt fastener
Belvoir hound
bend sinister
benefactress
Bengal monkey
Benjamin tree
bent-wing moth
beta particle
betel nut palm
betrothal day
between decks
bible-thumper
bibliography
bibliologist
bibliomaniac
bibliopegist
bicentennial
bilateralism
billiard ball
bill of lading
billycock hat
biochemistry
biodiversity
biogeography
birdwatching
birthday cake
bitter almond
blackcurrant
black drummer
black rock-cod
bladderwrack
blanchimeter
blast furnace
block letters
block machine
block signals
blood brother
blotting book
bluestocking
blue trevally
boarding pike
board meeting
bobsleighing
body stocking
boiling point
bolting cloth
bomb disposal
bona vacantia
bond creditor
bonded stores
boogie-woogie
booking clerk
book reviewer
book scorpion
boolean logic
border collie
boring mussel
bottle opener
bottle-washer
bottomry bond
bounty hunter
bouquet garni
bow compasses
Bowland shale
bowling alley
brace-and-bits
brachygraphy
branch office
branding iron
brass rubbing
breakdown van
breakfast cup
breastplough
breeches buoy
breech loader
bridging loan
brigade major
bromo seltzer
bronze pigeon
brother-in-law
brown Burmese
brushed denim
buccal cavity
bucking stool
buffalo grass
building site
bullfighting
burglar alarm
burning glass
burnt almonds
burrowing-owl

bus conductor
bush fighting
business suit
butterfly net
butterscotch
buyer's market
buzzard clock
cabbage white
cabin cruiser
cabinet maker
cabin steward
cable's length
Cairn terrier
calisthenics
callable bond
calligrapher
camera lucida
camp bedstead
canalization
candleholder
candle sconce
cannon fodder
canonization
canvas length
capercaillie
capercailzie
capital gains
capital goods
capital stock
capitulation
caravanserai
carbohydrate
carbon dating
carbonic acid
cardinal bird
cardiologist
caricaturist
carpenter ant
carpenter bee
carpet beater
carpet fitter
carrying over
carry over day
cartographer
cartridge box
carving knife
case of thorns
cash and carry
catamountain
caulking iron
caulking tool
causa proxima
caution money
cavalry sword
cavalry twill
caveat emptor
cave painting
cecropia moth
cembal d'ambre
central canal
centre of mass
centrolinead
cerographist
chained snake
chain reactor
chaise longue
chamber music
champagne cup
championship
change course
chapel of ease
chapel of rest
charter party
chat potatoes
chaumontelle
chauvinistic
cheese fondue
cheesemonger
cherry brandy
cherry laurel
chesterfield
chicken snake
chief cashier
chief justice
chief mourner
chief of staff
chief officer
chief skipper
chief steward
chimneypiece
chimney shaft
chimney sweep
Chinaman's hat
chip potatoes
chiropractic
chiropractor
chlorambucil
chlorbutanol
chlorhexadol
chlorination
chocolate nut
chondrometer
choreography
Christ's thorn
chromaticism
chromosphere
chronography
chronologist
chrysophrase
church living
church member
church parade
church school
churchwarden
cinema studio
cinnabar moth
circuit board
circuit rider
circumcision
cirrocumulus
cirrostratus
civil defence
civil servant
civil service
clapperboard
clarinettist
clavicembalo
clearing bank
clerid beetle
clerk of works
client server
closing price
clothes brush
clothes drier
clothes horse
cloth shearer
clotted cream
cloud chamber
club swinging
clutchspring
coach-and-four
coach-and-pair
coachbuilder
coachwhip ray
coalitionist
coasting boat
coasting ship
coaxial cable
cochineal fig
cockfighting

cockle stairs
coleopterist
collaborator
collar and tie
collared dove
college scarf
collision mat
colour circle
combinations
comedy ballet
cometography
commiserator
commissariat
commissioned
commissioner
committee man
common market
commonwealth
communicator
companionway
compass plant
compensation
competitress
complimenter
concert grand
concert party
concert pitch
conchologist
condensation
conductivity
confectioner
confessional
confirmation
conglomerate
congregation
conic section
conning tower
conquistador
conscription
consecration
consequences
conservatism
conservative
conservatory
consistorial
console table
constabulary
constipation
constituency
constitution
construction
constructure
contemplator
contemporary
contour lines
contract note
contrapuntal
control tower
control valve
controverter
convalescent
conventicler
conventional
conventioner
conveyancing
convivialist
cooking apple
co-respondent
corn chandler
Cornish pasty
corn marigold
corn on the cob
cornu-ammonis
corporealist
cosmographer
cosmopolitan
costermonger
cost of living
cottage piano
council of war
counter-brace
counter gauge
countermarch
counter-paled
counterpoint
counterpoise
counterscarp
countershaft
counter-tenor
country house
court-martial
covalent bond
covered court
covering fire
cow's lungwort
CPU memory bus
cradle scythe
crafts master
cramping iron
craniologist
crash barrier
crash landing
credit rating
credit titles
crême de cacao
creosote bush
crêpe-de-chine
crested grebe
cricket match
crime and tort
crimping iron
crisping iron
critical mass
cross-bedding
cross-examine
cross heading
crown-equerry
crown witness
crow's foot elm
cryptogamist
cubic measure
cuckoo flower
cuckoo-shrike
cucumber fish
cucumber tree
culver-tailed
cup and saucer
curds and whey
curling stone
curling tongs
current price
current ratio
currocumulus
currostratus
curvirostral
custard apple
customs union
cylinder head
Cyprus sherry
cytogenetics
Dall porpoise
danger signal
Danish pastry
danse macabre
Dartmoor pony
deadly carrot
death penalty
debrisoquine
declinometer
decommission

deep-sea diver
deer stalking
default value
deflationary
dehumidifier
deinotherium
deliquescent
demimondaine
demonologist
demonstrator
dendrologist
denitrifying
denomination
dentirostres
deponent verb
depreciation
deregulation
despatch boat
despatch case
dessertspoon
determinator
device driver
diadem spider
dialectician
diamagnetism
dichlorophen
dictatorship
diesel engine
differential
dimerosomata
dinner jacket
diploblastic
dipterygians
direct labour
disaccharide
disaffection
disbursement
disc coupling
disciplinant
discommender
discontinuer
discount rate
disenchanter
disestablish
disinflation
disintegrate
disorganizer
dispatch boat
dispatch case
dispensation
displacement
dispossessor
disseminator
dissertation
dissociation
dissyllabify
distillation
distributary
distribution
distributive
divertimento
divided skirt
dodecahedron
domino theory
donkey engine
donkey jacket
donkey's years
doppelganger
Doppler shift
dormer window
double acting
double-banked
double boiler
double-braced
double-dealer
double-decker
double-manned
double octave
double sequin
draft dodging
dragon's blood
drama therapy
dramaturgist
draughtboard
draught horse
draughtproof
drawing board
drawing paper
dress clothes
dressing case
dressing gown
dressing room
drill grubber
drinking bout
drinking horn
drip-dry shirt
driving chain
driving shaft
driving wheel
dry-core cable
ductilimeter
dumdum bullet
Dunmow flitch
duodecennial
dusky morwong
Dutch auction
earned income
Easter bonnet
eavesdropper
eccentricity
ecclesiastic
ecclesiology
echinocactus
econometrics
economy class
economy drive
ectoparasite
educationist
eggs and bacon
ejection seat
elaterometer
electric bulb
electric fire
electric fuse
electric iron
electric lamp
electric wire
electrolysis
electrometer
electromotor
electropathy
electrophone
electroscope
elecutionist
elephant seal
ellipsograph
elliptograph
elocutionist
Embering days
embezzlement
emblazonment
emergent year
emery grinder
encroachment
encumbrancer
endless screw
endoparasite
endoskeleton
endosmometer
enfranchiser

engine driver
enorthotrope
ensign bearer
enthronement
entomologist
entrance hall
entrepreneur
epidemiology
epigrammatic
epirrheology
episcopalian
episodically
epithalamium
equinoctials
erythromycin
erythroxylon
escapologist
escutcheoned
eternity ring
ethnographer
etymological
evangelicism
evaporometer
evening class
evening dress
event horizon
exchange rate
exclusionist
excursionist
exhaust valve
exhibitioner
exotic dancer
experimenter
export credit
expostulator
express train
express trust
ex-serviceman
extemporizer
extensionist
exterminator
extractor fan
extravaganza
facing matter
fairy penguin
falcon-gentle
false-bedding
false cadence
false prophet
fan regulator
fan-tailed ray
farm labourer
fatherlasher
fatigue party
featherbrain
feather grass
feature story
federal union
feeding stock
female thread
fennel flower
ferae naturae
fermentation
ferry steamer
fibrillation
field glasses
field kitchen
field marshal
field officer
fighter pilot
fighting fish
figured stone
figure skater
filibusterer
film director
film festival
film producer
Finnan haddie
fire detector
first-nighter
first officer
first quarter
first refusal
fiscal policy
fishing smack
fish strainer
fixed capital
flame-thrower
fleet admiral
flexible wire
flexor muscle
flittermouse
float chamber
floating debt
floating dock
floor timbers
floriculture
flour dredger
flour dresser
flow cleavage
flower basket
flower beetle
flowering ash
flower making
fluoxuridine
flying bridge
flying circus
flying column
flying doctor
flying lizard
flying pinion
flying saucer
folding chair
folding doors
folding stool
fool's parsley
footplateman
forehead fish
forestay sail
forest marble
formaldehyde
forward march
foster father
foster mother
foster parent
foster sister
foul mesdames
foundationer
founder's dust
founder's sand
fowling piece
frankincense
freewheeling
freezing rain
French window
friendly fire
frozen assets
fuel injection
fuller's earth
funeral march
funky chicken
furniture van
futtock plate
galactometer
galvanometer
galvanoscope
garden suburb
gargoyle fish
garlic butter
garnet schist

garrison town
gas condenser
gas container
gas regulator
gastronomist
gastrulation
gate-leg table
gazelle hound
gear changing
general synod
genuflection
geochemistry
geodesic dome
geometrician
geriatrician
German collie
German millet
German silver
gesticulator
giant herring
giant shallot
ginger brandy
glacial phase
glacial snout
Gladstone bag
glass blowing
glass furnace
glass grinder
Glauber's salt
gliding angle
globe thistle
globe-trotter
glockenspiel
glossologist
going concern
gold bracelet
gold earrings
golden oriole
golden plover
golden wattle
gold standard
googly bowler
go over the top
Gordon setter
grammaticism
grammaticize
grand assizes
graphics card
grass warbler
gray tuskfish
greasemonkey
great hundred
green tree boa
grey eminence
grey squirrel
greyweathers
ground beetle
ground tackle
ground thrush
ground troops
group captain
group therapy
guanethidine
guarana bread
guardianship
guerrilla war
guest chamber
guest speaker
guild brother
guitar string
Haber process
hackney coach
hackney horse
hagiographer
hair of the dog
hair's breadth
hair-splitter
half-quartern
half-timbered
haliographer
Halley's comet
halogenation
handkerchief
hanging valve
hard-aweather
hard currency
hard shoulder
harlequinade
harmonic mean
harmonometer
harness maker
harvest goose
harvest mouse
hasty pudding
hat stretcher
headmistress
headquarters
headshrinker
heart disease
heather bells
heavy cruiser
hebdomatical
hedge sparrow
hedgehopping
heir apparent
heliotropism
hempagrimony
herpetofauna
heterocercal
heteroclitic
heterogamete
heterozygous
hexametrical
high pressure
hippopotamus
hire purchase
holidaymaker
hollow square
holy of holies
honeybuzzard
hoodman-blind
horned clerid
horned iguana
horned lizard
horn-of-plenty
horse breaker
horse chestnut
horse courser
horse knacker
horsemanship
horseshoe bat
horse soldier
horse stinger
horticulture
host computer
hot cupboard
hotel manager
hot gospeller
hot water tank
hound's tongue
housekeeping
house of peers
house sparrow
house steward
house surgeon
housewarming
hubble-bubble
humanitarian
humpty dumpty
Hungarian cap

hunting horse
huntsmanship
hyaloid canal
hydraulic ram
hydrochloric
hydrodynamic
hydrogen bomb
hydrogen bond
hydrographer
hydropathist
hydrostatics
hydrotherapy
hydrothermal
hymnographer
hypertension
hypnotherapy
hypochondria
hypothalamus
hypothecator
ice-cream soda
iced lemon tea
Iceland poppy
illumination
illustration
immunologist
impersonator
impoverisher
imprisonment
incense cedar
inclinometer
incontinence
indeclinable
indefensible
Indian cotton
Indian millet
Indian turnip
India pale ale
indirect cost
indomethacin
inescutcheon
inflammation
inflationary
infringement
inharmonious
inherent vice
inking roller
inner sanctum
insemination
inspectorate
installation
instructress
instrumental
intellectual
intelligence
intercession
intercipient
interdiction
interest rate
interference
interglacial
interlocutor
intermeddler
intermediary
intermundane
interpleader
interpolator
interrogator
intersection
interstadial
interstellar
intimidation
intransitive
introduction
invagination
invalidation
invalid chair
invertebrate
investigator
invoice clerk
invulnerable
Ionian column
Irish spaniel
Irish terrier
Irish whiskey
ironing board
ironing table
irredeemable
irregularist
isoprenaline
jack-o'-lantern
jacob's ladder
jet-propelled
jewel bearing
jigsaw puzzle
joint account
joint tenancy
joint trustee
julienne soup
jurisconsult
juvenile lead
kaleidoscope
keep accounts
keep standing
kilowatt-hour
kindergarten
king's counsel
king's proctor
kirschwasser
kitchen range
kitchen table
kleptomaniac
klipspringer
knee breeches
kneehole desk
knife cleaner
knife grinder
knife machine
knife thrower
knight errant
Komodo dragon
labour market
labour-saving
lady's slipper
lager and lime
laissez-faire
lake dwelling
Lancaster gun
landed gentry
landing barge
landing craft
landing light
landing party
landing speed
landing wires
land surveyor
land transfer
laryngoscope
laser printer
lateen-rigged
lath-splitter
launching pad
leader writer
leading light
least squares
leather skirt
legacy hunter
leopard snake
letter writer
lexicography
lexicologist

life interest
light cavalry
light cruiser
light therapy
lightning rod
line of battle
lines per inch
link bracelet
liquid assets
literacy hour
lithographer
liver sausage
lobster patty
lock-up garage
London editor
longshoreman
looking-glass
lord advocate
lord chairman
lord of appeal
lord temporal
losing hazard
loss adjuster
loudspeakers
lounge lizard
louvre window
low water mark
lubrifaction
luggage train
lumber dealer
lumber jacket
lunar eclipse
lunar rainbow
lymphography
machicolated
machine ruler
machine tools
macrotherium
madam speaker
mademoiselle
magazine page
magazine rack
magic lantern
magnetic mine
magnetic pole
magnetograph
magnetometer
magnetomotor
magnotherapy
maiden flight
maiden voyage
maid of honour
maitre d'hotel
major general
make-and-break
make-up artist
malnutrition
mammary gland
man-about-town
mandrel lathe
mangel wurzel
manilla paper
manned rocket
man overboard
mansion house
manslaughter
manual worker
manufacturer
marathon race
marcatissimo
march against
marginal cost
marginal lake
marine boiler
marine engine
market garden
marking board
marline spike
married woman
marrying kind
marsh harrier
marshmallows
marsh warbler
marsupial rat
mass producer
mass-produced
master-at-arms
master gunner
master of arts
master-singer
master spring
maturity date
maypole dance
measured mile
measuregraph
measuring cup
measuring jug
meat salesman
medical corps
medicine ball
medullary ray
meeting house
megalichthys
melancholist
melodramatic
melon thistle
mensa et thoro
mercantilism
merchant bank
merchant ship
merry-go-round
merrythought
metallurgist
metamorphism
metaphorical
method acting
mezzo-relievo
mezzo-soprano
microbiology
microcoustic
microscopist
miles per hour
militaristic
military band
milk-white ant
Mills grenade
mine detector
mineralogist
minesweeping
mini-computer
minnesingers
minstrel show
misbehaviour
misconstruer
misdemeanour
misdirection
misinformant
missel thrush
mission house
miss milligan
mistle thrush
mitochondria
mitrailleuse
mixed bathing
mixed doubles
mixed economy
mobilization
modern ballet
monetization
money changer

moneyspinner
monkey jacket
monkey puzzle
monkey wrench
monographist
morality play
morning dress
morning glory
morris dancer
mosaic artist
mosaic worker
mosquito boat
motorcyclist
motor drifter
motor scooter
motor trawler
mountain cork
mountain flax
mountain hare
mountain lion
mountain milk
mountain rice
mountain soap
mourning dove
mouse opossum
mulled claret
mulligatawny
multitasking
musicologist
music teacher
music therapy
musk parakeet
muzzle loader
myelin sheath
mythographer
nail scissors
name in lights
national bank
national debt
natural break
natural child
nautical mile
naval command
navigability
nearest offer
near relation
negative pole
neoplatonist
nerve impulse
neuroanatomy
neurobiology
newspaperman
night classes
nightcrawler
night fighter
night glasses
nimble-footed
noctambulist
nominal price
nominal value
nonagenarian
non-combatant
non-conductor
none-so-pretty
northeastern
northwestern
Norway spruce
notary public
nouveau riche
novel reading
nuclear power
number theory
nunc dimittis
nursery rhyme
nutmeg butter
nutmeg grater
nutmeg pigeon
nutritionist
oak eggar moth
obedientiary
obscurantist
obstacle race
obstetrician
oceanography
octogenarian
office bearer
office junior
officer cadet
official list
old-fashioned
old gentleman
old man's beard
omnipresence
onomatopoeia
opening price
opera comique
opera glasses
oral evidence
orange brandy
orange flower
orange squash
orchestra pit
orchestrator
organ builder
organ grinder
organ of Corti
organography
organ recital
ornithoscopy
orthalmology
orthodontist
orthodromics
orthographer
orthopaedics
oscillograph
oscilloscope
osteoporosis
otacousticon
outer gateway
outmanoeuvre
output device
outward-bound
ovariotomist
overcapacity
oxolinic acid
oxy-acetylene
oyster-blenny
ozone therapy
packing cloth
packing paper
packing sheet
painted quail
painted saury
palaeography
palette knife
palification
pallid cuckoo
palma christi
pandean pipes
pantechnicon
paper stainer
paraffin lamp
parallel bars
parallel port
paramilitary
parietal bone
parish priest
parking light
parking meter
parking place

parlour games
parquet floor
pasque flower
passion fruit
passion music
pattern maker
pay as you earn
pay in advance
paying-in-slip
peace-breaker
peaceful dove
peacekeeping
peace officer
peach bitters
peanut butter
pease pudding
pediatrician
pelican's foot
pendente lite
penitentiary
penny whistle
pentacrinite
peppered moth
perambulator
peregrinator
perfect bound
perfect tense
permanganate
permeability
permittivity
persona grata
petrogenesis
petrol engine
petrol filter
petty officer
pharmacology
pheasant's ego
philharmonic
philomusical
philosophist
phonographer
phospholipid
photographer
photogravure
photomontage
phototropism
phrenologist
physiography
physiologist
pickerel weed
picnic basket
picnic hamper
picture frame
piked dogfish
pillion rider
pilot balloon
pilot officer
pinhole borer
pioneer corps
piperidolate
pirate cutter
pisciculture
pistachio nut
pitch and putt
pitch-and-toss
pitcher plant
plain clothes
plant manager
platinum ring
platonic year
playing cards
pleasure boat
pleasure trip
pleated skirt
plectognathi
Plimsoll line
Plimsoll mark
ploughwright
plumber's mate
plummer block
plum porridge
plutonic rock
pneumatology
poet laureate
point-to-point
poisoned dart
polarization
pole vaulting
police launch
policy holder
polymorphism
polytonality
pond tortoise
pontoon crane
poor relation
porridge bowl
postage stamp
post-diluvial
post-diluvian
postgraduate
post meridiem
postmistress
postponement
postposition
potato masher
potato peeler
potter's wheel
pouched mouse
powder monkey
power station
powerful-fowl
practitioner
pralltriller
precipitator
prednisolone
prescription
prescriptive
present tense
present worth
press officer
pressure pump
pressure suit
prestigiator
prevaricator
price ceiling
price control
price current
price rigging
primary cache
primogenitor
Prince's metal
principal boy
principality
printer's ream
prison warder
privateering
privy council
prize fighter
prize-winning
productivity
professional
profiteering
profit margin
profit motive
profit taking
propagandist
proprietress
proselytizer
prostitution
protectorate

prothalamium
protozoology
pruning knife
psychiatrist
psychologist
psychrometer
public figure
publicity man
public orator
public sector
pudding basin
pudding cloth
puddingstone
pulley blocks
pumpernickel
punk cockatoo
pupil-teacher
puppet player
purbeck stone
purification
purpose-built
pursuit plane
pyrazinamide
pyro-electric
pyrotechnics
pyrotechnist
Pythian games
quadragesima
quaking grass
quarry master
quarter horse
quartern loaf
quarter noble
quarterstaff
quartz schist
queen-consort
queen-dowager
queen-regnant
quinquennial
racing driver
racing stable
radar scanner
radial engine
radiator muff
radiobiology
radiographer
raiding party
railway train
rainbow trout
ratchet wheel
rate constant
rate of growth
ratification
rat-tailed ray
raw materials
razor-grinder
reading clerk
reading glass
Reaumur scale
receivership
receptionist
recommission
reconsecrate
record player
recriminator
red blood cell
red cedar moth
redemptioner
redeployment
red-head finch
red-letter day
reductionism
red wine punch
reefer jacket
refreshments
refrigerator
regent master
registration
reindeer moss
religious war
relinquisher
remembrancer
remonstrator
remuneration
remunerative
repair outfit
repercussion
reproduction
reserve price
residentiary
resolutioner
response time
restaurateur
resuscitator
retiring room
retrenchment
Rhenish wines
rhesus monkey
rhododendron
ride at anchor
riding master
right-hand man
rig the market
ripstop nylon
rising prices
river capture
river garfish
river gunboat
river terrace
road junction
roan antelope
roasting rack
Rochelle salt
rock climbing
rock flathead
rock pinnacle
rock squirrel
rocket attack
rocket mortar
rocking chair
rocking horse
Rogation days
roller blader
roller skater
rolling press
rolling stock
rolling stone
rope climbing
rope spinning
rope throwing
royal charter
royal warrant
rubber grader
running block
running board
running costs
saddle oyster
sage-thrasher
sailboarding
sale or return
sales manager
salesmanship
salvationist
sandfly fever
sand yachting
saprophagans
sarsaparilla
Saturn's rings
savoy cabbage
scala tympani

scarab beetle
scarificator
scarlet bream
scarlet fever
scatterbrain
scene painter
scene shifter
scene stealer
schoolfellow
schoolmaster
sclerenchyma
Scotch barley
scotch hopper
Scotch whisky
scraper board
screen filter
screenwriter
scribing iron
scriptwriter
scullery maid
sculling boat
sea butterfly
sea-porcupine
search engine
second cousin
second fiddle
second master
security lock
sedge warbler
seed merchant
seeing-eye dog
seismography
seismologist
seltzer water
semicircular
semi-detached
senior purser
sentinel crab
sequestrator
serial access
serpent eater
serpentstone
serviceberry
service cable
service dress
sesquialtera
severance pay
sexagenarian
sexton beetle
share capital
sharecropper
shareholding
share options
sharpshooter
shell account
shell-shocked
shepherd's pie
sheriff clerk
Shetland pony
Shetland wool
ship chandler
shipping line
ship's biscuit
ship's husband
ship's surgeon
shirtwaister
shock tactics
shock therapy
shoe repairer
shooting star
short circuit
shoulder arms
shoulder belt
show business
shrike-thrush
shrimping net
shunt winding
sidereal time
sidereal year
siege warfare
signal rocket
silver beater
silver glance
silver mullet
silver screen
silver-stater
silver-wattle
silviculture
single acting
single-decker
single mother
single parent
single person
skater's waltz
skipping rope
skittle alley
slack in stays
slaughterman
sledge hammer
sleeping suit
sleep therapy
sleeve button
sliding bevel
sliding scale
slitting mill
smallholding
smooth angler
smooth collie
smooth-haired
smooth muscle
snail trefoil
snake charmer
snap division
snowball tree
social credit
social worker
socket chisel
soft currency
soil mechanic
solar battery
solar eclipse
sole occupant
Solomon's seal
somnambulist
somniloquist
song and dance
sound barrier
sound effects
sounding-post
southeastern
southernwood
southwestern
space capsule
space lattice
space shuttle
space station
space vehicle
span farthing
Spanish broom
Spanish cedar
Spanish grass
Spanish onion
sparking plug
sparrow grass
spear thistle
special agent
special needs
specie points
specific heat
speckled wood

spectrograph
spectrometer
spectroscope
spectroscopy
specular iron
speechwriter
speed counter
speed skating
spermatology
spermatozoid
spheremelody
sphygmometer
spice blender
spider monkey
spinal column
spinning mill
spiral galaxy
spiral stairs
spiritualist
splash screen
sportscaster
sports editor
sports jacket
sportswriter
spotted hyena
sprig crystal
spring beetle
spring greens
spring onions
spruce sawfly
square-rigged
square-rigger
staff officer
stage manager
stage whisper
stained glass
stamping mill
standard lamp
standard time
starboard bow
starring role
starter motor
starting post
state lottery
state of siege
statistician
steak pudding
steal the show
steam gondola
steam heating
steam turbine
steam whistle
steeplechase
steering gear
steering lock
stenographer
step aerobics
stepdaughter
sterling area
stern-wheeler
stilt walking
stirrup strap
stock company
stockingette
stock in trade
stockjobbery
stockjobbing
stonebreaker
stone-chatter
stonedresser
stone's-mickle
stonesquarer
storm brewing
stormtrooper
stormy petrel
storytelling
straightedge
straightener
straight line
straight part
strangleweed
stratigraphy
stratosphere
straw bolster
stream anchor
street trader
street urchin
streptomycin
striped hyena
stubble goose
stubble quail
studding sail
stuffed shirt
styloglossus
sub-committee
subdirectory
submaxillary
subpurchaser
substitution
substruction
substructure
subterranean
suction valve
sugar refiner
suit of armour
sulphonamide
summer savory
Sunday driver
Sunday school
sunshine roof
supernaculum
supply rating
supreme court
surplus value
surveillance
survey vessel
swamp cypress
swamp harrier
swashbuckler
swathe turner
sweating bath
sweating room
sweet and sour
sweet William
swimming gala
swine thistle
swingle knife
sworn enemies
sylviculture
synchronized
syndesmology
synosteology
systematizer
table croquet
table lighter
table service
table turning
tape recorder
taramasalata
tartaric acid
tax avoidance
tax collector
tax exemption
taxing master
tax inspector
technologist
telegraphese
telegraphist
temporal bone
tennis player

tennis racket
tercentenary
terminal post
terms of trade
tessellation
testamentary
test engineer
testificator
tetracycline
thalassaemia
Thames bawley
thanksgiving
theatre-going
theatre of war
therapeutics
therapeutist
thermocouple
third officer
thorough bass
thoroughbred
three-ply wood
three-wheeler
thundercloud
thunderstorm
tidal barrage
tiddley-winks
tiger bittern
tiger economy
timber-framed
time contract
timothy grass
tin-lined case
tittle-tattle
toasting fork
tobacco plant
tobacco pouch
toilette case
toll gatherer
toothed wheel
top of the bill
torch thistle
touch needles
tourist class
tower bastion
town planning
toxicologist
tracer bullet
tracing cloth
tracing linen
tracing paper
trade balance
trade deficit
trading stamp
training ship
tramp steamer
transfer deed
transgressor
transhipment
transmigrant
transmigrate
transmission
transplanter
transvestite
traumatology
treacle water
treasury bill
treasury bond
treasury note
tree kangaroo
tree of heaven
trench mortar
trench plough
trial balance
tribute penny
tricentenary
trichologist
trigonometry
trimeprazine
tripe de roche
troop carrier
tropical heat
tropical year
troublemaker
truce-breaker
trumpet major
truncheoneer
trustee stock
tuberculosis
tuning hammer
turbit pigeon
turfing spade
Turkey carpet
turner pigeon
turning lathe
turnip cutter
two-pound coin
two-speed gear
tympanometer
typhoid fever
ugly customer
ugly duckling
ukulele banjo
ulotrichales
umbrella palm
underclothes
undercurrent
undermanager
underwriting
unemployment
unfathomable
universalist
unmechanical
unmodernized
unornamental
unornamented
untenantable
unvanquished
unventilated
upright piano
urban renewal
urbanization
user friendly
valance board
valproic acid
valued policy
variable star
velocipedist
venetian door
Venus flytrap
versificator
veterinarian
vicar-general
Victoria plum
village idiot
vinegar plant
vin ordinaire
viola da gamba
virgin forest
Virginia reel
Virgin's bower
visitors' book
V-neck sweater
vocalization
vodka and lime
volcanic bomb
volcanic plug
wainscotting
waiting woman
walking boots
walking staff

walking stick
warehouseman
war insurance
warning light
washing board
water bailiff
water battery
water bellows
water boatman
water diviner
water hemlock
watering cart
water opossum
water parsnip
water pitcher
water quality
water soldier
water spaniel
water turbine
water wagtail
wattle-psylla
wattle turkey
wave equation
way passenger
ways and means
weatherboard
weatherbound
weather cloth
weather glass
weatherproof
weather woman
wedding dress
weeding tongs
weeping birch
welfare state
Welsh dresser
Welsh flannel
Welsh rarebit
Welsh terrier
westerly wind
wheel-and-axle
wheel cutting
whip-poor-will
white admiral
white cabbage
white campion
white currant
white cypress
white feather
white goshawk
whitlow grass
who goes there
whortleberry
wicker basket
wicket keeper
wild Williams
will-o'-the-wisp
Windsor chair
wine decanter
wine merchant
winning horse
winter barley
winter cherry
winter citron
winter garden
winter savory
winter sports
wood engraver
wool gatherer
woolly monkey
working class
working model
works council
works manager
writer's block
writers' cramp
writing paper
writing table
yellow rattle
yellowhammer
zamiostrobus
zenith sector
zero emission
zoophytology

13

acceptilation
accommodation
accompaniment
accoutrements
acorn barnacle
Adelie penguin
adminiculator
administrator
admission pipe
adult learning
advanced guard
advertisement
aerated waters
affenpinscher
affreightment
age of marriage
agriculturist
aircraftwoman
air stewardess
airworthiness
alcoholimeter
alcoholometer
alectoromachy
alectryomachy
alligator pear
allotment note
allports perch
alpha particle
alpine flowers
Alpine spaniel
ambulance cart
aminophylline
amitriptyline
amphiprostyle
anagrammatist
ancient forest
ancient lights
annexationist
anthropometry
anthropophagi
antichristian
antique dealer
antisocialist
aperitif wines
apothegmatist
apple dumpling
apportionment
appropriation
approximation

apricot brandy
aquatic lizard
aquatic sports
aqueous humour
arachnologist
arboriculture
archaeologist
archbishopric
archdeaconate
architectonic
architectural
archpresbyter
archtreasurer
arithmetician
armed services
armourer's mate
army commander
arteriography
articled clerk
Asian elephant
assembly rooms
auction bridge
audio cassette
auditory nerve
average clause
back staircase
backwardation
bacteriophage
Bactrian camel
bagpipe player
ballad singing
ball cartridge
ballet dancing
ball lightning
ballroom dance
balneotherapy
Baltimore bird
banded pigfish
bank statement
barber surgeon
barnacle goose
barrack master
barrack square
barred garfish
battlecruiser
battle fatigue
bearded collie
bearded lizard
beatification
Beaufort scale
béchamel sauce
Belisha beacon
bendy-sinister
Bermuda cutter
Bermuda shorts
betamethasone
bibliographer
bibliophilist
bicuspid valve
bidding prayer
bijou cocktail
billiard balls
billiard table
binary fission
biodegradable
bioenergetics
biotechnology
bird's-eye maple
black and white
black cockatoo
black king fish
black lecanium
black trevally
blanket flower
blank transfer
bleeding heart
bleeding tooth
blended whisky
blind man's buff
blister beetle
blood relation
blotting paper
border terrier
borough master
Boston terrier
Boston two-step
bothrodendron
bougainvillea
bouillabaisse
braided rivers
branchiostoma
brass knuckles
breakfast room
breakfast time
Bristol flower
Bronx cocktail
brucite marble
bubble blowing
bubble chamber
bubonic plague
buffing spring
bulbourethral
bullion market
burden of proof
burial service
burlesque show
burning mirror
burnt offering
business class
business cycle
butcher's broom
butler's pantry
butobarbitone
calendar month
calico printer
camera obscura
campanologist
Canadian canoe
canonical hour
captain's chair
captain's clerk
carbenicillin
carbon dioxide
carboniferous
carbonization
cardiac arrest
carpenter's bee
carpet bombing
carpet sweeper
carriage horse
carrier pigeon
cartridge case
cashmere shawl
castle-builder
catastrophism
catchment area
Catherine pear
cat-o'-nine-tails
cephalization
cephaloglycin
cephalography
cephalosporin
chain adjuster
chain bracelet
chain reaction
chalk hill blue
chamber-fellow
Chantilly lace
Chapman's zebra
charging order

charter flight
chartographer
cheddar cheese
chemoreceptor
cherry blossom
chief armourer
chief engineer
chili con carne
chilled margin
chimney corner
chirographist
chlormezanone
chondrography
chopping block
chopping board
chopping knife
choral singing
choreographer
chose in action
chrematistics
Christmas cake
Christmas rose
Christmas tree
chromatometer
chronographer
chrysanthemum
chuck farthing
church service
cinematograph
cinnamon stone
circumference
circumvallate
civil engineer
clearing house
clearstarcher
climate change
climatography
climbing perch
close quarters
clouded yellow
coachwhip-bird
cocker spaniel
co-educational
coffee grinder
coffee planter
collaboration
colour therapy
combat fatigue
combinatorics
cometographer
common assault
compass signal
compass window
compatibility
complementary
composing room
compound-wound
comprehension
comprehensive
comprovincial
conceptualist
concessionist
confectionery
confessionary
connecting rod
Connemara pony
conservatoire
consideration
constellation
consul-general
consumer goods
contabulation
contact lenses
container ship
contamination
contemplative
context switch
contortionist
contract curve
control column
control theory
conventionist
convertiplane
convocational
cooling system
copper pyrites
coral necklace
co-religionist
cornet-a-piston
Cornish boiler
Cornish engine
correspondent
co-trimoxazole
cottage cheese
cotton spinner
count palatine
counterattack
counterfeiter
counterstroke
counterweight
county council
coursing joint
courtesy light
court of appeal
credit account
credit control
credit squeeze
creeping jenny
crême de menthe
crested pigeon
cribbage board
cricket ground
cricket stumps
criminal libel
critical angle
Crohn's disease
croquet mallet
cross-crosslet
crossed cheque
crown imperial
cruise control
cruise missile
cruising speed
crustaceology
cryptographer
cumulostratus
current assets
curtain-raiser
custard coffin
cylinder press
dactylopterus
daddy-long-legs
daguerreotype
damage feasant
dance festival
dandelion wine
Darjeeling tea
daughter-in-law
dead reckoning
deck billiards
deck passenger
decomposition
decompression
decorative art
deipnosophist
demonstration
deputy premier
deputy speaker
dermatologist
deus ex machina

devotionalist
dexamethasone
diagnostician
diamond beetle
diamond cutter
diaphonometer
diathiazinine
digital camera
dihydralazine
dipleidoscope
dipping needle
diprophylline
direct current
discharge tube
disconformity
discount house
discriminator
disengagement
disharmonious
dispatch rider
distinguisher
district judge
divertisement
dividend yield
division lobby
doctor of music
dog's-tail grass
dog-wood wattle
dolichosaurus
dollar premium
double glazing
double or quits
double-sculler
Dow-Jones index
draught engine
draughtswoman
drawing master
dress designer
dressing table
drill sergeant
driving mirror
drummond light
dusky flathead
Dutch clinkers
dwelling house
dwelling place
eccentric gear
editor-in-chief
eightsome reel
ejection order
elastic impact
electric cable
electric clock
electric drill
electric field
electric fluid
electric light
electric mixer
electric motor
electric power
electric razor
electric shock
electric stove
electric truck
electrifiable
electromagnet
electromotive
electron shell
electrophorus
electroplater
electrostatic
electrotypist
elephant grass
elephant's foot
elephant's tusk
elephantiasis
elevator shoes
emerald copper
emergency exit
emigrationist
éminence grise
encaustic tile
endocrinology
engine-turning
English setter
entertainment
entomostomata
entomostracan
entozoologist
entrance lobby
environmental
epigrammatist
erector muscle
establishment
estate manager
esthesiometer
European bison
exchequer bill
excommunicate
exhibitionist
expansion card
expansion gear
expansion slot
expeditionary
experimentist
expressionism
extracellular
extractor hood
Fair Isle shawl
Fallopian tube
family therapy
fantail pigeon
fashion-monger
fatigue parade
feather pillow
featherweight
feeding bottle
fell sandstone
fencing master
ferro-concrete
fertilization
field of battle
fighter bomber
fighting force
fig-leaf beetle
figure skating
file extension
filing cabinet
financial year
finnan haddock
first offender
fishing tackle
fishnet tights
flexible cable
flitch of bacon
floating light
floodlighting
flowering fern
flowering rush
fluid flywheel
flying colours
flying gurnard
flying officer
folding screen
food processor
foot passenger
football boots
football scarf
forced landing
foreign editor

fork lightning
forklift truck
fortification
fortune-hunter
fortune-teller
foster brother
four-oared boat
fourth officer
free trade area
free trade zone
freezing point
freight broker
French bulldog
frequentative
fresh-air fiend
friction balls
friction cones
frilled lizard
future perfect
futures market
galvanologist
gastriloquist
gastrocnemius
Geiger counter
generalissimo
geochronology
geometric mean
geomorphology
German measles
German sausage
giant boarfish
giant molecule
giant tortoise
gigot de mouton
ginger cordial
ginger pudding
glass painting
glibenclamide
global warming
globalization
globe amaranth
glorification
glossographer
glyphographer
golden hamster
golden jubilee
golden thistle
golden wedding
goliath beetle
googly-bowling
goose barnacle
governess cart
grammar school
granddaughter
grand-seigneur
grape hyacinth
grappling-iron
gravitational
Grecian temple
greenhouse gas
green tree frog
Gregorian year
gross receipts
ground-angling
ground bailiff
ground control
Gruyère cheese
guarantee fund
guard of honour
guided missile
gynaecologist
hacking jacket
Haflinger pony
handbrake turn
harbourmaster
hard bargainer
hard-shell clam
hare-and-hounds
harmonic chord
head-up display
helminthology
hepatic portal
hereditaments
hermaphrodite
hexobarbitone
hieroglyphist
high churchman
high constable
high-explosive
Highland fling
high priestess
high water mark
holiday season
holy communion
holy innocents
home secretary
homoiothermic
horizontal bar
horse chestnut
horse cucumber
horse mackerel
horse-milliner
horseshoe crab
housebreaking
hovelling boat
humpback whale
hundredweight
huntsman's horn
hurricane deck
hydraulic jack
hydrodynamics
hydrokinetics
hypochondriac
hypoglycaemia
ichneumon wasp
ichthyography
ichthyologist
illegal action
incense burner
incomes policy
Indian buffalo
Indian tobacco
induction coil
induction pipe
industrialist
infallibility
inflexibility
injection cock
in-line engines
insectivorous
inside measure
inspection pit
insulated wire
intelligencer
interim report
interlocutory
international
interrogative
intracellular
invincibility
irregular verb
issued capital
Japanese cedar
Japanese maple
jigsaw puzzles
Job's comforter
jollification
judge-advocate
jumping spider
justification

kerosene shale
keyhole limpet
kinetic energy
king's shilling
kiss-in-the-ring
knuckleduster
lacrimal gland
ladies' fingers
lamellibranch
lance corporal
land measuring
land surveying
lattice energy
lattice window
laughing hyena
laughing stock
law of property
leading seaman
leading stoker
leafy seahorse
leatherjacket
leishmaniasis
lemon squeezer
lepidodendron
leptospirosis
letter founder
letters patent
lexicographer
liberty bodice
licence holder
lichenography
life-annuitant
lifeguardsman
life preserver
lifting bridge
light infantry
lime-tree borer
linear algebra
linear measure
liqueur brandy
liqueur whisky
liquid starter
literary agent
livery company
long-dated bill
long-finned eel
long-tailed tit
long underwear
lord president
lord privy seal
lord spiritual
lubrification
lunisolar year
lyrical poetry
machiavellian
machicolation
machine gunner
machine junket
made-to-measure
magazine rifle
magnetic field
magnetic fluid
magnetic north
magnetic poles
magnetization
magpie-morwong
maid-of-all-work
making-up price
mangold beetle
marbled angler
marine biology
marrowfat peas
marsh marigold
marsupial mole
martello tower
master builder
master mariner
mathematician
matriculation
matrix algebra
mature student
meadow saffron
medicinal herb
medicine glass
mermaid's purse
meteorography
meteorologist
methanderione
methylene blue
metoposcopist
microcomputer
microwave oven
millennialist
millennium bug
millstone grit
mineral waters
miracle worker
misanthropist
mischief-maker
mission church
mister speaker
mistletoe-bird
mitochondrion
mitrobronitol
mizzen rigging
model yachting
molecular mass
moral majority
morello cherry
morphogenesis
mortar carbine
mother-of-pearl
motor cruising
motor lifeboat
mountain tract
mountain trout
mountain zebra
mounted police
mournful widow
mourning coach
mourning dress
mourning ring
movement maker
mowing machine
multinucleate
mushroom cloud
musical chairs
musical comedy
music festival
music mistress
nalidixic acid
nature reserve
naval dockyard
naval ordnance
navigableness
netting needle
New Forest pony
newspaper rack
night watchman
Nile crocodile
no-claims bonus
nolle prosequi
non-conducting
nonconformist
non-cumulative
Norman doorway
northeasterly
northeastward
northeast wind
northerly wind

northwesterly
northwestward
northwest wind
not negotiable
objective case
occipital bone
office manager
Olympian games
once upon a time
one for the road
operatic music
ophthalmology
orange bitters
orange blossom
orchestration
order of battle
ordinary share
ordnance depot
ornithologist
orthographist
outside broker
overhead price
overshot wheel
ovoviviparity
owlet-nightjar
ox-eyed herring
Oxford sausage
oystercatcher
packing needle
paddle steamer
paediatrician
paid-up capital
palaeontology
palisade cells
paper nautilus
parallel ruler
parallelogram
paramagnetism
parasitic cone
park attendant
parliamentary
parlour tricks
par of exchange
Parry's wallaby
parthenocarpy
participating
partridge wood
paschal candle
passenger boat
passenger ship

passion flower
paste necklace
patent leather
paterfamilias
pattern cutter
pearl necklace
penicillamine
penny farthing
people carrier
percussion cap
perfectionist
periodic table
periodicalist
perpendicular
Persian blinds
Persian carpet
petrification
petrochemical
petrol lighter
petty sessions
pharmaceutics
pharmaceutist
phenothiazine
phenylephrine
philhellenist
philosophizer
photoelectric
photoreceptor
physiognomist
physiographer
phytoplankton
pillion riding
pinafore dress
ping-pong table
pink champagne
pitched battle
plain-wanderer
plane geometry
planters' punch
plasmodesmata
plateau basalt
platform shoes
platform soles
pneumatic tyre
pneumatometer
poetic licence
point of impact
poisoned arrow
poliomyelitis
pontoon bridge

porcupine fish
portland stone
potientiometer
poultry farmer
power function
power steering
prairie oyster
prayer meeting
praying mantis
precious stone
precipitation
predestinator
premium income
pressure-gauge
primal therapy
primary colour
prime minister
printer driver
printing press
prisoner of war
prisoner's base
privateersman
private sector
privatization
prize fighting
probe scissors
process server
profitability
profit sharing
projectionist
proprioceptor
proselytizing
protectionist
protriptylene
proverbialist
psalmographer
psychoanalyst
psychometrics
psychophysics
psychotherapy
pteridologist
public company
public speaker
public trustee
purple emperor
pyrheliometer
quadrilateral
quantum meruit
quantum number
quantum theory

quarter dollar
quarter florin
quarter laurel
quartermaster
quota sampling
racing tipster
rack-and-pinion
radio operator
radioactivity
radiolocation
rallying point
ranz-des-vaches
raspberry bush
rateable value
razor stropper
reaction order
receptor cells
recognizances
record breaker
rectification
recurviroster
Red-Indian fish
red-wattle bird
re-embarkation
reflectometer
refractometer
regular troops
reincarnation
reinforcement
remote control
reprobationer
restructuring
revenue cutter
revolutionary
riding teacher
right bisector
right of appeal
ring-tail coati
roll and butter
roller-bearing
roller skating
root directory
rosella parrot
rose of Jericho
rotten borough
roulette table
royal dockyard
running battle
Russell's viper
Russia leather
Russian ballet
sable antelope
saccharometer
saccharometry
sacerdotalism
sacred concert
sadomasochist
safety curtain
sailing master
sailing vessel
salad dressing
sales forecast
salicylic acid
salmon catfish
saltwater fish
sanctuary lamp
sandpaper fish
sandstone dyke
satellite dish
satellite town
saucepan brush
scalping knife
scarlet angler
scarlet runner
schaapsticker
schizophrenia
schoolteacher
science master
scintillation
Scotch collops
Scotch terrier
Scotch thistle
scribing block
scripturalist
sea gooseberry
seaman recruit
search warrant
second officer
secretary bird
security guard
sedimentology
semi-automatic
semiconductor
sergeant major
series winding
servo-assisted
sesamoid bones
settlement day
Seville orange
sewing machine
shadow cabinet
shalwar kameez
share transfer
sherry cobbler
shield volcano
shining parrot
ship of the line
ship's chandler
shock absorber
shooting brake
shop assistant
shot-hole borer
shoulder blade
shoulder strap
shrapnel shell
shrink wrapped
sidereal clock
signal officer
silent partner
silicious ooze
silk throwster
silver batfish
silver drummer
silver wedding
simple larceny
single chamber
sirloin of beef
skirting board
slaty cleavage
sleight-of-hand
slender weevil
smoke detector
smoothing iron
snorkel jacket
snub-nosed dart
social climber
social realism
soft-shell clam
soldering bolt
soldering iron
sol-fa notation
solid geometry
solid solution
solitaire ring
sophisticator
sound engineer
sounding board
southeasterly
southeastward
southeast wind

southerly wind
southern tunny
southwesterly
southwestward
southwest wind
sowing machine
spade-foot toad
sparkling hock
sparkling wine
special forces
specification
spectinomycin
speed merchant
spider-catcher
spider phaeton
spike lavender
spilling lines
spindleshanks
spinning jenny
spinning wheel
spiny anteater
spiny dormouse
spiny flathead
spiny seahorse
spiral binding
spirit rapping
spiritualizer
splanchnology
splinterproof
sponge pudding
sportsmanship
spotted lizard
spring balance
spring cabbage
square measure
squash rackets
staff corporal
staff notation
staff sergeant
stalking horse
standard gauge
standing waves
starboard beam
starboard side
starting motor
starting point
state carriage
state criminal
state prisoner
station master
statute barred
steam carriage
steeplechaser
steering wheel
stenographist
stereoscopist
sternomastoid
stethoscopist
stiletto heels
Stilton cheese
stink-pheasant
stocking frame
stoichiometry
stop press news
storming party
strategically
straw mattress
street sweeper
strike-breaker
string octette
string of beads
string quartet
striped angler
striped muscle
studio manager
styptic pencil
subcontractor
sub-lieutenant
submachine gun
submandibular
submarine mine
subsoil plough
suicide bomber
sulphadiazine
sulphuric acid
summer cypress
superdominant
superintender
supernumerary
supply teacher
suspender belt
Sussex spaniel
swallow-shrike
swanee whistle
sweating house
sweet calabash
sweet marjoram
switch selling
sword fighting
swordsmanship
symmetry class
sympiesometer
synchronicity
tankard turnip
Tasmanian wolf
taxable income
tectonic plate
telegraph line
telegraph pole
telegraph wire
telephone line
telephone wire
televangelism
televangelist
temperate zone
ten-pin bowling
terpsichorean
tetradiapason
thaumaturgics
thaumaturgist
theatre school
thermo current
thermonuclear
thigmotropism
thimble rigger
third engineer
three-foot rule
three-line whip
thresher shark
throttle valve
thrust bearing
thunder shower
tiger-flathead
toad-in-the-hole
toll collector
torpedo gunner
tortoiseshell
track and field
trade discount
trade unionist
trading vessel
traffic signal
tramcar driver
tram conductor
tranquillizer
translocation
transmigrator
transmutation
transom window
transpiration

transposition
traveller's joy
treasure trove
tree porcupine
trench warfare
trial by combat
trial by ordeal
triamcinolone
triumphal arch
tropical storm
trumpet flower
tumbler pigeon
tunnel of corti
turkey-buzzard
turkey vulture
Turkish angora
turnover table
two-hole pliers
twopenny piece
umbrella stand
unarmed combat
unconquerable
unconsecrated
undercarriage
underclothing
undergraduate
underpainting
understrapper
unevangelical
ungrammatical
uninhabitable
unscutcheoned
vacuum cleaner
value added tax
vantage ground
vaulting horse
vaulting shaft
veal-and-ham pie
vendor's shares
venetian blind
ventriloquist
Venus's fly trap
vervain mallow
vice-president
vice-principal
victor ludorum
video cassette
video recorder
Viennese waltz
vinyl emulsion
violoncellist
viper's bugloss
virtual memory
visiting cards
vodka and tonic
vote of censure
wall pennywort
war department
wash-hand stand
waste disposal
wasting assets
water calamint
water crowfoot
water drainage
water hyacinth
water moccasin
water softener
watt-hour meter
wattle and daub
wave mechanics
wayfaring tree
way of the cross
weather report
weeding chisel
weeping willow
weightlifting
wheel carriage
wheeler-dealer
whippet racing
whirling table
white cockatoo
whooping cough
wicket keeping
willow warbler
window cleaner
window curtain
window dresser
wing commander
winning hazard
winter aconite
wire stitching
Witney blanket
Wolf-Rayet star
word processor
works councils
writing master
X-ray apparatus
yellow bunting
yellow wagtail
young offender
zodiacal light
zoophysiology
zygomatic bone

14

account current
action painting
act of indemnity
adjusting screw
administration
administratrix
advance freight
aesthesiometer
aircraftswoman
airing cupboard
air raid shelter
air thermometer
air vice-marshal
all-in wrestling
Ambrosian chant
ambulance wagon
ammunition dump
amylobarbitone
analog computer
angina pectoris
anglepoise lamp
annular eclipse
anthropologist
antiaristocrat
antimony glance
antiscriptural
apple Charlotte
apprenticeship
archchancellor
architectonics
arithmetic mean
armchair critic
armour-piercing
artificial silk
auditor-general
aurora borealis
Australian bear
autobiographer
automatic pilot
auxiliary force
axes of symmetry
babbling thrush
bachelor of arts
bacteriologist
balance of trade
ballet mistress
bamboo cocktail
banded sea-perch
banjo mandoline
banner headline
barbadoes penny
Barbados cherry
barrage balloon
bathing costume
bathing machine
bearer security
beclomethasone
bendrofluazide
benzodiazepine
bifocal glasses
billiard marker
billiard player
bill of exchange
bimia longicorn
bioclimatology
bird of paradise
bird's foot delta
bituminous coal
blackberry bush
black letter day
black stingaree
bladder angling
blank cartridge
Blenheim orange
blockade runner
blocked account
blood poisoning
blowing machine
blue couch grass
blue suede shoes
boa constrictor
boarding school
boatswain's mate
Bologna sausage
Born-Haber cycle
Bowen technique
branchiostegan
bread and butter
bread and cheese
break-even point
bridled wallaby
Bright's disease
britannia metal
brownfield site
brown haematite
brown-sweetlips
brown tree snake
Brunner's glands
Burchell's zebra
bureau de change
butterfly bream
cabbage-root fly
cabinet picture
Cairngorm stone
calcareous ooze
Canterbury bell
canvasback duck
Cape gooseberry
capital account
capital gearing
capitalization
caramel custard
carbon monoxide
carboxylic acid
cardinal flower
carding machine
carline thistle
cassette player
central heating
chamber counsel
chamber hanging
chamois leather
champagne cider
champagne punch
character space
chemosynthesis
Cheshire cheese
chest of drawers
chief constable
children's party
chimney sweeper
chloral hydrate
chlorcyclizine
chlorite schist
chlorothiazide
chlorpropamide
chlorthalidone
chocolate-point
chromatic scale
chromatography
church assembly
church planting
cinematography
circuit breaker
circumferentor
circumnavigate
citizen-soldier
classics master
claustrophobia

clumber spaniel
coach-whip snake
coasting vessel
cobra de capello
cocktail shaker
coin collecting
colonel-in-chief
Colorado beetle
colour sergeant
commissionaire
common entrance
common nuisance
common sergeant
communion table
companies court
compass bearing
complex numbers
compression tap
computer dating
concealed fraud
conchyliaceous
Conestoga wagon
conference pear
conjugal rights
conjunctivitis
constitutional
constructivism
consumer credit
contact breaker
continuity girl
contract bridge
contra rotation
convertibility
convexo-concave
corporation tax
corpuscularian
counterchanged
counter-passant
country dancing
county judgment
court of justice
crab-eating seal
criminal appeal
crockery washer
croque monsieur
crown solicitor
crystal lattice
crystal therapy
cubic decimetre
current account
current balance
current bedding
customs officer
cyclobarbitone
cyclopentamine
cystic fibrosis
dancing academy
data protection
debenture stock
decimalization
default summons
deferred rebate
deferred shares
deltidial plate
demisemiquaver
demobilization
deposit account
deputy chairman
deputy sergeant
desert pavement
desk calculator
despatch cutter
destructionist
dexamphetamine
dextromoramide
diamond sparrow
diesel electric
diethylpropion
dihydrocodeine
dimethisterone
dinactinometer
direct interval
discharge valve
discharging rod
disciplinarian
discount broker
discount market
discus throwing
disembarkation
disintegration
distaff thistle
divertissement
domestic comedy
dormouse possum
double jeopardy
double patience
double-bar finch
double-declutch
double-foolscap
double-imperial
dowager duchess
downhill skiing
draining engine
draining plough
dramatic critic
drawing teacher
driving licence
drying cupboard
ducks-and-drakes
duelling pistol
eccentric strap
eccentric wheel
ecclesiastical
ecclesiologist
economic growth
edible dormouse
educationalist
eiderdown quilt
eight-oared boat
ejusdem generis
elastic bitumen
electric blanket
electric cooker
electric cut-out
electric energy
electric geyser
electric guitar
electric kettle
electric launch
electrobiology
electrodynamic
electrostatics
electrotherapy
electrothermic
elephant beetle
enaliosaurians
encyclopaedist
engagement ring
engine mounting
epigrammatical
escape velocity
estuary catfish
ethacrynic acid
eustachian tube
exchange broker
exhaust-cam axle
expanded memory
explosive rivet
extended memory
extensor muscle

extreme unction
Fair Isle jumper
false eyelashes
false pretences
feather bolster
featherbedding
features editor
fenestra ovalis
ferromagnetism
ferro-manganese
fiduciary issue
fifth columnist
figbranch borer
file conversion
filling station
finance company
fin-backed whale
fire salamander
flag-lieutenant
floating bridge
floating charge
Florence fennel
flotilla leader
fluid mechanics
flying buttress
flying squirrel
fortifications
foster daughter
founders' shares
four-lined snake
fourth engineer
four-wheel drive
fraternity ring
French vermouth
friction clutch
friction wheels
friendship band
fringe benefits
fuelless cooker
full employment
fuller's thistle
futtock shrouds
galactophagist
galvanized iron
galvanized pail
garden designer
garnishee order
general average
general manager
general reserve
gentleman-usher
geothermometer
German shepherd
gerrymandering
gestalt therapy
giant groundsel
globe artichoke
glove-stretcher
glutethimidine
golden lungwort
golden mouse-ear
golden pheasant
golden tree frog
good-for-nothing
gooseberry bush
grammaticaster
graphic granite
grease injector
greenfield site
Greenland shark
Greenland whale
Gregorian chant
grey nurse shark
ground squirrel
hair extensions
half-commission
handicraftsman
hard-astarboard
haunch of mutton
Haversian canal
heavier-than-air
heptabarbitone
heraldic emblem
Hercules beetle
heresiographer
high court judge
Himalayan viper
hippopathology
holder for value
holding company
holding pattern
Hong Kong dollar
horned screamer
horn-nosed viper
horn-rim glasses
horse whisperer
horticulturist
hostess trolley
hot water bottle
house decorator
house furnisher
household bread
hunt the slipper
hunt the thimble
hydraulic press
hydrobarometer
hydrocortisone
hydrolic action
hydrophytology
hyperglycaemia
hyperinflation
ichthyophagist
identical twins
identification
identity parade
incendiary bomb
incised meander
Indian elephant
Indian pangolin
indicative mood
indifferentist
inflatable chair
infrastructure
innominate bone
inscribed stock
instruction set
insulated cable
interferometer
interplanetary
intrusive rocks
inverted commas
invisible trade
Irish wolfhound
ironbark sawfly
Isabelline bear
joint stock bank
junior wrangler
Kaposi's sarcoma
king barracouta
king-lory parrot
king parrotfish
king's messenger
kitchen dresser
knickerbockers
knife sharpener
knitting needles
lacrimal gland
language master
lath and plaster
latitudinarian

leading steward
leather dresser
letter of credit
letter of marque
Lewisian gneiss
liaison officer
light fantastic
lighter-than-air
lighting-up time
light pollution
limited company
liquid paraffin
liquidity ratio
literary editor
little numbfish
loan conversion
local authority
long-arm balance
long-nosed viper
longshore drift
looping the loop
lord chancellor
lord lieutenant
lord of the manor
lords and ladies
love-in-idleness
Lowland bagpipe
lubricating oil
luggage carrier
luggage trailer
Macquarie perch
macroeconomics
magnetic needle
major intrusion
managing agents
managing editor
mandarin orange
mandolin player
manifold writer
man in the street
manual labourer
Manx shearwater
many-banded sole
marine annelida
market gardener
market research
marmoset monkey
marsupial mouse
mashed potatoes
master sergeant
mechanized army
mechanotherapy
medical officer
meerschaum pipe
meibomian gland
merchant tailor
meteorological
methoserpidine
mezzanine floor
Michaelmas term
microeconomics
microprocessor
miles per gallon
military police
milk of magnesia
mincing machine
ministerialist
minor intrusion
miscellanarian
misinterpreter
mock turtle soup
money scrivener
monosaccharide
monthly account
Morocco leather
mortgage broker
mother superior
mountaineering
mountain sorrel
mountain thrush
mourning brooch
multi-core cable
multiplication
mushroom anchor
nail extensions
nankeen kestrel
natural history
naturalization
natural numbers
natural science
naval architect
nether garments
new issue market
nitroglycerine
noise pollution
nominal capital
Norfolk spaniel
Norfolk terrier
Norwich terrier
nuclear reactor
nuclear warfare
nuclear weapons
obstructionist
office building
off-road vehicle
offset printing
one-finned shark
ophthalmoscope
option dealings
orderly officer
ordinary seaman
ordinary shares
organo-metallic
osmoregulation
otolaryngology
oversubscribed
oxidizing agent
oxyhaemoglobin
page impression
painted gurnard
painter-stainer
paragrammatist
paramethadione
parapsychology
parmesan cheese
parochial board
partial denture
Patagonian cavy
pavement artist
pearly nautilus
penal servitude
pentobarbitone
perfect binding
personal column
petrol strainer
pharmacologist
phenethicillin
philanthropist
phosphor bronze
photogrammetry
photoperiodism
photosynthesis
phytopathology
picture gallery
pincer movement
plaster of paris
plate tectonics
pneumatic drill
pneumatologist
poikilothermic

political agent
polysaccharide
Pontefract cake
portable engine
portland cement
positive degree
possessive case
powder magazine
prairie chicken
predestination
preferred stock
prehistoric age
preserved fruit
pressure cooker
prevailing wind
prima ballerina
prince's feather
privet hawk moth
procrastinator
prognosticator
progress chaser
progressionist
prohibitionist
promise-breaker
promissory note
propeller shaft
property master
provost-marshal
psalmographist
psychonosology
purple broccoli
purple sea-perch
push technology
Pyrrhic victory
quadragenarian
quality control
quarter guilder
Queen's evidence
Queen's pleasure
quodlibetarian
radio astronomy
radio telescope
radiochemistry
random sampling
rate of exchange
rate of interest
rating observer
rat-tailed snake
reading glasses
reaping machine
rear-wheel drive
receiving order
reception clerk
reclining seats
reconnaissance
reconsecration
reconstruction
record breaking
recrystallized
red gurnet-perch
redemptionists
regimental band
reinforcements
release therapy
representative
requisitionist
resino-electric
restorationist
resultant force
revenue account
rhinoceros bird
riding breeches
riding mistress
right ascension
right to silence
ripple-drifting
river blackfish
river blindness
Rob Roy cocktail
robin-redbreast
rocket launcher
rubicon bezique
running rigging
sabbath-breaker
sabbatical year
sacramentarian
saddle of mutton
sales assistant
sanctification
saponification
sawn-off shotgun
saw-scaled viper
scala vestibuli
schoolmistress
school of acting
schooner-rigged
science fiction
science teacher
screw propeller
scrubbing brush
seaplane tender
second corporal
second division
second engineer
secondary cache
security forces
seidlitz powder
senior wrangler
sensationalist
sensitive plant
sentimentalist
septuagenarian
sergeant-at-arms
service station
sheet lightning
shellac varnish
shepherd's crook
shepherd's pouch
shepherd's purse
shepherd's staff
Shetland jumper
ship's carpenter
shooting script
short-finned eel
short-term gains
shove-halfpenny
shovel-nosed ray
shunt regulator
side impact bars
siderographist
sign of the cross
signals officer
silver pheasant
simple fracture
Singapore sling
skittles player
slide projector
smallbore rifle
smoking concert
smooth flathead
smooth operator
smoothing plane
snake's-head iris
snake-eyed skink
snapping turtle
snowshoe rabbit
social democrat
social security
sodium sulphate
sonic altimeter

sound projector
space traveller
Spanish bayonet
Spanish leather
sparkling water
sparkling wines
special licence
spectacle maker
spectroscopist
spotted harrier
spotted whiting
squadron leader
squandermaniac
stage carpenter
stamp collector
standing orders
starch hyacinth
starched collar
starting handle
steel engraving
steeplechasing
steering column
store detective
string of pearls
strip the willow
striped catfish
striped gudgeon
striped sea-pike
sulphacetamide
summer solstice
sunshine wattle
superannuation
superintendent
superior person
superstructure
supreme command
surrender value
sustainability
swingling knife
swivel rowlocks
symptomatology
syndesmography
synodical month
syringodendron
systems analyst
tallow chandler
Tasmanian devil
tawny frogmouth
teleconference
temporary files
tequila slammer
thermodynamics
thermoelectric
thigh-high boots
third-party risk
three-core cable
three-metre rule
three-point turn
three-speed gear
threshing floor
thrusting screw
Tibetan mastiff
tintinnabulary
tintinnabulate
toasted teacake
tobacco stopper
topgallant mast
top hat and tails
torpedo gunboat
torrential rain
total immersion
touring company
traction engine
trading account
transformation
transit of Venus
transmigration
treacle mustard
Turkish delight
two-guinea piece
uberrimae fidei
ultramontanist
unearned income
universal joint
unknown soldier
valetudinarian
vanishing point
variety theatre
vascular bundle
vegetable cutter
venetian blinds
venetian window
vermouth cassis
version control
vertical circle
vice-chancellor
vitreo electric
vitreous humour
vodka and orange
voltaic battery
volunteer force
waifs and strays
walking wounded
war of attrition
warrant officer
washing machine
watercolourist
wave telegraphy
wayside station
weather prophet
weeding forceps
weight training
weightlessness
welcome swallow
whippersnapper
whispering dome
whistling eagle
white horsefish
white wine punch
wholemeal bread
wind instrument
winter overcoat
winter quarters
winter solstice
wire micrometer
word processing
working capital
wrongful arrest
xylometazoline
Yorkshire coble
zenith distance

15

Aberdeen terrier
acrobatic troupe
act of bankruptcy
adjutant-general
advocate-general
African elephant
air chief marshal
air conditioning
aircraft carrier
Airedale terrier
air-to-air missile
Alaskan malamute
alternative fuel
American buffalo
antepenultimate
anti-aircraft-gun
arboriculturist
archchamberlain
armillary sphere
assistant master
astronomer royal
attorney general
Australian perch
Australian smelt
autograph hunter
autrefois acquit
average adjuster
aversion therapy
Bakewell pudding
ballroom dancing
basilar membrane
beaked coral-fish
Belgian sheepdog
benefit of clergy
Bennett's wallaby
binomial theorem
biological clock
black rhinoceros
black-cap pudding
block signalling
blue Gascon hound
boarding officer
bolt action rifle
bonded warehouse
bottlenose shark
Bow Street runner
brass instrument
broccoli sprouts
Brussels griffon
Brussels sprouts
bubble and squeak
building society
bulletproof vest
cabinet minister
cable-laying ship
cable-repair ship
calcareous shale
calendered paper
capital employed
carbonated water
cardinal virtues
carpenter's bench
carriage builder
cascade cocktail
casualty station
celestial sphere
centre of gravity
champagne cognac
chargé d'affaires
charitable trust
chemical balance
chloramphenicol
chlormethiazole
chocolate éclair
chocolate fondue
Christmas flower
cinderella dance
cinematographer
circumnavigable
circumnavigator
classical ballet
classics teacher
clearing station
clerk of the house
comedy of manners
command of the sea
commercial court
commissary court
commission agent
common stingaree
compound a felony
compound larceny
computer science
concentric cable
consignment note
consistory court
consolation race
constitutionist
contempt of court
conversationist
cornelian cherry
corporal-of-horse
cosmetic surgeon
creative writing
crimping machine
crossing sweeper
cross-lamination
crossword puzzle
crown green bowls
crustaceologist
crusted flounder
crusted weed-fish
crystal necklace
crystallization
crystallography
Cuban bloodhound
cubic centimetre
cyclobranchiata
daily-wear lenses
dampproof course
dancing mistress
decarbonization
definite article
defragmentation
desertification
Devonshire cream
diamond bracelet
diamond earrings
diamond merchant
diamond necklace
differentiation
digital computer
dirt-track racing
discharge papers
discharging arch
displaced person
disposable nappy
district officer
dividend warrant
doctor of science
domestic servant
double-barrelled
double-tongueing
dramatic society
draughtsmanship
drawing mistress
dredging machine
dressing station
drilling machine

dual carriageway
duchess cocktail
early closing day
edriophthalmata
egg-eating snakes
Egyptian bassett
election auditor
electric battery
electric blanket
electric circuit
electric current
electric heating
electric machine
electrification
electrochemical
electrodynamics
electrokinetics
electromagnetic
electronegative
electronic brain
electronic music
electropositive
emancipationist
emergency powers
energy-efficient
English springer
entrenching tool
entrepreneurial
envelope machine
ethnic cleansing
exchange control
excommunication
ex-gratia payment
expansion engine
experimentalist
Fahrenheit scale
Fair Isle sweater
feather boarding
feather mattress
fellow traveller
fenestra rotunda
fife-and-drum band
finless porpoise
first-degree burn
first lieutenant
five-guinea piece
flight attendant
foreign exchange
forked lightning
forwarding agent
foundation stone
Fraunhofer lines
friction rollers
frigate mackerel
front-wheel drive
frost shattering
funeral director
furniture beetle
galvanic battery
garden furniture
gastroenteritis
gate-legged table
general election
gentleman-at-arms
gentleman farmer
glacial stairway
golden delicious
golden handshake
golden retriever
golden saxifrage
golden tree snake
governor-general
greyhound racing
Grignard reagent
guerilla warfare
gunnery sergeant
hackney carriage
hackney coachman
hairback herring
hall of residence
harbour porpoise
harvest festival
haunch of venison
heart specialist
heir presumptive
helminthologist
hierogrammatist
high density disk
higher education
high-heeled shoes
Highland bagpipe
Highland terrier
historic present
historiographer
Hodgkin's disease
honorary colonel
household troops
humpbacked whale
hydraulic cement
hydromica schist
impure limestone
infernal regions
inflatable chair
instrument panel
instrumentalist
instrumentation
insulating paper
insurance broker
insurance policy
insurrectionary
insurrectionist
intellectualist
interim dividend
invalid carriage
investment trust
invulnerability
irrigation canal
Italian rye grass
Italian vermouth
jack-of-all-trades
Japanese spaniel
javelin throwing
Jerusalem cherry
king-of-the-castle
knee-length boots
knee-length socks
knitting needles
labour-intensive
Lakeland terrier
lance bombardier
language teacher
lapsang souchong
latent ambiguity
lily of the valley
linotype machine
liquidity ratios
little cling-fish
little conger eel
local government
long-finned perch
long-tailed shirt
machine language
magnetic battery
magneto-electric
magnifying glass
marbled flathead
maribou feathers
marine insurance
mariner's compass
marital coercion

marriage licence
married quarters
master of science
messenger-at-arms
metamorphic rock
meteoric showers
methylcellulose
Michaelmas daisy
military academy
military college
military funeral
military honours
military two-step
minister of state
missile launcher
Molotov cocktail
morning sickness
mountain leather
mounted infantry
mourning clothes
mousetrap cheese
multilateralism
multiple fission
Muscovite schist
musical director
musical festival
musique concrete
nationalization
neurophysiology
nitrogen mustard
non-commissioned
non-contributory
Norfolk springer
numismatologist
observation post
official secrets
offshore breezes
ohmic resistance
onion weathering
operating system
operation orders
ophthalmologist
orderly corporal
orderly sergeant
ordnance officer
ostrich feathers
overflow channel
oxytetracycline
oyer and terminer
painted dragonet
painted terrapin
palaeontologist
parliamentarian
parthenogenesis
people's republic
perpetual motion
personality cult
persona non grata
personification
pestle and mortar
phenolphthalein
photograph album
photograph frame
physiotherapist
Planck's constant
plastic raincoat
platform speaker
pleasure gardens
pleasure grounds
plenipotentiary
pneumatic pillow
point-blank range
political science
portrait painter
potential energy
power of attorney
prairie schooner
preference bonds
preference share
preference stock
preferred shares
prevailing winds
privy councillor
programme seller
provision dealer
provost sergeant
psychopathology
psychotherapist
public enclosure
public ownership
public relations
pump screwdriver
purchasing power
quarter sessions
queen's messenger
rabbit bandicoot
Radiolarian ooze
railway carriage
railway engineer
rain cats and dogs
rationalization
rational numbers
reaction profile
redemption yield
reducing balance
refreshment room
resurrectionist
reversing lights
ring-tailed lemur
Rogerian therapy
running headline
sabretooth tiger
sawed-off shotgun
school inspector
school of dancing
science mistress
Scottish dancing
Scottish terrier
scripture reader
Sealyham terrier
seating capacity
secondary modern
secured creditor
seedling gum moth
semi-retractable
serricorn beetle
shepherd's needle
sheriff's officer
short-arm balance
short suckerfish
shrinking violet
single-barrelled
situation comedy
sleeping partner
small-headed sole
smelting furnace
smooth stingaree
soft contact lens
solar microscope
spangled grunter
Spanish chestnut
Spanish mackerel
sparkling waters
specific gravity
spigot-and-socket
spiral staircase
split infinitive
spotted cat-shark
spotted eagle-ray
spotted pipefish

springer spaniel
square decimetre
St Bernard's waltz
stage properties
stamp collecting
stapedius muscle
star of Bethlehem
sterling balance
stretcher bearer
string quartette
strolling player
suffragan bishop
summer lightning
supernaturalist
surveyor-general
symphony concert
synchronization
systems analysis
tableaux-vivants
talking pictures
Tasmanian possum
tectibranchiata
tensile strength
thermal capacity
thermochemistry
thickset chalcid
third-degree burn
Thomson's gazelle
three-legged race
thyrocalcitonin
ticket collector
tightrope walker
tonsorial artist
topsail schooner
totalitarianism
transfiguration
trembling poplar
trifluoperazine
trinitrotoluene
triple tongueing
tropical climate
TV remote control
two-guilder piece
unissued capital
unleavened bread
unsportsmanlike
upper memory area
vegetable cutter
vegetable marrow
Venus's navelwort
vertebral column
vestibular nerve
vice-chamberlain
victualling yard
video conference
virginia creeper
vitruvian scroll
water-tube boiler
weather boarding
weather forecast
weighing machine
wheel animalcule
white-spotted ray
whitworth thread
wind chill factor
wind instruments
windscreen wiper
winter underwear
withdrawing room
woody nightshade
yellow longicorn
youth hostelling

16

Alphonsine tables
altitude sickness
astronomical unit
ballistic missile
behaviour therapy
benzyl penicillin
brass instruments
bread and dripping
brigadier general
Caerphilly cheese
cassette recorder
centre of symmetry
Circassian circle
classics mistress
cognitive therapy
collateral damage
colour separation
compound fracture
computer literacy
condensation trap
cone of depression
continental drift
control character
costume jewellery
counteroffensive
cyclophosphamide
data transfer rate
deadly nightshade
deathwatch beetle
deoxyribonucleic
dextromethorphan
dial up connection
diamanté bracelet
diamanté earrings
diamanté necklace
digital video disk
disposable lenses
Doberman pinscher
double-edged sword
double Gloucester
electoral college
elephant hawk moth
emissions trading
fishnet stockings
flight lieutenant
Forsterite marble
further education
gastroenterology
general of the army
greenhouse effect
high capacity disk
hysteron proteron
interior designer
Italian greyhound
language mistress
lighthouse keeper
lithium carbonate
little black dress
long combinations
long underclothes
long-sleeved dress
long-sleeved shirt
Magellanic clouds
meta-aromatherapy
mousseline de soie
nervous breakdown
paraformaldehyde
passing-out parade
personal computer
phenoxybenzamine
photolithography
pillion passenger
plastic explosive
precision bombing
preemptive attack
preemptive strike

psychogeriatrics
quantity surveyor
repertory theatre
representational
satellite decoder
second lieutenant
secondary deposit
second-degree burn
Shetland sheepdog
soldier of fortune
stand to attention
support stockings
terminal velocity
tetrahydrozoline
thermal underwear
thigh-length boots
tintinnabulation
turtleneck jumper
twinset and pearls
tympanic membrane
varifocal glasses
war establishment
Wheatstone bridge
white tie and tails

17

admiral of the fleet
angels on horseback
antipersonnel mine
anti-virus software
Bedlington terrier
biological warfare
chattering classes
concentration camp
confirmed bachelor
continental lentil
conversation piece
demilitarized zone
desktop publishing
devils on horseback
domestic shorthair
English toy spaniel
fragmentation bomb
helicopter gunship
humanistic therapy
Huntington's chorea
landscape gardener
lieutenant colonel
lieutenant general
Manchester terrier
master of foxhounds
multiple sclerosis
muscular dystrophy
Parkinson's disease
peacekeeping force
regression therapy
relaxation therapy
rules of engagement
Scottish deerhound
semicircular canal
sickle-cell anaemia
special operations
technical sergeant
tectorial membrane
veterinary surgeon
weather forecaster

18

Alexander technique
bilingual secretary
central reservation
chicken tikka masala
command interpreter
conventional memory
dark night of the soul
death's head hawk moth
electronic commerce
expeditionary force
genetic engineering
greenstick fracture
heat-seeking missile
King Charles spaniel
landscape architect
membrane of reissner
Old English sheepdog
recruiting sergeant
Rhodesian ridgeback
thirty-nine articles
transubstantiation

19

cross-country running
electroshock therapy
environment friendly
hummingbird hawk moth
legionnaire's disease
lieutenant-commander
occupational therapy
recreational therapy
recreational vehicle
ridge of high pressure
surface-to-air missile
thermonuclear weapon

20 and over

artificial intelligence (22)
central processing unit (21)
confrontation therapy (20)
conscientious objector (21)
continuous assessment (20)
direct cable connection (21)
electroconvulsive therapy (24)
general of the air force (20)
general protection fault (22)
intercontinental ballistic missile (32)
marshal of the Royal Air Force (25)
surface-to-surface missile (23)

Section 2

Abbreviations

1

b. born
C Celsius, Centigrade, Conservative
c cent(s)
c. circa (around, about)
d old penny, old pence (denarius)
d. died
E east, Ecstasy
F Fahrenheit
f feminine, franc(s), forte
g gram(s)
h hour(s)
J Joule
K Kelvin, kilobyte
L large, Latin, Liberal, learner
l litre(s)
M monsieur, medium
m masculine, metre(s), minute(s)
m. married
N Newton, north
n neuter
p penny, pence, piano
p. page
q. query, question
R Royal, Rex (King), Regina (Queen)
S small, south
s second(s)
V volt(s)
v verse, versus (against), very
W watt(s), west

2

AA Alcoholics Anonymous, Automobile Association
AC air conditioning, alternating current
A/C air conditioning
a/c account
AD Anno Domini (in the year of our Lord)
AI Amnesty International, artificial insemination, artificial intelligence
a.m. ante meridiem (before noon)
AS Anglo-Saxon
BA Bachelor of Arts
BC Before Christ
BD Bachelor of Divinity
BS Bachelor of Science
BT British Telecommunications
Bt Baronet
ca circa (around, about)
cc carbon copy, cubic centimetre(s)
CD compact disc
cf. compare
ch. chapter
cl centilitre(s)
cl. class, clause
cm centimetre(s)
CO commanding officer
Co. company, county
c/o care of
CV curriculum vitae
DA District Attorney (US)
DC direct current
DD Doctor of Divinity
DJ disc jockey, dinner jacket
DM Deutschmark
do ditto
Dr doctor
ea. each
Ed. editor
e.g. exempli gratia (for example)
eq. equal
ER Elizabeth Regina (Queen)
EU European Union
ex. example, without, from
FA Football Association
FC football club
ff fortissimo
FM frequency modulation
Fr. French, Friday
ft foot, feet
GB Great Britain, gigabyte(s)
GC George Cross
GI general issue (US)
Gk Greek
gm gramme(s)
GM George Medal, genetically modified
GP General Practitioner
GR Georgius Rex (King George)

Gr. Greek
Gt great
HM His/Her Majesty
HP hire purchase
hp horsepower
HQ headquarters
hr hour
Hz Hertz
ID identification
i.e. id est (that is)
in inch(es)
IQ intelligence quotient
JP Justice of the Peace
Jr junior
KC King's Counsel
kg kilogram(s)
km kilometre(s)
Kt knight
lb libra (pound)
Lt Lieutenant
MA Master of Arts
MB Bachelor of Medicine, megabyte(s)
MC Master of Ceremonies, Military Cross
MD Doctor of Medicine
ME Middle English, myalgic encephalomyelitis
mf mezzo forte
mg milligram(s)
mm millimetre(s)
MO medical officer
MP Member of Parliament, military police
Mr mister
MS manuscript, multiple sclerosis
Mt mount
NB nota bene (note well)
NE north-east
no number (numero)
nr near
NT New Testament
NW north-west
NY New York
NZ New Zealand
OE Old English
OM Order of Merit
Op. opus (work)
OT Old Testament
oz ounce(s)
PA personal assistant, public-address system
PC personal computer, police constable, politically correct
pd paid
PE physical education
pf pianoforte
pl plural
PM Prime Minister
p.m. post meridiem, post mortem
PO post office
pp pianissimo
pp. pages
p.p. per procuration (by proxy)
PR proportional representation, public relations
PS postscript
pt pint
QC Queen's Counsel
qr quarter
qt quart
q.v. quod vide (which see)
RA Royal Academy
RC Roman Catholic
Rd road
RE Religious Education
SE south-east
SF science fiction
SJ Society of Jesus
SM sadomasochism, Sergeant-Major
sq. square
Sr senior
SS steamship
St Saint, street
SW south-west
TA Territorial Army
TB tuberculosis
TV television
UK United Kingdom
UN United Nations
US United States
VC Victoria Cross
VD venereal disease
v.g. very good
VR Victoria Regina (Queen)
vs versus
vv verses
WC water closet

wt weight
XL extra large
yd yard
yr your

3

AAA Amateur Athletic Association, American Automobile Association
ABC alphabet, American Broadcasting Company
ADC aide-de-camp
Adm. Admiral
AGM annual general meeting
aka also known as
AOB any other business
AOR adult-oriented rock
APR annual percentage rate
Apr. April
arr. arrive(s, ed)
ATM automated or automatic teller machine
ATS Auxiliary Territorial Service
Aug. August
aux. auxiliary
Ave avenue
BBC British Broadcasting Corporation
BDS Bachelor of Dental Surgery
bhp brake horsepower
BMA British Medical Association
BNP British National Party
Bro. brother
BSc Bachelor of Science
BSE bovine spongiform encephalopathy
BST British Summer Time
Btu British Thermal Unit(s)
BVM Blessed Virgin Mary
cap. capital
CBE Commander of the British Empire (Order)
CBI Confederation of British Industry
CBS Columbia Broadcasting System US)
CFC chlorofluorocarbon
CIA Central Intelligence Agency
CID Criminal Investigation Department
c.i.f. cost, insurance, freight
CIO Congress of Industrial Organizations (US)
CJD Creutzfeldt-Jakob disease
CNN Cable News Network (US)
COD cash/collect on delivery
cwt hundredweight
DBE Dame Commander of the British Empire (Order)
DDT dichlorodiphenyltrichloro-ethane
DEA Drug Enforcement Agency (US)
Dec. December
DFC Distinguished Flying Cross
DFM Distinguished Flying Medal
DIY do it yourself
DNA deoxyribonucleic acid
DOS disc operating system
doz. dozen
DSC Distinguished Service Cross
DSc Doctor of Science
DSM Distinguished Service Medal
DSO Distinguished Service Order
DTI Department of Trade and Industry
EEC European Economic Community
ENE east-north-east
ESE east-south-east
Esq. Esquire
etc. etcetera
FBI Federal Bureau of Investigation (US)
FDA Food and Drug Administration (US)
Feb. February
fem. feminine
fig. figure
f.o.b. free on board
FRS Fellow of the Royal Society
gal. gallon(s)
GBE Knight Grand Cross of the British Empire

Gen.	General
GHQ	General Headquarters
GHz	gigahertz
Gib.	Gibraltar
GMO	genetically modified organism
GMT	Greenwich Mean Time
HIV	Human Immunodeficiency Virus
HMS	His/Her Majesty's Ship
Hon.	honorary, Honourable
HRH	His/Her Royal Highness
hrs	hours
HRT	hormone replacement therapy
IBA	Independent Broadcasting Authority
ILO	International Labour Organization
Inc.	incorporated
INS	Immigration and Naturalization Service (US)
ins	inches
IOU	(acknowledgment of debt)
IRA	Irish Republican Army
IRS	Internal Revenue Service (US)
ITV	Independent Television
IUD	intrauterine device
Jan.	January
Jun.	junior
KBE	Knight Commander of the British Empire (Order)
KGB	Komitet Gosudarstvennoi Bezopasnosti (Committee for State Security)
KKK	Ku Klux Klan
kph	kilometres per hour
Lab.	Labour
lbw	leg before wicket
LCD	liquid crystal display
LLB	Bachelor of Laws
LLD	Doctor of Laws
loq.	loquitur (speaks)
LSD	lysergic acid diethylamide
L.S.D.	librae (pounds), solidi (shillings), denarii (pence)
LSE	London School of Economics
Ltd	Limited
Maj.	Major
Mar.	March
MBA	Master of Business Administration
MBE	Member of the British Empire (Order)
MCC	Marylebone Cricket Club
MCP	male chauvinist pig
MEP	Member of the European Parliament
MHz	megahertz
Mme	Madame
MOD	Ministry of Defence
MOT	Ministry of Transport
mph	miles per hour
MSc	Master of Science
MSG	monosodium glutamate
MSS	manuscripts
MTV	Music Television
NBC	National Broadcasting Company (US)
NCO	non-commissioned officer
NFU	National Farmers' Union
NHS	National Health Service
NNE	north-north-east
NNR	National Nature Reserve
NNW	north-north-west
Nos	numbers
Nov.	November
NRA	National Rifle Association (US)
NSW	New South Wales
NUJ	National Union of Journalists
NUM	National Union of Mineworkers
NUS	National Union of Seamen, National Union of Students
NUT	National Union of Teachers
NVQ	National Vocational Qualification
NYC	New York City
OAP	old age pensioner
OBE	Officer of the British Empire (Order)
Oct.	October
OTC	Officer Training Corps
PBS	Public Broadcasting Service (US)

PhD	Doctor of Philosophy
PLO	Palestine Liberation Organization
PMS	premenstrual syndrome
PMT	premenstrual tension
pop.	population
POW	prisoner of war
pro	professional
PTO	please turn over
PVC	polyvinyl chloride
QED	quod erat demonstrandum (which was to be demonstrated)
RAC	Royal Automobile Club
RAF	Royal Air Force
RAM	random access memory
ref	referee, reference
rep	repertory, representative
Rev.	Reverend
RIP	requiescat in pace (may he/she rest in peace)
RMS	Royal Mail steamer
RNA	ribonucleic acid
ROM	read-only memory
RSI	repetitive strain injury
RUC	Royal Ulster Constabulary
SAS	Special Air Service
SAT	Standard Assessment Task or Test (UK), Scholastic Aptitude Test (US)
Sec.	secretary
Sen.	senator
SNP	Scottish National Party
Soc.	society
SOS	(distress signal)
SSE	south-south-east
SSW	south-south-west
STD	sexually transmitted disease, subscriber trunk dialling
SUV	sports utility vehicle (US)
tbs	tablespoon(s)
TNT	trinitrotoluene (explosive)
TUC	Trades Union Congress
UDA	Ulster Defence Association
UDI	unilateral declaration of independence
UFO	unidentified flying object
UHF	ultra-high frequency
UHT	ultra heat treated
UNO	United Nations Organization
USA	United States of America, United States Army
USN	United States Navy
USS	United States Ship
VAT	value-added tax
VDU	visual display unit
VHF	very high frequency
VIP	very important person
viz.	videlicet (namely)
vol	volume
VSO	Voluntary Service Overseas
WNW	west-north-west
WPC	Woman Police Constable
WSW	west-south-west
WTO	World Trade Organization

4

AIDS	Acquired Immune Deficiency Syndrome
asst	assistant
Bart	baronet
Beds	Bedfordshire
Brit	British
Bros	brothers
BUPA	British United Provident Association
Capt.	Captain
chap.	chapter
C of E	Church of England
Corp.	Corporal, corporation
dept	department
DfES	Department for Education and Skills
DLit	Doctor of Literature
GATT	General Agreement on Tariffs and Trade
GCSE	General Certificate of Secondary Education
Glos	Gloucestershire
GNVQ	General National Vocational Qualification
ibid.	ibidem (in the same source)
inst.	instant (in the present month)
ISBN	International Standard Book Number
Mlle	Mademoiselle

MusB Bachelor of Music
MusD Doctor of Music
NASA National Aeronautics and Space Administration
NATO North Atlantic Treaty Organization
OECD Organization for Economic Co-operation and Development
OHMS On His/Her Majesty's Service
OPEC Organization of Petroleum Exporting Countries
Oxon Oxfordshire, of Oxford
PAYE pay as you earn
PDSA People's Dispensary for Sick Animals
Prof. professor
recd received
Regt regiment
RIBA Royal Institute of British Architects
RSPB Royal Society for the Protection of Birds
RSVP répondez s'il vous plait (please reply)
Sept. September
Serg. Sergeant
SSSI Site of Special Scientific Interest
tbsp tablespoon(s)
TEFL teaching English as a foreign language
TGWU Transport and General Workers' Union
USAF United States Air Force
USSR Union of Soviet Socialist Republics
WASP white Anglo-Saxon Protestant
YMCA Young Men's Christian Association
YWCA Young Women's Christian Association

5

ad lib ad libitum (as much as desired)
ANZAC Australian and New Zealand Army Corps
ASCII American standard code for information interchange
assoc. associate, association
B&B bed and breakfast
Berks Berkshire
Bucks Buckinghamshire
Cambs Cambridgeshire
CD-ROM compact disc read-only memory
CITES Convention on International Trade in Endangered Species
DEFRA Department for Environment, Food and Rural Affairs
DLitt Doctor of Letters
et seq. et sequens (and what follows)
Hants Hampshire
Herts Hertfordshire
Lancs Lancashire
Lieut. Lieutenant
NAAFI Navy, Army and Air Force Institutes
NSPCC National Society for the Prevention of Cruelty to Children
op. cit. opere citato (in the work cited)
P & O Peninsular and Oriental
RSPCA Royal Society for the Prevention of Cruelty to Animals
Rt Hon. Right Honourable
Rt Rev. Right Reverend
Salop Shropshire
UNHCR United Nations High Commission for Refugees
Wilts Wiltshire
Yorks Yorkshire

6

Cantab. of Cambridge
E. and OE. errors and omissions excepted
Messrs Messieurs
Ofsted Office for Standards in Education

per pro per procurationem (by proxy)
Staffs Staffordshire
UNESCO United Nations Educational, Scientific and Cultural Organization
UNICEF United Nations International Children's Emergency Fund

7
mod cons modern conveniences

8
UNPROFOR United Nations Protection Force

Alphabets

GREEK

2
mu
nu
pi
xi

3
chi
eta
phi
psi
rho
tau

4
beta
iota
zeta

5
alpha
delta
gamma
kappa
omega
sigma
theta

6
lambda

7
epsilon
omicron
upsilon

HEBREW

2
He
Pe

3
Ain
Jod
Mem
Nun
Tau
Yod

4
Ayin
Beth
Caph
Heth
Kaph
Koph
Resh
Shin
Teth
Vain
Zade

5
Aleph
Cheth
Gimel
Lamed
Schin
Zayin

6
Daleth
Samech
Samekh
Tzaddi

PHONETIC

4
Echo
Golf
Kilo
Lima
Mike
Papa
X-ray
Zulu

5
Alpha
Bravo
Delta
Hotel
India
Oscar
Romeo
Tango

6
Juliet
Quebec
Sierra
Victor
Whisky
Yankee

7
Charlie
Foxtrot
Uniform

8
November

Archaeological Periods

6
Ice Age
La Tène
Minoan

7
Azilian
Iron Age

8
Asturian
Helladic

9
Acheulean
or Acheulian
Bronze Age
Levallois
Mycenaean
Neolithic
Solutrean

10
Eneolithic
Gravettian
Mesolithic
Mousterian

11
Aurignacian
Magdalenian
New Stone Age
Old Stone Age

12
Chalcolithic
Levalloisian
Palaeolithic

13
Neo-Babylonian
Old Babylonian

15
Châtelperronian

Asteroids

4
Eros
Hebe
Juno

5
Ceres
Vesta

6
Icarus
Pallas

8
Hyperion

Artists, Architects, Cartoonists and Sculptors

3
Arp
Cox
Dix
Dou
Egg
Fox
Gow
Key
Lam
Lee
Low
May
Pei
Poy
Puy
Ryn

4
Adam
Arno
Beck
Bell
Bird
Bone
Both
Burn
Capp
Caro
Cima
Cole
Cuyp
Dadd
Dali
Dick
Dine
Dodd
Dore
Dufy
Dyce
Dyck
Emin
Etty
Eves
Eyck
Faed
Fehr
Ford
Gabo
Gere
Gill
Gogh
Good
Gore
Goya
Gray
Gris
Gros
Guys
Hals
Hand
Hart
Held
Hemy
Herp
Holl
Home
Hone
Hook
Hunt
Jack
Kahn
Kane
Kerr
King
Klee
Lamb
Lane
Lear
Lely
Lion
Loos
Maes
Marc
Miro
Mola
Nash
Nast
Neer
Opie
Owen
Pyne
Reid
Reni
Rich
Rohe
Rosa
Ross
Sant
Shaw
Sime
Sims
Spee
Swan
Todd
Toft
Tuke
Wade
Wain
Ward
Watt
Webb
West
Wood
Wren

5
Aalto
Abbey
Adams
Adler
Allan
Allen
Amiet
André
Appel
Avery
Bacon
Baily
Baker
Balla
Banks
Barry
Barye
Bates
Beale
Berry
Bezzi
Blake
Block
Boehm
Booth
Bosch
Bough
Brett
Brock
Brown
Buell
Bundy
Burra
Carra
Chast
Clark
Clint

Cohen
Cooke
Corad
Corot
Cossa
Costa
Cotes
Craig
Crane
Crane
Credi
Crome
Cross
Crumb
Danby
David
Davie
Davis
Degas
Devis
Dirks
Dixon
Drury
Durer
Ensor
Ernst
Flagg
Foley
Freud
Frink
Frith
Furse
Gaddi
Gaudi
Gaunt
Gibbs
Giles
Gotch
Gould
Goyen
Grant
Grosz
Haden
Haghe
Hanna
Hatio
Hayes
Hurst
Innes
Johns
Jones
Keane
Keene
Kelly
Kirby
Klein
Klimt
Koren
Lance
Lantz
Leech
Leger
Lemon
Le Vau
Lewis
Lippi
Lotto
Lowry
Lucas
Manet
Maris
Mason
Mauve
McCay
Mingo
Moira
Monet
Moore
Munch
Myers
Nebot
Nervi
Nicol
Noble
Nolde
North
Opper
Orpen
Palma
Pater
Payne
Penny
Piper
Plaas
Platt
Ponte
Ponti
Poole
Price
Prout
Pugin
Redon
Rodin
Rooke
Rossi
Sands
Scott
Segar
Segna
Short
Sitko
Sleap
Small
Smith
Soane
Soest
Speed
Stael
Stark
Steen
Steer
Steig
Stone
Stott
Studd
Terry
Tobey
Tonks
Unwin
Uwins
Velde
Vicky
Vonet
Watts
Wells
White
Wiens
Woods
Wyatt
Wyeth
Wylie
Yeats
Young
Zoppo

6

Abbott
Addams
Albers
Allori
Archer
Arnold
Ashton
Barker
Barton
Baskin
Behnes
Benson
Benton
Berman
Bettes
Bewick
Birley
Bodley
Boxall
Braque
Breuer
Briggs
Brough
Browne
Brunel
Buchel
Burnet
Burton
Butler
Calder
Callow
Campin
Caniff
Carter
Casson
Claude
Clouet
Colton
Conder
Cooper
Copley
Corbet
Cotman
Cowper
Cozens
Currie
Dahmen
Dawson
DeBeck
Derain
De Wint
Disney
Dobson
Draper
Duccio
Dunbar
Elwell
Ferber
Fildes
Fisher
Forbes
Foster
Fraser
Fuller
Fuseli
Geddes
Gibson
Gilman
Ginner
Giotto
Girtin
Glover
Gordon
Graham
Greuze
Guardi
Gulich
Hacker
Harral
Haydon
Heckel
Hilton
Holmes
Howard
Hudson
Hughes
Hunter
Ingres
Jagger
Joseph
Kaprow
Kettle
Keyser
Kilban
Knight
Krauze
Laroon
Larson
Laszlo
Lavery
Lawson
Leader
Lebrun
Ledoux
Legros
Le Nain
Leslie
Levine
Linton
Mabuse
Manson
Marini
Martin
Massys
McEvoy
Mesdac
Millet
Monaco
Moores
Morley
Morone
Morris
Muller
Mullin
Murray
Newton
Nisbet
Noland
Oliver
Olsson
O'Neill
Palmer
Panini
Parker
Parton
Paxton
Pegram
Penley
Perret
Peters
Pettie
Piombo
Pisano
Potter
Ramsay
Renoir
Ribera
Ridley
Rivera
Rivers
Robbia
Robert
Romano
Romney

Rothko
Rubens
Ruskin
Sadler
Sandby
Sandys
Sansom
Seddon
Serres
Seurat
Siegel
Sisley
Smirke
Smythe
Soglow
Spence
Stokes
Storck
Storey
Strang
Strube
Stuart
Stubbs
Tadema
Tanguy
Tayler
Taylor
Thaves
Thomas
Titian
Turner
Vacher
Van Ryn
Varley
Vernet
Walker
Waller
Wallis
Walton
Wardle
Warhol
Watson
Weekes
Weenix
Weyden
Wilkie
Wilson
Windus
Wright
Wyllie
Yeames

7

Alberti
Aretino
Baldung
Barbera
Barlach
Bassano
Bateman
Beechey
Behrens
Belcher
Bellini
Bennett
Berchem
Bernini
Blondel
Bomberg
Bonnard
Boucher
Boullee
Bramley
Bridell
Brouwer
Calvert
Cameron
Campion
Cellini
Cerceau
Cezanne
Chagall
Chardin
Charles
Cheston
Chirico
Christo
Cimabue
Clausen
Cockram
Collier
Collins
Connard
Corinth
Cortona
Courbet
Cranach
Crucker
Cundell
Dalziel
Daniell
Darling
Daumier
Da Vinci
De Hooch
De Lazlo
Delorme
Dicksee
Dighton
Douglas
Downman
Duchamp
Edridge
Edwards
El Greco
Emanuel
Epstein
Feiffer
Flaxman
Fouquet
Fox-Pitt
Francia
Freieng
Gabriel
Garnier
Garstin
Gauguin
Gertler
Gibbons
Gilbert
Gillray
Goodall
Goodwin
Greaves
Gregory
Gropius
Guarini
Guevara
Guthrie
Harding
Hartung
Hayward
Herbert
Herring
Hobbema
Hockney
Hofland
Hogarth
Hokusai
Holbein
Holroyd
Hoppner
Hopwood
Horsley
Housman
Indiana
Israels
Jackson
Jaggers
Johnson
Ketcham
Kneller
Knights
Kooning
Lambert
Lancret
Lanteri
Latrobe
Lazarus
Lessore
Linnell
Llander
Lucidel
Lutyens
Macbeth
Maccoll
Maclise
Maillol
Mansart
Maratti
Martini
Matisse
Mauldin
McManus
Memlinc
Merritt
Messick
Meunier
Michaux
Millais
Montana
Morandi
Morisot
Morland
Morrice
Murillo
Nasmith
Nattier
Neumann
Orcagna
Orchard
Osborne
Pacchia
Parrish
Parsons
Pasmore
Peacock
Peruzzi
Phidias
Philips
Phillip
Phil May
Philpot
Picabia
Picasso
Pickard
Pinwell
Pomeroy
Poussin
Poynter
Prinsep
Rackham
Raeburn
Raphael
Raymond
Riviere
Roberts
Rouault
Roussel
Russell
Sargent
Schetky
Schiele
Schultz
Shannon
Sickert
Siddall
Simpson
Smetham
Solomon
Spencer
Stanley
Stevens
Teniers
Tenniel
Thirtle
Thomson
Thurber
Tiepolo
Trudeau

Uccello
Ugolino
Utrillo
Van Dyck
Van Eyck
Van Gogh
Vermeer
Watteau
Webster
Westall
Whiting
Willard
Woolner
Wynants
Zoffany

8

Allinson
Anderson
Angelico
Armitage
Armstead
Aumonier
Beaumont
Beckmann
Beerbohm
Boccioni
Boffrand
Boughton
Brabazon
Bramante
Brancusi
Brangwyn
Brearley
Breathed
Brooking
Brueghel
Bulfinch
Caldecot
Calderon
Callcott
Calthorp
Carracci
Chambers
Chantrey
Crawhall
Creswick
Daubigny
De Keyser
Delaunay
De Laszlo
Del Prete
Deverell
Dietrich
Dressler
Dubuffet
Eastlake
Fielding
Fleisher
Fontaine
Frampton
Garofalo
Ghiberti
Giovanni
Goldberg
Gottlieb
Groening
Hartwell
Hepworth
Herkomer
Herriman
Highmore
Hilliard
Hodgkins
Hokinson
Holloway
Houghton
Ibbetson
Inchbold
Jacobsen
Jan Steen
John Opie
Johnston
Jordaens
Kaufmann
Kokoshka
Kollwitz
Kurtzman
Lambardo
Landseer
Lawrence
Leighton
Leonardo
Logsdail
Macallum
MacNelly
Macquoid
Magritte
Maitland
Mantegna
Mariette
Marshall
Masaccio
Melville
Mondrian
Montalba
Montegna
Muirhead
Mulready
Munnings
Naviasky
Nevinson
Niemeyer
Oliphant
Outcault
Palladio
Paolozzi
Paul Nash
Perugino
Phillips
Pissarro
Pontormo
Redgrave
Reynolds
Richmond
Ricketts
Rirchner
Robinson
Rossetti
Rousseau
Rugendas
Rushbury
Saarinen
Sassetta
Scamozzi
Schinkel
Segonzac
Severini
Simmonds
Solimena
Stanhope
Stothard
Stringer
Sullivan
Terbosch
Tinguely
Topolski
Vanbrugh
Van Goyen
Van Steen
Vasarely
Verbeeck
Veronese
Vlaminck
Waterlow
Westover
Wheatley
Whistler
Willcock
Williams
Woodward
Zakharov
Zurbaran

9

Ackermann
Alexander
Appleyard
Aston Webb
Bakhinzen
Beardsley
Biederman
Bonington
Borromini
Botticini
Branwhite
Canaletto
Carpaccio
Collinson
Constable
Correggio
Delacroix
d'Erlanger
Donaldson
Donatello
Farington
Feininger
Fragonard
Franz Hals
Friedrich
Gastineau
Giorgione
Griffiths
Grunewald
Guido Reni
Guisewite
Halswelle
Hatherell
Hawksmoor
Henderson
Hollander
Honthorst
Hurlstone
Jawlensky
Kandinsky
Kemp-Welch
Kokoschka
Lancaster
Lanfranco
La Thangue
Lee-Hankey
Lightfoot
Louis Wain
MacGregor
MacKennal
Martineau
Maundrell
Mazzolino
McLachlan
McWhirter
Mestrovic
Mondriaan
Nicholson
Nollekens
Northcote
Pisanello
Rembrandt
Salisbury
Sansovino
Schalcken
Singleton
Stanfield
Steenwyck
Stevenson
Strudwick
Thornhill
Velázquez
Verrochio
von Erlach
Waterford
Watterson
Whitcombe

10

Alma-Tadema
Archipenko
Botticelli
Breenbergh
Brockhurst
Burne-Jones

Bushmiller
Caravaggio
Cattermole
Cruikshank
Del Pacchia
di Giovanni
Fiddes-Watt
Friedenson
Fulleylove
Giacometti
Glendening
Hershfield
Hirschfeld
Holman-Hunt
Jan van Eyck
Kennington
La Fresnaye
Lethbridge
Liebermann
Lorenzetti
Mackintosh
McCutcheon
Meissonier
Michelozzo
Modigliani
Onslow Ford
Orchardson
Peppercorn
Pollaiuolo
Richardson
Rowlandson
Saint-Aubin
Sanmicheli
Shackleton
Simon Vonet
Somerville
Spiegelman
Sutherland
Tintoretto
Van de Velde
Van der Goes
Van der Meer
Waterhouse
Winstanley

11
Apollodorus
Butterfield
Churriguera
Copley Heath
Della Robbia
Farquharson
Fra Angelico
Ghirlandaio
Hondecoeter
Le Corbusier
Lloyd Wright
Margaritone
Pickersgill
Poelenburgh
Rippingille
San Severino
Somerscales
Thornycroft
Van der Plaas
Van Ruisdael

12
Brunelleschi
Fantin-Latour
Gainsborough
Grandma Moses
Huchtenburgh
Lichtenstein
Loutherbourg
Michelangelo
Muirhead-Bone
Rauschenberg
Sassoferrato
Sidney Cooper
Spencer Pryse
Van der Weyden
Winterhalter
Witherington

13
de Hondecoeter
Heath Robinson
Hughes-Stanton
Van Ochtervelt

14
de Loutherbourg
Della Francesca
Ford Madox Brown
Gaudier-Brzeska
Haynes-Williams

15 *and over*
Gilbert and George (16)
Leonardo da Vinci (15)
Puvis de Chavannes (16)
Rembrandt van Ryn (15)
Toulouse-Lautrec (15)
Van Huchtenburgh (15)

Bays and Harbours

NB: *St* can also be spelled as *Saint*, which may affect letter counts.

NB: letter counts do not include the words *bay* or *harbour*.
B. = Bay; H = Harbour

Australia
Botany B. (6)
Broken B. (6)
Broughton B. (9)
Bustard B. (7)
Denial B. (6)
Discovery B. (9)
Encounter B. (9)
Geographe B. (9)
Halifax B. (7)
Hermitage B. (9)
Hervey B. (6)
Moreton B. (7)
Port Jackson B. (11)
Portland B. (8)
Port Philip B. (10)
Princess Charlotte B.(17)
Sharks B. (6)
Sydney H. (6)

Baltic Sea
Pomeranian B. (10)

Canada
Baffin B. (6)
Chaleur B. (7)
Conception B. (10)
Fortune B. (7)
Frobisher B. (9)
Fundy B. (5)
Georgian B. (8)
Hudson B. (6)
Mackenzie B. (9)
Notre Dame B. (9)
Placentia B. (9)
St George's B. (9)
Trinity B. (7)

China
Hang-Chow B. (8)

England
Barnstaple B. (10)
Bridgwater B. (10)
Lyme B. (4)
Morecambe B.(9)
Mounts B. (6)
Plymouth H. (8)
Portland H. (8)
Portsmouth H. (10)
Robin Hood's B.(10)
Tees B. (4)
Tor B. (3)
Weymouth B. (8)

France
Biscay, B. of (6)
Quiberon B. (8)

Germany
Heligoland B. (10)
Kiel B. (4)
Lubeck B. (6)

India
Bengal, B. of (6)

Ireland (Republic of)
Bantry B. (6)
Clew B. (4)
Dingle B. (6)
Donegal B. (7)
Dublin B. (6)
Galway B. (6)

Israel
Acre, B. of (4)

Italy
Naples, B. of (6)

Japan
Volcano B. (7)

Mexico
Campeche, B. of (8)

New Zealand
Admiralty B. (9)
Cloudy B. (6)
Evans B. (5)
Hawke B. (5)
Kaipara H. (7)
Otago H. (5)
Pegasus B. (7)
Plenty, B. of (6)
Tasman B. (6)

Scotland
Dundalk B. (7)
Enard B. (5)
Luce B. (4)

South Africa
Algoa B. (5)
Delagoa B. (7)
False B. (5)
Table B. (5)
Walvis B. (6)

South America
St George's B. (9)

USA
Buzzard's B. (8)
Chesapeake B. (10)
Delaware B.(8)
Drake's B. (6)
Galveston B. (9)
San Francisco B. (12)
San Pablo B. (8)

Wales
Cardigan B. (8)
Carmarthen B. (10)
Colwyn B. (6)
St Bride's B. (8)
Tremadoc B. (8)

Bights, Estuaries, Fiords, Firths and Gulfs

NB: letter counts do not include the words *bight, firth*, etc.
Bt = Bight; E. = Estuary; F. = Firth; Fd = Fiord; G. = Gulf

Adriatic Sea
Trieste, G of (7)

Arabian Sea
Arabian G. (7)
Persian G. (7)

Australia
Cambridge G. (9)
Carpentaria, G. of (11)
Great Australian Bt (15)
Spencer's G. (8)
St Vincent G. (9)
Van Diemen G. (9)

Baltic Sea
Finland, G. of (7)

Burma
Martaban, G. of (8)

Canada
Boothia, G. of (6)
St Lawrence, G. of (10)

Central America
Honduras, G. of (8)
Panama, G. of (6)

China
Chi-Li, G. of (5)
Liau-Tung, G. of (8)
Pe-Chi-Li, G. of (7)

Denmark
Ringkøbing Fd (10)

England
Severn E. (6)
Thames E. (6)
Wash (the) (4)

France
St Malo, G. of (6)

Greece
Aegina, G. of (6)
Argolis, G. of (7)
Lepanto, G. of (7)
Salonika, G. of (8)

India
Cambay, G. of (6)
Cutch, G. of (5)
Manaar, G. of (6)

Italy
Cagliari, G. of (8)
Genoa, G. of (5)
Salerno, G. of (7)
Taranto, G. of (7)
Venice, G. of (6)

Latvia
Riga, G. of (4)

Mediterranean
Lions, G. of (5)

Mexico
California, G. of (10)
Mexico, G. of (6)
Tehuantepec, G. of (11)

New Guinea
Papua, G. of (5)

New Zealand
Canterbury Bt (10)

North Africa
Hammamet, G. of (8)
Tunis, G. of (5)

Norway
Christiania Fd (11)

Poland
Danzig, G. of (6)

Red Sea
Aqaba, G. of (5)
Suez, G. of (4)

Russia
Ob, G. of (2)

Scotland
Clyde, F. of (5)
Cromarty F. (8)
Dornoch F. (7)
Forth, F. of (5)
Inverness F. (9)
Lorne, F. of (5)
Moray F. (5)
Pentland F. (8)
Solway F. (6)
Tay, F. of (3)

South America
Darien, G. of (6)
Paria, G. of (5)
San Jorge, G. of (8)
San Matias, G. of (9)
Venezuela, G. of (9)

South China Sea
Siam, G. of (4)
Thailand, G. of (8)
Tongking, G. of (8)
Tonkin, G. of (6)

Sweden
Bothnia, G. of (7)

Turkey
Izmir, G. of (5)
Smyrna, G. of (6)

West Africa
Benin, Bt of (5)
Biafra, Bt of (6)
Guinea, G. of (6)

Books of the Bible

Ap. = Apocrypha; NT = New Testament; OT = Old Testament

3
Job (OT)

4
Amos (OT)
Ezra (OT)
Joel (OT)
John (NT)
Jude (NT)
Luke (NT)
Mark (NT)
Ruth (OT)

5
Hosea (OT)
James (NT)
Jonah (OT)
Kings (OT)
Micah (OT)
Nahum (OT)
Peter (NT)
Titus (NT)
Tobit (Ap.)

6
Baruch (Ap.)
Daniel (OT)
Esdras (Ap.)
Esther (OT, Ap.)
Exodus (OT)
Haggai (OT)
Isaiah (OT)
Joshua (OT)
Judges (OT)
Judith (Ap.)
Psalms (OT)
Romans (OT)
Samuel (OT)
Sirach (Ap.)

7
Ezekiel (OT)
Genesis (OT)
Hebrews (NT)
Malachi (OT)
Matthew (NT)
Numbers (OT)
Obadiah (OT)
Susanna (Ap.)
Timothy (NT)

8
Habakkuk (OT)
Jeremiah (OT)
Nehemiah (OT)
Philemon (NT)
Proverbs (OT)

9
Ephesians (NT)
Galatians (NT)
Leviticus (OT)
Maccabees (Ap.)
Zechariah (OT)
Zephaniah (OT)

10
Chronicles (OT)
Colossians (NT)
Revelation (NT)

11
Corinthians (NT)
Deuteronomy (OT)
Philippians (NT)

12
Ecclesiastes (OT)
Lamentations (OT)

13
Song of Solomon (OT)
Thessalonians (NT)

14 and over
Acts of the Apostles (17) (NT)
Bel and the Dragon (15) (Ap.)
Ecclesiasticus (14) (Ap.)
Epistle of Jeremy (15) (Ap.)
Song of the Three Holy Children (26) (Ap.)
The Prayer of Manasseh (19) (Ap.)
The Wisdom of Solomon (18) (Ap.)

Boxing Weights

9
flyweight

11
heavyweight
lightweight

12
bantamweight
middleweight
welterweight

13
cruiserweight
featherweight

14
light flyweight
super flyweight

16
light heavyweight
super heavyweight
super lightweight

17
junior lightweight
light middleweight
light welterweight
super bantamweight
super middleweight
super welterweight

18
super featherweight

Branches of Study

6
botany
oology
optics
syntax

7
algebra
anatomy
biology
bionics
ecology
history
myology
nealogy
noology
orology
otology
ovology
photics
physics
statics
urology
zoology

8
abiology
aerology
agrology
agronomy
algology
apiology
areology
aretaics
atmology
avionics
axiology
azoology
batology
bryology
cetology
cryology
cynology
cytology
demology
halology
heraldry
kinesics
kinetics
merology
mycology
nidology
oenology
oncology
orthoepy
pedology
penology
polemics
pomology
pyrology
robotics
semitics
serology
sinology
taxonomy
tenology
theology
topology
toponymy
virology
xylology
zymology

9
acarology
adenology
aerometry
aetiology
agriology
ambrology
anemology
angiology
archology
astronomy
audiology
avigation
bionomics
cambistry
carpology
casuistry
chemistry
chorology
cosmology
ctetology
diabology
didactics
dioptrics
economics
emetology
genealogy
helcology
hippology
histology
horometry
hydrology
hygienics
hygrology
hypnology
ichnology
isagogics
koniology
limnology
lithology
logistics
mammalogy
metrology
micrology
momiology
muscology
nephology
neurology
ombrology
ophiology
orthology
osteology
pantology
pathology
petrology
phenology
philology
phonetics
phorology
photology
phytology
pistology
radiology
rhinology
semantics
semiotics
sindology
sociology
tectonics
teleology

10
actinology
aerography
aerolitics
aesthetics
agmatology
antinology
arthrology
astrognosy
autecology
ballistics
bibliology
bibliotics
bioecology
biostatics
cacogenics
cardiology
caricology
catoptrics
chrysology
codicology
conchology
crustalogy
cryogenics
demography
demonology
dendrology
deontology
echinology
Egyptology
heparology
hepatology
herniology
heterology
hydraulics
iamatology
kinematics
lexicology
malacology
metaethics
metallurgy
miasmology
mineralogy
morphology
morphonomy
neontology
neossology
nephrology
obstetrics
odontology
oneirology
onomastics
organology
orthoptics
oryctology
paedeutics
palaeology
pasimology
pathognomy
pelycology
phaenology
philosophy
phletology
phyllotaxy
physiology
pneumology
ponerology
potamology
praxeology
proctology
psephology
psychiatry
psychology
pyretology
selenology
somatology
sophiology
speleology
spongology
sumerology
synecology
teratology
theoretics
toxicology
trichology
trophology
typhlology
urbanology
zenography
zoobiology

11
aeronautics
aerophysics
aerostatics
agrobiology

agrogeology
agrostology
alethiology
allergology
apologetics
arachnology
archaeology
Assyriology
astrogation
autoecology
biodynamics
cartography
cecidiology
chondrology
Christology
climatology
cliometrics
coccidology
criminology
cybernetics
dactylology
dermatology
diagnostics
dipterology
eccrinology
hagiography
herpetology
hippiatrics
hydroponics
hyetography
hypsography
hysterology
ichthyology
insectology
laryngology
lichenology
linguistics
mathematics
mensuration
metaphysics
meteoritics
meteorology
methodology
metoposcopy
myrmecology
neonatology
olfactology
ornithology
orthography
paediatrics
paedogogics
pedodontics
perastadics
physiognomy
pteridology
siagonology
sphagnology
sphygmology
stomatology
telmatology
thanatology
uranography
uredinology
venereology
vexillology
viticulture
volcanology

12

aerodynamics
alimentology
ampelography
amphibiology
anthoecology
anthropogeny
anthropology
astrogeology
astronautics
astrophysics
bacteriology
bibliography
biochemistry
biogeography
chromatology
cryptography
desmidiology
ecclesiology
hamartiology
hermeneutics
horticulture
hydrogeology
hydrostatics
liturgiology
macrobiotics
microbiology
oceanography
orthodontics
orthopaedics
osmonosology
palaeobotany
palaeography
paroemiology
periodontics
petrogenesis
pharmacology
pharyngology
physiography
phytobiology
protozoology
seismography
stratigraphy
syndesmology
testaceology
thaumatology
traumatology
trigonometry
zoogeography
zoopathology
zoophytology

13

aerolithology
anthropometry
biophysiology
biotechnology
chrematistics
crustaceology
cytochemistry
dactylography
diplomatology
emblematology
helminthology
hemipterology
hydrodynamics
hydrokinetics
lalopathology
ophthalmology
palaeobiology
palaeoecology
palaeontology
palaeozoology
photodynamics
psychotherapy
radiogenetics
splanchnology
stirpiculture
thermostatics
thremmatology
zoophysiology
zoopsychology

14

aeroballistics
anthropography
archaeogeology
architectonics
astrolithology
bioclimatology
biolinguistics
cardiodynamics
cinematography
coleopterology
cytotechnology
desmopathology
electrobiology
hippopathology
hydromechanics
iatrochemistry
immunogenetics
neuropterology
orthopterology
otolaryngology
palaeopedology
parapsychology
phytogeography
thalassography
thermodynamics

15

bioastronautics
cardioangiology
hymenopterology
lepidopterology
metalinguistics
metamathematics
neuropsychiatry
orthopsychiatry
palaeoethnology
palaeogeography
palaeomammalogy
palaeopathology
psychopathology
thermogeography

16

dendrochronology
palaeornithology
thermokinematics

17

anthropogeography

anthroposociology
palaeoichthyology
psychodiagnostics
psycholinguistics

18
psychopharmacology

British Prime Ministers

4
Bute, Lord
Eden, Sir Anthony
Grey, Lord
Peel, Sir Robert
Pitt, William (Pitt the Younger)

5
Blair, Tony
Derby, Lord
Heath, Edward
Major, John
North, Lord

6
Attlee, Clement
Pelham, Henry
Wilson, Sir Harold

7
Asquith, Herbert
Baldwin, Stanley
Balfour, Arthur
Canning, George
Chatham, Lord (Pitt the Elder)
Grafton, Duke of
Russell, Lord John
Walpole, Sir Robert

8
Aberdeen, Lord
Bonar Law, Andrew
Disraeli, Benjamin
Goderich, Lord
Perceval, Spencer
Portland, Duke of
Rosebery, Lord
Thatcher, Margaret

9
Addington, Henry
Callaghan, James
Churchill, Sir Winston
Gladstone, William
Grenville, George
Grenville, Lord
Liverpool, Lord
MacDonald, Ramsay
Macmillan, Harold
Melbourne, Lord
Newcastle, Duke of
Salisbury, Marquis of
Shelburne, Lord

10
Devonshire, Duke of
Palmerston, Lord
Rockingham, Marquis of
Wellington, Duke of
Wilmington, Lord

11 and over
Beaconsfield, Lord (12)
Campbell-Bannerman, Sir Henry (17)
Chamberlain, Neville (11)
Douglas-Home, Sir Alec (11)
Lloyd George, David (11)

Business, Commerce and Economics

2
A1
CA
EU
FT

3
bid
buy
COD
cut
Dow
DTI
dun
ECU
EEC
EMU
fee
f.o.b.
GDP
GNP
IMF
job
lot
Ltd
net
owe
par
pay
PIN
plc
rig
sum
tax
tip
VAT
WTO

4
back
bail
bank
bear
bill
bond
boom
bull
bust
call
cash
cess
chip
City (the)
coin
cost
deal
dear
debt
deed
dole
dues
dump
duty
earn
easy
EFTA
euro
even
fine
firm
fisc
free
FTSE
fund
gain
GATT
gild
gilt
giro
glut
gold
good
hire

idle
lend
levy
lien
loan
long
loss
mart
mint
nett
note
OPEC
owed
paid
PAYE
poll
pool
post
PSBR
puff
punt
ramp
rate
real
rent
ring
risk
sale
scot
sell
sink
sold
spot
stag
tare
term
turn
vend
wage

5
agent
angel
asset
at par
audit
award
batch
bid up
block
board
bonds
bonus
books
brand
bribe
buyer
buy in
buy up
by-law
cargo
cheap
check
chips
clear
clerk
costs
cover
crash
cycle
debit
draft
entry
ex cap.
ex div.
float
folio
funds
gilts
goods
gross
hedge
House
index
issue
lease
limit
money
notes
offer
order
owing
panic
paper
payee
payer
plant
pound
price
proxy
quota
quote
rally
rates
remit
repay
rider
score
scrip
share
shark
short
sight
slump
stock
talon
taxes
tight
tithe
token
trade
trend
trust
usury
value
wages
worth
yield

6
accept
accrue
advice
agency
amount
assets
assign
at cost
avails
bailee
bailor
banker
barter
bearer
borrow
bought
bounce
bounty
bourse
branch
broker
bubble
budget
burden
buying
buy out
by-laws
cartel
change
charge
cheque
client
corner
coupon
credit
crisis
cum. div.
dealer
deal in
debtor
defray
demand
dicker
docket
dot.com
drawee
drawer
equity
estate
excise
expend
export
factor
figure
fiscal
freeze
go down
growth
hammer
holder
honour
import
in cash
income
in debt
indent
insure
jobber
job lot
labour
ledger
lender
liable
liquid
Lloyd's
lock-up
margin
market
mark-up
mature
merger
minute
mutual
nem. con.
Nikkei
notice
office
on call
on cost
one-off
option
outbid
outlay
outlet
output
packet
parity
pay day
paying
pay-off
pay out
pledge
plunge
policy
profit
public
punter
quango
quorum
racket
rating
realty
rebate
recoup
redeem
refund
remedy
rental
report
resale
retail
return
salary
sample
save up
saving
sell in
sell up
set off
settle
shares
shorts
silver
simony
specie
spiral
spread
staple
stocks
strike
supply
surety
surtax
tariff
taxman
teller
tender
ticket
trader
unload
unpaid
usance
usurer
valuta
vendor
vendue
volume
wampan
wealth
wind up

7
account
actuary
advance
allonge
annuity
arrears
at sight
auction
auditor

average
backing
bad debt
balance
banking
bank run
bargain
bidding
bonanza
bullion
buy back
buydown
cambist
capital
cashier
ceiling
certify
chamber
charter
company
consols
convert
crossed
customs
cut-rate
damages
day book
dealing
declare
default
deficit
deflate
deposit
douceur
draw out
dumping
duopoly
economy
embargo
endorse
engross
entrust
ex bonus
expense
exploit
exports
ex works
factory
failure
fall due
finance
flutter
forward
freight
funding
futures
gearing
haulage
hedging
holding
imports
imprest
indorse
inflate
in funds
insured
interim
invoice
jobbers
jobbing
killing
lay days
leasing
lending
limited
lockout
lottery
lump sum
manager
mint par
minutes
name day
nest egg
net gain
no funds
nomimal
on offer
on order
package
partner
payable
pay cash
payment
payroll
pay slip
pension
per cent
pre-empt
premium
prepaid
pricing
product
profits
promote
pro rata
pyramid
realize
receipt
reissue
renewal
reserve
returns
revenue
rigging
royalty
salvage
selling
sell-out
service
sold out
solvent
squeeze
stipend
storage
subsidy
surplus
swindle
takings
tax-free
tonnage
trade in
trading
traffic
trustee
utility
vending
venture
war bond
war loan
warrant
way bill
write up
year end

8

above par
acceptor
accounts
act of God
after tax
agiotage
amortize
antedate
appraise
assignee
assigner
auditing
back bond
bailment
bank bill
bankbook
bank giro
bank loan
banknote
bank rate
bankrupt
barratry
basic pay
below par
berthage
blue chip
book debt
borrower
bottomry
business
buying in
carriage
cashbook
cash down
cash flow
cash sale
clearing
commerce
consumer
contango
contract
creditor
credit to
cum bonus
currency
customer
cut-price
dealings
defrayed
delivery
director
disburse
discount
dividend
Dow Jones
drawings
dry goods
earnings
embezzle
employee
employer
emporium
endorsee
endorser
entrepot
equities
estimate
evaluate
exchange
ex gratia
expenses
exporter
ex rights
feedback
finances
flat rate
goodwill
gratuity
hallmark
hammered
hard cash
hard sell
importer
increase
indebted
industry
interest
in the red
investor
lame duck
manifest
mark down
markings
maturing
maturity
merchant
monetary
monetize
monopoly
mortgage
net price
novation
on credit
on demand
on strike

operator
ordinary
overhead
overtime
par value
passbook
poundage
price cut
price war
proceeds
producer
property
purchase
receipts
receiver
recovery
reinvest
reserves
retailer
retainer
scarcity
schedule
security
shipment
sideline
sinecure
solvency
spending
spot cash
sterling
straddle
supertax
swindler
takeover
taxation
tax dodge
tax haven
taxpayer
trade gap
transfer
Treasury
turnover
undercut
unquoted
variable
wage rate
warranty
windfall
write off

9

actuarial
ad valorem
aggregate
allotment
allowance
annuitant
ante-dated
anti-trust
appraisal
appraiser
arbitrage
arrearage
assurance
averaging
bank stock
bilateral
blank bill
book value
bordereau
borrowing
brokerage
by-product
call money
call price
carry over
certified
chartered
clearance
commodity
cost price
cum rights
debenture
debit card
debit note
deck cargo
deduction
defaulter
deflation
demurrage
depletion
depositor
dishonour
easy money
easy terms
economics
economies
economist
economize
emolument
endowment
exchequer
executive
extortion
face value
fair price
fair trade
fiat money
fiduciary
financial
financier
fine paper
firm offer
firm price
first call
first cost
flotation
franchise
free trade
fully paid
garnishee
gilt-edged
globalism
going rate
guarantee
guarantor
hard money
import tax
in arrears
incentive
income tax
indemnify
indemnity
indenture
inflation
insolvent
insurance
inventory
leasehold
liability
liquidate
liquidity
list price
long-dated
mail order
marketing
middleman
mortgagee
mortgagor
near money
negotiate
net income
order book
outgoings
overdraft
overdrawn
overheads
packaging
paymaster
pecuniary
petty cash
piecework
PIN number
portfolio
post-dated
preferred
price list
price rise
prime cost
principal
privatize
profiteer
promotion
purchaser
put option
quittance
quotation
ratepayer
ready cash
recession
redundant
reflation
reimburse
repayable
repayment
resources
restraint
reversion
royalties
sell short
shift work
short bill
shortfall
short time
sight bill
slush fund
speculate
spot price
stamp duty
statement

stock list
stockpile
subscribe
subsidize
surcharge
syndicate
tax return
ticket day
trade fair
trademark
trade name
tradesman
treasurer
undersell
unit trust
utilities
valuation
vendition
viability
wage claim
warehouse
wealth tax
wholesale
winding up
work force
work sheet
work study
World Bank

10

acceptance
accountant
account day
accounting
accumulate
active bond
adjustment
advice note
appreciate
assessment
assignment
attachment
auctioneer
automation
average out
bank credit
bank return
bankruptcy
bearer bond
bear market
bill broker
bill of sale
block grant
bondholder
bonus issue
bonus share
bookkeeper
bucket shop
bulk buying
bull market
calculator
call option
capitalism
capitalist
capitalize
capitation
chain store
chequebook
closed shop
collateral
colporteur
commercial
commission
compensate
competitor
consortium
conversion
credit bank
credit card
credit note
credit slip
cumulative
defalcator
del credere
depreciate
depression
deregulate
direct cost
dirty money
drawn bonds
elasticity
employment
encumbered
engrossing
evaluation
excise duty
ex dividend
first offer
fiscal year
fixed costs
fixed price
fixed trust
floor price
forwarding
free market
funded debt
gross value
ground rent
growth area
honorarium
import duty
income bond
indexation
industrial
insolvency
instalment
in the black
investment
joint stock
lighterage
liquidator
living wage
long period
loss leader
management
marked down
marketable
mass market
mercantile
monetarism
monetarist
money order
monopolize
moratorium
negotiable
non-payment
no par value
note of hand
obligation
open cheque
open credit
opening bid
open market
open policy
option rate
overcharge
paper money
pawnbroker
percentage
plough back
pre-emption
preference
prepayment
price index
production
profitable
profits tax
prospector
prospectus
prosperity
prosperous
provide for
purchasing
pure profit
pyramiding
quarter day
ready money
real estate
real income
recompense
redeemable
redemption
redundancy
remittance
remunerate
rock bottom
sales force
scrip issue
second-hand
securities
selling day
selling out
settlement
serial bond
share index
short bonds
short-dated
sole agency
speculator
statistics
stockpiles
stock split
subscriber
tax evasion
ticker tape
tight money
trade cycle
trade price
trade union
ultra vires

underwrite
unemployed
upset price
wage freeze
Wall Street
wholesaler
working day
work to rule
written off

11

accountancy
account book
acquittance
advance note
advertising
arbitration
asking price
auction ring
auction sale
average bond
bank account
bank balance
bank of issue
bear squeeze
beneficiary
big business
billionaire
bill of entry
bimetallism
black market
blank cheque
bonded goods
bonus scheme
bookkeeping
budget price
businessman
capital gain
cash account
central bank
certificate
circulation
commitments
commodities
common stock
competition
competitive
consignment
consumption
convergence
co-operative
corporation
counterfeit
cum dividend
customs duty
days of grace
death duties
demand curve
demand draft
demutualize
deposit rate
deposit slip
devaluation
discounting
dishonoured
distributor
dividend tax
double-entry
down payment
endorsement
expenditure
fixed assets
fixed charge
fixed income
fluctuation
foreclosure
free on board
freight note
Gresham's Law
gross income
high finance
hypothecate
income stock
indirect tax
industrials
issuing bank
job analysis
joint return
labour force
legal tender
liquidation
loan capital
manufacture
market overt
market price
mass-produce
merchandise
middle price
millionaire
minimum wage
money lender
money market
money supply
nationalize
negotiation
net interest
net receipts
open account
option price
outstanding
overpayment
overtrading
package deal
partnership
pay on demand
point of sale
postal order
poverty line
premium bond
price fixing
price freeze
property tax
purchase tax
Queer Street
raw material
realization
reinsurance
reserve bank
restructure
revaluation
rights issue
risk capital
safe deposit
sales ledger
savings bank
sell forward
shareholder
single-entry
sinking fund
small trader
sold forward
speculation
stagflation
stakeholder
stockbroker
stockjobber
stock market
stockpiling
stocktaking
subsistence
supermarket
syndicalism
take-home pay
takeover bid
time deposit
transaction
undercharge
undervalued
underwriter
with profits

12

above the line
account payee
ad valorem tax
amalgamation
amortization
appreciation
assembly line
balance sheet
banker's draft
banker's order
bargain price
below the line
bilateralism
bill of lading
board meeting
Board of Trade
bond creditor
bonded stores
bottomry bond
branch office
bridging loan
buyer's market
callable bond
capital gains
capital goods
capital stock
carrying over
carry over day
cash and carry
caveat emptor
charter party
clearing bank
closing price
common market
compensation
contract note
cost of living
credit rating

current price
current ratio
customs union
deflationary
denomination
depreciation
deregulation
differential
direct labour
disbursement
discount rate
disinflation
distribution
Dutch auction
earned income
econometrics
economy drive
embezzlement
entrepreneur
exchange rate
export credit
first refusal
fiscal policy
fixed capital
floating debt
frozen assets
going concern
gold standard
hard currency
hire purchase
indirect cost
inflationary
interest rate
invoice clerk
irredeemable
joint account
keep accounts
labour market
laissez-faire
life interest
liquid assets
manufacturer
marginal cost
mass-produced
maturity date
mercantilism
merchant bank
mixed economy
monetization
money changer
national bank
national debt
nearest offer
nominal price
nominal value
official list
opening price
overcapacity
pay as you earn
pay in advance
paying-in-slip
policy holder
present worth
price ceiling
price control
price current
price rigging
productivity
profiteering
profit margin
profit motive
profit taking
public sector
rate of growth
raw materials
receivership
redeployment
remuneration
remunerative
reserve price
rig the market
rising prices
running costs
sale or return
sales manager
salesmanship
severance pay
share capital
shareholding
share options
sliding scale
social credit
soft currency
specie points
statistician
sterling area
stock in trade
stockjobbery
stockjobbing
surplus value
tax avoidance
tax collector
tax exemption
terms of trade
tiger economy
trade balance
trade deficit
trading stamp
transfer deed
treasury bill
treasury bond
treasury note
trial balance
trustee stock
underwriting
unemployment
valued policy
welfare state
works council

13

acceptilation
allotment note
appropriation
articled clerk
average clause
backwardation
bank statement
blank transfer
bullion market
business cycle
clearing house
consumer goods
contract curve
credit account
credit control
credit squeeze
crossed cheque
current assets
discount house
dividend yield
dollar premium
Dow-Jones index
exchequer bill
financial year
free trade area
free trade zone
futures market
globalization
gross receipts
guarantee fund
incomes policy
interim report
issued capital
livery company
Lombard Street
long-dated bill
making-up price
non-cumulative
not negotiable
ordinary share
outside broker
overhead price
paid-up capital
par of exchange
participating
premium income
private sector
privatization
profitability
profit sharing
public company
quota sampling
rateable value
restructuring
sales forecast
settlement day
share transfer
silent partner
specification
Stock Exchange
switch selling
taxable income
trade discount
value added tax
vendor's shares
wasting assets
wheeler-dealer
works councils

14

account current
advance freight
apprenticeship
balance of trade
bearer security
bill of exchange
blocked account
break-even point
bureau de

change
capital account
capital gearing
capitalization
consumer credit
convertibility
corporation tax
current account
current balance
debenture stock
decimalization
deferred rebate
deferred shares
deposit account
discount market
economic growth
featherbedding
Federal Reserve
fiduciary issue
finance company
floating charge
founders' shares
fringe benefits
full employment
garnishee order
general average
general manager
half-commission
holder for value
holding company
hyperinflation
infrastructure
inscribed stock
invisible trade
joint stock bank
letter of credit
limited company
liquidity ratio
Lloyd's Register
loan conversion
macroeconomics
managing agents
market research
microeconomics
monthly account
mortgage broker
new issue market
nominal capital
option dealings
ordinary shares
oversubscribed
preferred stock
progress chaser
promissory note
quality control
random sampling
rate of exchange
rate of interest
receiving order
revenue account
short-term gains
social security
superannuation
surrender value
trading account
uberrimae fidei
unearned income
working capital

15

average adjuster
bonded warehouse
building society
capital employed
commission agent
consignment note
dividend warrant
entrepreneurial
exchange control
ex-gratia payment
foreign exchange
golden handshake
interim dividend
investment trust
labour-intensive
liquidity ratios
marine insurance
multilateralism
nationalization
non-contributory
political science
preference bonds
preference share
preference stock
preferred shares
public ownership
public relations
purchasing power
rationalization
redemption yield
reducing balance
secured creditor
sleeping partner
sterling balance
unissued capital

Capes, Points, Headlands and Peninsulas

NB: letter counts do not include the words *cape, head*, etc.
C. = Cape; Hd = Head; Pen. = Peninsula; Pt = Point

Antarctic
Antarctic Pen. (9)

Arctic
Thorsden, C. (8)
Washington, C. (10)

Asia
Arabia (6)
Arabian Pen. (7)
Indo-China (9)

Australia
Adieu, C. (5)
Barren, C. (6)
Bauer, C. (5)
Blanche C. (6)
Bridewater, C. (10)
Byron, C. (5)
Catastrophe, C. (11)
Claremont Pt (9)
Coffin Bay Pen. (9)
Cuvier, C. (6)
Eyre Pen. (4)
Howe, C. (4)
Leeuwin, C. (7)
Melville, C. (Austral.) (8)
Northumberland, C. (14)
Otway, C. (5)
Palmerston, C. (10)
Sand Patch Pt (9)
Sandy C. (5)
Sidmouth, C. (8)
Slade Pt (5)
Sorell, C. (6)
Tribulation, C. (11)
Upstart, C. (7)
Wiles, C. (5)
York, C. (4)
Yorke Pen. (5)

Brazil
Frio, C. (4)
Maranhão, C. (8)
São Roque, C. (8)
São Tome, C. (7)

Bulgaria
Kaliakra, C. (8)

Burma
Negrais, C. (7)
Tavoy Pt (5)

Canada
Bathurst, C. (8)
Bonavista, C. (9)
Breton, C. (6)
Breakheart Pt (10)
Clark Pt (5)
East Pt (4)
Esquimaux, C. (9)
Fogo, C. (4)
Gaspé C. (5)
Gaspé Pen. (5)
Gregory, C. (7)
Icy C. (3)
Labrador (8)
Murchison C . (9)
Race, C. (4)
Roxo, C. (4)
Sable, C. (5)
St Francis, C. (9)
St George, C. (8)
St Margaret Pt (10)
St Mary, C. (6)
Sambro, C. (6)
Snettisham Pt (10)
Walsingham, C. (10)

Central America
Blanco, C. (6)
Gracias a Dios, C. (12)

China
South C. (5)
Yang-tsi, C. (7)

Corsica
Corso, C. (5)

Crete
Busa, C. (4)
Krio, C. (4)
Sidero, C. (6)

Croatia
Istria (6)
Istrian Pen. (7)

East Africa
Amber, C. (5)
Cayenne Pt (7)

Egypt
Sinai Pen. (5)

England
Ayre Pt (4)
Beachy Hd (6)
Cornwall, C. (8)
Dodman Pt (6)
Dungeness (9)
Flamborough Hd (11)
Foreland (the) (8)
Formby Hd (6)
Hartland Pt (8)
Land's End (8)
Lizard (the) (6)
Lizard Pen. (6)
Lizard Pt (6)
Naze (the) (4)
Needles (the) (7)
North Foreland (13)
Orford Ness (10)
Portland Bill (12)
Prawle Pt (6)
St Albans Hd (8)
St Bees Hd (6)
Selsey Bill (10)
Spurn Hd (5)
Start Pt (5)
Wirral (6)

Europe
Balkan Pen. (6)
Iberian Pen. (7)
Scandinavia (11)

France
De Talbert Pt (9)
Gris-Nez, C. (7)
La Hague, C. (7)
St Gilda's Pt (8)
St Matthieu Pt (10)

Greece
Colonna, C. (7)
Gallo, C. (5)
Malia, C. (5)
Matapan, C. (7)
Peloponnese (11)

Greenland
Bismark, C. (7)
Farewell, C. (8)

Haiti
Haitien, C. (7)

India
Comorin, C. (7)
Palmyras Pt. (8)

Indonesia
Bantam, C. (6)

Ireland (Republic of)
Béara Pen. (5)
Clare, C. (5)
Clogher Hd (7)
Dingle Pen. (6)
Galley Hd (6)
Greenore Pt (8)
Inishowen Hd (9)
Loop Hd (4)
Sheep Hd (5)
Slea Hd (4)
Slyne Hd (5)
Streedagh Pt (9)

Israel
Carmel, C. (6)

Italy
Bizzuto, C. (7)
Nao, C. (3)
Vaticano, C. (8)

Japan
Kataska, C. (7)
King, C. (4)
Patience, C. (8)
Sima, C. (4)
Soya, C. (4)
Yerimo, C. (6)

Malaysia
Romania, C. (7)

Mexico
San Antonio Pt (10)
San Lucas, C. (8)
Tegupan Pt (7)
Yucatán Pen. (7)

New Zealand
Castle Pt (6)
East C. (4)
Egmont, C. (6)
Farewell, C. (8)
North C. (5)
Palliser, C. (8)
Runaway C. (7)

North Africa
Blanco, C. (6)
Bon, C. (3)
Spartel, C. (7)
Wad Nun, C. (6)

Northern Ireland
Bengore Hd (7)
Downpatrick Hd (11)
Fairhead, C. (8)

Norway
Naze (the) (4)
Nord, C. (4)
North C. (5)

Philippines
Bataan Pen. (6)

Portugal
Carvoeira, C. (9)
De Roca, C. (6)
De Sines C. (7)
Espicher, C. (8)
Mondego, C. (7)
St Vincent, C. (9)
Santa Maria, C. (10)

Russia
Aniva, C. (5)
Kola Pen. (4)
Yakan, C. (5)

Sardinia
Comino, C. (6)
Teulada, C. (7)

Scotland
Aird Pt (4)
Arisaig Pt (7)
Ardnamurchan Pen. (12)
Ardnamurchan Pt (12)
Brims Ness (9)
Buddon Ness (10)
Burrow Hd (6)
Burrow Pt (6)
Duncansbay Hd (10)
Dunnet Hd (6)
Farr Pt (4)
Fife Ness (8)
Gallon Hd (6)
Greenstone Pt (10)
Hoe Pt (3)
Kinnaird Hd (8)
Noss Hd (4)
Rattray Hd (7)
Rhynns Pt (6)
Roray Hd (5)
St Abb's Hd (6)
Sanaig Pt (6)
Sleat Pt (5)
Strathy Pt (7)
Sumburgh Hd (8)
Tarbat Ness (10)
Toe Hd (3)
Tolsta Hd (6)
Troup Hd (5)
Turn Ness (8)

Vaternish Pt (9)
Whiten Hd (6)
Wrath, C. (5)

Sicily
Granitola, C. (9)
Milazzo, C. (7)
Orlando, C. (7)
Santo Vito, C. (9)

South Africa
Agulhas, C. (7)
Good Hope, C. of (8)
Hangklip, C. (8)
Murraysburg, C. (11)
Quoin Pt (5)
Recife, C. (6)
St Lucia, C. (7)
Sordwana Pt (8)

South America
Andres Pt (6)
Cruz, C. (4)
Gallinas Pt (8)
Horn, C. (4)
Rayes Pt (5)
San Diego, C. (8)
San Francisco, C. (12)
San Lorenzo, C. (10)
Sur Pt (3)

Spain
Creus, C. (5)
De Gata, C. (6)
De Palos, C. (7)
De Penas, C. (7)
De San Adrian, C. (11)
Finisterre, C. (10)
Ortegal, C. (7)
Tarifa, C. (6)
Trafalgar, C. (9)

Tasmania
Sandy C. (5)

Thailand
Cambodia Pt (8)

Turkey
Baba, C. (4)
Glossa, C. (6)

Ukraine
Crimea (6)

USA
Ann, C. (3)
Canaveral, C. (9)
Charles C. (7)
Cod, C. (5)
Conception Pt (10)
Fear, C. (4)
Flattery, C. (8)
Florida (7)
Friars Pt (6)
Girardeau, C. (9)
Hatteras, C. (8)
Kennedy, C. (7)
May, C. (3)
Mendocino C. (9)
Sable, C. (5)
San Blas, C. (7)
Vincent, C. (7)
Sur Pt (3)

Vietnam
San Ho, C. (5)

Wales
Great Ormes Hd (10)
Gower Pen. (5)
Little Ormes Hd (11)
Lleyn Pen. (5)
Mumbles Hd (7)
Nash Pt (4)
Orme's Hd (5)
St David's Hd (8)
St Gowan's Hd (8)
Strumble Hd (8)
Worms Hd (5)

West Africa
Formosa C. (7)
Frio, C. (4)
Lopez C. (5)
Mirik, C. (5)
Negro, C. (5)
Nun, C. (3)
Palmas, C. (6)
St Paul, C. (6)
Three Points, C. (11)
Verde, C. (5)

Capital Cities

* = former

4
Aden* (Yemen)
Apia (Samoa)
Baku (Azerbaijan)
Bern (Switzerland)
Bonn* (Germany)
Dili (East Timor)
Doha (Qatar)
Kiev (Ukraine)
Lima (Peru)
Lomé (Togo)
Malé (Maldives)
Nuuk (Greenland)
Oslo (Norway)
Riga (Latvia)
Rome (Italy)
Suva (Fiji)
Vila (Vanuatu)

5
Abuja (Nigeria)
Accra (Ghana)
Agaña (Guam)
Ajman (Ajman)
Amman (Jordan)
Berne (Switzerland)
Cairo (Egypt)
Dacca (Bangladesh)
Dakar (Senegal)
Delhi (India)
Dubai (Dubai)
Hanoi (Vietnam)
Kabul (Afghanistan)

Koror (Belau)
Lagos* (Nigeria)
La Paz (Bolivia)
Minsk (Belarus)
Paris (France)
Praia (Cape Verde Is.)
Quito (Ecuador)
Rabat (Morocco)
Sana'a (Yemen)
Seoul (South Korea)
Sofia (Bulgaria)
Sucre (Bolivia)
Tokyo (Japan)
Tunis (Tunisia)
Vaduz (Liechtenstein)
Yaren (Nauru)

6

Akmola (Kazakhstan)
Almaty* (Kazakhstan)
Ankara (Turkey)
Aqmola (Kazakhstan)
Asmara (Eritrea)
Astana* (Kazakhstan)
Athens (Greece)
Bagdad (Iraq)
Bamako (Mali)
Bangui (Central African Republic)
Banjul (Gambia)
Beirut (Lebanon)
Berlin (Germany)
Bissau (Guinea-Bissau)
Bogotá (Colombia)
Brunei (Brunei)
Dodoma (Tanzania)
Dublin (Republic of Ireland)
Havana (Cuba)
Harare (Zimbabwe)
Hobart (Tasmania)
Kigali (Rwanda)
Lisbon (Portugal)
London (England, UK)
Luanda (Angola)
Lusaka (Zambia)
Madrid (Spain)
Majuro (Marshall Is.)
Malabo (Equatorial Guinea)
Manama (Bahrain)
Manila (Philippines)
Maputo (Mozambique)
Maseru (Lesotho)
Masqat (Oman)
Moroni (Comoros)
Moscow (Russia)
Muscat (Oman)
Nassau (Bahamas)
Niamey (Niger)
Ottawa (Canada)
Peking (China)
Prague (Czech Republic)
Riyadh (Saudi Arabia)
Roseau (Dominica)
Saigon* (Vietnam)
Skopje (Macedonia)
Taipei (Taiwan)
Tarawa (Kiribati)
Tehran (Iran)
Tirana (Albania)
Valley (Anguilla)
Vienna (Austria)
Warsaw (Poland)
Zagreb (Croatia)

7

Abidjan* (Ivory Coast)
Algiers (Algeria)
Alma-Ata* (Kazakhstan)
Baghdad (Iraq)
Bangkok (Thailand)
Beijing (China)
Belfast (Northern Ireland)
Bishkek (Kyrgystan)
Caracas (Venezuela)
Chisnau (Moldova)
Colombo (Sri Lanka)
Conakry (Guinea)
Cotonou (Benin)
Douglas (Isle of Man)
El Aaiun (Western Sahara)
Honiara (Solomon Is.)
Jakarta (Indonesia)
Kampala (Uganda)
Managua (Nicaragua)
Mbabane (Swaziland)
Nairobi (Kenya)
Nicosia (Cyprus)
Palermo (Sicily)
Rangoon (Burma)
St John's (Antigua)
San José (Costa Rica)
São Tomé (São Tomé and Principe)
Sharjah (Sharjah)
Stanley (Falkland Is.)
Tallinn (Estonia)
Teheran (Iran)
Tbilisi (Georgia)
Thimphu (Bhutan)
Tripoli (Libya)
Valetta (Malta)
Vatican (Vatican)
Vilnius (Lithuania)
Yaoundé (Cameroun)
Yerevan (Armenia)

8

Abu Dhabi (UAE)
Ashgabat (Turkmenistan)
Asunción (Paraguay)
Belmopan (Belize)
Belgrade (Serbia)
Brasilia (Brazil)
Brussels (Belgium)
Budapest (Hungary)
Canberra (Australia)
Cape Town (South Africa)
Castries (St Lucia)
Damascus (Syria)
Djakarta (Indonesia)
Djibouti (Djibouti)
Dushanbe (Tajikistan)
Freetown (Sierra Leone)
Fujairah (Fujairah)
Funafuti (Tuvalu)
Gaborone (Botswana)
Hamilton (Bermuda)
Helsinki (Finland)
Honolulu (Hawaii)
Istanbul* (Turkey)

Katmandu (Nepal)
Khartoum (Sudan)
Kingston (Jamaica)
Kinshasa (Democratic Republic of the Congo)
Kishinev (Moldova)
La Habana (Cuba)
Lilongwe (Malawi)
Monrovia (Liberia)
N'Djamena (Chad)
New Delhi (India)
Plymouth (Montserrat)
Pretoria (South Africa)
St Helier (Jersey)
Santiago (Chile)
Sarajevo (Bosnia and Herzegovina)
Tashkent (Uzbekistan)
Titograd* (Montenegro)
Tórshavn (Faroe Is.)
Valletta (Malta)
Victoria (Seychelles)
Windhoek (Namibia)

9

Amsterdam (Netherlands)
Ashkhabad (Turkmenistan)
Bucharest (Romania)
Bujumbura (Burundi)
Edinburgh (Scotland)
Gaberones (Botswana)
Grand Turk (Turks and Caicos Is.)
Islamabad (Pakistan)
Jamestown (St Helena)
Jerusalem (Israel)
Kathmandu (Nepal)
Kingstown (St Vincent)
Ljubliana (Slovenia)
Macao City (Macao)
Mogadishu (Somalia)
Nuku'alofa (Tonga)
Phnom Penh (Cambodia)
Podgorica (Montenegro)
Port Louis (Mauritius)
Porto Novo (Benin)
Pyongyang (North Korea)
Reykjavik (Iceland)
St George's (Grenada)
San Marino (San Marino)
Singapore (Singapore)
Stockholm (Sweden)
Thorshavn (Faroe Is.)
Ulan Bator (Mongolia)
Vientiane (Laos)

10

Addis Ababa (Ethiopia)
Basseterre (St Kitts and Nevis)
Belize City* (Belize)
Basseterre (St Christopher-Nevis-Anguilla)
Bratislava (Slovakia)
Bridgetown (Barbados)
Brunei City* (Brunei)
Copenhagen (Denmark)
Georgetown (Cayman Is., Guyana)
Kuwait City (Kuwait)
Libreville (Gabon)
Luxembourg (Luxembourg)
Mexico City (Mexico)
Montevideo (Uruguay)
Nouakchott (Mauritania)
Ougadougou (Burkina Faso)
Panama City (Panama)
Paramaribo (Surinam)
Quezon City* (Philippines)
Tananarive* (Madagascar)
Wellington (New Zealand)

11

Brazzaville (Congo)
Buenos Aires (Argentina)
Dar es Salaam* (Tanzania)
Kuala Lumpur (Malaysia)
Monaco-Ville (Monaco)
Port Moresby (Papua New Guinea)
Port of Spain (Trinidad and Tobago)
St Peter Port (Guernsey)
San Salvador (El Salvador)
Tegucigalpa (Honduras)
Ulaanbaatar (Mongolia)
Vatican City (Vatican City)

12

Antananarivo (Madagascar)
Bloemfontein (South Africa)
Cockburn Town (Turks and Caicos Is.)
Port-au-Prince (Haiti)
Ras al-Khaimah (Ras al-Khaimah)
Santo Domingo (Dominican Republic)
Umm al-Qaiwain (Umm al-Qaiwain)
Washington DC (USA)

Yamoussoukro (Ivory Coast)

Yaren District (Nauru)

13
Guatemala City (Guatemala)

14 and over
Andorra la Vella (Andorra) (14)
Bandar Seri Begawan (Brunei) (17)
Lourenço Marques* (Mozambique) (15)

Champagne Bottle Sizes

6
bottle
magnum (2 bottles)

8
Jeroboam (4 bottles)
Rehoboam (6 bottles)

9
Balthazar (16 bottles)

10
Methuselah (8 bottles)

11
Salamanazar (12 bottles)

14
Nebuchadnezzar (20 bottles)

Channels and Straits

NB: letter counts do not include the words *strait*, *channel*, etc.; place references are given as a general guideline on location.

Ch. = Channel; P. = Passage; Sd = Sound; St.(s) = Strait(s)

Australia
Bass St. (4)
Queen's Ch. (6)
Torres St. (6)

Canada
Barrow St. (6)
Cabot St. (5)
Davis St. (5)
Dolphin St. (7)
Fox Ch. (3)
Georgia, St. of (7)
Hecate St. (6)
Hudson St. (6)
King George Sd (10)
Lancaster Sd (9)
Nootka Sd (6)
Northumberland St. (14)
Queen Charlotte Sd (14)
Smith Sd (5)

Central America
Panama Canal (11)

China
Formosa St. (7)

Denmark
Cattegat (the) (8)
Great Belt (the) (9)
Kattegat (the) (8)
Little Belt (the) (10)
Skagerrak (9)

East Africa
Mozambique Ch. (10)

East Indies
Malacca St. (7)
Molucca P. (7)
Sunda St. (5)

England
Bristol Ch. (7)
Dover, Sts of (5)
Downs (the) (5)
English Ch. (7)
Goodwin Sands (12)
Nore (the) (4)
Plymouth Sd (8)
St George's Ch. (9)
Solent (the) (6)
Spithead (8)

France
Biscay (6)
Pas de Calais (11)

Greenland
Denmark St. (7)

India
Palk St. (4)

Iran
Ormuz, St. of (5)

Ireland (Republic of)
Achill Sd (6)

Italy
Messina, St. of (7)
Otranto, St. of (7)

Japan
Korea St. (5)
Van Diemen St. (9)

Mediterranean
Bonifacio, St. of (9)
Suez Canal (9)

Mexico
Yucatán Ch. (7)

New Zealand
Cook St. (4)
Foveaux St. (7)

North Sea
Dogger Bank (10)

Norway
Skagerrak (9)
Tromsø Sd (6)

Pacific
Bering St. (6)

Red Sea
Bab-el-Mandeb St. (11)
Suez Canal (9)

Russia
Behring St. (7)

Scotland
Caledonian Canal (15)
Coll, P. of (4)
Colonsay, P. of (8)
Cuillin Sd (7.)
Harris, St. of (6)
Jura Sd (4)
Kilbrennan Sd (10)
Little Minch (the) (11)
Minch (the) (5)
Minches (the) (7)
North Ch. (5)
Scapa Flow (9)
Sleat, Sd of (5)

South America
Le Maire St. (7)
Magellan St (8)

Spain
Gibraltar, Sts of (9)

Sweden
Sound (the) (5)

Turkey
Bosphorus (the) (9)
Dardanelles (the) (11)
Golden Horn (10)

USA
Florida St. (7)
Golden Gate (10)
Pamlico Sd (7)
Puget Sd (5)
Hampton Roads (12)

Wales
Menai Sts (5)

West Indies
Mona P. (4)
Windward P. (8)

Chemical Elements and Symbols

actinium, Ac (8)
aluminium, Al (9)
americium, Am (9)
antimony, Sb (8)
argon, Ar (5)
arsenic, As (7)
astatine, At (8)
barium, Ba (6)
berkelium, Bk (9)
beryllium, Be (9)
bismuth, Bi (7)
bohrium, Bh (7)
boron, B (5)
bromine, Br (7)
cadmium, Cd (7)
caesium, Cs (7)
calcium, Ca (7)
californium, Cf (11)
carbon, C (6)
cerium, Ce (6)
chlorine, Cl (8)
chromium, Cr (8)
cobalt, Co (6)
columbium, Cb (9)
copper, Cu (6)
curium, Cm (6)
dubnium, Db (7)
dysprosium, Dy (10)
einsteinium, Es (11)
erbium, Er (6)
europium, Eu (8)
fermium, Fm (7)
fluorine, F (8)
francium, Fr (8)
gadolinium, Gd (10)
gallium, Ga (7)
germanium, Ge (9)
gold, Au (4)
hafnium, Hf (7)
helium, He (6)
holmium, Ho (7)
hydrogen, H (8)
indium, In (6)
iodine, I (6)
iridium, Ir (7)
iron, Fe (4)
krypton, Kr (7)
lanthanum, La (9)
lawrencium, Lr (10)
lead, Pb (4)
lithium, Li (7)

lutetium, Lu (8)
magnesium, Mg (9)
manganese, Mn (9)
mendelevium, Md (11)
mercury, Hg (7)
molybdenum, Mo (10)
neodymium, Nd (9)
neon, Ne (4)
neptunium, Np (9)
nickel, Ni (6)
niobium, Nb (7)
nitrogen, N (8)
nobelium, No (8)
osmium, Os (6)
oxygen, O (6)
palladium, Pd (9)
phosphorus, P (10)
platinum, Pt (8)
plutonium, Pu (9)
polonium, Po (8)
potassium, K (9)
praseodymium, Pr (12)
promethium, Pm (10)
protactinium, Pa (12)
radium, Ra (6)
radon, Rn (5)
rhenium, Re (7)
rhodium, Rh (7)
rubidium, Rb (8)
ruthenium, Ru (9)
samarium, Sm (8)
scandium, Sc (8)
selenium, Se (8)
silicon, Si (7)
silver, Ag (6)
sodium, Na (6)
strontium, Sr (9)
sulphur, S (7)
tantalum, Ta (8)
technetium, Tc (10)
tellurium, Te (9)
terbium, Tb (7)
thallium, Tl (8)
thorium, Th (7)
thulium, Tm (7)
tin, Sn (3)
titanium, Ti (8)
tungsten, W (8)
uranium, U (7)
vanadium, V (8)
xenon, Xe (5)
ytterbium, Yb (9)
yttrium, Y (7)
zinc, Zn (4)
zirconium, Zr (9)

Chess Pieces and Abbreviations

Bishop (6)	B
King (4)	K
King's bishop (11)	KB
King's knight (11)	KN
King's rook (9)	KR
Knight (6)	N
Pawn (4)	P
Queen (5)	Q
Queen's bishop (12)	QB
Queen's knight (12)	QN
Queen's rook (10)	QR

Cities and Towns

See also **Capital Cities**.

Afghanistan
Herat (5)
Jalalabad (9)
Kandahar (8)

Algeria
Oran (4)

Argentina
Bahia Blanca (11)
Cordoba (7)
La Plata (7)

Australia
Adelaide (8)
Alice Springs (12)
Brisbane (8)
Darwin (6)
Melbourne (9)
Newcastle (9)
Perth (5)
Sydney (6)

Austria
Innsbruck (9)
Salzburg (8)

Bangladesh
Chittagong (10)

Belgium
Antwerp (7)
Bruges (6)
Ghent (5)
Liège (5)
Ostend (6)
Ypres (5)

Brazil
Bahia (5)
Belo Horizonte (13)
Recife (6)
Rio de Janeiro (13)
São Paulo (8)

Bulgaria
Varna (5)

Burma
Mandalay (8)

Canada
Calgary (7)
Edmonton (8)
Fredericton (11)
Halifax (7)
Hamilton (8)
Kingston (8)
Montreal (8)
Niagara Falls (12)
Quebec (6)
Regina (6)
St John's (7)
Toronto (7)
Vancouver (9)
Victoria (8)
Winnipeg (8)

China
Anshan (6)
Canton (6)
Changchun (9)
Dairen (6)
Fushun (6)
Harbin (6)
Kunming (7)
Nanking (7)
Shanghai (8)
Shenyang (8)
Sian (4)
Taiyuan (7)
Tientsin (8)
Tsinan (6)
Wuhan (5)

Colombia
Cartagena (9)
Medellín (8)

Congo, Democratic Republic of the
Lubumbashi (10)

Croatia
Split (5)

Czech Republic
Brno (4)

Egypt
Alexandria (10)
Aswan (5)
Giza (4)
Luxor (5)
Mansura (7)
Memphis (7)
Ismailia (8)
Port Said (8)

England

3
Ely
Eye
Rye
Usk

4
Bath
Bray
Bude
Bury
Clun
Deal
Diss
Eton
Holt
Hove
Hull
Hyde
Ince
Leek
Looe
Lydd
Ross
Ryde
Shap
Ware
Wark
Wern
Yarm
York

5
Acton
Alton
Bacup
Blyth
Bourn
Calne
Chard
Cheam
Colne
Cowes
Crewe
Derby
Dover
Egham
Epsom
Filey
Fowey
Frome
Goole
Grays
Hawes
Hedon
Hurst
Hythe
Leeds
Leigh
Lewes
Louth
Luton
March
Olney
Otley
Poole
Reeth
Ripon
Risca
Rugby
Sarum
Selby
Stoke
Stone
Tebay
Thame
Tring
Truro
Wells
Wigan

6
Alston
Alford
Ashton
Barnet
Barrow
Barton
Batley
Battle
Bawtry
Bedale
Belper
Bodmin
Bognor
Bolton
Bootle
Boston
Bruton
Bungay
Burton
Buxton
Castor
Cobham
Cromer
Darwen
Dudley
Durham
Ealing
Eccles
Epping
Exeter
Goring
Hanley
Harlow
Harrow
Havant
Henley
Hexham
Howden
Ilford
Ilkley
Ilsley
Jarrow
Kendal
Leyton
London
Ludlow
Lynton
Lytham
Maldon
Malton
Marlow
Masham
Morley
Naseby
Nelson
Neston
Newark
Newent
Newlyn
Newton
Norham
Oakham
Oldham
Ormsby
Ossett
Oundle
Oxford
Penryn
Pewsey
Pinner
Pudsey
Putney
Ramsey
Redcar
Ripley
Romney
Romsey
Rugely
St Ives
Seaham
Seaton
Selsey
Settle
Snaith
Strood
Stroud
Sutton
Thirsk
Thorne
Totnes
Walmer
Walton
Watton
Welwyn
Weston
Whitby
Widnes
Wigton
Wilton

Witham
Witney
Wooler
Yeovil

7
Alnwick
Andover
Appleby
Arundel
Ashford
Aylsham
Bampton
Banbury
Barking
Beccles
Bedford
Belford
Berwick
Bewdley
Bexhill
Bickley
Bilston
Bourton
Bowfell
Brandon
Bristol
Brixham
Bromley
Burnham
Burnley
Burslem
Caistor
Cafford
Cawston
Charing
Chatham
Cheadle
Cheddar
Chesham
Chester
Chorley
Clacton
Clifton
Crawley
Croydon
Darsley
Datchet
Dawlish
Devizes
Dorking
Douglas
Dunster
Elstree
Enfield
Everton
Evesham
Exmouth
Fareham
Farnham
Feltham
Glossop
Gosport
Grimsby
Halifax
Hampton
Harwich
Haworth
Helston
Heywood
Hitchin
Honiton
Hornsea
Hornsey
Horsham
Ipswich
Ixworth
Keswick
Kington
Lancing
Langton
Ledbury
Leyburn
Lincoln
Malvern
Margate
Matlock
Molesey
Moreton
Morpeth
Mossley
Newbury
Newport
Norwich
Oldbury
Overton
Padstow
Penrith
Poulton
Prescot
Preston
Rainham
Reading
Redhill
Redruth
Reigate
Retford
Romford
Rossall
Royston
Runcorn
St Neots
Salford
Saltash
Sandown
Saxelby
Seaford
Shifnal
Shipley
Shipton
Silloth
Skipton
Spilsby
Staines
Stilton
Sudbury
Sunbury
Swanage
Swindon
Swinton
Taunton
Telford
Tenbury
Tetbury
Thaxted
Tilbury
Torquay
Twyford
Ventnor
Walsall
Waltham
Wantage
Wareham
Warwick
Watchet
Watford
Wembley
Wickwar
Windsor
Winslow
Winster
Wisbeck
Worksop

8
Abingdon
Alfreton
Alnmouth
Amesbury
Ampthill
Axbridge
Aycliffe
Bakewell
Barnsley
Berkeley
Beverley
Bicester
Bideford
Bolsover
Brackley
Bradford
Brampton
Bridport
Brighton
Bromyard
Broseley
Caerleon
Camborne
Carlisle
Caterham
Chepstow
Chertsey
Clevedon
Clovelly
Coventry
Crediton
Dartford
Daventry
Debenham
Dedworth
Deptford
Dewsbury
Egremont
Eversley
Fakenham
Falmouth
Foulness
Grantham
Grantown
Hadleigh
Hailsham
Halstead
Hastings
Hatfield
Helmsley
Hereford
Herne Bay
Hertford
Hinckley
Holbeach
Hunmanby
Ilkeston
Keighley
Kingston
Lavenham
Lechlade
Liskeard
Longtown
Lynmouth
Maryport
Midhurst
Minehead
Monmouth
Nantwich
Newhaven
Nuneaton
Ormskirk
Oswestry
Penzance
Pershore
Peterlee
Petworth
Pevensey
Plaistow
Plymouth
Ramsgate
Redditch
Richmond
Ringwood
Rochdale
Rothbury
St Albans
St Helens
Saltburn
Sandgate
Sandwich
Sedbergh
Shanklin
Shelford
Shipston

Sidmouth
Skegness
Sleaford
Southend
Spalding
Stafford
Stamford
Stanhope
Stanwell
Stockton
Stratton
Swaffham
Surbiton
Tamworth
Thetford
Thornaby
Tiverton
Tunstall
Uckfield
Uxbridge
Wallasey
Wallsend
Wanstead
Westbury
Wetheral
Wetherby
Weymouth
Woodford
Woolwich
Worthing
Yarmouth

9
Aldeburgh
Aldershot
Allendale
Alresford
Ambleside
Ashbourne
Ashburton
Avonmouth
Aylesbury
Blackburn
Blackpool
Blandford
Blisworth
Bracknell
Braintree
Brentford
Brentwood
Brighouse
Broughton
Cambridge
Carnforth
Castleton
Chesilton
Chingford
Clitheroe
Congleton
Cranborne
Cranbrook
Crewkerne
Cricklade
Cuckfield
Dartmouth
Devonport
Doncaster
Donington
Droitwich
Dronfield
Dungeness
Dunstable
Ellesmere
Faversham
Fleetwood
Gateshead
Godalming
Gravesend
Greenwich
Grinstead
Guildford
Harrogate
Haslemere
Haverhill
Hawkhurst
Holmfirth
Ilchester
Immingham
Kettering
King's Lynn
Kingswear
Lambourne
Lancaster
Leicester
Lichfield
Liverpool
Longridge
Lowestoft
Lyme Regis
Lymington
Maidstone
Mansfield
Middleton
Newcastle
Newmarket
New Romney
Northwich
Otterburn
Pembridge
Penistone
Penkridge
Penyghent
Pickering
Rochester
Rotherham
St Austell
Salisbury
Saltfleet
Sevenoaks
Sheerness
Sheffield
Sherborne
Smethwick
Southgate
Southport
Southwell
Southwold
Starcross
Stevenage
Stockport
Stokesley
Stourport
Stratford
Tarporley
Tavistock
Tenterden
Todmorden
Tonbridge
Towcester
Tynemouth
Ulverston
Upminster
Uppingham
Uttoxeter
Wainfleet
Wakefield
Warkworth
Weybridge
Whernside
Wimbledon
Wincanton
Wokingham
Woodstock
Worcester
Wymondham

10
Accrington
Aldborough
Altrincham
Barnstaple
Beaminster
Bedlington
Bellingham
Billericay
Birkenhead
Birmingham
Bridgnorth
Bridgwater
Bromsgrove
Broxbourne
Buckingham
Canterbury
Carshalton
Chelmsford
Cheltenham
Chichester
Chippenham
Chulmleigh
Coggeshall
Colchester
Cullompton
Darlington
Dorchester
Dukinfield
Eastbourne
Eccleshall
Farningham
Folkestone
Freshwater
Gillingham
Gloucester
Halesworth
Hartlepool
Haslingdon
Heathfield
Horncastle
Hornchurch
Hungerford
Hunstanton

Huntingdon
Ilfracombe
Kenilworth
Kingsclere
Kirkoswald
Launceston
Leamington
Leominster
Littleport
Maidenhead
Malmesbury
Manchester
Mexborough
Micheldean
Middlewich
Mildenhall
Nailsworth
Nottingham
Okehampton
Orfordness
Pangbourne
Patrington
Peacehaven
Pontefract
Portishead
Portsmouth
Potter's Bar
Ravenglass
Rockingham
St Leonards
Saxmundham
Shepperton
Sheringham
Shrewsbury
Stalbridge
Stowmarket
Sunderland
Teddington
Teignmouth
Tewkesbury
Thamesmead
Torrington
Trowbridge
Twickenham
Warminster
Warrington
Washington
Wednesbury
Wellington
Westward Ho!
Whitchurch
Whitehaven
Whitstable
Whittlesey
Willenhall
Winchelsea
Winchester
Windermere
Windlesham
Wirksworth
Withernsea
Wolsingham
Woodbridge
Workington

11

Basingstoke
Berkhamsted
Bognor Regis
Bournemouth
Bridlington
Buntingford
Cleethorpes
Cockermouth
East Retford
Glastonbury
Great Marlow
Guisborough
Haltwhistle
Hampton Wick
Hatherleigh
High Wycombe
Ingatestone
Leytonstone
Littlestone
Lostwithiel
Ludgershall
Lutterworth
Mablethorpe
Manningtree
Market Rasen
Marlborough
Much Wenlock
New Brighton
Newton Abbot
Northampton
Petersfield
Pocklington
Rawtenstall
St. Margaret's
Scarborough
Shaftesbury
Southampton
South Molton
Stalybridge
Stourbridge
Tattershall
Wallingford
Walthamstow
Westminster
Whitechurch
Woodhall Spa

12

Attleborough
Bexhill-on-Sea
Castle Rising
Chesterfield
Christchurch
Gainsborough
Great Grimsby
Great Malvern
Huddersfield
Ingleborough
Long Stratton
Loughborough
Macclesfield
Milton Keynes
Morecambe Bay
North Shields
North Walsham
Peterborough
Shoeburyness
Shottesbrook
South Shields
Stoke-on-Trent

13

Barnard Castle
Bishop's Castle
Boroughbridge
Brightlingsea
Burton-on-Trent
Bury St Edmunds
Chipping Ongar
Finchampstead
Godmanchester
Great Yarmouth
Higham Ferrers
Kidderminster
Kirkby Stephen
Knaresborough
Littlehampton
Lytham St Annes
Market Deeping
Market Drayton
Melcombe Regis
Melton Mowbray
Middlesbrough
Northallerton
Saffron Walden
Shepton Mallet
Wolverhampton
Wootton Basset

14

Berwick-on-Tweed
Bishop Auckland
Bishops Waltham
Chipping Barnet
Chipping Norton
Hemel Hempstead
Kirkby Lonsdale
Market Bosworth
Mortimer's Cross
Stockton-on-Tees
Stony Stratford
Sutton Courtney
Tunbridge Wells
Wellingborough
West Hartlepool

15

Ashton-under-Lyne
Barrow-in-Furness
Burnham-on-Crouch
Castle Donington
Leighton Buzzard
Newcastle-on-Tyne
St Leonards-on-Sea
Stratford-on-Avon
Sutton Coldfield

Weston-super-Mare

16
Bishop's Stortford
Welwyn Garden City

France
Abbeville (9)
Aix (3)
Ajaccio (7)
Albi (4)
Alencon (7)
Amiens (6)
Arles (5)
Armentières (11)
Arras (5)
Avignon (7)
Bayonne (7)
Besancon (8)
Bordeaux (8)
Boulogne (8)
Brest (5)
Caen (4)
Calais (6)
Cherbourg (9)
Clermont-Ferrand (15)
Dieppe (6)
Dijon (5)
Dunkirk (7)
Grenoble (8)
Laon (4)
Le Havre (7)
Le Mans (6)
Lille (5)
Lourdes (7)
Lyon (4)
Marseille (9)
Marseilles (10)
Metz (4)
Montelimar (10)
Nancy (5)
Nantes (6)
Nice (4)
Nimes (5)
Orange (6)
Orléans (7)
Reims (5)
Rheims (6)
Rouen (5)
St Malo (6)
Soissons (8)
Strasbourg (10)
Toulon (6)
Toulouse (8)
Tour (4)
Verdun (6)
Versailles (10)

Germany
Aachen (6)
Aix-la-Chapelle (13)
Augsburg (8)
Baden Baden (10)
Bad Homburg (10)
Bochum (6)
Bremen (6)
Brunswick (9)
Cassel (6)
Chemnitz (8)
Coblenz (7)
Cologne (7)
Cottbus (7)
Darmstadt (10)
Dortmund (8)
Dresden (7)
Dusseldorf (10)
Erfurt (6)
Essen (5)
Frankfurt (9)
Gera (4)
Halle (5)
Hamburg (7)
Hannover (8)
Hanover (7)
Heidelberg (10)
Homburg (7)
Kassel (6)
Kiel (4)
Koblenz (7)
Köln (4)
Leipzig (7)
Magdeburg (9)
Mainz (5)
Mannheim (8)
Munich (6)
Munchen (7)
Nuremberg (9)
Nurnberg (8)
Potsdam (7)
Rostock (7)
Saarbrucken (11)
Schwerin (8)
Stuttgart (9)
Suhl (4)
Treves (6)
Trier (5)
Wiesbaden (9)
Wuppertal (9)

Greece
Corinth (7)
Mycenae (7)
Piraeus (7)
Salonika (8)
Sparta (6)

India
Agra (4)
Agartala (8)
Ahmedabad (9)
Ajmer (5)
Allahabad (9)
Alwar (5)
Amritsar (8)
Bangalore (9)
Baroda (6)
Benares (7)
Bhopal (6)
Bhubaneswar (11)
Bombay (6)
Calcutta (8)
Cawnpore (8)
Chandigarh (10)
Darjeeling (10)
Delhi (5)
Gwalior (7)
Howrah (6)
Hyderabad (9)
Imphal (6)
Indore (6)
Jaipur (6)
Jamalpur (8)
Jamshedpur (10)
Jhansi (6)
Jodhpur (7)
Kanpur (6)
Kohima (6)
Kotah (5)
Lucknow (7)
Madras (6)
Meerut (6)
Mumbai (6)
Mysore (6)
Nagpur (6)
Patna (5)
Poona (5)
Pune (4)
Rampur (6)
Shillong (8)
Simla (5)
Srinagar (8)
Trivandrum (10)
Varanasi (8)

Indonesia
Bandung (7)
Surabaya (8)

Iran
Abadan (6)
Isfahan (7)
Mashhad (7)
Shiraz (6)
Tabriz (6)

Iraq
Basra (5)
Mosul (5)

Ireland (Republic of)
Arklow (6)
Athlone (7)
Balla (5)
Ballymurphy (11)
Bantry (6)
Blarney (7)
Boyle (5)
Bray (4)
Carlow (6)
Cashel (6)

Clonmel (7)
Clontarf (8)
Cobh (4)
Cork (4)
Drogheda (8)
Dundalk (7)
Ennis (5)
Galway (6)
Kildare (7)
Kilkenny (8)
Killarney (9)
Limerick (8)
Listowel (8)
Maynouth (8)
Rathdrum (8)
Roscommon (9)
Shillelagh (10)
Sligo (5)
Tipperary (9)
Waterford (9)
Wexford (7)
Youghal (7)

Israel
Beersheba (9)
Gaza (4)
Haifa (5)
Jaffa (5)
Tel Aviv (7)

Italy
Agrigento (9)
Bari (4)
Bologna (7)
Genoa (5)
Messina (7)
Milan (5)
Naples (6)
Ostia (5)
Padua (5)
Palermo (7)
Parma (5)
Pisa (4)
Ravenna (7)
Reggio (6)
Rieti (5)
Salerno (7)
San Remo (7)
Siena (5)
Syracuse (8)
Trent (5)
Turin (5)
Trieste (7)
Vatican (7)
Venice (6)
Verona (6)

Japan
Hiroshima (9)
Kobe (4)
Kyoto (5)
Nagasaki (8)
Nagoya (6)
Osaka (5)
Sapporo (7)
Yokohama (8)

Kenya
Mombasa (7)

Lebanon
Sidon (5)
Tyre (4)

Libya
Tobruk (6)

Mali
Timbuktu (8)

Mexico
Acapulco (8)
Guadalajara (11)
Juárez (6)
Monterrey (9)
Puebla (6)

Morocco
Casablanca (10)
Fez (3)
Marrakech (9)
Marrakesh (9)
Tangier (7)
Tangiers (8)

Netherlands
Arnhem (6)
Dordrecht (9)
Eindhoven (9)
The Hague (8)
Leiden (6)
Leyden (6)
Rotterdam (9)
Utrecht (7)

New Zealand
Auckland (8)
Christchurch (12)
Dunedin (7)
Napier (6)
Nelson (6)

Northern Ireland

5
Derry
Doagh
Glynn
Keady
Larne
Newry
Omagh
Toome

6
Antrim
Augher
Bangor
Belcoo
Beragh
Comber
Lurgan

7
Belfast
Belleek
Caledon
Carrick
Clogher
Dervock
Dundrum
Dunmore
Fintona
Gilford
Glenarm
Lisburn

8
Ahoghill
Dungiven
Hilltown
Portrush
Strabane
Trillick

9
Ballintra
Ballymena
Banbridge
Bushmills
Coleraine
Cookstown
Dungannon
Kircubbin
Moneymore
Newcastle
Portadown
Rasharkin
Rostrevor
Tobermore
Tovermore

10
Ballyclare
Ballymoney
Ballyroney
Castlederg
Cushendall
Donaghadee
Glengariff
Markethill
Portaferry
Saintfield
Strangford
Tanderagee

11
Ballycastle
Ballygawley
Carrickmore
Crossmaglen
Downpatrick
Draperstown
Enniskillen
Londonderry
Magherafelt
Portglenone

Randalstown
Rathfriland

12
Castle Dawson
Castlewellan
Five Mile Town
Hillsborough
Inishtrahull
Stewartstown

13
Brookeborough
Carrickfergus
Derrygonnelly

14
Newtown Stewart

Norway
Bergen (6)
Trondheim (9)

Pakistan
Hyderabad (9)
Karachi (7)
Lahore (6)
Peshawar (8)
Quetta (6)
Rawalpindi (10)

Peru
Ayacucho (8)
Cuzco (5)

Poland
Breslau (7)
Danzig (6)
Gdansk (6)
Krakow (6)
Lodz (4)
Lublin (6)
Posen (5)
Przemysl (8)

Portugal
Coimbra (7)
Faro (4)
Oporto (6)
Porto (5)

Russia
Archangel (9)
Astrakhan (9)
Cherkessk (9)
Gorky (5)
Irkutsk (7)
Kalinin (7)
Kaliningrad (11)
Kazan (5)
Konigsberg (10)
Kuibyshev (9)
Leningrad (9)
Novgorod (8)
Novosibirsk (11)
Omsk (4)
Petrograd (9)
Pskov (5)
Rostov (6)
St Petersburg (12)
Smolensk (8)
Stalingrad (10)
Sverdlovsk (10)
Ufa (3)
Vladivostok (11)
Volgograd (9)
Yakutsk (7)

Saudi Arabia
Jeddah (6)
Jidda (5)
Mecca (5)
Medina (6)

Scotland

3
Ayr
Uig

4
Alva
Barr
Duns
Elie
Kirn
Luss
Nigg
Oban
Reay
Rona
Stow
Wick

5
Alloa
Annan
Appin
Avoch
Ayton
Banff
Beith
Brora
Bunaw
Busby
Ceres
Clova
Clune
Crail
Cupar
Denny
Downe
Elgin
Ellon
Errol
Fyvie
Govan
Insch
Islay
Keiss
Keith
Kelso
Lairg
Largs
Leith
Nairn
Perth
Salen
Troon

6
Aboyne
Alford
Barvas
Beauly
Bervie
Biggar
Bo'ness
Buckie
Carron
Cawdor
Comrie
Crieff
Cullen
Culter
Dollar
Drymen
Dunbar
Dundee
Dunlop
Dunnet
Dunoon
Dysart
Edzell
Findon
Forfar
Forres
Girvan
Glamis
Hawick
Huntly
Irvine
Killin
Kilmun
Lanark
Lauder
Leslie
Linton
Lochee
Meigle
Moffat
Pladda
Reston
Rhynie
Rosyth
Rothes
Shotts
Thurso
Tongue
Wishaw
Yarrow

7
Airdrie
Balfron
Balloch
Banavie
Bowmore
Braemar
Brechin
Brodick

Canobie
Cantyre
Carbost
Cargill
Carluke
Crathie
Culross
Cumnock
Denholm
Douglas
Dunkeld
Dunning
Evanton
Fairlie
Falkirk
Galston
Gifford
Glasgow
Glencoe
Golspie
Gourock
Granton
Guthrie
Halkirk
Kenmore
Kessock
Kilmory
Kilmuir
Kilsyth
Kinross
Kintore
Lamlash
Larbert
Lybster
Macduff
Maybole
Meldrum
Melrose
Melvich
Methven
Monikie
Muthill
Newport
Paisley
Peebles
Polmont
Poolewe
Portree
Portsoy
Renfrew
Saddell
Sarclet
Scourie
Selkirk
Stanley
Strathy
Tarbert
Tarland
Tayport
Tranent
Turriff
Tundrum
Ullster
Yetholm

8

Aberdeen
Aberlady
Abington
Annadale
Arbroath
Arrochar
Auldearn
Ballater
Banchory
Barrhill
Beattock
Blantyre
Burghead
Canisbay
Carnwath
Creetown
Cromarty
Dalkeith
Dalmally
Dingwall
Dirleton
Dufftown
Dumfries
Dunbeath
Dunblane
Dunscore
Earlston
Eyemouth
Findhorn
Fortrose
Glenluce
Greenlaw
Greenock
Hamilton
Inverary
Inverury
Jeantown
Jedburgh
Kilbride
Kilniver
Kilrenny
Kinghorn
Kirkwall
Langholm
Latheron
Leuchars
Loanhead
Markinch
Marykirk
Moniaive
Montrose
Monymusk
Muirkirk
Neilston
Newburgh
Newmilns
Penicuik
Pitsligo
Pooltiel
Quiraing
Rothesay
St Fergus
Stirling
Strichen
Talisker
Taransay
Traquair
Whithorn
Ullapool
Woodside

9

Aberfeldy
Aberfoyle
Ardrossan
Berridale
Bettyhill
Blacklarg
Bracadale
Braeriach
Broadford
Broughton
Buckhaven
Cairntoul
Callander
Carstairs
Dumbarton
Edinburgh
Ferintosh
Fochabers
Inchkeith
Inveraray
Inverness
Johnstone
Kildrummy
Kingussie
Kirkcaldy
Leadhills
Lochgelly
Lochinvar
Lochnagar
Lockerbie
Logierait
Mauchline
Milngavie
Peterhead
Pitlochry
Port Ellen
Prestwick
Riccarton
Ronaldsay
Rothiemay
St Andrews
St Fillans
Saltcoats
Shieldaig
Slamannan
Stewarton
Stranraer
Strathdon
Strontian
Tobermory
Thornhill
Tomintoul

10

Abbotsford
Achnasheen
Anstruther
Applecross
Ardrishaig
Auchinleck
Ballantrae
Blackadder

Carnoustie
Carsphairn
Castletown
Coatbridge
Coldstream
Coldingham
Dalbeattie
Drumlithie
East Linton
Galashiels
Glenrothes
Johnshaven
Kilcreggan
Killenaule
Kilmainham
Kilmalcolm
Kilmarnock
Kilwinning
Kincardine
Kingsbarns
Kirkmaiden
Kirkoswald
Kirriemuir
Lennoxtown
Lesmahagow
Linlithgow
Livingston
Milnathort
Motherwell
Pittenweem
Portobello
Rutherglen
Stonehaven
Stonehouse
Stoneykirk
Strathaven
Strathearn
Strathmore
Tweedmouth
West Calder
Wilsontown

11
Aberchirder
Balquhidder
Bannockburn
Blairgowrie
Campbeltown
Charlestown
Cumbernauld
Drummelzier
Dunfermline
Ecclefechan
Fettercairn
Fort William
Fraserburgh
Helensburgh
Invergordon
Kirkmichael
Lossiemouth
Maxwelltown
Musselburgh
Port Glasgow
Port Patrick
Prestonpans
Pultneytown
Strathblane

12
Auchterarder
Ballachulish
East Kilbride
Fort Augustus
Garelochhead
Innerleithen
Lawrencekirk
North Berwick
Portmahomack
Strathpeffer
Tillicoultry

13
Auchtermuchty
Castle Douglas
Cockburnspath
Dalmellington
Inverkeithing
Inverkeithnie
Kirkcudbright
Kirkintilloch
Newton Stewart
Rothiemurchus

South Africa
Bloemfontein (12)
Durban (6)
Grahamstown (11)
Johannesburg (12)
Kimberley (9)
Ladysmith (9)
Mafeking (8)
Pietermaritzburg (16)
Port Elizabeth (13)
Sharpeville (11)
Simonstown (10)
Soweto (6)

Spain
Alicante (8)
Badajoz (7)
Barcelona (9)
Bilbao (6)
Cadiz (5)
Cartagena (9)
Cordoba (7)
Ferrol (6)
Granada (7)
Las Palmas (9)
Pamplona (8)
Salamanca (9)
San Sebastián (12)
Santander (9)
Santiago de Compostela (20)
Saragossa (9)
Seville (7)
Valencia (8)
Vigo (4)
Zaragoza (8)

Sri Lanka
Galle (5)
Kandy (5)

Sudan
Berber (6)
Dongola (7)
Omdurman (8)

Sweden
Goteborg (8)
Gothenburg (10)
Helsingborg (11)
Malmö (5)
Uppsala (7)

Switzerland
Basel (5)
Basle (5)
Geneva (6)
Lausanne (8)
Lucerne (7)
Zurich (6)

Syria
Aleppo (6)
Palmyra (7)

Turkey
Erzerum (7)
Istanbul (8)
Izmir (5)
Smyrna (6)

Ukraine
Dnepropetrovsk (14)
Donetsk (7)
Kharkov (7)
Krivoi Rog (9)
Lemberg (7)
Lvov (4)
Odessa (6)
Sevastopol (10)
Yalta (5)

USA

4
Gary
Lima
Reno
Troy
York
Waco

5
Akron
Miami
Omaha
Salem

Selma
Tulsa

6
Albany
Austin
Bangor
Biloxi
Boston
Dallas
Dayton
Denver
El Paso
Fresno
Irvine
Mobile
Nassau
Newark
Peoria
St Paul
Topeka
Tucson

7
Anaheim
Atlanta
Boulder
Buffalo
Chicago
Concord
Detroit
Hampton
Houston
Jackson
Lincoln
Madison
Memphis
Modesto
New York
Oakland
Orlando
Phoenix
St Louis
San Jose
Seattle

8
Berkeley
Columbus
Honolulu
Las Vegas
New Haven
Palo Alto
Pasadena
Portland
Richmond
San Diego
Santa Ana
Stamford
Syracuse

9
Anchorage
Arlington
Baltimore
Cambridge
Cleveland
Des Moines
Fairbanks
Fort Worth
Galveston
Lexington
Long Beach
Manhattan
Milwaukee
Nashville
Princeton
Rochester
Tombstone

10
Baton Rouge
Birmingham
Charleston
Cincinnati
Harrisburg
Jersey City
Kansas City
Little Rock
Los Angeles
Louisville
Miami Beach
Montgomery
New Bedford
New Orleans
Pittsburgh
Providence
Sacramento
San Antonio

11
Albuquerque
Chattanooga
Grand Rapids
Minneapolis
Palm Springs
Springfield

12 and over
Atlantic City (12)
Colorado Springs (15)
Fort Lauderdale (14)
Indianapolis (12)
New Brunswick (12)
Niagara Falls (12)
Oklahoma City (12)
Philadelphia (12)
Salt Lake City (12)
San Francisco (12)
Santa Barbara (12)
Washington DC (12)

Uzbekistan
Samarkand (9)
Tashkent (8)

Vietnam
Danang (6)
Haiphong (8)
Hue (3)

Wales

4
Bala
Holt
Mold
Pyle
Rhyl

5
Chirk
Flint
Neath
Nevin
Tenby
Towyn

6
Amlwch
Bangor
Brecon
Builth
Conway
Ruabon
Ruthin

7
Carbury
Cardiff
Cwmbran
Denbigh
Maesteg
Newport
Newtown
St Asaph
Swansea
Wrexham

8
Aberavon
Aberdare
Abergele
Barmouth
Bridgend
Cardigan
Dolgelly
Hawarden
Holyhead
Kidwelly
Knighton
Lampeter
Llanelly
Llanrwst
Pembroke
Pwllheli
Rhayader
Skerries
Skifness
Talgarth
Tredegar
Tregaron

9
Aberaeron
Aberdovey
Aberffraw
Beaumaris
Carnarvon
Criccieth
Festiniog
Fishguard
Llanberis
Llandudno
New Radnor
Pontypool
Porthcawl
Portmadoc
Welshpool

10
Cader Idris
Caernarvon
Carmarthen
Crickhowel
Ffestiniog
Llandovery
Llanfyllin
Llangadock
Llangollen
Llanidloes
Montgomery
Plinlimmon
Porth Nigel
Presteigne

11
Aberystwyth
Abergavenny
Braich-y-Pwll
Llantrisant
Machynlleth
Oystermouth

12
Llandilofawr

13
Merthyr Tydfil
Haverfordwest

Zimbabwe
Bulawayo (8)
Harare (6)

Classic English Horse Races

Derby (5) (colts, Epsom)
Oaks (4) (fillies, Epsom)
One Thousand Guineas (18) (fillies, Newmarket)
St Leger (7) (colts and fillies, Doncaster)
Two Thousand Guineas (18) (colts, Newmarket)

Coffees

4
iced
Java

5
black
brown
latte
mocha
white

6
Kenyan
filter

7
arabica
bourbon
caturra
cortado
dopiata
instant
robusta
Turkish

8
café noir
espresso
Honduras

9
Americano
Brazilian
café crème
canephora
Colombian
New Guinea

10
café au lait
caffe latte
cappuccino
Costa Rican
Guatemalan
maragogype
mochaccino

11
Continental
French roast

12
Blue Mountain

13 and over
decaffeinated (13)
espresso doppio (14)
espresso macchiato (17)
espresso vistretto (17)
Sumatra lingtong (15)

Collective Terms

3

cry (of hounds)
gam (of porpoises, whales)
mob (of kangaroos, people)
nye (of pheasants)
pod (of peas, seals, whales)
rag (of colts)
run (of fish, poultry)
set (of various articles)

4

army (of frogs)
bale (of turtles)
bask (of crocodiles)
bevy (of larks, quails, swans)
bury (of rabbits)
cast (of hawks)
cete (of badgers)
crew (of sailors)
dole (of doves)
dout (of wild cats)
down (of hares)
dule (of doves)
erst (of bees)
fall (of woodcock)
gang (of elk, prisoners, thieves, workmen)
herd (of antelopes, buffalo, cattle, cranes, curlews, deer, donkeys, elephants, giraffes, goats, horses, oxen, pigs, ponies, seals, swans, wolves)
hive (of bees)
host (of angels, sparrows)
husk (of hares)
knob (of pochards, teal, toads, widgeon)
knot (of toads)
leap (of leopards)
lepe (of leopards)
mute (of hounds)
nest (of mice, rabbits, rumours, wasps)
nide (of pheasants)
pace (of asses)
pack (of dogs, grouse, hounds, wolves)
peal (of bells)
rope (of onions, pearls)
rout (of wolves)
rush (of pochards)
safe (of ducks)
sawt (of lions)
sord (of mallards, wild fowl)
span (of mules)
stud (of mares)
sute (of mallards, wild fowl)
team (of ducks, oxen)
trip (of goats)
turn (of turtles)
walk (of snipe)
wing (of plovers)
wisp (of snipe)
yoke (of oxen)
zeal (of zebras)

5

batch (of bread and various)
bench (of aldermen, bishops, judges, magistrates)
blast (of hunters)
bloat (of hippopotami)
blush (of boys)
board (of directors)
brace (of ducks, partridges, etc.)
brood (of grouse, hens)
bunch (of flowers, grapes, teal, widgeon)
caste (of bread)
catch (of fish)
charm (of goldfinches)
cloud (of gnats)
covey (of grouse, partridges)
crash (of rhinos)
crowd (of people)
doylt (of tame pigs)
drift (of swans, pigs)
drove (of cattle, horses, oxen)
field (of racehorses)
fleet (of cars, ships)
flock (of geese, hens, pigeons, sheep, swifts)
flush (of mallards)
glean (of herrings)
grist (of bees, flies)
leash (of bucks, hounds)
plump (of wild fowl)
posse (of police)
pride (of lions)
sedge (of bitterns, cranes, herons)
shoal (of fish)
siege (of cranes, herons)
skein (of geese)
skulk (of foxes)
sloth (of bears)
smack (of jellyfish)
smuth (of jellyfish)
squad (of beaters, soldiers)
stalk (of foresters)
stand (of plovers)
stuck (of jellyfish)
swarm (of bees and other insects)
tribe (of goats)
troop (of boy scouts, Brownies, kangaroos, lions, monkeys)

watch (of nightingales)
wedge (of swans)

6

ambush (of tigers)
barren (of mules)
budget (of inventions, papers)
bundle (of asparagus, firewood and various)
clutch (of eggs, hens)
colony (of ants, gulls, rats)
covert (of coots)
desert (of lapwings)
family (of otters)
flight (of aeroplanes, doves, dunlins, pigeons, swallows)
gaggle (of geese)
galaxy (of beauties)
harras (of horses)
kennel (of dogs)
kindle (of kittens)
labour (of moles)
litter (of cubs, kittens, pigs, pups)
melody (of harpers)
murder (of crows)
muster (of peacocks, soldiers)
parade (of elephants)
parcel (of penguins)
rabble (of remedies)
rafter (of turkeys)
rosary (of quotations)
school (of dolphin, porpoises, whales)
sleuth (of bears)
spring (of teal)
string (of pearls, racehorses)
tiding (of magpies)
troupe (of actors, dancers, minstrels)
warren (of rabbits)

7

battery (of guns)
bouquet (of flowers)
cavalry (of kangaroos, lions, monkeys)
clamour (of rooks)
clouder, clowder (of cats)
cluster (of grapes, stars)
company (of actors, capitalists, widgeon)
descent (of woodpeckers)
dopping (of sheldrakes)
draught (of butlers)
fluther (of jellyfish)
rookery (of rooks, seals)
shrivel (of critics)
sounder (of pigs)

8

audience (of people)
building (of rooks)
business (of ferrets)
paddling (of ducks)
richesse (of martens)
singular (of boars)
subtlety (of sergeants)

9

anthology (of stories)
badelynge (of ducks)
bellowing (of bullfinches)
cowardice (of curs)
morbidity (of majors)
mustering (of storks)
obstinacy (of buffalos)
sachemdom (North American Indians)
shrubbery (of shrubs)
syndicate (of capitalists)
tittering (of magpies)

10

chattering (of choughs)
exaltation (of larks)
observance (of hermits)
parliament (of owls)
shrewdness (of apes)
simplicity (of subalterns)
tabernacle (of bakers)
unkindness (of ravens)

11 and over

congregation (of birds, people, worshippers) (12)
mellificium (of quotations) (11)
murmuration (of starlings) (11)
pandemonium (of parrots) (11)

Collectors and Enthusiasts

7
diarist

8
apiarist
zoophile

9
herbalist
medallist
oenophile

10
arctophile
audiophile
discophile

11
ailurophile
bibliophile
numismatist
philatelist
scripophile

12
automobilist
cartophilist
deltiologist
fusilatelist
phillumenist

13
brolliologist
campanologist
lepidopeterist
phraseologist
vexillologist

14
cruciverbalist

15
paranumismatist

Colours

3
aal
aba
dun
jet
red
tan

4
bleu
blue
bois
bure
cuir
drab
ebon
ecru
gold
grey
gris
hopi
iris
jade
lake
lark
navy
noir
onyx
opal
pied
pink
plum
puce
rose
ruby
sand
shot
vert

5
amber
beige
black
brown
camel
capri
cocoa
coral
cream
cymar
delft
flesh
green
hazel
henna
ivory
jaune
jewel
khaki
lemon
loden
maize
mauve
ochre
olive
ombre
peach
prune
rouge
sepia
shade
taupe
topaz
umber
white

6
acajou
alesan
argent
auburn
bistre
blonde
bronze
burnet
castor
cerise
cherry
chroma
citron
claret
copper
dorado
flaxen
garnet
golden
indigo
jasper
madder
maroon
matara
motley
orange
orchid
oyster
pastel
pearly
pirned
purple
rachel
raisin
reseda
russet
salmon
shrimp
silver
titian
violet
yellow
zircon

7
anamite
apricot
ardoise
aureate
biscuit
caldron
caramel
carmine
chamois
corbeau
crimson
emerald
filbert
fuchsia
heather
ingénue
jacinth
jonquil
lacquer
lavande
magenta
mottled
mustard
nacarat
natural
neutral
old rose
pearled
platina
saffron
scarlet
sea blue
sky blue
tea rose
thistle
tile red
tilleul
tussore

violine

8
absinthe
alizarin
amaranth
aurulent
baby blue
baby pink
bordeaux
burgundy
capucine
chaldera
chestnut
ciel blue
cinnamon
crevette
cyclamen
eau de nil
eggplant
eggshell
gun metal
hazelnut
hyacinth
larkspur
lavender
mahogany
mole grey
mulberry
navy blue
pea green
pistache
poppy red
primrose
sapphire
sea green
shagreen
spectrum

viridian

9
alice blue
aubergine
azure blue
blue-green
cadet blue
cadet grey
carnation
carnelian
champagne
chocolate
cochineal
delph blue
dutch blue
flesh pink
green-blue
harlequin
leaf green
lime green
moonstone
moss green
nile green
olive drab
parchment
pearl grey
raspberry
royal blue
tangerine
tomato red
turkey red
turquoise
verdigris
vermilion
wally blue

10
aquamarine
bois de rose
café au lait
castor grey
cobalt blue
congo brown
ensign blue
liver brown
marina blue
marine blue
oxford blue
petrol blue
polychrome
powder blue
terracotta
zenith blue

11
bottle green
burnt almond
cardinal red
clair de lune
forest green
gobelin blue
horizon blue
hunter's pink
lapis lazuli
lemon yellow
lipstick red
parrot green
peacock blue
pomegranate
smoked pearl
solid colour
ultramarine
versicolour
walnut brown

yellow ochre

12
ball park blue
canary yellow
carrot colour
Castilian red
celadon green
hunter's green
hyacinth blue
logwood brown
midnight blue
overseas blue
sapphire blue
solferino red
tyrian purple
verdant green

13
bishop's purple
bishop's violet
Cambridge blue
mother-of-pearl
pepper-and-salt
tortoiseshell

14
periwinkle blue
pistachio green

15
Caledonian brown
chartreuse green

16
chartreuse yellow

Composers

EARLY AND RENAISSANCE

4
Bull
Byrd

5
Dufay

6
Carver
Lassus
Morley
Tallis

7
Dowland
Gibbons
Joachim
Machaut
Perotin
Weelkes
Zarlino

8
Binchois
Gabrieli
Gesualdo
Marenzio
Ockeghem
Taverner
Victoria

9 and over
Dunstable (9)
Gabrielli (9)
Josquin des Pres (14)
Palestrina (10)

CLASSICAL AND ROMANTIC

3
Cui

4
Arne
Lalo
Wolf

5
Bizet
Boyce
Falla
Gluck
Grieg
Haydn
Lehar
Liszt
Sousa
Spohr
Verdi
Wagner

6
Brahms
Busoni
Chopin
Dvorak
Foster
Franck
Glinka
Gounod
Hummel
Mahler
Mozart
Pleyel

7
Bellini
Berlioz
Borodin
Delibes
Puccini
Rossini
Smetana
Stamitz
Strauss

8
Bruckner
Cimarosa
Kreisler
Massenet
Paganini
Respighi
Schubert
Schumann
Sibelius
von Weber

9
Balakirev
Beethoven
Cherubini
Donizetti
MacDowell
Meyerbeer
Offenbach
Paisiello

10
Boccherini
Kabalevsky
Ponchielli
Saint Saens
Sammartini

11 and over
Dittersdorf (11)
Mendelssohn (11)
Tchaikovsky (11)
Moussorgsky (11)
Charpentier (11)
Humperdinck (11)
Leoncavallo (11)
Rimsky Korsakov (14)

TWENTIETH-CENTURY

3
Bax
Suk

4
Berg
Bush
Cage
Ives
Nono
Orff

5
Berio
Bliss
Bloch
Brian
Carse
Dukas
Elgar
Fauré
Glass
Henze
Holst
Ibert
Nyman
Parry
Ravel
Reich
Riley
Satie
Weill
Ysaye

6
Barber
Bartok
Boulez
Carter
Delius
Kodaly
Piston
Walton
Webern

7
Albeniz
Arriaga
Babbitt
Bantock
Beamish
Bennett
Britten
Copland
Debussy
Gorecki
Ireland
Janacek
Martinu
Menotti
Milhaud
Nielsen
Novello
Poulenc
Quilter
Tavener
Tippett
Warlock
Xenakis

8
Dohnanyi
Gershwin
Glazunov
Grainger
Granados
Honegger
Mascagni
Messiaen
Scriabin
Sibelius
Thompson

9
Bernstein

Hindemith
Macmillan
Prokofiev

10
Birtwistle
Penderecki
Rubinstein
Schoenberg
Skalkottas
Stravinsky
Villa-Lobos

11 and over
Dallapiccola (12)
Khachaturian (12)
Lennox Berkeley (14)
Lutoslawski (11)
Maxwell Davies (13)
Rachmaninov (11)
Racine Fricker (13)
Richard Strauss 14)
Shostakovich (12)
Stockhausen (11)
Vaughan Williams (15)

Constellations and Groups of Stars

* = popular name

3
Ara
Cup*
Leo
Ram*

4
Apus
Argo
Bull*
Crab*
Crow*
Crux
Grus
Hare*
Lion*
Lynx*
Lyra
Lyre*
Pavo
Swan*
Vela
Wolf*

5
Aries
Arrow*
Cetus
Crane*
Draco
Eagle*
Hydra
Indus
Lepus
Libra
Lupus
Mensa
Musca
Norma
Orion
Pyxis
Tucan*
Twins*
Virgo

6
Antlia
Aquila
Archer*
Auriga
Boötes
Caelum
Cancer
Carina
Corvus
Crater
Cygnus
Dipper*
Dorado
Dragon*
Fishes*
Fornax
Gemini
Hydrus
Indian*
Lizard*
Octans
Octant*
Persei
Pictor
Pisces
Plough
Puppis
Scales*
Scutum
Square*
Taurus
Tucana
Virgin*
Volans

7
Centaur*
Cepheus
Columba
Dolphin*
Furnace*
Giraffe*
Lacerta
Peacock*
Pegasus
Perseus
Phoenix*
Pleiads
Sagitta
Scorpio
Sea Goat*
Serpens
Serpent*
Sextans
Unicorn*

8
Aquarius
Circinus
Equuleus
Eridanus
Great Dog*
Hercules*
Leo Minor
Pleiades
Scorpion*
Scorpius
Sculptor
Ship Argo*
Triangle*

9
Andromeda*
Centaurus
Chameleon
Compasses*
Delphinus
Great Bear*
Little Dog*
Monoceros
Noah's Dove*
Ophiuchus
Ploughman*
Reticulum
Swordfish*
Telescope*
Ursa Major
Ursa Minor
Vulpecula

10
Atlantides
Canis Major
Canis Minor
Cassiopeia*
Charioteer*
Flying Fish*
Greyhounds*
Horologium
Little Bear*
Little Lion*
Microscope*
Piscis Aust
Sea Monster*
Triangulum
Watersnake*

11
Capricornus
Hunter Orion*
Little Horse*
Sagittarius
Southern Fly*
Telescopium
Water-bearer*
Winged Horse*

12
Charles's Wain
Flying Dragon*
Microscopium
Southern Fish*

13
Berenice's Hair*
Canes Venatici
Coma Berenices
Crux Australis
Northern Crown*
Painter's Easel*
River Eridanus*
Serpentbearer*
Southern Cross*
Southern Crown*

14
Bird of Paradise*
Camelopardalis
Corona Borealis
Musca Australis
Sculptor's Tools*

15
Corona Australis
Piscis Australis
Sculptor's Chisel

Continents

Africa (6)
Asia (4)
Australasia (11)
Australia (9)
Europe (6)
Antarctica (10)
North America (12)
South America (12)

Counties of the UK and Ireland

England
Avon (4)
Bedford (7)
Bedfordshire (12)
Berkshire (9)
Buckingham (10)
Buckinghamshire (15)
Cambridge (9)
Cambridgeshire (14)
Cheshire (8)
Cleveland (9)
Cornwall (8)
Cumberland (10)
Cumbria (7)
Derby (5)
Derbyshire (10)
Devon (5)
Dorset (6)
Dorsetshire (11)
Durham (6)
Devonshire (10)
East Sussex (10)
Essex (5)
Gloucester (10)
Gloucestershire (15)
Hampshire (9)
Hereford (8)
Herefordshire (13)
Hertford (8)
Hertfordshire (13)
Humberside (10)
Huntingdon (10)
Huntingdonshire (15)
Isle of Wight (11)
Lancashire (10)
Leicester (9)
Leicestershire (14)
Lincoln (7)
Lincolnshire (12)
London (6)
Merseyside (10)
Middlesex (9)
Monmouth (8)
Monmouthshire (13)
Norfolk (7)
Northampton (11)
Northamptonshire (16)
Northumberland (14)
North Yorkshire (14)
Nottingham (10)
Nottinghamshire (15)
Oxford (6)
Oxfordshire (11)
Rutland (7)
Rutlandshire (12)
Shropshire (10)
Somerset (8)
Somersetshire (13)
South Yorkshire (14)
Stafford (8)
Staffordshire (13)
Suffolk (7)
Surrey (6)
Sussex (6)
Tyne and Wear (11)
Warwick (7)
Warwickshire (12)
West Midlands (12)
Westmorland (11)
West Sussex (10)
West Yorkshire (13)
Wiltshire (9)
Worcester (9)
Worcestershire (14)
Yorkshire (9)

Ireland (Republic of)
Carlow (6)
Cavan (5)
Clare (5)
Connaught (9)
Cork (4)
Donegal (7)
Dublin (6)
Galway (6)
Kerry (5)
Kildare (7)
Kilkenny (8)
King's County (11)
Laois (5)
Leitrim (7)
Leix (4)
Limerick (8)
Longford (8)
Louth (5)
Mayo (4)
Meath (5)
Monaghan (8)
Offaly (6)
Queen's County (12)
Roscommon (9)
Sligo (5)
Tipperary (9)
Waterford (9)
Westmeath (9)
Wexford (7)
Wicklow (8)

Northern Ireland
Antrim (6)
Armagh (6)
Down (4)
Fermanagh (9)
Londonderry (11)
Tyrone (6)

Scotland
Aberdeen (8)
Aberdeenshire (13)
Angus (5)
Argyll (6)
Argyllshire (11)
Ayr (3)

Ayrshire (8)
Banff (5)
Banffshire (10)
Berwick (7)
Berwickshire (12)
Bute (4)
Caithness (9)
Clackmannan (11)
Cromarty (8)
Dumfries (8)
Dumfriesshire (13)
Dunbarton (9)
Dunbartonshire (14)
East Lothian (11)
Edinburgh (9)
Elgin (5)
Fife (4)
Forfar (6)
Forfarshire (11)
Haddington (10)
Inverness (9)
Inverness-shire (14)
Kincardine (10)
Kinross (7)
Kircudbright (13)
Lanark (6)
Lanarkshire (11)
Linlithgow (10)
Midlothian (10)
Moray (5)
Nairn (5)
Orkney (6)
Peebles (7)
Perth (5)
Perthshire (10)
Renfrew (7)
Renfrewshire (12)
Ross (4)
Ross and Cromarty (15)
Roxburgh (8)
Selkirk (7)
Stirling (8)
Sutherland (10)
West Lothian (11)
Wigtown (7)
Wigtownshire (12)

Wales
Anglesey (8)
Brecon (6)
Brecknockshire (14)
Caernarvon (10)
Caenarvonshire (15)
Cardigan (8)
Cardiganshire (13)
Carmarthen (10)
Carmarthenshire (15)
Clwyd (5)
Denbigh (7)
Denbighshire (12)
Dyfed (5)
Flint (5)
Flintshire (10)
Glamorgan (9)
Glamorganshire (14)
Gwent (5)
Gwynedd (7)
Merioneth (9)
Merionethshire (14)
Mid Glamorgan (12)
Montgomery (10)
Montgomeryshire (15)
Pembroke (8)
Pembrokeshire (13)
Powys (5)
Radnor (6)
Radnorshire (11)
South Glamorgan (14)
West Glamorgan (13)

Countries of the World

* = former

2
UK

3
CIS
DDR*
GDR*
UAE
USA

4
Bali
Chad
Cuba
Eire
Fiji
Guam
Iran
Iraq
Java
Laos
Mali
Nejd
Oman
Peru
Siam*
Togo
USSR*

5
Belau
Benin
Burma
Chile
China
Congo
Egypt
Gabon
Ghana
Haiti
India
Italy
Japan
Kandy*
Kenya
Khmer*
Korea
Libya
Lydia*
Macao
Malta
Natal*
Nauru
Nepal
Niger
Palau*
Qatar
Samoa
Spain
Sudan
Syria
Tchad
Tibet
Timor
Tonga
Wales
Yemen
Zaire*

6
Angola
Arabia*
Azores
Belize
Bhutan
Brazil
Brunei
Canada
Cathay*
Ceylon*
Cyprus
Epirus*
Faroes
France
Gambia (the)
Greece
Guinea
Guyana
Hawaii

Israel
Jordan
Kuwait
Latvia
Malawi
Malaya*
Mexico
Monaco
Norway
Panama
Persia*
Poland
Russia
Rwanda
Serbia
Sicily
Sweden
Taiwan
Tobago
Turkey
Tuvalu
Uganda
Zambia

7

Albania
Algeria
Andorra
Antigua
Armenia
Ashanti*
Assyria*
Austria
Bahamas (the)
Bahrain
Bavaria*
Belarus
Belgium
Bermuda
Bohemia*
Bolivia
Britain
Burkina
Burundi
Comoros
Croatia
Dahomey*
Denmark
Ecuador
England
Eritrea
Estonia
Faeroes
Finland
Formosa*
Georgia
Germany
Grenada
Holland
Holy See
Hungary
Iceland
Ireland
Jamaica
Lebanon
Lesotho
Liberia
Livonia
Macedon*
Moldova
Morocco
Myanmar
Namibia
Nigeria
Prussia*
Romania
Rumania
St Kitts
St Lucia
São Tomé
Senegal
Somalia
Sumatra
Surinam
Tunisia
Ukraine
Uruguay
Vanuatu
Vatican
Vietnam

8

Barbados
Botswana
Bulgaria
Burgundy*
Byelarus
Cambodia*
Cameroon
Colombia
Djibouti
Dominica
Ethiopia
Honduras
Hong Kong
Kiribati
Malaysia
Maldives
Malvinas
Moldavia*
Mongolia
Pakistan
Paraguay
Portugal
Rhodesia*
Roumania
St Helena
Sardinia
Scotland
Slovakia
Slovenia
Sri Lanka
St Helena
Suriname
Tanzania
Tasmania
Thailand
Togoland*
Trinidad
Zanzibar
Zimbabwe

9

Abyssinia*
Argentina
Argentine (the)
Australia
Babylonia*
Caledonia*
Costa Rica
East Timor
Gibraltar
Greenland
Guatemala
Indonesia
Irian Jaya
Kampuchea*
Kirghizia*
Lithuania
Macedonia
Manchuria*
Mauritius
New Guinea
Nicaragua
Nyasaland*
Palestine
San Marino
Singapore
Swaziland
Transvaal*
Venezuela
West Irian

10

Azerbaijan
Bangladesh
Basutoland*
Belorussia
El Salvador
Ivory Coast
Kazakhstan
Kyrgyzstan
Luxembourg
Madagascar
Martinique
Mauretania*
Mauritania
Micronesia
Montenegro
Montserrat
Mozambique
New Zealand
North Korea
Seychelles
Somaliland
South Korea
South Yemen*
Tajikistan
Tanganyika*
Upper Volta*
Uzbekistan
Yugoslavia*

11

Afghanistan
Burkina Faso
Byelorussia
Cook Islands
Côte d'Ivoire
Dutch Guiana*
East Germany*
Mesopotamia*
Netherlands (the)
New Hebrides
Philippines
Saudi Arabia
Sierra Leone
South Africa
Soviet Union*
Switzerland
Transjordan*
Vatican City
West Germany*
White Russia*

12

Bechuanaland*
Belgian Congo*
Cocos Islands
Faero Islands
Faroe Islands
French Guiana
Great Britain
Guinea-Bissau
North Vietnam*
South Vietnam*
Tadzhikistan
Turkmenistan
United States

13

Afars and Issas*
British Guiana*
Cayman Islands*
Khmer Republic*
Liechtenstein
Norfolk Island
Trucial States*
United Kingdom
Virgin Islands

14
Czechoslovakia*
Gilbert Islands*
Irish Free State*
Mariana Islands
Papua New Guinea
Pitcairn Island
Slovak Republic
Society Islands
Solomon Islands

15
British Honduras*
Caroline Islands
Christmas Island
Falkland Islands
French Indo-China*
Marshall Islands
Northern Ireland
Orange Free State*
Southwest Africa*
St Kitts and Nevis

16 and over
Antigua and Barbuda (17)
Bosnia and Herzegovina (20)
Cape Verde Islands (16)
Central African Republic (22)
Democratic Republic of the Congo (28)
Dominican Republic (17)
Equatorial Guinea (16)
Malagasy Republic* (16)
Republic of the Congo (the) (18)
St Vincent and the Grenadines (25)
São Tomé and Principe (18)
Trinidad and Tobago (17)
Turks and Caicos Islands (21)
United Arab Emirates (18)
Vatican City State (16)

Currencies

3
kip
lat
lek
leu
lev
pul
won
yen

4
baht
birr
cedi
dông
euro
inti
kina
kuna
kyat
lira
loti
mark
peso
pula
punt
rand
real
rial
riel
taka
tala
vatu
yuan

5
colon
denar
dinar
dobra
franc
krona
krone
kroon
leone
litas
manat
naira
pound
riyal
rupee
sucre
tenge
tolar
zaire
zloty

6
balboa
dalasi
dirham
dollar
duktat
escudo
forint
gourde
koruna
kwacha
kwanza
markka
pa'anga
pataca
peseta
rouble
rupiah
shekel
tugrik

7
Bolivar
cordoba
drachma
guarani
guilder
lempira
metical
quetzal
ringgit
rufiyaa

8
cruzeiro
ngultrum
shilling

9
boliviano
lilangeni
schilling

Curries

3
red

4
dhal
phal

5
balti
bhuna
green
korma

6
achari
bhoona
chasni
karahi
madras
masala
pathia

7
dhansak
dopiaza
nentara
pasanda

8
jalfrezi
vindaloo

9
mussalman
rogan josh

Deserts

NB: letter count does not include the word *desert*.

4
Gobi
Thar

5
Namib
Negev
Ordos
Sinai
Sturt

6
Gibson
Mojave
Nubian
Sahara
Syrian

7
Alashan
An Nafud
Arabian
Atacama
Kara Kum
Simpson
Sonoran

8
Colorado
Kalahari
Kyzyl Kum

9
Dasht-e-Lut

10
Great Sandy
Rub al-Khali
Takla Makan

11
Death Valley

13
Great Victoria

Districts, Cantons, Provinces, Regions, Dependent States, etc.

Afghanistan
Herat (5)
Kandahar (8)

Africa
East Africa (10)
North Africa (11)
Sahara (6)
Sahel (5)
Senegambia (10)
Slave Coast (10)
Soudan (6)
Southern Africa (14)
West Africa (10)

Argentina
Entre Rios (9)
Jujuy (5)
Mendoza (7)
Salta (5)
Santa Fe (7)
Tucuman (7)

Asia
Asia Minor (9)
Bashan (6)
Bokhara (7)
Caucasia (8)
Hadramaut (9)
Hindustan (9)
Indo-China (9)
Judaea (6)
Judea (5)
Khiva (5)
Kurdistan (9)
Levant (6)
Palestine (9)
Samaria (7)
Tartary (7)
Tongking (8)
Turkestan (9)
Turkistan (9)
Turkmenia (9)

Australia
New South Wales (13)
Queensland (10)
South Australia (14)
Victoria (8)
Western Australia (16)
Wimmeria (8)

Austria
Burgenland (10)
Carinthia (9)
Carniola (8)
Lower Austria (12)
Salzburg (8)
Styria (6)
Tyrol (5)
Upper Austria (12)
Vorarlberg (10)

Azerbaijan
Caucasia (8)
Nagorno-Karabakh (15)

Bangladesh
Sylhet (6)

Belgium
Antwerp (7)
Brabant (7)
Eupen (5)
Flanders (8)
Hainault (8)
Liège (5)
Namur (5)
Wallonia (8)

Bolivia
La Paz (5)
Oruro (5)
Potosi (6)

Brazil
Alagoas (7)
Amazonas (8)
Bahia (5)
Ceara (5)
Espirito Santo (13)
Goias (5)
Maranhão (8)
Matto Grosso (11)
Minas Gerais (11)
Para (4)
Parahiba (8)
Paraiba (7)
Parana (6)
Pernambuco (10)
Rio de Janeiro (12)
Rio Grande do Sul (14)
Santa Catarina (13)
Santa Catharina (14)
Sergipe (7)

Burma
Mergui (6)
Shan State (9)
Tavoy (5)
Tenasserim (10)
Thayetmyo (9)

Canada
Alberta (7)
Baffinland (10)
British Columbia (15)
Labrador (8)
Manitoba (8)
New Brunswick (12)
Newfoundland (12)
Nova Scotia (10)
Ontario (7)
Quebec (6)
Saskatchewan (12)
Yukon (5)

Caribbean
West Indies (the) (10)

Central America
Latin America (12)

Chile
Iquique (7)
Linares (7)
Tacna (5)
Tarapaca (8)
Valdivia (8)
Valparaiso (10)

China
Anhwei (6)
Chekiang (8)
Fukien (6)
Heilungkiang (12)
Honan (5)
Hong Kong (8)
Hopeh (5)
Hunan (5)
Hupeh (5)
Inner Mongolia (13)
Kansu (5)
Kiangsi (6)
Kirin (5)
Kwangtung (9)
Kweichow (8)
Liaoning (8)
Macao (5)
Shansi (6)
Shantung (8)
Shensi (6)
Sinkiang (8)
Szechwan (8)
Tibet (5)
Tsinghai (8)
Yunnan (6)

Croatia
Dalmatia (8)
Slavonia (8)

Czech Republic
Bohemia (7)
Moravia (7)
Sudetenland (11)

Denmark
Jutland (7)
Viborg (6)

Egypt
Dakahlieh (9)
Fayum (5)

England
East Anglia (10)
Mercia (6)
New Forest (the) (9)
Northumbria (11)
Potteries (the) (9)
Romney Marshes (13)
Weald (the) (5)
Wessex (6)

Ethiopia
Tigre (5)

Europe
Banat (5)
British Isles (12)
Bukovina (8)
Gibraltar (9)
Lapland (7)
Ruthenia (8)

Finland
Tavastehus (10)

France
Ain (3)
Aisne (5)
Allier (6)
Alpes-Maritimes (14)
Alsace-Lorraine (14)
Alsace (6)
Anjou (5)
Aquitaine (9)
Ardennes (8)
Ariège (6)
Artois (6)
Aube (4)
Aude (4)
Aveyron (7)
Basque Country (13)
Bearn (5)
Berry (5)
Bourbonnais (11)
Brittany (8)
Burgundy (8)
Calvados (8)
Champagne (9)
Charente (8)
Cher (4)
Correze (7)
Côte-d'Or (7)
Côtes-du-Nord (11)
Creuse (6)
Dauphine (8)
Dordogne (8)
Doubs (5)
Drome (5)
Eure (4)
Eure-et-Loir (10)
Franche-Comte (11)
Gard (4)
Gascony (7)
Gers (4)
Guienne (7)
Haute-Garonne (12)
Haute-Loire (10)
Haute-Marne (10)
Haute-Saône (10)
Hautes-Alpes (11)
Haute-Savoie (11)
Hautes-Pyrenees (14)
Haute-Vienne (11)
Haut Rhin (8)
Herault (7)
Ile-de-France (11)
Ile-et-Vilaine (12)
Indre (5)
Indre-et-Loire (12)
Isère (5)
Jura (4)
Landes (6)
Languedoc (9)
Limousin (8)
Loire (5)
Loire-Atlantique (15)
Loiret (6)
Loir-et-Cher (10)
Lorraine (8)
Lot (3)

Lot-et-Garonne (12)
Lozère (6)
Lyonnais (8)
Maine (5)
Manche (6)
Marne (5)
Mayenne (7)
Meuse (5)
Morbihan (8)
Nièvre (6)
Nivernais (9)
Nord (4)
Normandy (8)
Oise (4)
Orléans (7)
Orne (4)
Pas de Calais (11)
Picardy (7)
Poitou (6)
Provence (8)
Rhône (5)
Riviera (the) (7)
Roussillon (10)
Sarthe (6)
Seine (6)
Seine-et-Marne (12)
Somme (5)
Tarn (4)
Tarn-et-Garonne (13)
Var (3)
Vaucluse (8)
Vendée (6)
Vienne (6)
Vosges (6)
Yonne (5)

Georgia
Caucasia (8)

Germany
Baden (5)
Baden-Württemberg (16)
Bavaria (7)
Brandenburg (11)
Eifel (5)
Franconia (9)
Hannover (8)
Hanover (7)
Hesse (5)
Hesse-Nassau (11)
Hohenzollern (12)
Holstein (8)
Lower Saxony (11)
Mecklenburg (11)
North Rhine-Westphalia (20)
Oldenburg (9)
Palatinate (10)
Pomerania (9)
Prussia (7)
Rhenish Prussia (14)
Rhineland (9)
Saar (4)
Saarland (8)
Saxe-Altenberg (13)
Saxe-Coburg-Gotha (15)
Saxe-Meiningen (13)
Saxony (6)
Schwarzwald (11)
Schaumberg-Lippe (15)
Schleswig (9)
Schleswig-Holstein (17)
Swabia (6)
Thuringia (9)
Waldeck (7)
Westphalia (10)
Württemberg (11)

Greece
Epirus (6)
Macedonia (9)
Morea (5)
Peloponnese (11)
Salonika (8)
Thessaly (8)
Thrace (6)

Hungary
Oedenburg (9)
Tokay (5)

India
Andhra Pradesh (13)
Assam (5)
Bengal (6)
Bihar (5)
Bihar and Orissa (14)
Bombay (6)
Cachar (6)
Diu (3)
Goa (3)
Gujarat (7)
Haryana (7)
Himachal Pradesh (15)
Johore (6)
Karnataka (9)
Kashmir (7)
Kerala (6)
Ladakh (6)
Madhya Pradesh (13)
Madras (6)
Maharashtra (11)
Manipur (7)
Meghalaya (9)
Mysore (6)
Nagaland (8)
Orissa (6)
Oudh (4)
Punjab (6)
Rajasthan (9)
Rajputana (9)
Rohilkhand (10)
Simla (5)
Surat (5)
Tamil Nadu (9)
Tanjore (7)
Terai (5)
Tripura (7)
United Provinces (15)
Uttar Pradesh (12)
West Bengal (10)

Indonesia
Achin (5)

Iran
Fars (4)
Ghilan (6)
Kaspan (6)
Kerman (6)
Kermanshah (10)
Khuzestan (9)
Korassan (8)
Kum (3)
Luristan (8)
Mazandaran (10)
Teheran (7)
Tehran (6)

Ireland (Republic of)
Connaught (9)
Leinster (8)
Munster (7)
Pale (the) (4)
Ulster (6)

Israel
Galilee (7)
Gaza (4)

Italy
Abruzzi (7)
Alto Adige (9)
Apulia (6)
Bari (4)
Basilicata (10)
Calabria (8)
Campania (8)

Emilia (6)
Emilia-Romagna (13)
Faenza (6)
Ferrara (7)
Florence (8)
Genoa (5)
Girgenti (8)
Latium (6)
Lecce (5)
Leghorn (7)
Liguria (7)
Lombardy (8)
Lucca (5)
Macerata (8)
Mantua (6)
Marches (7)
Milan (5)
Modena (6)
Molise (6)
Novara (6)
Padua (5)
Parma (5)
Pavia (5)
Perugia (7)
Piacenza (8)
Piedmont (8)
Pisa (4)
Potenza (7)
Ravenna (7)
Riviera (the) (7)
Rome (4)
Sardinia (8)
Savoy (5)
Sicily (6)
Sondrio (7)
Syracuse (8)
Trentino (8)
Tuscany (7)
Umbria (6)
Valle d'Aosta (11)
Venetia (7)
Veneto (6)

Malaysia
Johor (5)
Johore (6)
Malacca (7)
Pahang (6)
Perak (5)
Sabah (5)
Sarawak (7)
Selangor (8)

Mexico
Alisco (6)
Baja California (14)
Campeche (8)
Chiapas (7)
Chihuahua (9)
Coahuila (8)
Durango (7)
Guanajuato (10)
Guerrero (8)
Hidalgo (7)
Lower California (15)
Jalisco (7)
Michoacan (9)
Nuevo Leon (9)
Oaxaca (6)
Ojaca (5)
Queretaro (9)
Quintana Roo (11)
San Luis Potosi (13)
Simaloa (7)
Sonora (6)
Tabasco (7)
Tamaulipas (10)
Tepic (5)
Tiaxcala (8)
Vera Cruz (8)
Yucatán (7)
Zacatecas (9)

Moldova
Bessarabia (10)

Morocco
Ceuta (5)
Melilla (7)
Sus (3)
Tafilet (7)

Namibia
Damaraland (10)
Namaqualand (11)

Netherlands
Drenthe (7)
Friesland (9)
Gelderland (10)
Groningen (9)
Guelderland (11)
Holland (7)
Limburg (7)
North Brabant (12)
North Holland (12)
Overijssel (10)
Overyssel (9)
South Holland (12)
Utrecht (7)
Zealand (7)
Zeeland (7)

New Zealand
Auckland (8)
Canterbury (10)
Hawke Bay (8)
Nelson (6)
Otago (5)
Southland (9)
Taranaki (8)
Westland (8)

Nigeria
Benue-Plateau (12)
East-Central (11)
Kano (4)
Kwara (5)
Lagos (5)
Mid-Western (10)
North-Central (12)
North-Eastern (12)
North-Western (12)
Rivers (6)
Sokoto (6)
South-Eastern (12)
Western (7)

Northern Ireland
Ulster (6)

Norway
Bergen (6)
Christiansand (13)
Finmark (7)
Hamar (5)
Tromsø (6)
Trondheim (9)

Pacific
Melanesia (9)
Micronesia (10)
Polynesia (9)

Pakistan
Baluchistan (11)
Kashmir (7)
North-West Frontier (17)
Punjab (6)
Rawalpindi (10)
Sind (4)
Waziristan (10)

Peru
Ica (3)
Huancavelica (12)
Huanuco (7)
Lambayeque (10)
Lima (4)

Philippines
Iloilo (6)

Poland
Galicia (7)
Kielce (6)
Lublin (6)

Pomerania (9)
Posen (5)
Silesia (7)
West Prussia 11)

Portugal
Alentejo (8)
Algarve (7)
Beira (5)
Entre-Douro-e-Minho (16)
Estremadura (11)
Loreto (6)
Trás-os-Montes (12)
Villareal (9)
Vizeu (5)

Romania
Moldavia (8)
Transylvania (12)
Wallachia (9)

Russia
Astrakhan (9)
Caucasia (8)
Kamchatka (9)
Karelia (7)
Siberia (7)
Tomsk (5)
Transbaikalia (13)

Saudi Arabia
Hedjaz (6)
Hejaz (5)

Scotland
Highlands (9)
Lothian (7)
Lowlands (8)

Serbia
Kosovo (6)
Montenegro (10)

South Africa
Great Karroo (11)
Griqualand West (14)
Griqualand (10)
Karroo (6)
Marico (6)
Namaqualand (11)
Orange Free State (15)
Transvaal (9)
Witwatersrand (13)

South America
Guiana (6)
Latin America (12)
Pampas (6)
Patagonia (9)

Spain
Alicante (8)
Almeria (7)
Andalusia (9)
Aragon (6)
Asturias (8)
Basque Country (13)
Basque Provinces (15)
Biscay (6)
Caceres (7)
Cadiz (5)
Canary Islands (13)
Castile (7)
Catalonia (9)
Ceuta (5)
Estremadura (11)
Galicia (7)
Gerona (6)
Granada (7)
Guadalajara (11)
Guipuzcoa (9)
Huelva (6)
Huesca (6)
Jaen (4)
Leon (4)
Lerida (6)
Logroño (7)
Lugo (4)
Malaga (6)
Melilla (7)
Murcia (6)
Navarre (7)
New Castile (10)
Old Castile (10)
Orense (6)
Oviedo (6)
Palencia (8)
Pontevedra (10)
Salamanca (9)
Saragossa (9)
Segovia (7)
Seville (7)
Tarragona (9)
Toledo (6)
Valencia (8)
Valladolid (10)
Zamora (6)

Sudan
Darfur (6)
Kordofan (8)
Nubia (5)
Sennaar (7)

Sweden
Gothland (8)
Linkoping (9)
Norrland (8)
Scania (6)
Upsala (6)

Switzerland
Aargau (6)
Appenzell (9)
Basel (5)
Basle (5)
Bern (4)
Berne (5)
Fribourg (8)
Geneva (6)
Glarus (6)
Grisons (7)
Lucerne (7)
Neuchatel (9)
Oberland (8)
St Gall (6)
Schaffhausen (12)
Schwyz (6)
Thurgau (7)
Ticino (6)
Unterwalden (11)
Uri (3)
Valais (6)
Vaud (4)
Zug (3)
Zurich (6)

Turkey
Adana (5)
Adrianople (10)
Anatolia (8)
Ferghana (8)
Roumelia (8)
Sivas (5)
Trebizond (9)

Ukraine
Bessarabia (10)
Crimea (6)

USA
Alabama (7)
Alaska (6)
Arizona (7)
Arkansas (8)
California (10)
Colorado (8)
Connecticut (11)
Delaware (8)
District of Columbia (18)
Florida (7)
Georgia (7)
Hawaii (6)
Idaho (5)
Illinois (8)
Indiana (7)
Iowa (4)
Kansas (6)
Kentucky (8)
Louisiana (9)
Maine (5)
Maryland (8)
Massachusetts (13)

Michigan (8)
Minnesota (9)
Mississippi (11)
Missouri (8)
Montana (7)
Nebraska (8)
Nevada (6)
New Hampshire (12)
New Jersey (9)
New Mexico (9)
New York (7)
North Carolina (13)
North Dakota (11)
Ohio (4)
Oklahoma (8)
Oregon (6)
Pennsylvania (12)
Rhode Island (11)
South Carolina (13)
South Dakota (11)
Tennessee (9)
Texas (5)
Utah (4)
Vermont (7)
Virginia (8)
Washington (10)
West Virginia (12)
Wisconsin (9)
Wyoming (7)

Wales

Rhondda Valley (13)

Divination

ZODIAC SIGNS

Aquarius (8) (the water carrier)
Aries (5) (the ram)
Cancer (6) (the crab)
Capricorn (9) (the goat)
Gemini (6) (the twins)
Leo (3) (the lion)
Libra (5) (the scales)
Pisces (6) (the fish)
Sagittarius (11) (the archer)
Scorpio (7) (the scorpion)
Taurus (6) (the bull)
Virgo (5) (the virgin)

CHINESE ZODIAC

buffalo (7)
dog (3)
dragon (6)
goat (4)
horse (5)
monkey (6)
pig (3)
rabbit (6)
rat (3)
rooster (7)
snake (5)
tiger (5)

TAROT

3

Sun (the)
Tower (the)
Wands
World (the)

4

Cups
Fool (the)
Moon (the)
Pope (the)
Star (the)

5

Coins
Death
Devil (the)
Disks
Juggler (the)
Justice

6

Batons
Lovers (the)
Papess (the)
Staves
Swords

7

Chariot (the)
Emperor (the)
Empress (the)
High Priest (the)
House of God (the)
Temperance

8

Magician (the)
Strength

9

Hanged Man (the)
Judgement
Pentacles

10

Heirophant (the)

11

Major Arcana
Minor Arcana

12

Blasted Tower (the)

13

High Priestess (the)

Explorers

3
Cam, Diego
Rae, John

4
Back, Sir George
Byrd, Richard Evelyn
Cook, James
Diaz, Bartolomeu
Eyre, Edward John
Gann, Thomas
Park, Mungo
Polo, Marco
Ross, Sir James Clark
Soto, Hernando de

5
Anson, Lord George
Baker, Sir Samuel White
Brown, William
Bruce, James
Burke, Robert O'Hara
Cabot, John
Cabot, Sebastian
Clark, William
Davis, John
Drake, Sir Francis
Eanes, Gil
Evans, Edgar
Evans, George William
Forbe, Rosita
Fuchs, Sir Vivian Ernest
Gomes, Diogo
Hanno
Hedin, Sven Anders
Lewis, Meriwether
Nares, Sir George
Nuyts, Pieter
Oates, Lawrence
Ojeda, Alonso de
Parry (Admiral)
Peary, Robert Edwin
Scott, Robert Falcon
Smith, John
Speke, John Hanning
Welzl, Jan
Wills, William John

6
Baffin, William
Balboa, Vasco Núñez de
Barrow, Sir John
Bering, Vitus
Burton, Sir Richard
Cabral, Pedro Alvares
Carson, Kit
Conway, Sir Martin
Cortés, Hernando
Cortez, Hernando
Da Gama, Vasco
Duluth, Daniel Greysolon
Fraser, Simon
Hartog, Dirk
Hobson, William
Hudson, Henry
Landor, Savage
Larsen, Kohl
Mawson, Sir Douglas
Nansen, Fridtjof
Philby, H. St John
Pocock, Roger
Selous, Frederick Courteney
Siemel, Sascha
Tasman, Abel
Thomas, Bertram

7
Almeida, Lourenço de
Cameron, Verney Lovett
Cartier, Jacques
Charcot, Jean
Dampier, William
de Prado, Albert
Doughty, Charles Montagu
Fawcett (Col.)
Fiennes, Sir Ranulph
Fremont, John Charles
Gilbert, Sir Humphrey
Hawkins, Sir John
Hillary, Sir Edmund
Houtman, Cornelis de
Houtman, Frederik de
Jolliet, Louis
Kearton, Cherry
Kennedy, William
La Salle, Robert Cavelier
McClure, Sir Robert
Markham, Albert
Pizzaro, Francisco
Raleigh, Sir Walter
Shippee, Robert
Stanley, Sir Henry Morton
Tristam, Nuno
Wilkins, Sir George Hubert
William, Sir Hubert
Workman, Hunter

8
Amundsen, Roald
Columbus, Christopher
Coronado, Francisco Vázquez de
de Brazza, Pierre
de Torres, Louis
Filchner, Wilhelm
Flinders, Matthew
Franklin, Sir John
Humboldt, Alexander von
Johnston, Sir Harry Hamilton
Kingsley, Mary
Magellan, Ferdinand
Radisson, Pierre Esprit
Standish, Miles
Sverdrup, Otto
Thesiger, Wilfred
Thompson, David
Vespucci, Amerigo

9
Africanus
Cadamosto, Alvise
Champlain, Samuel de
Emin Pasha
Frobisher, Sir Martin
Gonsalvez, Antam
Heyerdahl, Thor
Jenkinson, Anthony
Mackenzie, Sir Alexander
Vancouver, George
Velasquez, Diego

10
Bransfield, Edward
Chancellor, Richard
Clapperton, Hugh
Erik the Red
Leichhardt, Friedrich Wilhelm Ludwig
Oglethorpe, James Edward
Richardson, Sir James
Shackleton, Sir Ernest Henry
Stefansson, Vzilhjalmur
Willoughby, Sir Hugh

11
La Vérendrye
Leif Ericson
Livingstone, Dr David

12
Bougainville, Louis-Antoine de
Cabeza de Vaca, Alvar Núñez
Leif Eriksson
Nordenskjold, Nils Adolf Erik
Younghusband, Sir Francis

14 *and over*
Bellingshausen, Fabian Gottlieb von (14)
Giovanni da Pian del Carpini (24)
Hanbury-Tenison, Robin Airling (14)
Oderic of Pordenone (17)
Prince Henry the Navigator (23)

Film, Theatre, TV and Radio

3
Day, Doris
Fry, Stephen
Lee, Christopher
Sim, Alistair

4
Bron, Eleanor
Cage, Nicholas
Cher
Cook, Peter
Dean, James
Depp, Johnny
Ford, John
Gish, Lillian
Hall, Sir Peter
Hill, Benny
Hope, Bob
Hurt, John
Kerr, Deborah
Lean, David
Lunt, Alfred
Marx Brothers (the)
More, Kenneth
Muir, Frank
Nunn, Trevor
Peck, Gregory
Peel, John
Pitt, Brad
Rigg, Diana
Swan, Donald
Tati, Jacques
Wise, Ernie

5
Adler, Larry
Allen, Dave
Allen, Woody
Bates, Alan
Benny, Jack
Brice, Fanny
Brook, Peter
Bruce, Lenny
Burke, Kathy
Burns, George
Caine, Michael
Clark, Lord
Close, Glenn
Cooke, Alistair
Cukor, George
Davis, Bette
Davis, Sammy
Dench, Dame Judi
Elton, Ben
Evans, Dame Edith
Finch, Peter
Flynn, Errol
Fonda, Henry
Fonda, Jane
Fosse, Bob
Frost, Sir David
Gable, Clark
Gabor, Zsa Zsa
Garbo, Greta
Gould, Elliot
Grade, Lord
Grant, Cary

Grant, Hugh
Greco, Juliette
Hanks, Tom
Hardy, Oliver
James, Clive
James, Sid
Kazan, Elia
Kelly, Grace
Korda, Alexander
La Rue, Danny
Leigh, Vivien
Magee, Patrick
Mason, James
Moore, Dudley
Niven, David
Quinn, Anthony
Reith, Lord
Smith, Dame Maggie
Stone, Oliver
Sykes, Eric
Terry, Dame Ellen
Tynan, Kenneth
Wayne, John
Welch, Raquel
Wogan, Terry

6

Bacall, Lauren
Bardot, Brigitte
Barnum, P.T.
Bogart, Humphrey
Brando, Marlon
Burton, Richard
Cagney, James
Chaney, Lon
Cleese, John
Cooper, Gary
de Niro, Robert
Disney, Walt
Divine
Fields, Gracie
Fields, W. C.
Finney, Albert
Garson, Greer
Godard, Jean-Luc
Harlow, Jean
Heston, Charlton
Howard, Trevor
Irving, Sir Henry
Jacobi, Derek
Keaton, Buster
Keitel, Harvey
Lauder, Sir Harry
Laurel, Stan
Monroe, Marilyn
Moreau, Jeanne
Morley, Robert
Mostel, Zero
Neeson, Liam
Newman, Paul
Norden, Dennis
O'Toole, Peter
Paxman, Jeremy
Quayle, Sir Anthony
Reiner, Rob
Renoir, Jean
Rogers, Ginger
Rooney, Mickey
Savile, Sir Jimmy
Sinden, Donald
Streep, Meryl
Taylor, Elizabeth
Temple, Shirley
Warner Brothers
Warner, David
Welles, Orson
Wilder, Billy
Wilder, Gene
Wolfit, Sir Donald

7

Andrews, Julie
Astaire, Fred
Bennett, Alan
Bentine, Michael
Bergman, Ingmar
Bergman, Ingrid
Blondin, Charles
Bogarde, Dirk
Branagh, Kenneth
Brynner, Yul
Campion, Jane
Chaplin, Sir Charles
Chester, Charlie
Cocteau, Jean
Collins, Joan
Connery, Sean
Coppola, Francis Ford
Cushing, Peter
De Palma, Brian
Douglas, Kirk
Douglas, Michael
Feldman, Marty
Fellini, Federico
Garland, Judy
Garrick, David
Gielgud, Sir John
Goldwyn, Sam
Guthrie, Sir Tyrone
Hancock, Sheila
Hancock, Tony
Handley, Tommy
Harding, Gilbert
Hawkins, Jack
Hepburn, Audrey
Hepburn, Katherine
Hoffman, Dustin
Hopkins, Sir Antony
Houdini, Harry
Jackson, Glenda
Jacques, Hattie
Karloff, Boris
Kennedy, Ludovic
Kubrick, Stanley
Langtry, Lillie
McQueen, Steve
Montand, Yves
Monteux, Pierre
Nichols, Mike
Olivier, Lord
Rantzen, Esther
Redford, Robert
Roberts, Julia
Roberts, Rachel
Rushton, William
Russell, Jane
Russell, Ken
Secombe, Sir Harry
Sellers, Peter
Seymour, Lynn
Shearer, Moira
Sherrin, Ned
Siddons, Mrs Sarah
Simmons, Jean
Stewart, James
Swanson, Gloria
Ustinov, Sir Peter
Wheldon, Sir Huw
Winfrey, Oprah

Winters, Shelley

8
Ashcroft, Dame Peggy
Brambell, Wilfred
Bygraves, Max
Campbell, Mrs Pat
Christie, Julie
Connolly, Billy
Crawford, Joan
Dietrich, Marlene
Dimbleby, Richard
Eastwood, Clint
Grenfell, Joyce
Grimaldi, Joseph
Guinness, Sir Alec
Harrison, Sir Rex
Laughton, Charles
Lawrence, Gertrude
Levinson, Barry
Limbaugh, Rush
McGregor, Ewan
Milligan, Spike
Pickford, Mary
Polanski, Roman
Redgrave, Sir Michael
Redgrave, Vanessa
Robinson, Edward G.
Robinson, Eric
Scofield, Paul
Scorsese, Martin
Stephens, Robert
Truffaut, François
Williams, Kenneth

9
Antonioni, Michelangelo
Barrymore, John
Bernhardt, Sarah
Cardinale, Claudia
Chevalier, Maurice
Courtenay, Tom
Davenport, Bob
Depardieu, Gérard
Fairbanks, Douglas
Hampshire, Susan
Hitchcock, Alfred
Humphries, Barry
Lyttelton, Humphrey
Monkhouse, Bob
Morecambe, Eric
Nicholson, Jack
Pleasence, Donald
Plowright, Joan
Preminger, Otto
Spielberg, Steven
Streisand, Barbra
Tarantino, Quentin
Thorndike, Dame Sybil

10
Bertolucci, Bernardo
Eisenstein, Sergei
Littlewood, Joan
Muggeridge, Malcolm
Richardson, Sir Ralph
Rutherford, Dame Margaret
Sutherland, Donald
Whitehouse, Paul

12
Attenborough, Sir David
Attenborough, Sir Richard
Stanislavsky, Constantin

Four Horsemen of the Apocalypse

Rider of the *Black Horse* (10, represents Famine)
Rider of the *Pale Horse* (9, represents Death)
Rider of the *Red Horse* (8, represents War and Bloodshed)
Rider of the *White Horse* (10, represents the Power of God)

Four Last Things

Death (5)
Heaven (6)
Hell (4)
Judgement (9)

Four Temperaments

choleric (8)
melancholic (11)
phlegmatic (lethargic) (10, 9)
sanguine (8)

Geological Ages

GEOLOGICAL ERAS

Cenozoic (8)
Mesozoic (8)
Palaeozoic (10)
Precambrian (11)

EPOCHS OF THE CENOZOIC ERA

Eocene (6)
Holocene (8)
Miocene (7)
Oligocene (9)
Palaeocene (10)
Pleistocene (11)
Pliocene (8)

GEOLOGICAL PERIODS

Archaeozoic (11)
Cambrian (8)
Carboniferous (13)
Cretaceous (10)
Devonian (8)
Jurassic (8)
Ordovician (10)
Permian (7)
Proterozoic (11)
Quaternary (10)
Silurian (8)
Tertiary (8)
Triassic (8)

Geometry

POLYGONS

triangle (8)
square (6)
pentagon (8)
hexagon (7)
heptagon (8)
octagon (7)
nonagon (7)
decagon (7)
undecagon (9)
dodecagon (9)

QUADRILATERALS (FOUR-SIDED POLYGONS)

square (6)
rectangle (9)
rhombus (7)
parallelogram (13)
trapezium (9)
kite (4)

TRIANGLES

equilateral (11)
isosceles (9)
hypotenuse (10)
scalene (7)
right angle (10)
obtuse angle (11)
acute angle (10)

Gods

NORSE

3
Ask
Bor
Hel
Hod
Ran
Sif
Tiw
Tyr
Ull

4
Buri
Garm
Gerd
Loki
Odin
Surt
Thor
Ymir

5
Aegir
Aesir
Alcis
Bragi
Donar
Embla
Freya
Freyr
Frigg
Hoder
Idunn
Jotun
Mimir
Nanna
Njord
Norns
Orcus
Sigyn
Vanir
Vidar
Woden
Wotan

6
Asgard
Balder
Fafnir
Fenrir
Freyja
Frigga
Gefion
Hermod
Hoenir
Kvasir
Weland

7
Alfheim
Audumla
Bifrost
Gungnir
Heimdal
Midgard
Muspell
Nerthus
Wayland
Weiland

8
Brynhild
Draupnir
Fjorgynn
Heimdall
Mjollnir
Niflheim
Ragnarok
Sleipnir
Valhalla
Vanaheim

9
Aurgelmir
Brunhilde
Jotunheim
Mannaheim
Siegfried
Valkyries
Yggdrasil

10
Jörmungand
Muspelheim
Nehallenia
Nidavellir

11
Skidbladnir
Svartalheim

12
Wayland Smith (the)
World Serpent

HINDU

3
Uma

4
Agni
Bana
deva
Devi
Kali
Kama
Ketu
Mara
Maya
puja
Rama
Sita
Siva
Soma
Teli
Veda
Yama
yoga

5
Aditi
asura
Durga
Ganga
Gauri
Indra
Kalki
karma
Kurma
Laxmi
Mitra
Nandi
prana
Radha
Rudra
Saiva
Sakti
Shiva
Sudra
Surya
Ushas
Vedas

6
ahimsa
ashram
Avatar
Brahma
Buddha
chakra
dharma
Ganesa
Ganesh
Garuda
Matsya
moksha
Natraj
Puchan
Purana
Shakti
Skanda
Vaisya
Vamana
Varaha
Varuna
Vishnu
Yaksha

7
Avatars
Brahman
Brahmin
chakras
darshan
Ganesha
Hanuman
Harijan
Krishna
Lakshmi
Narayan
Parvati
Rig Veda
Rukmani
Savitar
Vaisya

8
Balarama
Bhairavi
Ganapati
Narayana
Narsingh
Nataraja
Ramayana (the)
Shaivism
Shaivite
Tvashtar

9
Kartikeya
Kshatriya
kundalini
Narashina
Prajapati
Sarasvati
Saraswati
Vaishnava
Vajrayana

10
Jagannatha
Juggernaut
Kartikkaya
Narasingha
Prajapatis
Satyabhama
Upanishads (the)

11
Mahabharata (the)
Ramachandra

12
Bhagavad Gita (the)

13
reincarnation

EGYPTIAN

2
Ma
Nu
Ra

3
Bes
Geb
Min
Mut
Nun
Nut
Set
Shu

4
Amon
Amun
ankh
Apis
Aten
Bast
Hapi
Isis
Ma'at
Ptah
Sati
Seth
Shai

5
Ament
Ammon
Anhur
Horus
Khnum
Neith
Pasht
Sebek
Seker
Thoth

6
Amon-Ra
Anquet
Anubis
Bastet
Hathor
Khepri
Khonsi
Khunum
Osiris
Renpet
Selket
Tefnut
Upuaut

7
Behdety
Khepera
Renenet
Sakhmet
Sekhmet
Taueret

8
Haroeris
Meshkent
Nephthys

9
Harakhtes
Harmakhis
Harsaphes
Harsiesis
Mertseger
Renenunet

CLASSICAL MYTHOLOGY

Gk. = Greek only; R. = Roman only

2
Ge
Io

3
Ate
Bel
Bia
Deo (Gk)
Dis (R.)
Eos (Gk)
Ida
Ino
Ker
lar (R.)
Nix (Gk)
Nox (R.)
Nyx (Gk)
Ops (R.)
Pan (Gk)
Pax (R.)
Sol (R.)

4
Abas
Ajax
Amor (R.)
Ares (Gk)
Argo
Auge
Bias
Ceto
Ceyx
Core
Dido
Echo
Enyo (Gk)
Eros (Gk)
Fata (R.)
Faun
Fury
Gaea (Gk)
Gaia (Gk)
Hebe
Hera (Gk)
Hero
Idas
Ilus
Iole
Iris
Irus
Itys
Jove (R.)
Juno (R.)
Kore
Leda
Leto
Luna (R.)
Maia (Gk)
Mars (R.)
moly
Mors (R.)
Muse
Nike (Gk)
Opis
Otus
Rhea (Gk)
Rome
Styx
Tros
Troy
Upis
Zeus (Gk)

5
Actor
aegis
Aegle
Agave
Alope
Amata
Ampyx
Arete
Argos
Argus
Arion
Asius
Atlas
Attis
Belus
Beroe
Butes
Cacus
Calus
Canis
Capra
Capys
Ceres (R.)
Cetus
Chaos
Cilix
Circe
Creon
Crete
Cupid (R.)
Damon
Danaê
devas
Diana (R.)
Dione
Dirce

Dolon
Doris
dryad
Edoni
Epeus
Fates
Fauna (R.)
Flora (R.)
Gorge
Hades (Gk)
Harpy
Helen
Helle
Herse
Horae
Hydra
Hylas
Hymen
Iasus
Idmon
Iliad
Ilium
Ionia
Iphis
Irene
Iulus
Ixion
Janus (R.)
Jason
Ladon
Laius
Lamus
lares (R.)
lases (R.)
Lethe
Liber (R.)
Linus
Lotis
Lycus
manes
Maron
Medea
Medon
melia
Metis
Midas
Mimas
Minos
Muses
naiad
Niobe
Nisus
Notus
nymph
oread
Orion
Paean
Pales (R.)
Paris
Perse
Picus (R.)
Pluto (R.)
Poeas
Priam
Remus
satyr
Sibyl
Sinis
Sinon
Siren
Syren
Talus
Terra (R.)
Theia
Thoas
Thyia
Titan
Venus (R.)
Vesta (R.)
Zetes

6

Acamus
Adonis
Aeacus
Aeëtes
Aegeus
Aegina
Aeneas
Aeneid
Aeolus
Aerope
Aethra
Agenor
Aletes
Aloeus
Althea
Amazon
Amycus
Antion
Aphaea
Apollo
Aquilo
Asopus
Athena (Gk)
Athene (Gk)
Athens
Atreus
Augeas
Aurora (R.)
Balius
Baucis
Boreas
Byblis
Byblus
Cabiri
Cadmus
Calais
Canens
Castor
Caunus
Celeus
Charis
Charon
Chione
Chiron
Chthon
Clytie
Codrus
Consus (R.)
Cratos
Creusa
Cronus (Gk)
Cybele (R.)
Cycnus
Cyrene
Danaus
Daphne
Delphi
Dryope
Egeria (R.)
Elatus
Erebus
Euneus
Europa
Evadne
Evenus
Faunus (R.)
Furies
genius (R.)
Geryon
Gorgon
Graces
Graeae
Haemon
Hecabe
Hecate
Hector
Hecuba
Helice
Helios (Gk)
Hellen
Hermes (Gk)
Hestia (Gk)
Hyades
Hygeia
Hyllus
Hypnos (Gk)
Iasion
Icarus
Iolaus
Ismene
Italus
Ithaca
Latona (R.)
Lucina (R.)
Lycaon
maenad
meliae
Medusa
Megara
Memnon
Mentor
Merops
Mestra
Minyas
Moerae (Gk)
Moirae (Gk)
Mopsus
Mygdon
naiads
Neleus
Nereid
Nereus
Nessus
Nestor
nymphs
Oenone
Oeonus
Ogyges
Ogygia
Ogygus
Oileus
Olenus
Ophion
oracle
orphic
Orthus
Oxylus
Pallas
Parcae (R.)
Peleus
Pelias
Pelops
Peneus
Perdix
Pheres
Pholus
Phylas
Plutus (Gk)
Pollux
Pomona (R.)
Procne
Psyche
Pyrrha
Pythia
Python
Rhesus
Rhodes
Saturn (R.)
Scylla
Selene (Gk)
Semele
Semnai
Simois
Sirens
Sirius
Somnus (R.)
Sphinx
Syrinx
Talaus
Tellus (R.)
Tereus
Tethys
Teucer
Theano
Thebes
Themis
Thetis
Thisbe

Thyone
Titans
Tityus
Triton
Typhon
Ulixes
Uranus (Gk)
Vulcan (R.)
Xuthus
Zethus

7
Acastus
Acestes
Achaeus
Achates
Acheron
Actaeon
Admetus
Aepytus
Aesacus
Alcmene
Alcyone
Alpheus
Amazons
Amphion
Ampycus
Amymone
Amyntor
Ancaeus
Antaeus
Antenor
Antiope
Arachne
Arcadia
Ariadne
Artemis (Gk)
Asteria
Athamas
Autonoe
Avernus
Bacchae
Bacchus
Belenos
Bellona (R.)
Bona Dea (R.)
Briseis
Bromius
Busiris
Caeneus
Calchas
Calypso
Camenae (R.)
Camilla
Canthus
Cecrops
centaur
Cepheus
Cheiron
Chimera
Chloris
Chryses
Cinyras
Clymene
Cocytus
Copreus
Coresus
Coronus
Curetes
Cyclops
Dactyls
Daphnis
Demeter (Gk)
Echemus
Echidna
Electra
Elicius
Elpenor
Elysian
Elysium
Epaphus
Epigoni
Erigone
Erinyes
Eumaeus
Eumelus
Eurytus
evil eye
Fortuna (R.)
Galatea
Gelanor
Glaucus
Gordius
Gorgons
Gratiae (R.)
Gryphon
Harpies
Helenus
Hesione
Hilaira
Iacchus
Iapetus
Icarius
Iobates
Jocasta
Jupiter (R.)
Laertes
Laocoon
Laodice
Latinus
Leander
Lynceus
Macaria
Machaon
maenads
Mercury (R.)
Minerva (R.)
Mithras (R.)
Nemesis
Nephele
Neptune (R.)
Nereids
Nycteus
Oceanus (Gk)
Oedipus
Ogygian
Olympia
Olympus
Omphale
oracles
Orestes
Ormenus
Orpheus
Orphism
Orthrus
Pandion
Pandora
Pegasus
penates (R.)
Perseis
Perseus
Phegeus
Phemius
Phineus
Phoebus
Phoenix
Phorcus
Phrixus
Pierian
Pleiads
Pleione
Priapus
Procles
Procris
Proetus
Proteus
Pylades
Pyramus
Pyrrhus
Romulus
Silenus
Stentor
Telamon
Temenus
Thaumas
Theonoe
Theseus
Triopas
Troilus
Ulysses
vestals (R.)
Virbius (R.)
Xanthus

8
Absyrtus
Acheloüs
Achilles
Acrisius
Adrastia
Adrastus
Aegimius
Aegyptus
Agamedes
Aglauros
Agraulus
Alcestis
Alcimede
Alcinous
Alcmaeon
ambrosia
Anchises
Anticlea
Antigone
Antiphus
Aphareus
Apsyrtus
Arcesius
Arethusa
Argonaut

Arimaspi
Ascanius
Asterion
Asterius
Astraeus
Astyanax
Atalanta
Avernian
Bebryces
caduceus
Caeculus
Callisto
Carmenta (R.)
Carthage
Cephalus
Cerberus
Cercopes
Chalybes
Charites
Chimaera
Chryseis
Cretheus
Cylopes
Daedalus
Damocles
Dardanus
Deianira
Delphyne
Diomedes
Dionysus (Gk)
Dioscuri
Endymion
Enyalius
Epicasta
Eriphyle
Eteocles
Eumolpus
Euphemus
Euryclea
Eurydice
Eurynome
Ganymede
Harmonia
Heliades
Heracles
Hercules
Hermione
Hyperion
Iphicles
Juventas (R.)
Labdacus
Lampetie
Laodamas
Laodamia
Laomedon
Lapithae
Lupercus (R.)
Maeander
Marpessa
Megareus
Melampus
Meleager
Menelaus
Minotaur
Morpheus (R.)
Mulciber (R.)
Myrtilus
Nausicaa
Oceanids
Odysseus
Oenomaus
Olympian
Opheltes
Palaemon
Pandarus
Panopeus
Panthous
paradise
Pasiphae
Pelasgus
Penelope
Pentheus
Periphas
Phaethon
Philemon
Philomel
Phlegyas
Pierides
Pittheus
Pleiades
Podarces
Polyxena
Porthaon
Poseidon (Gk)
Psamathe
Quirinus (R.)
Sarpedon
Schedius
Silvanus (R.)
Sisyphus
Tantalus
Tartarus
Tecmessa
Telephus
Thamyris
Thanatos (Gk)
Theogony
Thyestes
Tiresias
Titaness
Tithonus
Victoria (R.)
Zephyrus

9

Aegisthus
Agamemnon
Alcathous
Alcyoneus
Androgeus
Andromeda
Aphrodite (Gk)
Argonauts
Aristaeus
Asclepius
Assaracus
Autolycus
Automeden
Aventinus
Bacchante
Carmentis (R.)
Cassandra
Chalcodon
Charybdis
Chthonius
Deiphobus
Demophoon
Deucalion
di penates (R.)
Enceladus
Ephialtes
Eumenides
Eurybates
Eurypylus
Eurysaces
Faustulus (R.)
Hamadryad
Hippolyte
Hypsipyle
Idomeneus
Iphigenia
Iphimedia
Melanippe
Melanthus
Menoeceus
Menoetius
Metaneira
Mnemosyne
Narcissus
Nyctimene
Oceanides
Palamedes
Palladium
Pandareos
Pandrosos
Parnassus
Patroclus
Philammon
Philomela
Phoroneus
Polydamas
Polydorus
Polynices
Pygmalion
Salmoneus
Scamander
sibylline
Sthenelus
Strophius
Teiresias
Telchines
Telegonus
Thersites
Tisamenus
Trojan War
Vertumnus (R.)

10

Aetholides
Amphictyon
Amphitrite
Amphitryon
Andromache
Antilochus
Archemoros
Callirrhoe
Cassiopeia
cornucopia
Corybantes
Cyparissus

Delphinius
Eileithyia
Epimetheus
Erechtheus
Erymanthus
Gorgophone
Hephaestus (Gk)
Hesperides
Hippocrene
Hippodamia
Hippolytus
Hippothous
Lifthrasir
Melanippus
Melantheus
Melanthius
Menestheus
Nausithous
Parnassian
Persephone (Gk)
Phlegethon
Polydectes
Polydeuces
Polymestor
Polyphemus
Porphyrion
Procrustes
Prometheus
Proserpine (R.)
Rhea Silvia (R.)
Samothrace
Scamandrus
Talthybius
Telemachus
Tlepolemus
Trophonius
Vortumnnus (R.)

11
Aesculapius (R.)
Arimaspians
Bellerophon
Britomartis
Gordian knot
Helen of Troy
Lotus-eaters
Semnai Theai

12
Clytemnestra
Golden Fleece (the)
Rhadamanthys
vestal virgin

13
Hundred-handed
Mother Goddess

14
Elysian Fields (the)
Hermaphroditus

15
Sword of Damocles (the)

Governments

7
anarchy (without law)
diarchy (2 rulers)

8
isocracy (all with equal power)
monarchy (hereditary head of state)
thearchy (God/gods)
triarchy (3 rulers)

9
andocracy (men)
autocracy (1 ruler, absolute power)
democracy (people)
gynocracy (women)
kritarchy (judges)
mobocracy (mob)
monocracy (1 person)
oligarchy (small, exclusive class)
theocracy (religious law)

10
ethnocracy (race/ethnic group)
hierocracy (priests)
matriarchy (mother(s))
patriarchy (eldest male)
plutocracy (wealthy)

11
aristocracy (nobility)
bureaucracy (officials)
ergatocracy (workers)
meritocracy (ability)
militocracy (military)
stratocracy (military)
technocracy (technical experts)

12
despotocracy (tyrant)
ecclesiarchy (clerics)
gerontocracy (old men)
kakistocracy (the worst)
pantisocracy (all with equal power)

The City Guilds

Livery Companies in order of precedence

Mercers (7)
Grocers (7)
Drapers (7)
Fishmongers (11)
Goldsmiths (10)
Merchant Taylors (15)
Skinners (8)
Haberdashers (12)
Salters (7)
Ironmongers (11)
Vintners (8)
Clothworkers (13)

NB Merchant Taylors and Skinners share 6/7 places

International Vehicle Registration Letters

A	Austria
ADN	Yemen
AFG	Afghanistan
AL	Albania
AND	Andorra
AUS	Australia
B	Belgium
BD	Bangladesh
BDS	Barbados
BER	Belarus
BG	Bulgaria
BH	Belize
BR	Brazil
BRN	Bahrain
BRU	Brunei
BS	Bahamas
BUR	Myanmar (Burma)
C	Cuba
CDN	Canada
CH	Switzerland
CI	Ivory Coast
CL	Sri Lanka
CO	Colombia
CR	Costa Rica
CRO	Croatia
CS	Czech Republic
CY	Cyprus
D	Germany
DK	Denmark
DOM	Dominican Republic
DY	Benin
DZ	Algeria
E	Spain
EAK	Kenya
EAZ	Tanzania
EAU	Uganda
EC	Ecuador
ES	El Salvador
ET	Egypt
ETH	Ethiopia
EW	Estonia
F	France
FJI	Fiji
FL	Liechtenstein
FR	Faroe Islands
GB	Great Britain
GBA	Alderney
GBG	Guernsey
GBJ	Jersey
GBM	Isle of Man
GBZ	Gibraltar
GCA	Guatemala
GH	Ghana
GR	Greece
GRU	Georgia
GUY	Guyana
H	Hungary
HKJ	Jordan
I	Italy
IL	Israel
IND	India
IR	Iran
IRL	Ireland
IRQ	Iraq
IS	Iceland
J	Japan
JA	Jamaica
K	Cambodia
KWT	Kuwait
L	Luxembourg
LAO	Laos
LAR	Libya
LB	Liberia
LR	Latvia
LS	Lesotho
LT	Lithuania
M	Malta
MA	Morocco
MAL	Malaysia
MC	Monaco
MEX	Mexico
MOL	Moldova
MS	Mauritius
MW	Malawi
N	Norway
NA	Netherlands Antilles
NIC	Nicaragua
NL	Netherlands
NZ	New Zealand
P	Portugal
PA	Panama
PAK	Pakistan
PE	Peru
PL	Poland
PNG	Papua New Guinea
PY	Paraguay
RO	Romania
RA	Argentina
RB	Botswana
RC	Taiwan
RCA	Central African Republic
RCB	Republic of Congo

RCH Chile
RH Haiti
RI Indonesia
RIM Mauritania
RL Lebanon
RM Madagascar
RMM Mali
RN Niger
ROK Republic of South Korea
RP Philippines
RSM San Marino
RU Burundi
RUS Russia
RWA Rwanda
S Sweden
SD Swaziland
SF Finland
SGP Singapore
SLO Slovenia
SME Surinam
SN Senegal
SQ Slovakia
SWA Namibia
SY Seychelles
SYR Syria
T Thailand
TG Togo
TN Tunisia
TR Turkey
TT Trinidad & Tobago
U Uruguay
UKR Ukraine
USA United States of America
V Vatican City
VN Vietnam
WAG Gambia
WAL Sierra Leone
WAN Nigeria
WD Dominica
WS Western Samoa
WV St Vincent and the Grenadines
YU Federal Republic of Yugoslavia
YV Venezuela
Z Zambia
ZA South Africa
ZRE Democratic Republic of Congo
ZW Zimbabwe

Islands

NB: letter counts do not include the words *island*, *archipelago*, etc. Arch.= Archipelago. I. = Island; Is. = Islands; (v.) = volcanic

Adriatic Sea
Brazza (6)
Bua (3)
Curzola (7)
Isola Grossa (11)
Lesina (6)
Lissa (5)

Aegean Sea
Euboea (6)
Imbros (6)
Lemnos (6)
Lesbos (6)
Limmos (6)

Africa
Bissagos Is. (8)
Comoros (7)
Corisco (7)
Fernando Po (10)
Ichaboe (7)
Johanna (7)
Madagascar (10)
Mayotte (7)
Nossi Be (v.) (7)
Pemba (5)
Perim (5)
St Marie (7)
St Thomas (8)
São Tomé (7)
Sherbro (7)
Zanzibar (8)

Antarctic
Balleny Is. (7)

Arabian Sea
Bahrain (7)
Kuria Muria Is. (10)
Laccadives (10)
Socotra (7)

Arctic
Diomede Is. (7)
Disco (5)
Disko (5)
Greenland (9)
Jan Mayen (8)
Liakhov Is. (7)
Mageroe (7)
Melville Land (11)
New Siberia (10)
North Devon (10)
North Somerset (13)
Novaya Zemlya (12)
Nova Zembla (10)
Parry Is. (5)
Spitsbergen (11)
West Spitsbergen (15)

Asia
Philippine Is. (10)
Philippines (11)
Singapore (9)
Sri Lanka (8)

Atlantic
Ascension (9)
Azores (6)

Banana Is. (6)
Bermuda (7)
Bermudas (Is.) (8)
Bissao (6)
Canaries (8)
Canary Is. (6)
Cape Verde Is. (9)
Corvo (5)
Desertas (8)
Faeroes (7)
Falkland Is. (8)
Falklands (9)
Faroes (6)
Fayal (5)
Ferro (5)
Flores (6)
Gomera (6)
Goree (5)
Gran Canaria (11)
Iceland (v.) (7)
Inaccessible I. (12)
Lanzarote (9)
Madeira (7)
Malvinas (8)
Rockall (7)
St Helena (8)
St Michael (9)
St Nicolas (9)
South Georgia (12)
South Shetlands (14)
Tenerife (8)
Tristan da Cunha (14)
Watling I. (7)
West Indies (10)

Australia
Alban (5)
Buccaneer Arch. (9)
Cape Barren I. (10)
Christmas I. (9)
Dampier Is. (7)
D'Entrecastreaux Is. (15)
Dirk Hartog (10)
Flinders (8)
Furneaux Is. (8)
Kangaroo Is. (8)
Lord Howe Is. (8)
Melville I. (8)
Norfolk I. (7)
Tasmania (8)
Thursday I. (8)
Wellesley Is. (9)

Baltic
Aland Is. (5)
Bornholm (8)
Falster (7)
Faro (4)
Fehmeru (7)
Gotland (7)
Oesel (5)

Canada
Anticosti (9)
Baffin I. (6)
Cape Breton I. (10)
Ellesmere (9)
Fortune Bay I. (10)
Magdalen Is. (8)
Miquelon (8)
Newfoundland (12)
Prince Albert (12)
Prince Edward I. 12)
Queen Charlotte I. (14)
Sable I. (5)
Southampton (11)
Thousand Is. (8)
Vancouver (9)
Victoria (8)

Central America
Bay Is. (3)

Channel Islands
Alderney (8)
Guernsey (8)
Herm (4)
Jersey (6)
Jethou (6)
Sark (4)

Chile
Tierra del Fuego (14)

China
Amoy (4)
Chusan (6)
Hainan (6)
Hong Kong (8)
Loo Choo Is. (7)
Matsu (5)
Quemoy (6)
Taiwan (6)

Denmark
Funen (5)
Laaland (7)
Langeland (9)
Moen (4)
Samsoe (6)

England
Channel Is. (7)
Dogs, I. of (4)
Farn Is. (4)
Farne Is. (5)
Hayling I. (7)
Holy I. (4)
Lindisfarne (11)
Lundy I. (5)
Man, I. of (3)
Portland, I. of (8)
Portsea I. (7)
Purbeck, I. of (7)
St Agnes (7)
Scillies (8)
Scilly, Is. of (6)
Sheppey, I. of (7)
Thanet, I. of (6)
Wight, I. of (5)

Europe
British Isles (12)
Great Britain (12)
Ireland (7)

Fiji
Vanua Levu (9)
Viti-Levu (8)

Finland
Dago (4)

France
Belle Isle (9)
Crozet Is. (6)
Lerins Is. (6)

Miquelon (8)
Oleron (6)
Re (2)
Ushant (6)

Germany
Borkum (6)
Fohr (4)
Norderney (9)
Rugen (5)
Sylt (4)
Usedom (6)

Greece
Aegina (6)
Andros (6)
Calamo (6)
Ceos (4)
Cephalonia (10)
Chios (5)
Corfu (5)
Cos (3)
Crete (5)
Cyclades Is. (8)
Delos (5)
Dodecanese (10)
Hydra (5)
Idra (4)
Ionian Is. (6)
Ithaca (6)
Leros (5)
Lesbos (6)
Melos (5)
Milo (4)
Milos (5)
Mitylene (8)
Mykonos (7)
Naxos (5)
Negropont (9)
Patmos (6)
Paxos (5)
Rhodes (6)
Salamis (7)
Samos (5)
Santorini (v.) (9)
Scio (4)
Serifos (7)
Seriphos (8)
Skopelos (8)
Skyro (5)
Skyros (6)
Syra (4)
Thera (5)
Zante (5)
Zea (3)

India
Andaman Is. (7)
Andamans (8)
Amindivi Is. (8)
Elephanta (9)
Lakshadweep Is. (11)
Nicobar Is. (7)
Salsette (8)

Indian Ocean
Amirante Is. (8)
Christmas I. (9)
Cocos Is. (5)
Hatia (5)
Keeling Is. (7)
Maldives (8)
Mascarene Is. (9)
Mauritius (9)
Réunion (7)
Rodrigues (9)
Seychelles (10)
Sri Lanka (8)

Indonesia
Albay (5)
Amboina (7)
Anamba Is. (6)
Arru Is. (4)
Bali (4)
Banda (5)
Billiton (8)
Borneo (6)
Buru (4)
Calamianes (10)
Celebes (7)
Ceram (5)
Flores (6)
Gilolo (6)
Halmahera (9)
Java (4)
Kei Is. (3)
Krakatoa (v.) (8)
Molucca Is. (7)
Moluccas (8)
Negros (6)
Sangir Is. (6)
Spice Is. (5)
Sulu Is. (4)
Sumatra (7)
Sumbawa (7)
Sunda Is. (5)
Ternate (7)
Timor (5)
Vaigen (6)
Zebu (4)

Iran
Kishni (4)
Ormuz (5)

Ireland (Republic of)
Achill (6)
Aran (4)
Arranmore (9)
Bere I. (4)
Clare (5)
Clear (5)
Copeland Is. (8)
Dursey (6)
Eagle I. (5)
Great Blasket (12)
High I. (4)
Inishbofin (10)
Inishshark (10)
Inishturk (9)
Lambay (6)
Tory (4)
Valentia (8)

Isles of Scilly
Bryher (6)
Gugh (4)
St Agnes (7)
St Martin's (9)
St Mary's (7)
Samson (6)
Tresco (6)

Italy
Capri (5)
Cherso (6)
Ischia (6)
Monte Cristo (11)
Sicily (6)

Japan
Hokkaido (8)
Hondo (5)
Honshu (6)
Iturup (6)
Kyushu (6)
Shikoka (7)
Yezo (4)

Korea
Cheja (5)
Dinding Is. (7)
Labuan (6)
Lombok (6)
Penang (6)
Prince of Wales I. (13)
Quelpart (8)
Sandlewood I. (10)
Timor (5)

Malaysia
Banca (5)

Mediterranean
Aegades Is. (7)
Aeolian Is. (v.) (7)
Balearic Is. (8)
Cabrera (7)
Candia (6)
Capraja (7)
Caprera (7)
Cerigo (6)
Cerigotto (9)
Corsica (7)
Cyprus (6)
Elba (4)
Formentera (10)
Gozo (4)
Ibiza (5)
Ivica (5)
Lampedusa (9)
Leucadia (8)
Lipari Is. (6)
Malta (5)
Majorca (7)
Mallorca (8)
Minorca (7)
Pantellaria (11)
Sardinia (8)
Scarpanto (9)
Sicily (6)
Stromboli (v.) (9)
Tenedos (7)

Netherlands
Ameland (7)
Beverland (9)
Dordrecht (9)
Frisian Is. (7)
Marken (6)
Rottum (6)
Texel (5)
Tholen (6)
Vlieland (8)
Voorn (5)
Walcheren (9)

New Zealand
Auckland Is. (8)
Bounty Is. (6)
Campbell (8)
North I. (5)
South I. (5)
Stewart I. (7)

Northern Ireland
Rathlin (7)

North Sea
Heligoland (10)

Norway
Lofoten Is. (7)
Tromso (6)

Pacific
Adi (3)
Admiralty Is. (9)
Aleutian Is. (8)
Banks (5)
Behring Is. (7)
Bismark Arch. (7)
Bonin Is. (5)
Bougainville (12)
Caroline Is. (8)
Chatham Is. (7)
Christmas I. (9)
Cook Is. (4)
Easter I. (6)
Ellice Is. (6)
Fanning (7)
Fiji Is. (4)
Friendlies (10)
Friendly Is. (8)
Galapagos Is. (v.) (9)
Gambier Is. (7)
Gilbert Is. (7)
Guadalcanal (11)
Guam (4)
Hall Is. (4)
Hawaii (6)
Isle of Pines (11)
Jaluit (6)
Juan Fernandez (13)
Kandava (7)
Kerguelen Land (13)
Kermadec Is. (8)
Kodiak (6)
Kurile Is. (6)
Ladrones (8)
Louisiade Arch. (9)
Low Arch. (3)
Loyalty Is. (7)
Malicolo (8)
Manihiki Is. (8)
Manitoulin Is. (11)
Marianne Is. (8)
Marquesas Is. (9)
Marshall Is. (8)
Melanesia (9)
Micronesia (10)
Molokai (7)
Nauru (5)
Navigators' I. (10)
New Britain (10)
New Hebrides (11)
New Zealand (10)
New Caledonia (12)
New Guinea (9)
Norfolk Island (13)
Oahu (4)
Oceania (7)
Otaheite (8)
Papua (5)
Pearl Is. (5)
Pelew Is. (5)
Phoenix Is. (7)
Pitcairn Is. (8)
Polynesia (9)
Pribilof Is. (8)

Pribylov Is. (8)
Raratonga (9)
Rat Is. (3)
Rotumah (7)
Samoa (5)
Sandwich Is. (8)
Savage I. (8)
Society Is. (7)
Solomon Is. (7)
Starbuck (8)
Tahiti (6)
Timor Laut Is. (9)
Tonga (5)
Tuamotu (7)
Tubugi Is. (6)
Yap (3)

Philippines
Leyte (5)
Luzon (5)
Mindanao (8)

Red Sea
Kamaran (7)
Massowa (7)

Russia
Kolonev (7)
Saghalien (9)
Sakhalin (8)

Scotland
Ailsa Craig (10)
Arran (5)
Barra (5)
Benbecula (9)
Bernera (7)
Berneray (8)
Burray (6)
Bute (4)
Canna (5)
Coll (4)
Colonsay (8)
Cumbrae (7)
Dabaz (5)
Eigg (4)
Eriskay (7)
Erromanga (9)
Ewe (3)
Fair Isle (8)
Flannan Is. (7)
Foula (5)
Great Cumbrae (12)
Harris (6)
Hebrides (8)
Hoy (3)
Inchcolm (8)
Inchgarvie (10)
Inchkeith (9)
Iona (4)
Islay (5)
Jura (4)
Lewis (5)
Little Cumbrae (13)
May, I. of (3)
Muck (4)
Mull, I. of (4)
North Uist (9)
Orkney Is. (6)
Orkneys (7)
Pomona (6)
Rhum (4)
Ronaldsay (9)
Rothesay (8)
St Kilda (7)
Scarba (6)
Shetland Is. (8)
Shetlands (9)
Skerryvore (10)
Skye, I. of (4)
Soay (4)
South Uist (9)
Staffa (6)
Stroma (6)
Uist (4)
Ulva (4)
Unst (4)
Tiree (5)
Whalsay (7)
Yell (4)

South Africa
Inyak (5)
Robben I. (6)

South America
Chiloe (6)
Chincha Is. (7)
Lobos Is. (5)
Marajo (6)
Pinos (5)

Spain
Balearic Is. (8)
Balearics (9)
Canaries (8)
Canary Is. (6)
Gomera (6)
Gran Canaria (11)
Ibiza (5)
Lanzarote (9)
Majorca (7)
Mallorca (8)
Minorca (7)
Tenerife (8)

Turkey
Princes Is. (7)

USA
Ellis (5)
Hart's I. (5)
Long I. (4)
Manhattan (9)
Martha's Vineyard (15)
Nantucket (9)
Prince of Wales I. (13)
Rhode I. (5)
Roanoke (7)
Staten I. (6)
Thousand Is. (8)
Tortugas Is. (8)
Unalaska (8)

Wales
Anglesey (8)
Caldy (5)
Puffin I. (6)

West Indies
Abaco (5)
Antigua (7)
Antilles Is. (8)
Aruba (5)
Bahama Is. (6)
Bahamas (7)
Barbados (Is.) (8)
Caicos I. (6)
Caribbee Is. (8.)
Cayman Is. (6)

Cuba (4)
Curacao (7)
Desirade (8.)
Domingo (7)
Dominica (8)
Eleuthera (9)
Grenada (7)
Grenadines (10)
Guadeloupe (10)
Haiti (5)
Hispaniola (10)
Inagua (6)
Isle of Pines (11)
Jamaica (7)
Leeward Is. (7)
Margarita (9)
Mariagalante (12)
Martinique (10)
Montserrat (10)
Nevis (5)
Porto Rico (9)
Puerto Rico (10)
Saba (4)
St Bartholomew (13)
St Christopher (13)
St John (6)
St Kitts (7)
St Lucia (7)
St Martin (8)
St Thomas (8)
St Vincent (9)
Tobago (6)
Tortola (7)
Tortuga (7)
Trinidad (8)
Turks and Caicos Is. (14)
Virgin Is. (6)
Watling I. (7)
Windward Is. (8)

Knights of the Round Table

Bedivere (8)
Bors (4)
Ector (5)
Galahad (7)
Gareth (6)
Gawain (6)
Kay (3)
Lancelot du Lac (12)
Lionel (5)
Mordred* (7)
Perceval (8)
Tarquin (7)
Tristan de Lyonnais (17)
Heaven (6)
Hell (4)
Judgement (9)

*Mordred was Arthur's son and responsible for his downfall

Lakes, Inland Lochs, Loughs and Sea Lochs

NB: letter counts do not include the words *lake, loch*, etc.
L. = Loch; Lou. = Lough

Afghanistan
Hamun (5)
Seistan (7)

Africa
Akamyara (8)
Albert (6)
Albert Edward Nyanza (18)
Albert Nyanza (12)
Bangweolo (9)
Cabora Bassa (11)
Chad (4)
Edward (6)
George (6)
Idi Amin (7)
Idi Amin Dada (11)
Kariba (6)
Kivu (4)
Kossu (5)
Leopold (7)
Malawi (6)
Mobuto Sésé Seko (14)
Moero (5)
Mweru (5)
Nyanza (6)
Nyasa (5)
Rudolf (6)
Shirwa (6)
Stefanie (8)
Tanganyika (10)
Tchad (5)
Tumba (5)
Victoria (8)
Victoria Nyanza (14)

Argentina
Argentino (9)
Viedma (6)

Armenia
Sevan (5)

Asia
Caspian Sea (10)
Dead Sea (7)
Issyk-Kul (8)
Khanka (6)

Australia
Austin (6)
Blanche (7)
Buloke (6)
Chowilla (8)
Cooroong (the) (8)
Eucumbene (9)
Eyre (4)
Frome (5)
Gairdner (8)
George (6)
Hindmarsh (9)
Humboldt (8)
Moore (5)
Torrens (7)
Tyrrell (7)

Bolivia
Roguaguado (10)

Burundi
Nyanza (6)

Cambodia
Sap (3)

Canada
Abitibi (7)
Athabasca (9)
Baker (5)
Camm (4)
Champlain (9)
Diefenbaker (11)
Dore (4)
Erie (4)
Etawney (7)
Garry (5)
Ghana (5)
Great Bear (9)
Great Slave (10)
Ha Ha (4)
Huron (5)
Kawarthi (8)
Kootenay (8)
Lachine (7)
Lake of the Woods (14)
Lesser Slave (11)
Mahood (6)
Manitoba (8)
Michikamau (10)
Minto (5)
Mistassini (10)
Muskoka (7)
Nipigon (7)
Nipissing (9)
Ontario (7)
Payne (5)
Playgreen (9)
Quesnal (7)
Rainy (5)
Reindeer (8)
Rideau (6)
Rosseau (7)
Simcoe (6)
St John (6)
Stuart (6)
Talka (5)
Timiskaming (11)
Winnipeg (8)
Winnipegosis (12)
Wollaston (9)

China
Dongting (8)
Koko Nor (7)
Tengri-Nor (9)
Tungting (8)

Congo, Democratic Republic of the
Mai-Ndombe (9)

Egypt
Bitter Lakes (11)
Mareotis (8)
Menzaleh (8)
Nasser (6)

England
Buttermere (10)
Coniston Water (13)
Derwentwater (12)
Ennerdale (9)
Grasmere (8)
Hawes Water (10)
Rydal Water (10)
Serpentine (10)
Thirlmere (9)
Ullswater (9)
Virginia Water (13)
Wastwater (9)
Windermere (10)

Estonia
Peipus (6)

Ethiopia
Abaya (5)
Tana (4)
Tsano (5)

Europe
Scutari (7)

Finland
Enara (5)

Ghana
Volta (5)

Hungary
Balaton (7)

India
Chilka (6)
Hirakud (7)

Indonesia
Toba (4)

Iran
Urmia (5)

Ireland (Republic of)
Allen, Lou. (5)
Derg, Lou. (4)
Ennell, Lou. (6)
Foyle, Lou. (5)
Key, Lou. (3)
Killarney, Lakes of (9)
Ree, Lou. (3)
Sheelin, Lou. (7)

Israel
Tiberias (8)
Sea of Galilee (12)

Italy
Como (4)
Garda (5)
Iseo (4)
Maggiore (8)
Perugia (7)
Trasimeno (9)

Japan
Biwa (4)

Kazakhstan
Aaköl (5)
Aral Sea (7)
Balqash (7)

Kyrgyzstan
Ysyk (4)

Mexico
Chapala (7)
Texcoco (7)
Tezcuco (7)
Xaltocan (8)
Xochimilco (10)

Netherlands
Ijssel Sea (9)
Ijsselmeer (10)
Yssel (5)
Zuider Zee (9)

New Zealand
Benmore (7)
Manipuri (8)
Oahu (4)
Rotomahana (10)
Tarawera (8)
Taupo (5)
Te Anau (6)
Wakatipu (8)
Wanaka (6)

Nicaragua
Nicaragua (9)

Northern Ireland
Belfast, Lou. (7)
Neagh, Lou. (5)
Strangford, Lou. (10)

Norway
Mjøsa (5)

Peru
Titicaca (8)

Russia
Baikal (6)
Elton (5)
Ilmen (5)
Kuibyshev (9)
Ladoga (6)
Onega (5)
Peipus (6)
Rybinsk (7)

Scotland
Affric, L. (6)
Ard, L. (3)
Arkaig, L. (6)
Assynt, L. (6)
Awe, L. (3)
Broom, L. (5)
Buie, L. (4)
Coille-Bharr, L. (11)
Earn, L. (4)
Eck, L. (3)
Ericht, L. (6)
Etive, L. (5)
Ewe, L. (3)
Fannich, L. (7)
Fyne, L. (4)
Gilp, L. (4)
Goil, L. (4)
Katrine, L. (7)
Leven L. (5)
Linnhe, L. (6)
Lochy, L. (5)
Lomond, L. (6)
Long, L. (4)
Loyal, L. (5)
Luichart, L. (8)
Maree, L. (5)
Morar, L. (5)
Moy, L. (3)
Ness, L. (4)
Quoich, L. (6)
Rannoch, L. (7)
Ryan, L. (4)
Seaforth, L. (8)
Shiel, L. (5)
Shin, L. (5)
Spey, L. (4)
Strathy, L. (7)
Sween, L. (5)
Tarbert, L. (7)
Tay, L. (3)
Tromlee, L. (7)
Torridon, L. (8)
Tummel, L. (6)
Urr, L. (3)
Voil, L. (4)

Sweden
Hjelmar (7)
Malar (5)
Wener (5)
Wetter (6)
Vänern (6)

Switzerland
Constance (9)
Geneva (6)
Lucerne (7)
Lugano (6)
Neuchatel (9)
Sempach (7)
Thun (4)
Zug (3)
Zurich (6)

Tibet
Tengri-Nor (9)

Turkey
Hirfanli (8)
Okhrida (7)
Tuz Gol (6)
Van (3)

Ukraine
Kakhovka (8)

USA
Bear (4)
Caillou (7)
Champlain (9)
Drummond (8)
Erie (4)
Grand Coulee (11)
Great Salt (9)
Honey (5)
Huron (5)
Indian (6)
Itasca (6)
La Crosse (8)
Lackawanna (10)
Lake of the Woods (14)
Mead (4)
Michigan (8)
Oneida (6)
Ontario (7)
Placid (6)
Pontchatrain (12)
Shasta (6)
Superior (8)
Utah (4)
Wenham (6)
Yellowstone (11)

Uzbekistan
Aral Sea (7)

Venezuela
Maracaibo (9)
Valencia (8)

Wales
Bala (4)
Vyrnwy (6)

Law Sittings

Hilary (6)
Easter (6)
Trinity (7)
Michaelmas (10)

London Boroughs

Barking & Dagenham (15)
Barnet (6)
Bexley (6)
Brent (5)
Bromley (7)
Camden (6)
Croydon (7)
Ealing (6)
Enfield (7)
Greenwich (9)
Hackney (7)
Hammersmith & Fulham (17)
Haringey (8)
Harrow (6)
Havering (8)
Hillingdon (10)
Hounslow (8)
Islington (9)
Kensington & Chelsea (17)
Kingston upon Thames (18)
Lambeth (7)
Lewisham (8)
Merton (6)
Newham (6)
Redbridge (9)
Richmond upon Thames (18)
Southwark (9)
Sutton (6)
Tower Hamlets (12)
Waltham Forest (13)
Wandsworth (10)

City status
Westminster (11)
Corporation of London (19)

London Underground Stations

4
Bank
Oval

5
Upney
Angel

6
Balham
Debden
Epping
Euston
Kenton
Leyton
Morden
Pinner
Temple

7
Aldgate
Archway
Arsenal
Barking
Borough
Bow Road
Brixton
Chesham
Croxley
East Ham
Edgware
Elm Park
Fairlop
Holborn
Kilburn
Mile End
Neasden
Oakwood
Pimlico
Ruislip
St Pauls
Wapping
Watford
West Ham

8
Alperton
Amersham
Barbican
Burnt Oak
Chalk Farm
Chigwell
Eastcote
Greenford
Hainault
Highgate
Ickenham
Loughton
Monument
Moor Park
Moorgate
New Cross
Northolt
Osterley
Perivale
Plaistow
Richmond
Royal Oak
Shadwell
Stanmore
Uxbridge
Vauxhall
Victoria
Wanstead
Waterloo
Woodford
Kingsbury
Maida Vale
Northwood
Old Street
Park Royal
Queensway
Redbridge
Southgate
Southwark
Stockwell
Stratford
Tower Hill
Upminster
Upton Park
West Acton
White City
Wimbledon
Wood Green

9
Acton Town
Bayswater
Becontree
Colindale
East Acton
Gants Hill
Green Park
Hampstead
Harlesden

10
Arnos Grove
Bermondsey
Bond Street
Brent Cross
Camden Town
Canons Park
Dollis Hill
Earls Court
East Putney

Embankment
Farringdon
Grange Hill
Hanger Lane
High Barnet
Hillingdon
Hornchurch
Kennington
Kew Gardens
Manor House
Marble Arch
Marylebone
North Acton
Paddington
Queens Park
Queensbury
Shoreditch
Tooting Bec
West Harrow

11

Aldgate East
Baker Street
Barkingside
Barons Court
Belsize Park
Blackfriars
Boston Manor
Bounds Green
Canada Water
Canary Wharf
Canning Town
Chorleywood
Cockfosters
Edgware Road
Gunnersbury
Hammersmith
Hatton Cross
Holland Park
Kensal Green
Kentish Town
Kilburn Park
Latimer Road
Leytonstone
Newbury Park
North Ealing
North Harrow
Northfields
Preston Road
Rayners Lane
Regents Park
Rotherhithe
Snaresbrook
South Ealing
South Harrow
South Kenton
Southfields
St James Park
St Johns Wood
Sudbury Hill
Sudbury Town
Surrey Quays
Theydon Bois
Tufnell Park
Wembley Park
West Ruislip
Westminster
Whitechapel

12

Bethnal Green
Bromley-by-Bow
Cannon Street
Chancery Lane
Charing Cross
Chiswick Park
Clapham North
Clapham South
Colliers Wood
Covent Garden
Dagenham East
Ealing Common
East Finchley
Euston Square
Finchley Road
Finsbury Park
Golders Green
Goldhawk Road
Goodge Street
Holloway Road
Hounslow East
Hounslow West
Lambeth North
London Bridge
Mansion House
Mill Hill East
New Cross Gate
North Wembley
Oxford Circus
Parsons Green
Putney Bridge
Roding Valley
Ruislip Manor
Seven Sisters
Sloane Square
South Ruislip
Stepney Green
Swiss Cottage
Turnham Green
Turnpike Lane
Warren Street
West Brompton
West Finchley
Woodside Park

13

Buckhurst Hill
Clapham Common
Hendon Central
Knightsbridge
Ladbroke Grove
Lancaster Gate
Northwick Park
Rickmansworth
Russell Square
Shepherds Bush
South Woodford
Stamford Brook
Tottenham Hale
Warwick Avenue
West Hampstead
Wimbledon Park

14

Black Horse Road
Caledonian Road
Ealing Broadway
Elephant & Castle
Fulham Broadway
Gloucester Road
Hyde Park Corner
North Greenwich
Northwood Hills
Ruislip Gardens
South Wimbledon
Wembley Central
West Kensington
Westbourne Park
Willesden Green

15
Chalfont & Latimer
Finchley Central
Harrow-on-the-Hill
Hounslow Central
Leicester Square
Liverpool Street
Notting Hill Gate
Ravenscourt Park
South Kensington
Stonebridge Park
Tooting Broadway
Upminster Bridge

16
Dagenham Heathway
Harrow & Wealdstone
Heathrow Terminal 4
Piccadilly Circus

17
Heathrow Terminals 1,2,3
Highbury & Islington
Kensington Olympia
Willesden Junction

18
Mornington Crescent
Tottenham Court Road
Walthamstow Central

19
Great Portland Street
Kings Cross St Pancras
Totteridge & Whetstone

20
High Street Kensington

Males, Females and Young of Animals

3
cob (M swan)
cow (F cow, elephant, whale)
cub (Y bear, fox, lion, wolf, tiger)
doe (F deer, hare, rabbit)
dog (M dog, fox)
ewe (F sheep)
fry (Y fish)
hen (F most birds, lobster, salmon)
hob (M ferret)
kid (Y goat)
kit (Y ferret)
pen (F swan)
pup (Y dog, seal)
ram (M sheep)
sow (F badger, pig)
tom (M cat)
tup (M sheep)

4
boar (M badger, pig)
buck (M deer, rabbit)
bull (M cow, elephant, whale)
calf (Y cow, elephant, whale)
cock (M most birds, lobster, salmon)
colt (Y horse)
duck (F duck)
eyas (Y hawk)
fawn (Y deer)
foal (Y horse, zebra)
gilt (F pig)
hind (F deer)
jill (F ferret)
joey (Y kangaroo)
lamb (Y sheep)
mare (F horse)
parr (Y fish)
stag (M deer)

5
billy (M goat)
bitch (F dog, wolf)
chick (Y most birds)
drake (M duck)
elver (Y eel)
goose (F goose)
nanny (F goat)
poult (Y pheasant, turkey)
puppy (Y dog)
queen (F cat)
shoat (Y pig)
steer (M cow)
vixen (F fox)
whelp (Y dog, wolf)

6
cygnet (Y swan)
eaglet (Y eagle)
gander (M goose)
heifer (F cow)
kitten (Y cat)
peahen (F peafowl)
piglet (Y pig)

7
bullock (M cow)
gosling (Y goose)
jackass (M donkey)
leveret (Y hare)
lioness (F lion)
peacock (M peafowl)
rooster (M chicken)
tadpole (Y frog, toad)
tigress (F tiger)

8
cockerel (M chicken)
jennyass (F donkey)

stallion (M horse)
yearling (Y horse)

10
leopardess (F leopard)
pantheress (F panther)

Military and Warfare Terminology

2
RN

3
arm
DMZ
dud
foe
gas
gun
HMS
jam
kit
man
map
MIA
RAF
sap
USA
USN
USS
van
war

4
ally
arms
army
AWOL
band
bang
base
bear
belt
berm
camp
D-day
draw
duck
duel
duty
fife
file
fire
flag
flak
foot
fort
fray
halt
host
jeep
kepi
kill
levy
line
loot
mess
mine
moat
NATO
navy
park
PIAT
plan
post
push
raid
rake
ramp
rank
rape
raze
rear
rout
ruse
sack
shot
sink
slay
spot
spur
take
tank
taps
tent
tilt
trap
unit
USAF
wage
ward
wing
yomp
zero
zone

5
abort
agent
alert
annex
armed
armor
array
baton
beret
beset
blast
blitz
booty
busby
cadre
cells
clean
corps
cover
craft
decoy
demob
depot
ditch
draft
dress
drill
enemy
enrol
equip
feint
field
fight
flank
flare
fleet
foray
front
group
guard
guide
harry
Jerry
jihad
khaki
leave
lines
march
medal
melee
mufti
onset
parry
peace
power
prime
radar
rally
range
ranks
rebel
recce
relay
repel
rifle
round
route
sally
salvo
scale
seize
shako
shell
shift
shock
shoot
siege
smart
snipe
sonar
sonic
squad
staff
stand
storm
strap
track
troop
truce
wound

6
ack-ack
action
allies
all out
ambush
animus
armada
armour
assail
at ease
attack
backup
bailey
banner
battle
billet
blow up
breech
bunker
castle
charge
cohort
colour
column
combat
convoy
cordon
curfew
debris
decamp
defeat
defect
defend
deploy
desert
detach
detail
disarm
dog tag
donjon
dugout
embark
embody
engage
Enigma
enlist
enmity
ensign
escape
escarp
escort
firing
flight
forces
forted
gabion
glacis
guards
guidon
harass
hawhaw
helmet
impact
impale
inroad
invade
invest
inwall
killed
kitbag
legion
maquis
marker
mining
mobile
muster
mutiny
occupy
oppose
orders
outfit
parade
parley
parole
patrol
permit
pocket
pursue
puttee
raider
ransom
rapine
rappel
ration
ravage
rebuff
recoil
redcap
relais
relief
report
resist
retake
retire

review
riddle
rioter
roster
saddle
salute
sconce
sensor
signal
sign up
sniper
sortie
spoils
square
stores
strafe
strife
strike
stripe
stroke
subdue
supply
target
tattoo
thrust
treaty
trench
trophy
turret
unhurt
vallum
valour
victor
volley
walled
war cry

7
advance
airdrop
airlift
air raid
alcazar
archery
armoury
arsenal
assault
baldric
baggage
barrack
barrage
bastion
battery
besiege
bivouac
body bag
bombard
bomb bay
bombing
bomblet
brigade
bulwark
canteen
carrier
cashier
cavalry
charger
chevron
citadel
cold war
colours
command
company
conchie
conquer
counter
courage
cruiser
crusade
curtain
debouch
defence
defiant
degrade
destroy
détente
disband
dismiss
dungeon
echelon
envelop
epaulet
evacuee
fallout
fanfare
fatigue
fend off
fighter
flanker
fortify
fortlet
forward
foxhole
frigate
gallery
gas mask
germ war
go to war
guérite
gunboat
gunfire
gunnery
gunroom
gunship
gunshot
harness
Harrier
holster
holy war
hostage
hostile
invader
jamming
jankers
jump jet
Kremlin
landing
lookout
looting
lunette
maniple
mantlet
march on
Marines
martial
megaton
militia
missing
mission
neutral
nuclear
on guard
outpost
outwork
overrun
paladin
parados
parapet
pass out
patriot
pennant
phalanx
pillbox
platoon
postern
priming
protect
pursuit
quarter
rampage
rampart
rations
ravages
ravelin
Red Army
redoubt
refugee
regular
repulse
reserve
retreat
reverse
salient
sandbag
section
service
sinking
sniping
standby
subvert
support
tactics
trailer
traitor
treason
triumph
unarmed
uniform
valiant
vanfoss
victory
wage war
ward off
warfare
war game
warlike
warlord
warpath
war song
warworn
windage
wounded

8
accoutre
activate
advanced
airborne
aircraft
air force
alliance
armament
armorial
armoured
arms race
Army List
attacker
baldrick
barbette
barbican
barracks
bartizan
bawdrick
bearskin
blockade
bomb site
buttress
campaign
casemate
casualty
cenotaph
chivalry
civil war
collapse
conflict
conquest
corvette
decimate
decisive
defector
defender
demilune
despatch
detonate
disarray
dispatch
dive-bomb
division
dogfight
drumfire

duelling
earth bag
embattle
embodied
enceinte
enfilade
entrench
escalate
evacuate
eyes left
fencible
field day
fighting
flagpole
flagpost
flotilla
fortress
furlough
garrison
gauntlet
gonfalon
guerilla
hang fire
hill fort
hold fire
infantry
informer
invasion
janizary
jingoism
kamikaze
knapsack
Land Army
Landwehr
last post
lay siege
lay waste
lodgment
loophole
Mameluke
mantelet
marching
mark time
martello
massacre
militant
military
mobilize
movement
Mulberry
musketry
mutineer
mutinous
near miss
on parade
open fire
opponent
ordnance
outflank
outguard
overcome
overkill
pacifist
palisade
paradrop
parallel
partisan
password
pavilion
pay corps
prisoner
quarters
quisling
radio fix
railhead
ramparts
rear line
rearward
re-embark
regiment
reprisal
reveille
ricochet
rifle pit
roll call
sabotage
saboteur
saluting
scramble
security
sentry-go
services (the)
shabrack
shelling
shooting
shot hole
skirmish
soldiery
squadron
stalward
stampede
standard
star fort
stave off
stockade
stoppage
storming
straddle
strafing
strategy
strength
struggle
supplies
surprise
surround
sword arm
tactical
total war
training
transfer
traverse
trenches
turbojet
turncoat
unallied
unharmed
uprising
vanguard
vanquish
vigilant
war crime
war dance
war grave
warhorse
weaponry
yeomanry
world war
zero hour

9

aggressor
air attack
air strike
alarm post
armistice
army corps
artillery
assailant
atomic war
attention
attrition
ballistic
banderole
bandolier
banquette
barricade
battalion
battle cry
beachhead
beleaguer
bellicose
bloodshed
body count
bombed-out
bombproof
bombs away
bombshell
bombsight
bomb squad
bugle call
camouflet
cannonade
captaincy
cashiered
cavalcade
ceasefire
challenge
chevalier
cold steel
colonelcy
combatant
combative
conqueror
conscript
crack shot
crossfire
crow's foot
defection
defensive
desertion
destroyer
devastate
discharge
disengage
earthwork
embattled
encompass
encounter
enemy camp
enemy fire
enrolment
epaulette
equipment
espionage
eyes front
eyes right
field army
firepower
flagstaff
flash burn
forage cap
fortalice
front line
fusillade
gallantry
gas attack
gladiator
guardroom
guerrilla
gun battle
gun turret
haversack
heavy fire
home front
Home Guard
hostility
incursion
insurgent
invalided
irregular
janissary
land force
Landsturm
legionary
lifeguard
logistics
loopholed
Luftwaffe
manoeuvre
march-past
megadeath
mercenary
militancy
minefield
mujahedin
objective
offensive
onslaught
operation
overpower

overthrow
overwhelm
packdrill
parachute
patriotic
phoney war
pressgang
projector
protector
rearguard
rebellion
reconquer
red ensign
reinforce
rencontre
revetment
Royal Navy
safe haven
safe house
sally port
sea battle
semaphore
sentry box
shellfire
slaughter
slope arms
slow march
stack arms
stand fast
stand fire
strategic
submarine
surrender
sword knot
task force
terrorism
terrorist
trainband
transport
treachery
tricolour
troopship
under fire
unguarded
uniformed
uninjured
unopposed
unscathed
unsheathe
vigilance

war effort
War Office
watchword
Wehrmacht
white flag

10

active duty
active list
Air Command
air defence
amphibious
annexation
annihilate
antagonism
Armageddon
armed truce
attackable
ballistics
barbed wire
battle flag
battle hymn
battle line
battlement
battleship
blitzkrieg
blockhouse
bombing run
breastwork
bridgehead
bugle corps
call to arms
camel corps
camouflage
campaigner
cantonment
capitulate
chauvinism
checkpoint
combat zone
commandeer
commission
decampment
declare war
defendable
defensible
demobilize
deployment
despatches
detachment

detonation
direct fire
dispatches
dive-bomber
divisional
dragonnade
drawbridge
duty roster
embankment
encampment
engagement
engarrison
enlistment
entrenched
epauletted
escalation
evacuation
expedition
firing line
flying camp
Foot Guards
garrisoned
glasshouse
ground fire
guardhouse
hand-to-hand
heliograph
inspection
insurgency
investment
invincible
jingoistic
lay siege to
Life Guards
light horse
limited war
line of fire
manoeuvres
martial law
militiaman
militarism
muster book
muster roll
need to know
nerve agent
neutralize
night watch
no man's land
nuclear war
occupation

operations
over the top
patriotism
patrolling
point blank
portcullis
prison camp
projectile
propaganda
protection
provision
quick march
raking fire
reconquest
recruiting
regimental
rencounter
rendezvous
resistance
revolution
rifle corps
rifle range
route march
rules of war
sabretache
sentry duty
sentry post
shellproof
shell shock
siege train
signal fire
signalling
slit trench
soldiering
stand guard
state of war
stronghold
subjection
subsection
submission
subversion
superpower
surrounded
sword fight
take up arms
terreplein
trajectory
trench foot
undefended
under siege

unsheathed
victorious
vulnerable
war council
war machine
watchtower

11

area bombing
armed combat
armed forces
at the double
barrack room
battledress
battlefield
battlegroup
battle order
battle royal
besiegement
bombardment
bulletproof
castellated
change sides
collaborate
conquerable
countermine
declaration
defenceless
devastation
disarmament
disbandment
dive-bombing
draft dodger
dress parade
ejector seat
embarkation
emplacement
envelopment
fatigue duty
fifth column
firing party
firing squad
flying corps
flying party
forced march
friend or foe
germ warfare
gun carriage
Horse Guards
hostilities
impregnable
indefensive
machicolate
Maginot line
Marine Corps
minesweeper
peacekeeper
peace treaty
platoon fire
postern gate
present arms
put to flight
rangefinder
rank and file
reconnoitre
recruitment
regular army
requisition
running fire
safe-conduct
searchlight
shock troops
shoot to kill
smokescreen
stand at ease
stray bullet
supply depot
take by storm
thin red line
unconquered
underground
unprotected
war criminal
war memorial
white ensign

12

advance guard
annihilation
anti-aircraft
armour-plated
Bailey bridge
battleground
battlemented
beat a retreat
bomb disposal
bush fighting
cannon fodder
capitulation
chauvinistic
civil defence
collaborator
commissariat
commissioned
conscription
council of war
countermarch
counterscarp
court-martial
covering fire
decommission
draft dodging
ejection seat
fatigue party
field kitchen
flying column
forward march
friendly fire
garrison town
go over the top
ground troops
guerrilla war
headquarters
hollow square
indefensible
intelligence
invulnerable
landing craft
landing party
Light Brigade
light cavalry
line of battle
machicolated
march against
medical corps
militaristic
mine detector
mobilization
non-combatant
outmanoeuvre
paramilitary
peacekeeping
pioneer corps
raiding party
religious war
retrenchment
rocket attack
Royal Marines
Royal Signals
shell-shocked
shock tactics
shoulder arms
shoulder belt
siege warfare
signal rocket
state of siege
surveillance
theatre of war
unvanquished
white feather
who goes there

13

accoutrements
advanced guard
armed services
barrack square
battle cruiser
battle fatigue
carpet bombing
carrier pigeon
circumvallate
collaboration
combat fatigue
counterattack
counterstroke
expeditionary
fatigue parade
field of battle
fighting force
flying colours
fortification
guard of honour
invincibility
King's shilling
light infantry
machicolation
martello tower
mounted police
mushroom cloud
order of battle
ordnance depot
pitched battle
point of impact
pontoon bridge
rallying point
re-embarkation
regular troops
reinforcement
Royal Air Force

running battle
shoulder strap
special forces
splinterproof
storming party
strategically
suicide bomber
swordsmanship
trench warfare
unarmed combat
unconquerable
Victoria Cross
war department

14
air raid shelter
ammunition dump
auxiliary force
barrage balloon
blockade runner
demobilization
fifth columnist
fortifications
general reserve
mechanized army
military police
nuclear warfare
pincer movement
Pyrrhic victory
reconnaissance
reinforcements
Royal Artillery
Royal Engineers
Royal Tank Corps
security forces
standing orders
supreme command
volunteer force
walking wounded
war of attrition
winter quarters

15
aircraft carrier
casualty station
clearing station
discharge papers
displaced person
dressing station
ethnic cleansing
guerilla warfare
invulnerability
married quarters
military academy
military college
military funeral
military honours
mounted infantry
non-commissioned
observation post
point-blank range

16
collateral damage
counteroffensive
passing-out parade
precision bombing
preemptive attack
preemptive strike
soldier of fortune
stand to attention
war establishment

17 *and over*
biological warfare (17)
concentration camp 17)
conscientious objector (21)
demilitarized zone (17)
expeditionary force (18)
helicopter gunship (17)
peacekeeping force (17)
post-traumatic stress disorder (27)
recruiting sergeant 18)
rules of engagement (17)
Special Air Service (17)
Special Boat Service (18)
special operations (17)

Modern Musicians

3
Lee, Peggy
Piaf, Edith
Ross, Diana

4
Baez, Joan
Bilk, Acker
Cash, Johnny
Cole, Nat King
Gaye, Marvin
Getz, Stan
John, Elton
Kern, Jerome
Lynn, Dame Vera
Monk, Thelonious
Jones, Tom
Melba, Dame Nellie
Melly, George
Smith, Bessie
Starr, Ringo
Swann, Sir Michael

5
Basie, Count
Berry, Chuck
Black, Cilla
Bowie, David
Clark, Petula
Davis, Miles
Dylan, Bob
Haley, Bill
Holly, Buddy
Horne, Lena

6
Bassey, Shirley
Berlin, Irving
Coward, Sir Noel
Crosby, Bing
Jagger, Mick
Joplin, Janis

Joplin, Scott
Lennon, John
Miller, Glenn
Mingus, Charlie
Morton, Jelly Roll
Parker, Charlie
Parton, Dolly
Porter, Cole
Seegar, Peggy
Seegar, Pete
Waller, Fats
Waters, Muddy

7
Beatles, the
Brubeck, Dave
Clapton, Eric
Collins, Judy
Garland, Judy
Gilbert, William S.
Goodman, Benny
Guthrie, Woody
Hendrix, Jimi
Holiday, Billie
Jackson, Mahalia
Jackson, Michael
MacColl, Ewan
Madonna
Novello, Ivor
Richard, Sir Cliff
Rodgers, Richard
Sinatra, Frank
Stevens, Cat
Vaughan, Sarah
Warwick, Dionne

8
Coltrane, John
Flanders, Michael
Harrison, George
Liberace
MacGowan, Shane
Mitchell, Joni
Morrison, Van
Sondheim, Stephen
Sullivan, Arthur S.
Williams, Andy
Williams, Hank

9
Armstrong, Louis
Beach Boys, the
Belafonte, Harry
Ellington, Duke
Gillespie, Dizzy
Leadbelly
McCartney, Paul
Reinhardt, Django

10 ***and over***
Fitzgerald, Ella (10)
Hammerstein, Oscar (11)
Led Zeppelin (11)
Lloyd-Webber, Andrew (11)
Sex Pistols, the (10)

Mountains, Mountain Ranges and Volcanoes

NB: letter counts do not include the words *hill*, *mountain*, *range*, etc.
H. = Hill; Hs. = Hills; M. = Mountain; Ms. = Mountains; Mt = Mount; Rge = Range; (v.) = volcanic

Afghanistan
Koh-i-Baba (8)
Khyber Pass (10)

Africa
Atlas Ms. (5)
Kong Ms. (4)
Milanji, Mt (7)
Miltsin, Mt (7)
Livingstone Ms. (11)

Alps
Bernima, Mt (7)
Breithorn (9)
Cenis, Mt (5)
Grossglockner (13)
Matterhorn (the) (10)
Mont Blanc (9)
Monte Rosa (9)

Antarctic
Erebus, Mt (v.) (6)
Terror (v.) (6)

Argentina
Aconcagua, Mt (v.) (9)
Maipu (v.) (5)

Asia
Hermon, Mt (6)
Himalaya Rge (8)
Himalayas (9)
Hindu Kush (9)
Karakoram Rge (9)
Kuenluiv Ms. (8)
Pamirs (6)
Tian Ms. (4)
Tien Shan Ms. (8)
Yablonoi Ms. (8)

Australia
Barry Ms. (5)
Blue Ms. (5)
Bogong, Mt (6)
Darling, Mt (7)
Flinders Ms. (8)
Koseiusko, Mt (9)
Liverpool Rge (9)
Townsend, Mt (8)

Austria
Ortler Spitz (11)

Bolivia
Illampa, Mt (7)
Illimani, Mt (8)

Borneo
Kinabalu, Mt (v.) (8)

Canada
Hooker M. (6)

Laurentian Ms. (10)
Logan, Mt (5)
Robson (6)
St Elias, Mt (7)
Wrangell, Mt (8)

Chile
Descapezado (v.) (11)
Las Yeguas (v.) (9)
Licancaur, Mt (9)
Llullaillaco (v.) (12)
Tinguiririca (v.) (12)

China
Wenchow, Mt (7)

Congo, Democratic Republic of the
Ruwenzori Ms. (9)

Crete
Ida, Mt (3)

Ecuador
Chimborazo (v.) (10)
Cotopaxi (v.) (8)

Egypt
Sinai, Mt (5)

England
Blencathra (10)
Bow Fell (7)
Cheviot Hs. (7)
Cheviots (8)
Chiltern Hs. (8)
Chilterns (9)
Cotswold Hs. (8)
Cotswolds (9)
Cross Fell (9)
Downs (the) (5)
Edgehill (8)
Helvellyn (9)
Ingleborough (12)
Malvern Hs. (7)
Mendip Hs. (6)
Mendips (7)
Peak District (the) (12)
Pennine Chain (12)
Pennines (8)
Quantock Hs. (8)
Quantocks (9)
Scafell Pike (11)
Scafell Rge (7)
Scaw Fell Rge (8)
Skiddaw (7)
Wolds (the) (5)

Europe
Alps (4)
Balkan Ms. (6)
Balkans (7)
Carpathian Ms. (10)
Carpathians (11)
Caucasus Ms. (8)
Dinaric Alps (8)
Graian Alps (10)
Jura Ms. (4)
Pennine Alps (11)
Pyrenees (8)
Riesengebirge Ms. (13)
Sudetes Ms. (7)

France
Auvergne Ms. (8)
Faucilles Ms. (9)
Maritime Alps (12)
Vosges Ms. (6)

Georgia
Elbrus, Mt (6)
Kazbek, Mt (6)

Germany
Brocken, Mt (7)
Drachenfels, Mt (11)
Erzgebirge (10)
Fichtelgebirge (14)
Harz Ms. (4)
Swabian Alps (11)
Taunus Ms. (6)
Zug M. (3)

Greece
Athos, Mt (5)
Olympus, Mt (7)
Ossa, Mt (4)
Parnassus, Mt (9)
Pelion, Ms. (6)
Pindus Ms. (6)
St Elias, Mt (7)

Hawaii
Hualalai (v.) (8)
Kilauea (v.) (7)
Mauna Kea (v.) (8)
Mauna Loa (v.) (8)

Himalayas
Altai Ms. (5)
Annapurna (9)
Dapsang, Mt (7)
Everest, Mt (7)
Dhaulagiri, Mt (10)
Godwin Austen, Mt (12)
Haramokh, Mt (8)
Jonsong, Mt (7)
K2 (2)
Kamet, Mt (5)
Kanchenjunga, Mt (12)
Lhotse, Mt (6)
Makalu, Mt (6)
Nanga Parbat (11)
Nanga-Devi (9)
Nuptse, Mt (6)
Rakaposhi (9)

Iceland
Hecla (v.) (7)
Skaptarjokull (v.) (13)
Vatnajokull (11)

India
Abu, Mt (3)
Aravalli Ms. (8)
Dardistan, Mt (9)
Eastern Ghats (12)
Jaintia Hs. (7)
Ghats (5)
Naga Hs. (4)
Nilgiri Hs. (7)
Nilgiris (8)
Rajmahal Hs. (8)
Siwalik Hs. (7)
Sulaiman Ms. (8)
Vindhya Ms. (7)
Western Ghats (12)

Indonesia
Carstensz, Mt (9)
Djaja, Mt (5)
Jaya, Mt (4)
Krakatoa (v.) (8)

Iran
Demavend, Mt (8)
Elburz Ms. (6)

Kuhi-Taftan (v.) (10)

Ireland (Republic of)
Caha Ms. (4)
Carrantuohill, Mt (13)
Galtee Ms. (6)
Knockmealdown Ms. (13)
Mamturk Ms. (7)

Isle of Man
Snaefell, Mt (8)

Israel
Carmel, Mt (6)
Olives, Mt of (6)
Tabor, Mt (5)

Italy
Apennines (9)
Averno, Mt (v.) (6)
Maritime Alps (12)
Monte Corno (10)
Solfatara (v.) (9)
Stelvio Pass (11)
Stromboli (v.) (9)
Vesuvius, Mt (8)
Vulcano (v.) (7)

Japan
Fuji, Mt (v.) (4)
Fujiyama (v.) (8)
Tomboro (v.) (7)

Jordan
Ebal, Mt (4)

Kenya
Kenya, Mt (5)

Kyrgyzstan
Lenin Peak (9)

Lebanon
Lebanon, Mt (7)

Lesotho
Mont Aux Sources (14)

Malaysia
Ophir, Mt (5)

Mexico
Citlaltepec, Mt (11)
Jorullo (v.) (7)
Orizaba (7)
Pico de Orizaba (13)
Popocatepetl (v.) (12)
Sierra Madre Ms. (11)

New Zealand
Cook M. (4)
Hochstetter, Mt (11)
Tarawera, Mt (8)
Tongariro (v.) (9)
Ruahine, Mt (7)

Nicaragua
Masaya (v.) (6)

North America
Cascade Ms. (7)
Rockies (7)
Rocky Ms. (5)

Northern Ireland
Mourne Ms. (6)

Oman
Akhdar Ms (6)
Sham, Mt (4)

Pakistan
Khyber Pass (10)

Papua New Guinea
Bougainville, Mt (12)
Owen Stanley Ms. (11)

Portugal
Estrela, Mt (7)

Pyrenees
Maladetta, Mt (9)
Mont Perdu (9)
Pic du Midi (9)
Roncesvalles (v) (12)

Russia
Elbrus, Mt (6)
Koshtan Tau (10)
Belukha (7)
Ural Ms. (4)
Urals (5)

Scotland
Ben Lawers (9)
Ben Lomond (9)
Ben Macdhui (10)
Ben More (7)
Ben Nevis (8)
Ben Venue (8)
Ben Wyvis (8)
Ben-y-Gloe (8)
Cairngorms (10)
Cairntoul (9)
Goatfell (8)
Grampians (9)
Lammermuir Hs. (10)
Lennox Hs. (6)
Moorfoot Hs. (8)
Ochil Hs. (5)
Pentland Hs. (8)
Schiehallion, Mt (12)
Sidlaw Hs. (6)

Sicily
Etna, Mt (v.) (4)

Skye
Cuillin Hs. (7)

South Africa
Cedar Berge, Mt (10)
Drakensberg Ms. (11)
Drakenstein, Mt (11)
Kwathlamba, Mt (10)
Table M. (5)
Zoutpansberg, Mt (12)

South America
Andes (5)
Cazambe, Mt (7)
El Potra, Mt (7)
Darwin, Mt (6)
Itaculomi, Mt (9)
Juncal (v.) (6)
Overo (v.) (5)
Peteroa (v.) (7)
Quizapu (v.) (7)
Roraima, Mt (7)
Sahama (v.) (6)
San José (v.) (7)
Sangay (v.) (6)
Sorata (6)
Tolima (v.) (6)
Tupungato (v.) (9)

Spain
Cantabrian Ms. (10)
Mulhacen, Mt (8)
Sierra Morena (12)

Sierra Nevada (12)

Sri Lanka
Adam's Peak (9)
Pidurutalagala (14)

Switzerland
Bernese Alps (11)
Dent du Midi (10)
Diablerets, Mt (10)
Eiger (5)
Finsteraahorn, Mt (13)
Jungfrau, Mt (8)
Mönch (5)
Pilatus, Mt (7)
Rigi, Mt (4)
St Bernard Pass (13)
St Gothard, Mt (9)
Simplon, Mt (7)
Splugen Pass (11)
Schreckhorn (11)
Wetterhorn (the) (10)

Tajikistan
Communism (9)
Lenin Peak (9)

Tanzania
Kibo, Mt (4)
Kilimanjaro, Mt (11)

Tasmania
Nelson, Mt (6)
Ossa, Mt (4)
Wellington, Mt (10)

Trinidad
Aripo M. (5)

Turkey
Ararat, Mt (6)
Rhodope, Mt (7)

Uganda
Ruwenzori Ms. (9)

USA
Adams M. (5)
Adirondack Ms. (10)
Allegheny Ms. (9)
Appalachian Ms. (11)
Baker (v.) (5)
Big Horn Ms. (7)
Black Ms. (5)
Black Dome Peak (13)
Blue Ms. (4)
Blue Ridge Ms. (9)
Brown M. (5)
Catskill Ms. (8)
Elk Ms. (3)
Green Ms. (5)
Hayden, Mt (6)
Hoffman, Mt (7)
Hoosac Ms. (6)
Iron M. (4)
Katahdin, Mt (8)
Lafayette, Mt (9)
Lookout M. (7)
McKinley, Mt (8)
Pike's Peak (5)
Rainier, Mt (7)
Rushmore, Mt (8)
San Juan Ms. (7)
Vinta, Mt (5)
White Ms. (5)
Whitney, Mt (7)
Wind River Ms. (9)

Wales
Black Ms. (5)
Moel Fammau, Mt (10)
Pinlimmon, Mt (9)
Preseley Ms. (8)
Snowdon, Mt (7)

West Indies
La Sonfrière (v.) (11)
Pelée (v) (5)

Musketeers

Athos (5)
Porthos (7)
Aramis (6)
D'Artagnan (9)

Nine Muses

Calliope (8)
Clio (4)
Erato (5)
Euterpe (7)
Melpomene (9)
Polyhymnnia (11)
Terpsichore (11)
Thalia (6)
Urania (6)

Nine Virtues

charity (7)
faith (5)
fortitude (9)
hope (4)
justice (7)
love (4)
modesty (7)
prudence (8)
temperance (10)

Opera, Ballet and Classical Music

4
Lind, Jennie
Wood, Sir Henry

5
Baker, Dame Janet
Boult, Sir Adrian
Brain, Dennis
Bream, Julian
Davis, Sir Colin
du Pré, Jacqueline
Gigli, Beniamino
Ogdon, John
Pears, Sir Peter
Sills, Beverly
Solti, Sir George
Stern, Isaac

6
Ashton, Sir Frederick
Callas, Maria
Caruso, Enrico
Casals, Pablo
Duncan, Isadora
Groves, Sir Charles
Irving, Sir Henry
Miller, Jonathan
Previn, Andre
Rattle, Sir Simon

7
Beecham, Sir Thomas
Domingo, Placido
Ferrier, Kathleen
Fiedler, Arthur
Fonteyn, Dame Margot
Karajan, Herbert von
Markova, Dame Alicia
Menuhin, Sir Yehudi
Nilsson, Birgit
Nureyev, Rudolf
Pavlova, Anna
Rambert, Dame Marie
Sargent, Sir Malcolm
Shankar, Ravi

8
Carerras, José
de Valois, Dame Ninette
Hoffnung, Gerard
Horowitz, Vladimir
Nijinski, Vaslav
Paganini, Niccolo
Te Kanawa, Dame Kiri
Williams, John

9
Ashkenazy, Vladimir
Barenboim, Daniel
Diaghilev, Serge
Pavarotti, Luciano
Toscanini, Arturo

10
Barbirolli, Sir John
Rubinstein, Artur
Soderstrom, Elizabeth
Sutherland, Dame Joan

11
Schwarzkopf, Elisabeth

Orders of Precedence

PEERAGE

duke/duchess (4,7)
marquis/marchioness (7,11)
earl/countess (4,8)
viscount/viscountess (8,11)
baron/baroness (5,8)

ARMY

Field Marshall (13)
General (7)
Lieutenant-General (17)
Major-General (12)
Brigadier (9)
Colonel (7)
Lieutenant-Colonel (17)
Major (5)
Captain (7)
Lieutenant (10)
Second Lieutenant (16)
Warrant Officer (14)
Staff Sergeant (13)
Sergeant (8)
Corporal (8)
Lance Corporal (13)
Private (7)

ROYAL NAVY

Admiral of the Fleet (17)
Admiral (7)
Vice-Admiral (11)
Rear-Admiral (11)
Commodore (9)
Captain (7)
Commander (9)
Lieutenant-Commander (19)
Lieutenant (10)
Sub-Lieutenant (13)
Midshipman (10)
Fleet Chief Petty Officer (22)
Chief Petty Officer (17)
Petty Officer (12)
Leading Rating (13)
Able Rating (10)
Junior Rating (12)

ROYAL AIR FORCE

Marshal of the RAF (15)
Air Chief Marshal (15)
Air Marshal (10)
Air Vice-Marshal (14)
Air Commodore (12)
Group Captain (12)
Wing Commander (13)
Squadron Leader (14)
Flight Lieutenant (16)
Flying Officer (13)
Pilot Officer (12)
Acting Pilot Officer (18)
Warrant Officer (14)
Flight Sergeant (14)
Sergeant (8)
Corporal (8)
Junior Technician (16)
Senior Aircraftman (17)
Leading Aircraftman (18)
Aircraftman (11)

METROPOLITAN POLICE

Commissioner (12)
Deputy Assistant Commissioner (27)
Commander (9)
Chief Superintendent (19)
Superintendent (14)
Chief Inspector (14)
Inspector (9)
Sergeant (8)
Constable (9)

Oxford and Cambridge Colleges

3
BNC (Brasenose, O.)
New (O.)

4
Hall (Trinity Hall, C.)

5
Caius (Gonville and) (C.)
Clare (C.)
Green (O.)
House (Christ Church, O.)
Jesus (C. and O.)
Keble (O.)
King's (C.)
Oriel (O.)

6
Darwin (C.)
Exeter (O.)
Girton (C.)
Merton (O.)
Queens' (C. and O.)
Selwyn (C.)
Wadham (O.)

7
Balliol (O.)
Christ's (C.)
Downing (C.)
Linacre (O.)
Lincoln (O.)
New Hall (C.) (w.)
Newnham (C.) (w.)
St Anne's (O.)
St Cross (O.)
St Hugh's (O.) (w.)
St John's (C. and O.)
Trinity (C. and O.)
Wolfson (C. and O.)

8
All Souls (O.)
Emmanuel (C.)
Hertford (O.)
Magdalen (O.)
Nuffield (O.)
Pembroke (C. and (O.)
Robinson (C.)
St Hilda's (O.) (w.)
St Peter's (O.)

9
Brasenose (O.)

Churchill (C.)
Clare Hall (C.)
Magdalene (C.)
Mansfield (O.)
St Antony's (O.)
Templeton (O.)
Worcester (O.)

10
Greyfriars (O.)
Hughes Hall (C.) (w.)
Osler House (O.)
Peterhouse (C.)
Somerville (O.)
University (O.)

11
Campion Hall (O.)
Fitzwilliam (C.)
Regent's Park (O.)
Rewley House (O.)
Trinity Hall (C.)

12
Christ Church (O.)
St Benet's Hall (O.)
St Catharine's (C.)
St Catherine's (O.)
St Edmund Hall (O.)
Sidney Sussex (C.)

13 and over
Corpus Christi (C. and O.) (13)
Gonville and Caius (C.) (16)
Lady Margaret Hall (O.) (16)
Lucy Cavendish (C.) (w.) (13)
St Edmund's House (C.) (14)

Patron Saints of the UK

England
George (6, 23 April)

Wales
David (5, 1 March)

Scotland
Andrew (6, 30 November)

Ireland
Patrick (7, 17 March)

Peoples, Languages and Nationalities

2
Ga
Wa
Wu

3
Edo
Ewe
Fon
Fox
Fur
Gur
Hun
Ibo
Ido
Ijo
Ila
Iru
Jew
Kru
Kui
Kwa
Lao
Luo
Mon
Shi
Suk
Tiv
Twi
Ute
Vai
Yao

4
Agni
Akan
Ambo
Arab
Avar
Baga
Bali
Beja
Bena
Bete
Bini
Bisa
Bodo
Boer
Bubi
Celt
Chad
Copt
Cree
Crow
Dane
Dari
Dyak
Efik
Erse
Fang
Finn
Fula
Garo
Gaul
Ge'ez
Gogo
Gond
Goth
Grig
Guro
Haya
Hehe
Hima
Hopi
Hupa
Hutu
Igbo
Iowa
Jute
Kelt
Kurd
Lala
Lapp
Lari
Lett
Loma
Lozi
Luba
Mali
Mano
Manx
Maya
Meru
Moki
Moor
Moxu
Naga
Nama
Nuba
Nuer
Nupe
Nyao
Pali
Pedi
Pict
Pima
Pole
Russ
Sauk
Scot
Sena
Serb
Shan
Sikh
Slav
Sobo
Susu
Teso
Thai
Tswa
Turk
Urdu
Wend
Yako
Yuma
Zend
Zulu
Zuni

5
Acoli
Afars
Aleut
Anuak
Aryan
Asian
Attic
Aztec
Bamum
Bantu
Bassa
Batak
Baule
Bemba

Benga
Berta
Bhili
Blood
Bulom
Bussi
Caddo
Campa
Carib
Chaga
Chewa
Chimu
Chopi
Creek
Croat
Cuban
Cymry
Czech
Dayak
Dinka
Dogon
Doric
Dutch
Dyold
Dyula
Fante
Frank
Galla
Ganda
Gbari
Gipsy
Gissi
Gondi
Grebo
Greek
Gypsy
Hadza
Haida
Hausa
Hindi
Huron
Idoma
Incas
Indic
Iraqi
Irish
Kadai
Kafir
Kamba
Kamla
Kansa
Karen
Kazak
Khasi
Khmer
Kiowa
Kissi
Kongo
Lamba
Lango
Latin
Lenge
Lipan
Lomwe
Lulua
Lunda
Malay
Mande
Maori
Masai
Mende
Miami
Moqui
Mossi
Munda
Nahua
Nandi
Naron
Ngala
Ngoni
Nguni
Nguru
Nkore
Norse
Nyong
Nyoro
Omaha
Oriya
Osage
Oscan
Parsi
Punic
Pygmy
Riffs
Roman
Ronga
Rundi
Sango
Saudi
Saxon
Scots
Shilh
Shona
Sinic
Sioux
Sotho
Swazi
Swede
Swiss
Tajik
Tamil
Tembu
Temne
Teton
Tigre
Tonga
Tussi
Tutsi
Uzbek
Venda
Wappo
Welsh
Wolof
Xhosa
Yaqui
Yuchi
Yunca
Yupik
Zande

6

Abnaki
Acholi
Aeolic
Afghan
Altaic
Angoni
Apache
Arabic
Arawak
Argive
Aymara
Aztecs
Bakota
Balega
Baltic
Baoule
Basque
Basuto
Bateke
Bayaka
Berber
Biloxi
Bokmal
Brahui
Breton
Briton
Bulgar
Caribs
Cayuga
Celtic
Chagga
Chokwe
Cocopa
Coptic
Creole
Cymric
Dakota
Danish
Dogrib
Dorian
Eskimo
Fijian
French
Fulani
Gaelic
Gallic
Gascon
German
Gothic
Hebrew
Herero
Ibibio
Indian
Inupik
Ionian
Italic
Jewish
Judaic
Kabyle
Kaffir
Kanuri
Kichai
Kikuyu
Korean
Kpelle
Kpessi
Kurukh
Libyan
Lumbwa
Luvale
Manchu
Mandan
Micmac
Mixtec
Mohave
Mohawk
Mongol
Murozi
Navaho
Ndonga
Nepali
Ngbaka
Ngombe
Ngwato
Nootka
Norman
Nsenga
Nubian
Nyanja
Ojibwa
Oneida
Ostiak
Ostman
Ottawa
Paiute
Papuan
Parian
Parsee
Pashto
Patois
Pawnee
Pequot
Pericu
Piegan
Polish
Pueblo
Pushto
Pushtu
Quakaw
Rajput
Rolong
Romaic
Romany
Rwanda
Ryukyu
Sabine
Salish
Sambaa
Samoan

Santee
Sarcee
Seneca
Senufo
Serere
Sindhi
Slavic
Slovak
Somali
Soviet
Sukuma
Syriac
Syrian
Telegu
Telugu
Teuton
Theban
Thonga
Tlokwa
Toltec
Tongan
Trojan
Tsonga
Tswana
Tuareg
Tungus
Turkic
Tuscan
Veddah
Viking
Votyak
Warega
Warrau
Yankee
Yemeni
Yoruba
Zenaga

7

Abenaki
Acadian
African
Amerind
Amharic
Angolan
Arabian
Aramaic
Aramean
Arapaho
Araucan
Arikara
Armoric
Ashanti
Asiatic
Avestan
Baganda
Bagirmi
Bakweii
Balanta
Balochi
Bambara
Bangala
Bapende
Barotse
Barundi
Basonge
Batonka
Batutsi
Bedouin
Belgian
Bengali
Berbers
Bisayan
British
Bunduka
Burmese
Bushmen
Catalan
Catawba
Chechen
Chilcal
Chilean
Chinese
Chinook
Choctaw
Cornish
Cypriot
Dagomba
Dalicad
English
Finnish
Flemish
Frisian
Gambian
Gaulish
Griquas
Guarani
Haitian
Hamitic
Hebraic
Hessian
Hidatsa
Hittite
Iberian
Ilocano
Iranian
Israeli
Italian
Karanga
Khoisan
Kirghiz
Kurdish
Kuwaiti
Laotian
Lappish
Latvian
Lingala
Lombard
Lugbara
Maduran
Mahican
Malinke
Maltese
Mandyak
Mapuche
Marathi
Mashona
Mexican
Mohegan
Mohican
Moorish
Mordvin
Morisco
Mozareb
Mulatto
Nahuatl
Namaqua
Natchez
Nauruan
Ndebele
Ngbandi
Nilotes
Nilotic
Nynorsk
Ojibway
Orejone
Ottoman
Pahlavi
Palaung
Persian
Prakrit
Punjabi
Quechua
Romance
Russian
Rwandan
Samburu
Samiote
Samoyed
Sandawe
Santali
Semitic
Serbian
Serrano
Shawnee
Shilluk
Siamese
Slovene
Songhai
Spanish
Spartan
Stonies
Swahili
Swedish
Tagalog
Tibetan
Tigrina
Tlingit
Tonkawa
Turkana
Turkish
Ugandan
Umbrian
Umbundu
Venetic
Walloon
Watutsi
Wichita
Wyandot
Yiddish
Zairean
Zambian

8

Abderite
Aguaruna
Akkadian
Albanian
Algerian
American

Andorran
Antiguan
Armenian
Assamese
Assyrian
Austrian
Bahamian
Balinese
Bavarian
Bergdama
Bermudan
Bohemian
Bolivian
Bushongo
Cambrian
Canadian
Chaldaic
Chaldean
Chamorro
Cherokee
Cheyenne
Comanche
Corsican
Cushitic
Cyrenaic
Delaware
Delphian
Dutchman
Egyptian
Estonian
Ethiopic
Etruscan
Eurasian
Frankish
Gallican
Georgian
Germanic
Ghanaian
Gujarati
Gujerati
Guyanese
Hawaiian
Hellenic
Helvetic
Honduran
Illinois
Illyrian
Irishman
Iroquois
Japanese
Javanese
Kashmiri
Kickapoo
Kimbundu
Kingwana
Kipsigis
Kootenay
Kuki-Chin
Kukuruku
Kwakiutl
Kwanyama
Lebanese
Liberian
Mahratti
Makassar
Malagasy
Malawian
Mamprusi
Mandarin
Mandingo
Mandinka
Matabele
Memphian
Menomini
Moroccan
Moru-Madi
Muskogee
Negritos
Nepalese
Nez Perce
Nigerian
Nuba-Fula
Nyamwesi
Old Norse
Old Saxon
Onondaga
Parthian
Pelasgic
Peruvian
Phrygian
Powhatan
Prussian
Quichuan
Romanian
Romansch
Rumanian
Sanskrit
Scotsman
Scottish
Seminole
Shoshoni
Shushwap
Sicilian
Slavonic
Spaniard
Sudanese
Sumerian
Tallensi
Teutonic
Tunisian
Turanian
Turkomen
Vandalic
Visigoth
Welshman

9

Abkhasian
Aborigine
Afrikaans
Afrikaner
Algonkian
Algonquin
Anatolian
Apalachee
Ashochimi
Barbadian
Bengalese
Blackfeet
Brazilian
Bulgarian
Byzantine
Cambodian
Cantonese
Caucasian
Ceylonese
Chari-Nile
Cheremiss
Chickasaw
Chipewyan
Chippeway
Cimmerian
Colombian
Congolese
Dravidian
Esperanto
Esquimaux
Ethiopian
Frenchman
Hanseatic
Hibernian
Hottentot
Hungarian
Icelander
Icelandic
Israelite
Jordanian
Kabardian
Kannarese
Karankawa
Kgalagedi
Low German
Malaysian
Mauritian
Menominee
Mongolian
Norwegian
Ostrogoth
Pakistani
Penobscot
Provençal
Rhodesian
Roumanian
Samaritan
Sardinian
Sere Mundu
Sinhalese
Sri Lankan
Sundanese
Taiwanese
Tanzanian
Tocharian
Tuscarora
Ukrainian
Ulotrichi
Uruguayan
Winnebago

10

Aboriginal
Abyssinian
Anglo-Saxon
Araucanian
Assiniboin
Athabascan
Australian
Autochthon
Babylonian
Bathlaping
Bella Coola

Circassian
Cornishman
Costa Rican
Dutchwoman
Ecuadorian
Englishman
Finno-Ugric
Florentine
Guatemalan
High German
Hindustani
Hottentots
Indonesian
Irishwoman
Israelitic
Karamojong
Leni-Lenape
Lithuanian
Melanesian
Mingrelian
Minnetaree
Monegasque
Montagnais
Neapolitan
Nicaraguan
Nicobarese
Old English
Panamanian
Paraguayan
Patagonian
Philippine
Philistine
Phoenician
Polynesian
Pomeranian
Portuguese
Rajasthani
Scotswoman
Senegalese
Serbo-Croat
Shoshonean
Venezuelan
Vietnamese
Welshwoman

11
Afro-Asiatic
Argentinian
Azerbaijani
Bangarwanda
Bangladeshi
Belorussian
Frenchwoman
Greenlander
Mauritanian
Narraganset
Palestinian
Scots Gaelic
Sino-Tibetan
Susquehanna
Trinidadian

12
Byelorussian
Cornishwoman
Englishwoman
Indo-European
Lunda-Bajokwe
Moru-Mangbetu
New Zealander
Plattdeutsch
Scandinavian
Tibeto-Burman

13
Middle English
Passamaquoddy
Pidgin English
Queen's English

Philosophers and Religionists

3
Fox, George
Hus, Jan
Lee, Ann

4
Ayer, A.J.
Eddy, Mary Baker
Hume, David
Kant, Immanuel
Knox, John
Marx, Karl
Mill, John Stuart
More, Thomas
Weil, Simone

5
Bacon, Francis
Bacon, Roger
Barth, Karl
Booth, William
Burke, Edmund
Dewey, John
Hegel, Georg Willhelm Friedrich
Keble, John
Plato

6
Boehme, Jakob
Berlin, Sir Isaiah
Calvin, John
Engels, Friedrich
Graham, Billy
Hobbes, Thomas
Luther, Martin
Popper, Sir Karl
Sartre, Jean-Paul
Tagore, Rabindranath
Wesley, John
Wyclif, John

7
Abelard, Peter
Aquinas, St Thomas
Bentham, Jeremy
Buchman, Frank
Diderot, Denis
Erasmus, Desiderius
Leibniz, Gottfried Wilhelm
Russell, Bertrand
Spinoza, Benedict
Steiner, Rudolf
Tyndale, William

8
Avicenna
Berkeley, George
Foucault, Michel
Rousseau, Jean Jacques
Socrates

9
Aristotle
Blavatsky, Madame Helena
Confucius
Descartes, René
Heidegger, Martin
Nietzsche, Friedrich

10
Macpherson, Aimee Semple
Swedenborg, Emanuel

11
Wilberforce, Samuel

12
Krishnamurti, Jiddu
Schopenhauer Arthur
Wittgenstein, Ludwig

Phobias

8
iophobia (poisons, rust)

9
apiphobia (bees)
atephobia (ruin)
urophobia (urinating)
zoophobia (animals)

10
acrophobia (heights)
aerophobia (fresh air, draughts, flying)
agiophobia (crossing streets)
agraphobia (sexual abuse)
algophobia (pain)
aphephobia (touching, being touched)
aurophobia gold)
autophobia (solitude)
barophobia (gravity)
basiphobia (walking)
batophobia (high buildings)
bogyphobia (demons, goblins)
cibophobia (food)
cryophobia (frost, ice)
cymophobia (waves, sea)
cynophobia (dogs)
demophobia (crowds)
dikephobia (justice)
dinophobia (dizziness)
doraphobia (animal skin, fur)
eosophobia (dawn)
gamophobia (marriage)
gelophobia (laughter)
genuphobia (knees)
hadephobia (hell)
hemaphobia (blood)
hodophobia (travel)
homophobia (homosexuals)
hylephobia (materialism)
ideophobia (ideas)
kenophobia (empty rooms)
kopophobia (fatigue)
kynophobia (pseudo-rabies)
levophobia (objects on left-hand side of the body)
logophobia (words)
menophobia (menstruation)
musophobia (mice)
mysophobia (dirt)
nosophobia (disease)
oenophobia (wine)
optophobia (opening one's eyes)
panophobia (everything)
papaphobia (pope)
pedophobia (dolls)
poinephobia (punishment)
potophobia (drink)
pyrophobia (fire)
sciophobia (shadows)
selaphobia (flashes of light)
sexophobia (opposite sex)
Sinophobia (China, Chinese)
tabophobia (wasting sickness)
theophobia (God)
tocophobia (childbirth)
tomophobia (surgery)
topophobia (certain places, performing (stagefright))
toxiphobia (being poisoned)
xenophobia (foreigners)
xerophobia (dryness)
zelophobia (jealousy)

11
acarophobia (mites, ticks)
acerophobia (sourness)
agoraphobia (open spaces)
amaxophobia (riding in vehicles)
androphobia (men)
anemophobia (draughts, winds)
Anglophobia (England, English)
anthophobia (flowers)
astraphobia (lightning)
atelophobia (imperfection)
bathophobia (bathing, depth)
cainophobia (novelty)
carnophobia (meat)

Celtophobia (Celts, Celtic)
cherophobia (gaiety)
chorophobia (dancing)
clinophobia (going to bed)
cnidophobia (insect stings)
coitophobia (sexual intercourse)
coprophobia (excrement)
cyclophobia (bicycles)
dentophobia (dentists)
dipsophobia (drinking alcohol)
emetophobia (emetics, vomiting)
enetophobia (needles)
erotophobia (sexual feelings)
geumophobia (flavours)
gymnophobia (nudity)
gynaephobia (women)
hagiophobia (saints)
heliophobia (sunlight)
hierophobia (sacred objects)
hippophobia (horses)
hormephobia (shock)
hydrophobia (rabies, water)
hygrophobia (dampness)
hypnophobia (sleep)
iatrophobia (doctors)
laliophobia (talking)
lepraphobia (leprosy)
leukophobia (white)
limnophobia (lakes)
lyssophobia (insanity, madness)
macrophobia (long waits)
maniaphobia (madness)
methyphobia (alcohol)
mnemophobia (memories)
motorphobia (motor vehicles)
mythophobia (lying, myths, stories)
necrophobia (corpses, death)
Negrophobia (Negroes)
nephophobia (clouds)
noctiphobia (night)
nostophobia (returning home)
nyctophobia (darkness)
obesophobia (becoming fat)
ombrophobia (rain)
pathophobia (disease, illness)
peniaphobia (poverty)
phagophobia (swallowing)
philiphobia (love)
phobophobia (fear)
phonophobia (speaking aloud)
photophobia (light)
placophobia (tombstones)
pnigophobia (choking)
prosophobia (progress)
radiophobia (radiation, X-rays)
rhypophobia (filth)
rhytiphobia (getting wrinkles)
Russophobia (Russian, Russian)
scopophobia (being looked at)
septophobia (decaying matter)
Slavophobia (Slavs, Slavic)
sophophobia (learning)
spacephobia (outer space)
stasiphobia (standing)
tachophobia (speed)
taphephobia (being buried alive)
taurophobia (bulls)
teleophobia (teleology)
testophobia (taking tests)
textophobia (particular fabrics)
tremophobia (trembling)
tropophobia (making changes)
uranophobia (the heavens)

12

ablutophobia (washing oneself)
aichmophobia (pointed objects)
ailurophobia (cats)
alliumphobia (garlic)
amathophobia (dust)
amychophobia (being scratched)
anginaphobia (narrowness)
ankylophobia (immobility of a joint)
anuptaphobia (staying single)
apeirophobia (infinity)
ataxiophobia (untidiness)
auroraphobia (auroral lights)
belonephobia (needles, pins)
bibliophobia (books)
blennophobia (slime)
botanophobia (plants)
brontophobia (thunder)
cardiophobia (heart disease)
chaetophobia (hair)
cheimaphobia (cold)
chionophobia (snow)

chromophobia (time)
chronophobia (colours)
cometophobia (comets)
cremnophobia (places, sleep)
decidophobia (decisions)
deipnophobia (dining, dinner conversation)
demonophobia (devils, evil spirits)
dextrophobia (objects on the right-hand side of the body)
domatophobia (home)
entomophobia (insects)
Francophobia (France, French)
graphophobia (writing)
hedonophobia (pleasure)
Japanophobia (Japan, Japanese)
Judaeophobia (Jews, Judaism)
kinesophobia (motion)
kleptophobia (thieves)
megalophobia (large objects)
meteorphobia (meteors)
musicophobia (music)
odontophobia (teeth)
ommatophobia (eyes)
oneirophobia (dreams)
papyrophobia (paper)
patriophobia (hereditary disease)
peladophobia (baldness)
phasmophobia (ghosts)
phengophobia (daylight)
pogonophobia (beards)
potamophobia (rivers)
proctophobia (rectal disease)
psychophobia (the mind)
pyrexiphobia (fever)
rhabdophobia (being beaten, magic)
Satanophobia (Satan)
selenophobia (moon)
siderophobia (stars)
soceraphobia (parents-in-law)
staurophobia (crucifixes)
taeniophobia (tapeworms)
tapinophobia (small objects)
technophobia (technology)
teletophobia (religious ceremonies)
teratophobia (monsters, or giving birth to a monster)
tetanophobia (tetanus (lockjaw))
thaasophobia (sitting down)
thermophobia (heat)
vestiophobia (clothes)

13

accoustiphobia (noise)
agrizoophobia (wild animals)
amnesiophobia (amnesia)
angionophobia (heart attack)
arachnophobia (spiders)
asthenophobia (weakness)
bacillophobia (bacteria)
cathisophobia (sitting still)
cholerophobia (cholera)
climacophobia (stairs)
clithrophobia (enclosed spaces)
cypridephobia (venereal disease)
dermatophobia (skin)
diabetophobia (diabetes)
electrophobia (electricity)
ergasiophobia (work)
erythrophobia (blushing, red)
gephyrophobia (crossing bridges)
gerascophobia (ageing)
Germanophobia (Germany, Germans)
hamartophobia (sin)
harpaxophobia (robbers)
herpetophobia (reptiles)
ichthyophobia (fish)
illyngophobia (vertigo)
keraunophobia (thunder and lightning)
koinoniphobia (crowded rooms)
lachanophobia (vegetables)
lilapsophobia (hurricanes)
mechanophobia (machinery)
metallophobia (metal)
myrmecophobia (ants)
olfactophobia (smells)
onomatophobia (particular word or name)
ophidiophobia (snakes)
ornithophobia (birds)
peccatiphobia (wrongdoing)
philosophobia (philosophy, philosophers)

pteronophobia (feathers)
scelerophobia (attack)
scoleciphobia (worms)
spectrophobia (ghosts)
symbolophobia (symbols)
syphiliphobia (syphilis)
theatrophobia (theatres)
trypanophobia (injections)
tyrannophobia (tyrants)
vaccinophobia (vaccines, vaccination)
venustaphobia (beautiful women)

14

allodoxaphobia (others' opinions)
anablepophobia (looking up at high places)
anthropophobia (people)
automysophobia (dirt on oneself)
ballistophobia (missiles)
batrachophobia (frogs, toads)
catapedaphobia (jumping)
catoptrophobia (mirrors)
chrematophobia (touching money)
claustrophobia (being locked in)
coimetrophobia (cemeteries)
computerphobia (computers)
cyprianophobia (prostitutes)
diplopiaphobia (double vision)
dystychiphobia (accidents)
homichlophobia (fog)
hypengyophobia (responsibility)
isopterophobia (termites)
katagelophobia (ridicule)
merinthophobia (being bound)
microbiophobia (microbes)
molysomophobia (infection)
nosocomephobia (hospitals)
paralipophobia (neglect of duty)
parasitophobia (parasites)
parthenophobia (young girls)
pediculophobia (lice)
pentheraphobia (mother-in-law)
pharmacophobia (drugs)
philemaphobia (kissing)
phronemophobia (thinking)
phthisiophobia (tuberculosis)
politocophobia (politicians)
porphyrophobia (purple)
thalassophobia (sea)
traumatophobia (physical injury, war)
trichinophobia (hair disease)

15

aeronausiphobia (air sickness)
carcinomophobia (cancer)
crystallophobia (glass)
dysmorphophobia (deformity)
eleutherophobia (freedom)
epistaxiophobia (nosebleeds)
meningitophobia (meningitis)
monopathophobia (particular disease)
neopharmaphobia (new drugs)
oneirogmophobia (wet dreams)
ostraconophobia (shellfish)
psellismophobia (stuttering)
stasibasiphobia (standing and walking)
syngenesophobia (relatives)
telephonophobia (telephones)

16

coprostasophobia (constipation)
dermatosiophobia (skin disease)
dishabillophobia (undressing in front of someone)
nucleomitophobia (nuclear energy)
photoaugiophobia (glaring lights)
primeisodophobia (losing one's virginity)
theologicophobia (theology)

17

bromhidrosiphobia (body odour)
Hellenologophobia (complex scientific or Greek terms)
siderodromophobia (railways)
triskaidekaphobia (thirteen)

18

defecalgesiophobia (painful defecation)
didaskaleinophobia (school)
kakorrhaphiophobia (failure)

Planets and Their Satellites

2
Io

4
Mars
Moon
Rhea

5
Ariel
Dione
Earth
Mimas
Pluto
Regel
Rigel
Spica
Titan
Venus

6
Deimos
Europa
Oberon
Phobos
Phoebe
Saturn
Tethys
Triton
Uranus

7
Iapetus
Jupiter
Mercury
Neptune
Titania
Umbriel

8
Callisto
Ganymede
Hesperus

9
Enceladus

11
Evening Star
Morning Star

Poisonous Substances and Gases

5
ozone
ricin
sarin

6
aldrin
arsine
bleach
curare
phenol
xylene

7
aconite
aniline
arsenic
benzene
brucine
cacodyl
coniine
cyanide
emetine
ethanol
hemlock
hexanes
lindane
ouabane
red lead
stibine
toluene
tropine

8
acrolein
adamsite
atropine
chlorine
cyanogens
gasoline
lewisite
methanol
nerve gas
phosgene
ratsbane
thallium
thebaine
urushiol

9
afterdamp
benzidine
digitalin
muscarine
poison gas
veratrine
whitedamp

10
chloroform
cyanic acid
hydrastine
mustard gas
oxalic acid
picrotoxin
silica dust
strychnine

11
hyoscyamine
prussic acid

12
allyl alcohol
formaldehyde
lead monoxide
zinc chloride

13
mercuric oxide
methyl bromide
nitrogen oxide
silver nitrate
sodium cyanide

14
asbestos fibres
carbon monoxide
hydrogen iodide
sodium fluoride
sulphur dioxide

15
barium hydroxide
hydrogen cyanide
nitrogen dioxide
osmium tetroxide

16
carbon disulphide
hydrogen fluoride
hydrogen sulphide
mercuric chloride
potassium cyanide
stannous fluoride

Politicians and Revolutionaries

3
Kun
Mao
Pym
Zia

4
Amin
Biko
Blum
Burr
Bush
Chou
Clay
Foot
Gore
Grey
Hess
Marx
Meir
Root
Tito

5
Banda
Benes
Bevan
Bevin
Blair
Burke
Ciano
Desai
Hague
Hiero
Hoxha
Husak
Jagan
Kadar
Laval
Lenin
Marat
Nehru
Paine
Peron
Putin
Sadat
Sands
Simon
Smith
Smuts
Solon
Tyler
Villa

6
Aquino
Arafat
Bhutto
Brandt
Bright
Castro
Cavour
Chiang
Chirac
Cicero
Cobden
Corday
Cripps
Cromer
Curzon
Danton
Dubcek
Dulles
Engels
Franco
Gadafy
Gandhi
Hitler
Horthy
Kaunda
Marcos
Mobuto
Mosley
Mugabe
Nasser
Pearse
Petain
Powell
Rhodes
Somoza
Stalin
Zapata

7
Allende
Bakunin
Batista
Bolivar
Bormann
Clinton
Giscard
Goldman
Gomulka
Himmler
Kennedy
Kosygin
Kreisky
Lumumba
Mandela
Masaryk
Menzies
Mintoff
Molotov
Nkrumah
Nyerere
Parnell
Pearson
Ptolemy
Redmond
Reynaud
Salazar
Sandino
Sukarno
Trotsky
Trudeau
Vorster
Wallace
Webster
Yeltsin

8
Abu Nidal
Adenauer
Ayub Khan
Bismarck
Brezhnev
Bukharin
Bulganin
Daladier
De Gaulle
De Valera
Dollfuss
Duvalier
Goebbels
Hamilton
Kenyatta
Lycurgus
Makarios
Morrison
Napoleon
Pinochet
Podgorny
Poincare
Pompidou
Proudhon
Verwoerd
Williams

9
Ben Gurion
Bonaparte
Bruntland
Chou En-Lai
Churchill
Garibaldi
Gorbachev
Ho Chi Minh
Kropotkin
Luxemburg
Milosevic
Mussolini
Spartacus

10
Che Guevara
Clemenceau
Hindenburg
Khrushchev
Lee Kuan-Yew
Mao Tse Tung
Metternich
Ribbentrop
Stroessner
Talleyrand

11
Castlereagh
Chamberlain
Robespierre
Shaftesbury

12
Bandaranaike
Hammarskjold
Kemal Ataturk

13 *and over*
Aung San Suu Kyi (13)
Chiang Kai-Shek (13)
Giscard d'Estaing (15)
Haile Selassie (13)

Ports

Algeria
Algiers (7)
Oran (4)
Port Arzew (9)
Skidda (6)

Angola
Lobito (6)

Argentina
Buenos Aires (11)
La Plata (7)
Rosario (7)

Asia
Hong Kong (8)
Singapore (9)

Australia
Adelaide (8)
Brisbane (8)
Dampier (7)
Darwin (6)
Fremantle (9)
Geelong (7)
Melbourne (9)
Newcastle (9)
Port Adelaide (12)
Port Jackson (11)
Sydney (6)

Azerbaijan
Baku (4)

Bangladesh
Chittagong (10)

Belgium
Antwerp (7)
Ostend (6)
Zeebrugge (9)

Benin
Cotonou (7)
Porto Novo (9)

Brazil
Belem (5)
Para (4)
Pernambuco (10)
Recife (6)
Rio de Janeiro (12)
Santos (6)
Tobarao (7)

Bulgaria
Varna (5)

Burma
Akyab (5)
Moulmein (8)
Rangoon (7)
Sittwe (6)

Cameroon
Douala (6)

Canada
Churchill (9)
Esquimault (10)
Halifax (7)
Kitimat (7)
Montreal (8)
Owen Sound (9)
Three Rivers (11)
Vancouver (9)

Canary Islands
Las Palmas (9)

Channel Islands
St Helier (8)
St Peter Port (11)

Chile
Arica (5)
Coquimbo (8)
Valparaiso (10)

China
Amoy (4)
Chefoo (6)
Dairen (6)
Foochow (7)
Hankow (6)
Hong Kong (8)
Port Arthur (10)
Shanghai (8)
Swatow (6)
Tientsin (8)
Weihai (6)
Yingkow (7)

Colombia
Barranquilla (12)
Buenaventura (12)
Cartagena (9)

Congo, Democratic Republic of the
Mahdi (5)
Mbuji-Mayi (9)

Corsica
Ajaccio (7)
Bastia (6)

Croatia
Dubrovnik (9)
Pula (4)
Rijeka (6)
Split (5)

Cuba
Santiago de Cuba (14)

Cyprus
Larnaca (7)

Denmark
Aalborg (7)
Copenhagen (10)
Elsinore (8)
Frederikshavn (13)
Helsingor (9)
Horsens (7)
Odense (6)

Djibouti
Djibouti (8)

Dubai
Dubai (5)

Ecuador
Guayaquil (9)

Egypt
Alexandria (10)
Damieth (7)
Port Said (8)
Suez (4)

England
Avonmouth (9)
Barnstaple (10)
Chatham (7)
Cinque Ports (11)
Colchester (10)
Deal (4)
Devonport (9)
Dover (5)
Falmouth (8)
Felixstowe (10)
Folkestone (10)
Gravesend (9)
Grimsby (7)
Hartlepool (10)
Harwich (7)
Hull (4)
King's Lynn (9)
Liverpool (9)

London (6)
Middlesbrough (13)
Newcastle (9)
Newhaven (8)
North Shields (12)
Penzance (8)
Plymouth (8)
Poole (5)
Portland (8)
Port Sunlight (12)
Portsmouth (10)
Rye (3)
Sandwich (8)
Sheerness (9)
Southampton (11)
Sunderland (10)
Teignmouth (10)
Tilbury (7)
Weymouth (8)
Whitstable (10)

Estonia
Reval (5)
Tallinn (7)

Finland
Helsinki (8)
Turku (5)

France
Bordeaux (8)
Boulogne (8)
Brest (5)
Calais (6)
Cannes (6)
Cherbourg (9)
Dieppe (6)
Dunkirk (7)
Fos-sur-Mer (9)
Honfleur (8)
La Rochelle (10)
Le Havre (7)
Marseilles (10)
Toulon (6)

French Guiana
Cayenne (7)

Germany
Bremen (6)
Bremerhaven (11)
Cuxhaven (8)
Emden (5)
Flensburg (9)
Hamburg (7)
Kiel (4)
Rostock (7)
Travemunde (10)
Wilhelmshaven (13)
Wismar (6)

Ghana
Takoradi (8)
Tema (4)

Greece
Canea (5)
Corfu (5)
Hermopolis (10)
Hermoupolis (11)
Navarino (8)
Patras (6)
Piraeus (7)
Rhodes (6)

Hawaii
Honolulu (8)
Pearl Harbor (11)

Hong Kong
Kowloon (7)

Hungary
Budapest (8)

India
Bombay (6)
Calcutta (8)
Cocanada (8)
Cochin (6)
Haldia (6)
Kakinada (8)
Kandla (6)
Madras (6)
Pondicherry (11)
Trincomalee (11)

Indonesia
Jakarta (7)
Macassar (8)
Makassar (8)
Padang (6)
Paradeep (8)

Iran
Bushire (7)

Iraq
Basra (5)
Umm Qasr (7)

Ireland (Republic of)
Cobh (4)
Cork (4)
Donegal (7)
Dundalk (7)
Dun Laoghaire (12)
Rosslare (8)
Youghal (7)

Isle of Man
Ramsey (6)

Israel
Acre (4)
Akko (4)
Ashdod (6)
Eilat (5)
Elat (4)
Haifa (5)

Italy
Ancona (6)
Bari (4)
Brindisi (8)
Gaeta (5)
Genoa (5)
Leghorn (7)
Marsala (7)
Messina (7)
Naples (6)
Ostia (5)
Palermo (7)
Salerno (7)
Trani (5)
Trapani (7)
Trieste (7)
Venice (6)

Ivory Coast
Abidjan (7)

Jamaica
Kingston (8)
Montego Bay (10)
Port Royal (9)

Japan
Hakodate (8)
Hiroshima (9)
Kagoshima (9)
Kobe (4)
Kochi (5)
Nagasaki (8)
Osaka (5)
Shimonoseki (11)
Yokohama (8)

Kenya
Mombasa (7)

Kuwait
Kuwait (6)
Mina al-Ahmadi (12)

Latvia
Riga (4)

Lebanon
Beirut (6)

Libya
Benghazi (8)
Tripoli (7)

Madagascar
Tamatave (8)

Majorca
Palma (5)

Malaysia
George Town (10)
Kotakinabalu (12)
Penang (6)
Port Klang (9)

Mauritania
F'derik (6)
Nouadhibou (10)

Mauritius
Port Louis (9)

Mediterranean
Gibraltar (9)

Mexico
Guaymas (7)
Vera Cruz (8)

Minorca
Mahon (5)
Port Mahon (9)

Montenegro
Bar (3)
Kotor (5)

Morocco
Agadir (6)
Casablanca (10)
Ceuta (5)
Essaouira (9)
Melilla (7)
Mina Hassan Tani (14)
Mogador (7)
Rabat (5)
Safi (4)
Tangier (7)
Tetuan (6)

Mozambique
Beira (5)

Netherlands
Amsterdam (9)
Delft (5)
Europort (8)
Flushing (8)
Rotterdam (9)
Vlissingen (10)

New Zealand
Auckland (8)
Gisborne (8)
Lyttelton (9)
Nelson (6)

Nigeria
Lagos (5)
Port Harcourt (12)

Northern Ireland
Belfast (7)
Larne (5)

Norway
Bergen (6)
Christiana (10)
Christiansund (13)
Larvik (6)
Narvik (6)
Oslo (4)
Stavangar (9)
Tromsø (6)
Trondheim (9)

Pakistan
Chalna (6)
Karachi (7)

Panama
Balboa (6)
Colón (5)
Cristobal (9)

Papua New Guinea
Port Moresby (11)

Peru
Callao (6)
Ilo (3)
Matarini (8)
San Juan Bay (10)

Philippines
Cebu (4)
Manila (6)

Poland
Danzig (6)
Gdansk (6)
Gdynia (6)
Kolobrzeg (9)
Szczecin (8)
Stettin (7)

Portugal
Lisbon (6)
Oporto (6)
Porto (5)

Puerto Rico
San Juan (7)

Romania
Constantsa (10)

Russia
Archangel (9)
Murmansk (8)
Nakhodka (8)
Okha (4)
Okhotsk (7)
Pechenga (8)
Petropavlovsk (13)
St Petersburg (12)
Taganrog (8)
Tiksi Bay (8)
Vladivostok (11)

Saudi Arabia
Jeddah (6)

Scotland
Ardrossan (9)
Dunbar (6)
Dundee (6)
Grangemouth (11)
Greenock (8)
Leith (5)
Port Glasgow (11)
Scapa (5)
Scapa Flow (9)
Stornaway (9)
Tain (4)
Wick (4)

Senegal
Dakar (5)

Sierra Leone
Freetown (8)

South Africa
Cape Town (8)
Durban (6)
East London (10)
Mossel Bay (9)
Port Elizabeth (13)
Port Natal (9)
Richard's Bay (11)
Simonstown (10)

South Korea
Pusan (5)

Spain
Algeciras (9)
Alicante (8)
Arrecife (8)
Barcelona (9)
Bilbao (6)
Cadiz (5)
Cartagena (9)
Corunna (7)
Ferrol (6)
Funchal (7)
La Coruña (8)
Malaga (6)
Palos (5)

Sri Lanka
Colombo (7)
Galle (5)
Lulea (5)
Malmo (5)

Sudan
Port Sudan (9)
Suakin (6)

Sweden
Goteborg (8)
Gothenburg (10)
Halmstad (8)
Helsingborg (11)
Kalmar (6)
Nykoping (8)
Stockholm (9)
Wisby (5)
Ystad (5)

Taiwan
Keelung (7)
Kaohsiung (9)
Tainan (6)

Tanzania
Dar es Salaam (11)
Mtwara (6)

Tasmania
Hobart (6)

Thailand
Bangkok (7)

Trinidad
Port of Spain (11)

Tunisia
Tunis (5)

Turkey
Istanbul (8)
Izmir (5)
Smyrna (6)

Ukraine
Izmail (6)
Kerch (5)
Odessa (6)
Yalta (5)

United Arab Emirates
Abu Dhabi (8)

Uruguay
Montevideo (10)

USA
Baltimore (9)
Boston (6)
Bridgeport (10)
Charleston (10)
Detroit (7)
Erie (4)
Galveston (9)
Houston (7)
Jersey City (10)
Los Angeles (10)
Nantucket (9)
New Bedford (10)
New Haven (8)
New Orleans (10)
New York (7)
Norfolk (7)
Pensacola (9)
Perth Amboy (10)
Portsmouth (10)
Rock Harbour (11)
San Francisco (12)
Seattle (7)

Venezuela
La Guiara (8)
Puerto Cabello (13)
Puerto Hierro (12)

Wales
Barry (5)
Cardiff (7)
Fishguard (9)
Holyhead (8)
Llanelli (8)
Milford Haven (12)
Pembroke (8)
Portmadoc (9)
Swansea (7)

Yemen
Aden (4)
Ahmedi (6)
Hodeida (7)
Mocha (5)

Presidents of the USA

4
Bush, George
Bush, George W.
Ford, Gerald
Polk, James K.
Taft, William

5
Adams, John
Adams, John Quincy
Grant, Ulysses S.
Hayes, Rutherford B.
Nixon, Richard M.
Tyler, John

6
Arthur, Chester A.
Carter, Jimmy
Hoover, Herbert
Munroe, James
Pierce, Franklin
Reagan, Ronald
Taylor, Zachary
Truman, Harry
Wilson, Woodrow

7
Clinton, Bill
Harding, Warren G.
Jackson, Andrew
Johnson, Andrew
Johnson, Lyndon B.
Kennedy, John F.

Lincoln, Abraham
Madison, James

8
Buchanan, James
Coolidge, Calvin
Fillmore, Millard
Garfield, James A.
Harrison, Benjamin
Harrison, William
McKinley, William
Van Buren, Martin

9
Cleveland, Grover
Jefferson, Thomas
Roosevelt, Franklin D.
Roosevelt, Theodore

10
Eisenhower, Dwight
Washington, George

Religions, Major

(largest first)

Christianity (12)
Islam (5)
Hinduism (8)
Buddhism (8)
Sikhism (7)
Judaism (7)
Confucianism (12)
Baha'ism (7)
Jainism (7)
Shintoism (9)

Rivers

R.= River (appears where this usually follows the name)

Afghanistan
Heri Rud (7)
Kabul R. (5)
Kuram (5)
Murghab (7)

Africa
Atbara (6)
Blue Nile (8)
Calabar (7)
Chambezi (8)
Congo (5)
Gambia (6)
Itimbiri (8)
Kafue (5)
Kagera (6)
Kubango (7)
Kwa (3)
Lomami (6)
Lualaba (7)
Luangwa (7)
Lugendi (7)
Niger (5)
Ogowai (6)
Prah (4)
Sankuru (7)
Semliki (7)
Senegal (7)
Shire (5)
Ubangi (6)
Welle (5)
White Nile (9)
Zaire (5)
Zambezi (7)

Asia
Amu Darya (8)
Amur (4)
Dnieper (7)
Hue (3)
Ili (3)
Mekong (6)
Oxus (4)
Selenga (7)
Shat-el-Arab (10)
Sungari (7)
Usuri (5)
Yarkand (7)
Zaratshan (9)

Australia
Albert (6)
Alice (5)
Avoca (5)
Barwon (6)
Brisbane R. (8)
Campaspe (8)
Clarence (8)
Darling (7)
Fitzroy (7)
Georgina (8)
Gilbert (7)
Glenelg (7)
Goulburn (8)
Hawkesbury (10)
Lachlan (7)
Loddon (6)
Lynd (4)
Macquarrie (10)
Mitchell (8)
Murray R. (6)
Murray-Darling (13)
Parramatta (10)
Peel (4)
Richmond (8)
Swan (4)
Thomson (7)
Warrego (7)
Yarra Yarra (10)

Austria
Enns (4)
Inn (3)
Traun (5)

Balkans
Stroma (6)

Belarus
Beresina (8)
Dnieper (7)
Niemen (6)

Belgium
Lys (3)
Meuse (5)
Sambre (6)
Schelde (7)
Scheldt (7)

Bosnia
Drina (5)

Brazil
Japura (6)
Paraná (6)
Parima (6)
Rio Grande (9)
São Francisco (12)

Burma
Chindwin (8)
Irrawaddy (9)
Salween (7)
Salwin (6)

Canada
Abbitibee (9)
Abitibi (7)
Albany (6)
Bonaventure (11)
Churchill (9)
Fraser (6)
French (6)
Gatineau (8)
Great Slave R. (10)
Ha Ha (4)
Klondyke R. (8)
Liard (5)
Mackenzie (9)
Mallagami (9)
Mattawa (7)
Mirimichi (9)
Missimabi (9)
Moose (5)
Nelson (6)
Nipisquit (9)
Ottawa (6)
Parsnip (7)
Peace R. (5)
Peel (4)
Restigouche (11)
Rimouski (8)
Saguenay (8)
St Claire (8)
St John (6)
St Lawrence (10)
Saskatchewan (12)
Severn (6)
Shubenacadia (12)
Thames (6)
Tobique (7)
Trent (5)
Winnipeg (8)
Yukon (5)

China
Canton R. (6)
Hankiang (8)
Hoang Ho (7)
Hsi (3)
Huang (5)
Hwangho (7)
Menam (5)
Pei Ho (5)
Tarim (5)
Yangtse (7)
Yangtse Kiang (12)
Yellow R. (6)

Czech Republic
Moldau (6)
Morava (6)
Oder (4)

East Africa
Hawash (6)
Ikopa (5)
Juba (4)
Komati (6)
Pungwe (6)
Rovuma (6)
Rufiji (6)
Shari (5)
Tana (4)

England
Adur (4)
Aire (4)
Aln (3)
Arun (4)
Avon (4)
Axe (3)
Beaulieu (8)
Blackwater (10)
Brent (5)
Bure (4)
Calder (6)
Cam (3)
Camel (5)
Chelmer (7)
Cherwell (8)
Cole (4)
Coln (4)
Colne (5)
Coquet (6)
Crouch (6)
Dart (4)
Deben (5)
Dee (3)
Derwent (7)
Dove (4)
Eden (4)
Evenlode (8)
Exe (3)
Fal (3)
Fleet (5)
Frome (5)
Great Ouse (9)
Hamble (6)
Humber (6)
Irwell (6)
Isis (4)
Itchen (6)
Kennet (6)
Lea (3)
Loddon (6)
Lune (4)
Medina (6)
Medway (6)
Mersey (6)
Mole (4)
Monnow (6)
Naze (4)
Nen (3)
Orwell (6)
Otter (5)
Ouse (4)
Parret (6)
Rede R. (4)
Ribble (6)
Roding (6)
Rother (6)
Rye (3)
Severn (6)
Sheaf (5)
Sid (3)
Sow (3)
Stour (5)
Swale (5)
Tamar (5)
Taw (3)
Tees (4)
Teign (5)
Test (4)
Thames (6)
Torridge (8)
Trent (5)
Tyne (4)
Ure (3)
Wandle (6)
Wansbeck (8)
Wash (4)
Waveney (7)
Wear (4)
Weaver (6)
Welland (7)
Wensum (6)
Wey (3)
Wharfe (6)
Windrush (8)
Witham (6)
Wye (3)
Yare (4)
Yeo (3)

Europe
Danube (6)
Moselle (7)
Roer (4)
Rur (3)

Finland
Tornio (6)

France
Adour (5)
Agout (5)
Ain (3)
Aisne (5)
Allier (6)
Cher (4)
Durance (7)
Garonne (7)
Ill (3)
Isère (5)
Loir (4)
Loire (5)
Lot (3)

Lys (3)
Marne (5)
Mayenne (7)
Oise (4)
Rance (5)
Rhône (5)
Saar (4)
Sambre (6)
Saone (5)
Sarthe (6)
Save (4)
Seine (5)
Somme (5)
Tarn (4)
Var (3)
Vienne (6)
Vire (4)
Yonne (5)

Germany
Aller (5)
Bober (5)
Eider (5)
Elbe (4)
Elster (6)
Ems (3)
Havel (5)
Isar (4)
Lahn (4)
Lech (4)
Main (4)
Memel (5)
Neckar (6)
Neisse (6)
Oder (4)
Rhine (5)
Ruhr (4)
Saale (5)
Saar (4)
Spree (5)
Werra (5)
Weser (5)
Wipper (5)

Greece
Maritza (7)

Hungary
Draava (6)
Drave (5)
Koros (5)
Leitha (6)
Neutra (6)
Temes (5)
Theiss (6)
Tisza (5)
Waag (4)
Zenta (5)

India
Beas (4)
Brahmaputra (11)
Cauvery (7)
Chambal (7)
Chenab (6)
Chumbal (7)
Dihong (6)
Gandak (6)
Ganges (6)
Godavari (8)
Gogra (8)
Gumti (5)
Hooghli (7)
Hugli (5)
Hunza (5)
Indus (5)
Jumna (5)
Kanawha (7)
Kaveri (6)
Kusi (4)
Mahanadi (8)
Narbuda (7)
Porali (6)
Ravi (6)
Sutlej (6)
Sutluj (6)
Tapti (5)
Tons (4)
Toombudra (9)

Iran
Karun (5)
Kizil Uzen (9)
Zarang (6)

Iraq
Euphrates (9)
Tigris (6)

Ireland (Republic of)
Barrow (6)
Blackwater (10)
Boyne (5)
Bride (5)
Erne (4)
Feale (5)
Foyle (5)
Lee (3)
Liffey (6)
Main (4)
Shannon (7)
Slaney (6)
Suck (4)
Suir (4)
Swilly (6)

Israel
Jordan (6)

Italy
Adda (4)
Adige (5)
Agogno (6)
Anio (4)
Arno (4)
Dora (4)
Mincio (6)
Oglio (5)
Po (2)
Rubicon (7)
Tanaro (6)
Tiber (5)

Jordan
Jordan (6)

Kazakhstan
Ishim (5)
Syr (3)
Syr Daria (8)
Ural (4)

Lithuania
Niemen (6)

Malaysia
Kelantan (8)
Perak (5)

Mexico
Bolsas (6)
Grande (6)
Rio del Norte (11)
Rio Grande (9)
Tampico (7)

Moldova
Dniester (8)

Netherlands
Lek (3)
Maas (4)
Rhine (5)
Schelde (7)
Scheldt (7)
Waal (4)
Yssel (5)

New Zealand
Buller (6)
Thames (6)
Waihou (6)
Walkato (7)
Wanganui (8)

North Africa
Habra (5)
Muluyar (7)

North America
Columbia (8)
Kootenay (8)
Niagara (7)

Northern Ireland
Bann (4)
Lagan (5)

Norway
Glommen (7)

Pakistan
Jelum (5)
Jhelum (6)

Papua New Guinea
Fly (3)

Poland
Bug (3)
Dunajec (7)
Nida (4)
Oder (4)
Vistula (7)
Warta (5)
Warthe (6)

Portugal
Douro (5)
Minho (5)
Tagus (5)
Tamega (6)

Romania
Maroo (5)
Pruth (5)
Sereth (6)

Russia
Angara (6)
Desna (5)
Dnieper (7)
Dunay (5)
Indigirka (9)
Irtish (6)
Kama (4)
Katun (5)
Ket (3)
Kur (3)
Lena (4)
Moskva (6)
Neva (4)
Ob (3)
Ob Irtysh (8)
Oka (3)
Onega (5)
Pechora (7)
Tara (4)
Tom (3)
Tunguska (8)
Ural (4)
Usa (3)
Vyatka (6)
Volga (5)
Yana (4)
Yenesei (7)

Scotland
Aire (4)
Allan (5)
Allen (5)
Allenwater (10)
Annan (5)
Beauly (6)
Bogie (5)
Carron (6)
Cart (4)
Clyde (5)
Deveron (7)
Devon (5)
Don (3)
Doon (4)
Earn (4)
Eden (4)
Esk (3)
Etive (5)
Ettrick (7)
Ettrickwater (12)
Forth (5)
Foyers (6)
Gala Water (9)
Leven (5)
Nith (4)
Shiel (5)
Spey (4)
Tay (3)
Teith (5)
Teviot (6)
Tummel (6)
Tweed (5)
Yarrow (6)
Yarrowwater (11)

South Africa
Blood R. (5)
Buffalo (7)
Crocodile R. (9)
Gamtoos (7)
Gauritz (7)
Great Fish R. (9)
Great Kei (8)
Hex R. (3)
Kowie (5)
Limpopo (7)
Modder R. (6)
Mooi (4)
Olifant (7)
Orange (6)
Pungwe (6)
Sunday (6)
Tugela (6)
Umsimkulu (9)
Umsimvubu (9)
Umvolosi (8)
Vaal (4)
Zontag (6)

South America
Amazon (6)
Arinos (6)
Caroni (6)
Demerara (8)
Desaguadero (11)
Esmeralda (9)
Essequibo (9)
Grande (6)
Guapore (7)
Huallaga (8)
La Plata (7)
Madeira (7)
Marañón (7)
Mazaruni (8)
Orinoco (7)
Paraguay (8)
Parahiba (8)
Paraíba (7)
Paraná (6)
Paranahiba (10)
Paranaíba (9)
Pilcomayo (9)
Plate (5)
Purus (5)
Putumayo (8)
Rio Branco (9)
Rio Negro (8)
San Juan (7)
Santiago (8)
Suriname (8)
Tapajos (7)
Teffe (5)
Tocantins (9)
Ucayali (7)
Upper Paraná (11)
Uruguay (7)
Xiugo (5)
Yavari (6)
Yuruari (7)

Spain
Aguada (6)
Alagon (6)
Douro (5)
Ebro (4)
Guadalete (9)
Guadalquivir (12)
Guadiana (8)
Manzanares (10)
Minho (5)
Rio Tinto (8)
Tormes (6)

Sweden
Gota (4)
Umea (4)

Switzerland
Aar (3)
Reuss (5)
Rhine (5)
Rhône (5)
Sulir (5)
Thur (4)
Ticino (6)

Syria
Abana (5)
Euphrates (9)
Jordan (6)
Orontes (7)

Thailand
Kwai (4)
Meklong (7)

Turkey
Euphrates (9)
Kizil Irmak (10)
Tigris (6)
Zab (3)

Ukraine
Alma (4)
Bug (3)

Dnieper (7)
Dniester (8)
Styr (4)

USA
Alabama (7)
Arkansas (8)
Big Black R. (8)
Big Blue R. (7)
Big Horn R. (7)
Big Sandy R. (8)
Big Sioux R. (8)
Black R. (5)
Brazos (6)
Cape Fear R. (8)
Catawba (7)
Colorado R. (8)
Delaware (8)
East R. (4)
Fall (4)
Feather (7)
Gila (4)
Genesee (7)
Grande (6)
Great Kanawka (12)
Green R. (5)
Hudson (6)
Humboldt (8)
James R. (5)
Juniata (7)
Kalamazoo (9)
Kankakee (8)
Kennebec (8)
Lackawanna (10)
Lehigh (6)
Merrimac (8)
Miami (5)
Mississippi (11)
Missouri (8)
Mobile (6)
Mohawk (6)
Monagahela (10)
Nebraska (8)
Neuse (5)
Niagara (7)
Ohio (4)
Oneida (6)
Passaic (7)
Pecos (5)
Penobscot (9)
Platte (6)
Potomac (7)
Racket (6)
Rappahannock (12)
Red R. (3)
Rio Grande (9)
Sabine (6)
Sacramento (10)
St John's (7)
Salt R. (4)
San Joaquin (10)
Santee (6)
Savannah (8)
Scioto (6)
Seneca (6)
Shenandoah (10)
Snake R. (5)
Spokane (7)
Sugar (5)
Susquehanna (11)
Suwanee (7)
Tennessee (9)
Trinity (7)
Wabash (6)
White R. (5)
Wichita (7)
Wisconsin (9)

Wales
Dovey (5)
Neath (5
Severn (6)
Taff (4)
Tawe (4)
Teiti (5)
Towy (4)
Usk (3)
Wye (3)
Ystwith (7)

West Africa
Benue (5)
Gallinas (8)
Geba (4)
Grande (6)
Kwanza (6)
Rio Grande (9)
St Paul (6)
Volta (5)

Roman Emperors

4
Geta
Nero
Otho

5
Carus
Galba
Nerva
Titus

6
Decius
Gallus
Probus
Trajan

7
Carinus
Hadrian
Tacitus

8
Balbinus
Caligula (Gaius Caesar)
Claudius
Commodus
Domitian
Floranus
Galerius
Jovianus
Julianus
Macrinus
Pertinax
Pupienus
Tiberius

9
Ballienus
Caracalla
Gordianus
Lincinius
Maxentius
Maximinus
Philippus
Vespasian
Vitellius

10
Aemilianus
Aurelianus
Diocletian
Elagabalus (Heliogabalus)
Maximianus
Numerianus
Quintillus
Valerianus
Volusianus

11 and over
Alexander Severus (16)
Antoninus Pius (13)
Constantine (11)
Constantius (11)
Gaius Caesar (Caligula) (11)
Glaudius Gothicus (16)
Heliogabalus (Elagabalus) (12)
Lucius Verus (11)
Marcus Aurelius (14)
Septimius Severus (16)

Rulers of the UK

Sovereigns of England (from 955) and of the United Kingdom (from 1801)

Saxon
Edwy (4)
Edgar (5)
Edward the Martyr (15)
Ethelred the Unready (18)
Edmund Ironside (14)

Danish
Canute (Cnut) (6)
Harold I (6)
Hardicanute (Harthacnut) (11)

Saxon
Edward the Confessor (18)
Harold II (Godwinson) (6)

House of Normandy
William I (The Conqueror) (7)
William II (7)
Henry I (5)
Stephen (7)

House of Plantagenet
Henry II (Curtmantel) (5)
Richard (The Lionheart) (7)
John (Lackland) (4)
Henry III (5)
Edward I (6)
Edward II (6)
Edward III (6)
Richard II (7)

House of Lancaster
Henry IV (5)
Henry V (5)
Henry VI (5)

House of York
Edward IV (6)
Edward V (6)
Richard III (7)

House of Tudor
Henry VII (5)
Henry VIII (5)
Edward VI (6)
Lady Jane Grey (12)
Mary I (Bloody Mary) (4)
Elizabeth I (The Virgin Queen) (9)

House of Stuart
James I of England and VI of Scotland (5)
Charles I (7)

Commonwealth (declared 1649)
Oliver Cromwell (14)
Richard Cromwell (15)

House of Stuart
Charles II (7)
James II of England and VII of Scotland (5)
William III and Mary II (7, 4)
Anne (4)

House of Hanover
George I (6)
George II (6)
George III (Farmer George) (6)
George IV (6)
William IV (Silly Billy) (7)
Victoria (8)

House of Saxe-Coburg-Gotha
Edward VII (6)

House of Windsor
George V (The Sailor King) (6)
Edward VIII (Our Smiling Prince) (6)
George VI (6)
Elizabeth II (9)

Sovereigns of Scotland (from 1058)

House of Dunkeld
Malcolm III (Canmore) (7)
Donald Ban (9)
Duncan II (6)
Donald Ban (restored) (9)
Edgar (5)
Alexander I (the Fierce) (9)
David I (the Saint) (5)
Malcolm IV (the Maiden) (7)
William I (the Lion) (7)
Alexander II (9)
Alexander III (9)
Margaret, Maid of Norway (20)
John Balliol (11)
Robert I (the Bruce) (6)
David II (5)

House of Stuart
Robert II (6)
Robert III (6)
James I (5)
James II (5)
James III (5)

James IV (5)
James V (5)
Mary, Queen of Scots (16)
James VI (ascended English throne, 1603) (5)

Scientists, Mathematicians and Engineers

3
Ohm
Ray

4
Bell
Bohr
Born
Bose
Davy
Ford
Gold
Hahn
Hall
Hess
Howe
Jung
Koch
Mond
Pare
Reed
Salk
Swan
Watt
Wren

5
Bacon
Banks
Barry
Bondi
Boole
Boyle
Bragg
Brahe
Crick
Curie
Debye
Euler
Ewing
Fermi
Freud
Galen
Galle
Gamov
Gauss
Gibbs
Haber
Henry
Hertz
Hooke
Hoyle
Jacob
Jeans
Joule
Klein
Krebs
Lodge
Maxim
Monod
Morse
Pauli
Pliny
Raman
Segrè
Smith
Tesla
Volta
White

6
Ampère
Brunel
Bunsen
Calvin
Cantor
Dalton
Darwin
Diesel
Edison
Euclid
Froude
Fulton
Galois
Halley
Harden
Harvey
Hubble
Hughes
Hutton
Huxley
Jenner
Kekule
Kelvin
Kepler
Kuiper
Liebig
Lister
Mendel
Morgan
Napier
Nernst
Newton
Pascal
Pavlov
Perutz
Planck
Ramsay
Stokes
Thales
Turing
Watson

7
Andrews
Babbage
Banting
Cassini
Charles
Compton
Crookes
Daimler
Da Vinci
Doppler
Ehrlich
Faraday
Fleming
Galileo
Galvani
Haldane
Hawking
Hilbert
Huggins
Huygens
Kapitsa
Kendrew
Lamarck
Leblanc
Leibniz
Lesseps
Lockyer
Lorentz
Marconi
Maxwell
Medawar
Moseley
Pasteur
Pauling
Piccard
Ptolemy
Rontgen
Rumford
Seaborg
Siemens
Spinoza
Thomson
Tyndall
Virchow
Wallace
Whitney

8
Agricola
Avogadro
Bessemer
Blackett
Chadwick
de Fermat
De Forest
Einstein
Foucault
Franklin
Goodyear
Harrison
Herschel
Humboldt
Lawrence
Linnaeus
Malpighi
Mercator
Millikan
Poincare
Rayleigh
Thompson
Van Allen
Van't Hoff
Zeppelin

9
Aristotle
Armstrong
Arrhenius
Becquerel
Bernoulli
Cavendish
De Broglie
de Coulomb
Descartes
Eddington
Fibonacci
Heaviside
Kirchhoff
Lankester
Michelson

10
Archimedes
Cannizzaro
Copernicus
Fahrenheit

Flammarion
Heisenberg
Hipparchus
Mendeleyev
Paracelsus
Pythagoras
Rutherford
Stephenson
Torricelli
Trevithick

11
Grosseteste
Le Chatelier
Leeuwenhoek
Oppenheimer
Schrodinger
Van der Waals

Seas and Oceans

3
Red S.

4
Aral S.
Azov, S. of
Dead S.
Java S.
Kara S.
Ross S.
Sava S.
Sulu S.

5
Banda S.
Black S.
Ceram S.
China S.
Coral S.
Irish S.
Japan, S. of
Malay S.
North S.
Timor S.
White S.

6
Aegean S.
Arctic O.
Baltic S.
Bering S.
Celtic S.
Flores S.
Gaelic S.
Indian O.
Ionian S.
Laptev S.
Scotia S.
Tasman S.
Yellow S.

7
Andaman S.
Arabian S.
Arafura S.
Barents S.
Behring S.
Caspian S.
Celebes S.
Marmora, S. of
Molucca S.
Okhotsk, S. of
Pacific O.
Weddell S.

8
Adriatic S.
Amundsen S.
Atlantic O.
Beaufort S.
Ligurian S.
Macassar S.
McKinley S.
Sargasso S.

9
Antarctic O.
Caribbean S.
East China S.
Greenland S.
Norwegian S.
Zuider Zee

10 ***and over***
Bellingshausen S. (14)
East Siberian S. (12)
King Haakon VIII S. (14)
Mediterranean S. (13)
South China S. (10)
Tyrrhenian S. (10)

Seven Against Thebes

Adrastus (8)
Amphiaraus (10)
Capaneus (8)
Hipomedon (9)
Parthenopaeus (13)
Polynices (9)
Tydeus (6)

Seven Deadly Sins

anger (5)
covetousness (12)
envy (4)
gluttony (8)
lust (4)
pride (5)
sloth (5)

Seven Dwarfs

Bashful (7)
Doc (3)
Dopey (5)
Grumpy (6)
Happy (5)
Sleepy (6)
Sneezy (6)

Seven Liberal Arts

arithmetic (10)
astronomy (9)
geometry (8)
grammar (7)
logic (5)
music (5)
rhetoric (8)

Seven Sacraments

anointing of the sick (18)
baptism (7)
confirmation (12)
eucharist (9)
matrimony (9)
ordination (10)
penance (7)

Seven Sages

Bias (4)
Chilon (6)
Cleobonlos (10)
Periander (9)
Pittacus (8)
Solon (5)
Thales (6)

Seven Seas

Antarctic Ocean (14)
Arctic Ocean (11)
Indian Ocean (11)
North Atlantic Ocean (18)
North Pacific Ocean (17)
South Atlantic Ocean (18)
South Pacific Ocean (17)

Seven Wonders of the Ancient World

Colossus of Rhodes (16)
Hanging Gardens of Babylon (23)
Pharos of Alexandria (18)
Pyramids of Egypt (15)
Statue of Jupiter at Olympia (24)
Temple of Diana at Ephesus (22)
Tomb of Mausolus (14)

Shakespeare's Plays

6
Hamlet
Henry V

7
Henry IV (Parts 1 and 2)
Henry VI (Parts 1, 2 and 3)
Macbeth
Othello

8
King John
King Lear
Pericles

9
Cymbeline
Henry VIII
Richard II

10
Coriolanus
King Henry V
Richard III
The Tempest

11
As You Like It
King Henry IV (Parts 1 and 2)
King Henry VI (Parts 1, 2 and 3)

12
Julius Caesar
Twelfth Night

13
King Henry VIII
King Richard II
Timon of Athens

14
King Richard III
Romeo and Juliet
The Winter's Tale

15 and over
A Comedy of Errors (15)
All's Well That Ends Well (20)
Hamlet, Prince of Denmark (21)
Love's Labour's Lost (16)
Measure for Measure (17)
The Merry Wives of Windsor (22)
A Midsummer Night's Dream (21)
Much Ado About Nothing (19)
Othello, the Moor of Venice (22)
Pericles, Prince of Tyre (20)
The Taming of the Shrew (19)
The Two Noble Kinsmen (18)
Troilus and Cressida (18)
Two Gentlemen of Verona (20)

Six Wives of Henry VIII

Anne Boleyn (10) (2, beheaded)
Anne of Cleves (12) (4, divorced)
Catherine Howard (15) (5, beheaded)
Catherine of Aragon (17) (1, divorced)
Catherine Parr (13) (6, survived)
Jane Seymour (11) (3, died)

Sports Personalities

ATHLETICS

3
Coe, Sebastian

4
Cram, Steve

5
Flo-Jo
Keino, Kip
Lewis, Carl
Lewis, Denise
Ovett, Steve
Owens, Jesse
Pirie, Gordon

6
Foster, Brendan
Peters, Mary

7
Elliott, Herb
Hopkins, Thelma
Johnson, Ben

8
Christie, Linford
Redgrave, Sir Steve

9 and over
Bannister, Sir Roger (9)
Grey-Thompson, Tanni (12)
Griffith-Joyner, Florence (14)
Whitbread, Fatima (9)

BOXING

3
Ali, Muhammad

4
Clay, Cassius
King, Don

5
Bruno, Frank
Hamad, Naseem "Prince")
Lewis, Lennox
Louis, Joe
Tyson, Mike

6
Bugner, Joe
Cooper, Henry
Eubank, Chris
Liston, Sonny

7
Dempsey, Jack
Foreman, George
Frazier, Joe

8
Marciano, Rocky
Robinson, Sugar Ray

11
Fitzsimmons, Bob

CHESS

6
Karpov, Anatoly

7
Fischer, Bobby
Spassky, Boris

8
Alekhine, Alexander
Kasparov, Gary

10
Capablanca, José

CRICKET

4
Amis, Dennis
Bird, Dickie
Khan, Imran
Lock, Tony
Snow, John

5
Close, Brian
Evans, Godfrey
Grace, Dr W.G.
Greig, Tony
Hobbs, Sir John
Knott, Alan
Laker, Jim
Lloyd, Clive

6
Bedser, Alec
Benaud, Richard
Botham, Ian

Dexter, Ted
Edrich, John
Hadlee, Sir Richard
Hutton, Sir Len
Kanhai, Rohan
Lillee, Dennis
Sobers, Sir Gary
Titmus, Fred
Willis, Bob

7
Boycott, Geoffrey
Bradman, Sir Don
Compton, Denis
Cowdrey, Colin
Thomson, Jeff
Trueman, Freddie
Worrell, Sir Frank

8
Chappell, Greg
Chappell, Ian
Graveney, Tom

9 and over
Constantine, Sir Leary (11)
D'Oliveira, Basil (9)
Fredericks, Roy (10)
Illingworth, Ray (11)
Underwood, Derek (9)

FOOTBALL

3
Law, Denis

4
Best, George
Owen, Michael
Pele

5
Banks, Gordon
Busby, Sir Matt
Moore, Bobby
Revie, Don
Stein, Jock

6
Clough, Brian
Keegan, Kevin
Ramsey, Sir Alf

7
Beckham, David
Cantona, Eric
Greaves, Jimmy
Lineker, Gary
Ronaldo

8
Charlton, Bobby
Charlton, Jack
Dalglish, Kenny
Docherty, Tommy
Ferguson, Sir Alex
Maradona, Diego
Matthews, Sir Stanley

9 and over
Beckenbauer, Franz (11)
Blancheflower, Danny (13)
Gascoigne, Paul (9)

GOLF

5
Hogan, Ben
Irwin, Hale
Woods, Tiger

6
Palmer, Arnold
Player, Gary

7
Jacklin, Tony
Trevino, Lee

8
Nicklaus, Jack
Weiskopf, Tom

10 and over
Ballesteros, Severiano (11)
Oosterhuis, Peter (10)

MOTOR RACING

4
Hill, Graham
Hunt, James
Moss, Stirling

5
Clark, Jim
Lauda, Niki
Senna, Ayrton

6
Fangio, Juan
Piquet, Nelson

7
Brabham, Jack
Ferrari, Enzo
Stewart, Jackie

10
Fittipaldi, Emerson
Schumacher, Michael
Villeneuve, Jacques

SWIMMING

4
Webb, Captain
Matthew

5
Spitz, Mark

6
Fraser, Dawn
Wilkie, David

7
Goodhew, Duncan

10 ***and over***
Lonsbrough, Anita (10)
Weissmuller, Johnny (11)

TENNIS

4
Ashe, Arthur
Borg, Bjorn
Cash, Pat
Graf, Steffi
King, Billie Jean
Wade, Virginia

5
Court, Margaret
Evert, Chris
Jones, Ann
Laver, Rod
Lendl, Ivan
Lloyd, Chris
Perry, Fred
Seles, Monica
Wills, Helen

6
Barker, Sue
Becker, Boris
Casals, Rosemary
Cawley, Yvonne
Edberg, Stefan
Henman, Tim
Taylor, Roger

7
Connors, Jimmy
Emerson, Roy
McEnroe, John
Mottram, Buster
Nastase, Ilie
Novotna, Jana
Sampras, Pete

8
Connolly, Maureen
Little Mo
Newcombe, John
Rosewall, Ken
Williams, Venus
Williams, Serena

9
Goolagong, Evonne

11
Navratilova, Martina

OTHER SPORTS

3
Fox, Uffa (yachting)
Kim, Nellie (gymnastics)

4
Cobb, Ty (baseball)
John, Barry (rugby)
Read, Phil (motorcycling)
Ruth, "Babe" (baseball)

5
Curry, John (skating)
Davis, Joe (billiards)
Davis, Steve (snooker)
Moore, Ann (showjumping)
Scott, Sheila (aviation)
Smith, Harvey (showjumping)

6
Broome, David (showjumping)
Carson, Willie (horseracing)
Hendry, Steven (snooker)
Korbut, Olga (gymnastics)
Smythe, Pat (showjumping)
Wilson, Jocky (darts)

7
Bristow, Eric (darts)
Carling, Will (rugby)
Higgins, Alex "Hurricane" (snooker)
Hillary, Sir Edmund (mountaineering)
Johnson, Amy (aviation)
Piggott, Lester (horseracing)
Tabarly, Eric (yachting)
Tensing, Sherpa (mountaineering)

8
Comaneci, Nadia (gymnastics)
Cordobés, El (bullfighting)
Cousteau, Jacques-Yves (diving)
Latynina, Larissa (gymnastics)
Richards, Sir Gordon (horseracing)

9
Bonington, Sir Chris (mountaineering)
Lindbergh, Charles (aviation)
Pattisson, Rodney (yachting)

10 ***and over***
Barrington, Jonah (squash) (10)
Chichester, Sir Francis (yachting) (10)
"Eddie the Eagle" (skiing) (13)
Schockemohle, Alwin (showjumping) (12)
Torvill and Dean (skating) (14)
Turischeva, Ludmila (gymnastics) (10)

Stars

4
Mira
Vega

5
Algol
Deneb
Hamal

6
Altair
Castor
Crucis
Pollux
Shaula
Sirius

7
Antares
Canopus
Capella
Dog Star
Lalande
Polaris
Procyon
Proxima
Regulus

8
Achernar
Alpherat
Arcturus
Barnard's
Centauri
Denebola
Kapteyn's
Lodestar
Pole Star

9
Aldebaran
Bellatrix
Fomalhaut

10
Betelgeuse

13
Alpha Centauri

States of the USA

State	*Abbreviations*	*Nickname*
Alabama (7)	AL, Ala	Yellowhammer State
Alaska(6)	AK, Alas	Last Frontier
Arizona (7)	AZ, Ariz	Grand Canyon State
Arkansas (8)	AR, Ark	The Natural State
California (10)	CA, Cal, Calif	Golden State
Colorado (8)	CO, Colo	Centennial State
Connecticut (11)	CT, Conn	Constitution State
Delaware (8)	DE, Del	Diamond State
Florida (7)	FL, Fla	Sunshine State
Georgia (7)	GA, Ga	Peach State
Hawaii (6)	HA	Aloha State
Idaho (5)	ID, Id, Ida	Gem State
Illinois (8)	IL, Ill	Land of Lincoln
Indiana (7)	IN, Ina	Hoosier State
Iowa (4)	IA, Ia	Hawkeye State
Kansas (6)	KS, Kan	Sunflower State
Kentucky (8)	KY, Ky, Ken	Bluegrass State
Louisiana (9)	LA, La	Pelican State
Maine (5)	ME	Pine Tree State
Maryland (8)	MD, Md	Old Line State
Massachusetts (13)	MA, Mass	Bay State
Michigan (8)	MI, Mich	Great Lakes State
Minnesota (9)	MN, Minn	North Star State
Mississippi (11)	MS, Miss	Magnolia State
Missouri (8)	MO, Mo	Show Me State
Montana (7)	MT, Mont	Treasure State
Nebraska (8)	NE, Neb	Cornhusker State
Nevada (6)	NV, Nev	The Silver State
New Hampshire (12)	NH	Granite State
New Jersey (9)	NJ	Garden State
New Mexico (9)	Nmex, NM	Land of Enchantment
New York (7)	NY	Empire State
North Carolina (13)	NC	Tar Heel State
North Dakota (11)	ND, N Dak	Peace Garden State
Ohio (4)	OH, O.	Buckeye State
Oklahoma (8)	OK, Okla	Sooner State
Oregon (6)	OR, Or.,Oreg	Beaver State
Pennsylvania (12)	PA, Penn	Keystone State
Rhode Island (11)	RI	The Ocean State
South Carolina (13)	SC	Palmetto State
South Dakota (11)	SD, S Dak	Mount Rushmore State
Tennessee (9)	TN, Tenn	Volunteer State
Texas (5)	TX, Tex	Lone Star State
Utah (4)	UT	Beehive State
Vermont (7)	VT	Green Mountain State
Virginia (8)	VA	The Old Dominion State
Washington (10)	WA, Wash	Evergreen State

State	Abbreviations	Nickname
West Virginia (12)	WV, W Va	Mountain State
Wisconsin (9)	WI, Wis	Badger State
Wyoming (7)	WY, Wyo	Equality State/Cowboy State

Teas

4	6	7	8	9 and over
mint	Ceylon	Chinese	black tea	Darjeeling (10)
	congou	iced tea	brick tea	English breakfast (16)
5	herbal	Russian	camomile	gunpowder (9)
Assam	Indian	twankay	Earl Grey	lapsang souchong (15)
bohea	oolong		Lady Grey	orange pekoe (11)
green			pouching	
lemon			souchong	

Three Fates

Atropos (7) Clotho (6) Lachesis (8)

Three Furies

Alecto (6) Megaera (7) Tisiphone (9)

Three Gorgons

Eurayale (8) Medusa (6) Stheno (6)

Three Graces

Aglaia (6) Euphrosyne (10) Thalia (6)

Three Harpies

Aello (6) Celaeno/Podargo (7) Ocypete (7)

Three Seasons

Dike (4) justice

Eirine (6) peace

Eunomia (7) order

Twelve Apostles

Andrew (6)
James (5)
James (son of Alphaeus) (5)
John (4)
Judas (brother of James) (5)
Judas Iscariot (13)
Matthew (7)
Nathanael (9)
Peter (5)
Philip (6)
Simon the Zealot (14)
Thomas (6)

Twelve Days of Christmas

(My true love sent to me)

A *partridge* in a *pear tree* (9, 8)
Two *turtle doves* (11)
Three *French hens* (10)
Four *calling birds* (12)
Five *gold rings* (9)
Six *geese a-laying* (12)
Seven *swans a-swimming* (14)
Eight *maids a-milking* (13)
Nine *ladies dancing* (13)
Ten *lords a-leaping* (13)
Eleven *pipers piping* (12)
Twelve *drummers drumming* (16)

Twelve Labours of Hercules

1 Kill the Nemean lion (17)
2 Kill the Hydra (12)
3 Capture the Cerynitian Hind (24)
4 Capture the boar of Erymanthus 26)
5 Clean out the Augean stables (24)
6 Kill the birds of Lake Stymphalos (28)
7 Capture the Cretan bull (20)
8 Bring back the horses of Diomedes (28)
9 Obtain the girdle of Hippolyte (26)
10 Bring back the cattle of Geryon (26)
11 Bring back the golden apples of the Hesperides (39)
12 Bring back Cerberus from the underworld (34)

Twelve Tribes of Israel

(sons of Jacob)

Asher (5)
Benjamin (8)
Dan (3)
Gad (3)
Issachar (8)
Joseph (6)
Judah (5)
Levi (4)
Naphtali (8)
Reuben (6)
Simeon (6)
Zebulun (7)

UK Shipping Areas

4
Sole
Tyne

5
Dover
Forth
Lundy
Malin
Wight
Bailey
Biscay
Dogger
Faroes
Fisher
Humber
Thames
Viking

7
Fastnet
FitzRoy
Forties
Rockall
Shannon

8
Cromarty
Fair Isle
Hebrides
Irish Sea
Plymouth
Portland

9
Trafalgar

11
German Bight
North Utsire
South Utsire

16
South-East Iceland

Waterfalls

Angel (5)
Churchill (9)
Gavarnie (8)
Giessbach (9)
Guaira (6)
Hamilton (8)
Krimmler (8)
Multnomah (9)
Niagara (7)
Ribbon (6)
Roraima (7)
Salto Ángel (10)
Sete Quedas (10)
Stanley (7)
Sutherland (10)
Trummelbach (11)
Vettisfos (9)
Victoria (8)
Upper Yosemite (13)

Wedding Anniversaries

Year	*Gift*
1	paper (5)
2	cotton (6)
3	leather (7)
4	linen (5)
5	wood (4)
6	iron (4)
7	copper (6)
8	bronze (6)
9	pottery (7)
10	tin (3)
11	steel (5)
12	silk (4)
13	lace (4)
14	ivory (5)
15	crystal (7)
20	china (5)
25	silver (6)
30	pearl (5)
35	coral (5)
40	ruby (4)
45	sapphire (8)
50	gold (4)
55	emerald (7)
60	diamond (7)

Wines

3
Dão

4
cava
Gavi
hock
mead
port
sack

5
durif
Fitou
gamay
lexia
Lirac
Mâcon
Médoc
mulse
Rioja
Roero
Rueda
Rully
syrah
Tavel
Tokay

6
Bandol
Barolo
Barsac
Cahors
canary
Carema
claret
Graves
Málaga
mataro
merlot
muscat
Pomard
Quincy
Saumur
sherry
shiraz
Tokaji

7
Amarone
Banyuls
bikavér
Bucelas
Chablis
chianti
cinsaut
Fleurie
Gaillac
Madeira
Margaux
Marsala
Moselle
Orvieto
Parrina
Pomerol
retsina
touriga
Vouvray

8
Bairrada
Bergerac
Bordeaux
Brouilly
Burgundy
carignan
Condrieu
dolcetto
Faugères
Frascati
Gigondas
grenache
jerepigo
Jurançon
marsanne
montilla
muscadet
muscatel
nebbiolo
palomino
Pauillac
riesling
Sancerre
semillon
vioghier

9
blistelle
Bourgogne
Bourgueil
Champagne
colombard
Corbières
Côte Rôtie
fruit wine
Fumé Blanc
Gattinara
Hermitage
Lambrusco
Meursault
Minervois
mourvèdre
pinot gris
pinot noir
Rhine wine
Rhône wine
roussanne
Sauternes
straw wine
trebbiano
ugni blanc
zinfandel

10
Barbaresco
beaujolais
Bulls Blood
Chambertin
chardonnay
Constantia
frontignac
muscadelle
Piesporter
Rosé d'Anjou
Saint-Véran
sangiovese
Valdepeñas
Verdicchio
vinho verde

11
chenin blanc
Monbazillac
Niersteiner
Pouilly-Fumé
Rosso Cònero
Rüdesheimer
Saint-Julien
scuppernong
tempranillo

12
Asti spumante
Barbera d'Albi
Barbera d'Asti
Côtes du Rhône
Moscato d'Asti
pinot meunier
Saint-Émilion
Saint-Estèphe
Valpolicella
vin ordinaire
Vosne-Romanée

13
blanc de blancs
cabernet franc
Entre-Deux-Mers
fortified wine
Liebfraumilch
Mâcon-Villages
Pessac-Léognan
Pouilly-Fuissé

14 and over
beaujolais nouveau (17)
Bereich Bernkastel (17)
cabernet sauvignon (17)
Crémant d'Alsace (14)
Crémant de Loire (14)
Crozes-Hermitage (15)
Gevrey-Chambertin (16)
gewürztraminer (15)
Grange Hermitage (15)
lachryma Christi (15)
muscat gordo blanco (17)
Nuits-Saint-Georges (17)
Quarts de Chaume (14)
Salice Salentino (15)
sauvignon blanc (14)

Woods

3
ash
elm
fir
koa
oak
yew

4
cade
pear
pine
poon
teak
toon

5
apple
balsa
beech
birch
cedar
ebony
hazel
holly
iroko
kauri
kiaat
larch
maple
olive
thorn

6
alerce
bog oak
cherry
gaboon
locust
padauk
poplar
red fir
red gum
red oak
spruce
sumach
tupelo
walnut
willow

7
amboyna
assegai
baywood
boxwood
camwood
cypress
durmast
gumtree
gumwood
hemlock
hickory
nutwood
quassia
rock elm

8
basswood
beefwood
chestnut
corkwood
crabwood
guaiacum
hard pine
hardwood
hornbeam
ironwood
jelutong
kingwood
mahogany
pulpwood
red cedar
rosewood
sandarac
sasswood
shagbark
softwood
sycamore
tamarack
tamarind

9
butternut
coachwood
eaglewood
hackberry
jacaranda
lancewood
narra wood
persimmon
pitch pine
quebracho
satinwood
Scots pine
shellbark
stinkwood
torchwood
tulipwood
white pine
whitewood
zebrawood

10
afrormosia
brazilwood
bulletwood
calamander
candlewood
citron wood
fiddlewood
greenheart
letterwood
marblewood
orangewood
ribbonwood
sandalwood
sappanwood
spotted gum
white cedar
yellowwood

11
black walnut
camphor wood
red mulberry

13 and over
patridgewood (13)
western red cedar (15)

Writers, Poets and Dramatists

NB: Authors are listed under the century in which they were born.

ANCIENT

4
Du Fu
Livy
Ovid

5
Aesop
Homer
Plato
Pliny

6
Cicero
Hesiod
Horace
Lao-Tse
Lucian
Pindar
Sappho
Seneca
Virgil

7
Juvenal
Tacitus
Terence

8
Catullus
Kalidasa
Menander

9
Aeschulus
Aristotle
Euripides
Herodotus
Lucretius
Sophocles
Suetonius

10
Propertius
Quintilian
Thucydides

11 ***and over***
Aristophanes (12)
Lucius Apuleius (14)
Omar Khayyam (11)
Valerius Flaccus (15)

MEDIEVAL

4
Bede

5
Dante
Gower
Sachs

6
Malory
Villon
Ariosto
Chaucer
Erasmus

7
Abelard
Aquinas

8
Langland
Petrarch
Rabelais

9
Boccaccio
Froissart

10 ***and over***
Chrétien de Troyes (16)
Christine de Pisan (16)
Duns Scotus (10)
Machiavelli (11)

1500–1600

3
Gay
Kyd

4
Behn
Pope

5
Basho
Defoe
Donne
Pepys
Swift
Tasso

6
Bunyan
Dryden
Jonson
Milton
Racine
Sidney

7
Addison
Cellini
Marlowe
Marvell
Molière
Spenser
Webster

8
Calderón
Congreve
Farquhar
Perrault
Voltaire

9
Cervantes
Corneille
La Fayette
Montaigne
Wu Chengen

10 ***and over***
Bradstreet (10)
Cyrano de Bergerac (16)
Juana Inés De la Cruz (17)
La Fontaine (10)
Richardson (10)
Shakespeare (11)

1700

3
Key

4
Gray
Lamb
Sade
Wyss

5
Blake
Burns
Byron
Clare
Heine
Keats
Moore
Paine
Scott
Staël

6
Austen
Balzac
Bryant
Burney
Cooper
Cowper
Goethe
Hammon
Irving
Laclos
Rowson
Sterne

7
Addison
Boswell
Carlyle
Freneau
Hazlitt
Johnson
Lessing
Manzoni
Pushkin
Shelley
Southey
Walpole

8
De Quincy
Fielding
Hoffmann
Rousseau
Schiller
Sheridan
Smollett
Stendhal
Wheatley

9
Coleridge
Goldsmith
Lomonosov
Radcliffe

10 ***and over***
Beaumarchais (12)
Brothers Grimm (the) (13)
Chateaubriand (13)

1800

2
Fo

3
Poe

4
Baum
Bely
Blok
Buck
Cain
Ford
Gale
Gide
Gray
Grey
Hall
Howe
Hugo
Kant
Lear
Loos
Mann
Owen
Rhys
Rice
Saki
Sand
Shaw
West
Zola

5
Adams
Agnon
Aiken
Akins
Alger
Babel
Benet
Brown
Bunin
Busch
Capek
Chase
Crane
Dario
Davis
Doyle
Dumas
Eliot
Field
Frost
Gogol
Gorky
Green
Hardy
Harte
Hasek
Henry
Hesse
Heyse
Ibsen
James
Joyce
Kafka
Kelly
Lewis
Marsh
Marti
McKay
Milne
Moore
O'Dell
Perse
Poole
Pound
Rilke
Sachs
Scott
Shute
Smith
Stein
Stout
Stowe
Svevo
Synge
Twain
Verne
Wells
White
Wilde
Woolf
Yeats
Zweig

6
Alcott
Alvaro
Andric
Arnold
Balzac
Barnes
Barrie
Belloc
Bierce
Blyton
Bolton
Borges
Brecht
Breton
Brontë
Brooke
Bryant
Buchan
Butler
Cather
Chopin
Coffin
Conrad
Coward
Cronin
Dubois
Dunbar
Fauset
Ferber
Flavin
France
Fuller
Gibran
Gilman
Graves
Hamsun
Harper
Harris
Holmes
Howard
Hughes
Huxley
Jerome
Jewett
Junger
Kilmer
Larsen
Le Fanu
London
Lowell
Machen
Miller
Mofolo
Morris
Mqhayi
Nesbit
Norris
O'Casey
O'Neill
Parker
Pessoa
Porter
Potter
Proust
Runyon
Ruskin
Sayers
Sewell
Stoker
Tagore
Toklas
Toomer
Traven
Undset
Valery
Wiggin
Wilder
Wilson

7
Bagnold
Bennett
Burnett
Carroll
Chekhov
Cocteau
Colette
Collins
Collodi
Delaney
Deledda
Dickens
Dinesen
Dreiser
Dunsany

Emerson
Falkner
Farjeon
Forster
Gallico
Gaskell
Grahame
Gregory
Haggard
Hammett
Hartley
Hillyer
Hodgson
Hopkins
Housman
Howells
Jackson
Jeffers
Jiménez
Johnson
Kästner
Kaufman
Kipling
Lardner
Lazarus
Lofting
Masters
Maugham
Mauriac
Mistral
Montale
Nabokov
Plaatje
Quiroga
Ransome
Reymont
Richter
Rimbaud
Rolland
Russell
Sassoon
Sitwell
Stevens
Thoreau
Thurber
Tolkien
Tolstoy
Travers
Wallace
Wharton
Whitman
Woolsey

8
Andersen
Anderson
Asturias
Bjornson
Browning
Brunhoff
Bulgakov
Carducci
Chandler
Chesnutt
Christie
Connelly
Cummings
De la Mare
Douglass
Faulkner
Flaubert
Fletcher
Forester
Glaspell
Kawabata
Kingsley
Lagerlof
Lawrence
Macaulay
Macleish
Mallarme
Marquand
Melville
Meredith
Nelligan
Peterkin
Rawlings
Remarque
Rinehart
Robinson
Rossetti
Sandburg
Sherwood
Sinclair
Tanizaki
Teasdale
Tennyson
Trollope
Turgenev
Van Doren
Verlaine
Wheatley
Whittier
Williams
Zamyatin

9
Akhmatova
Benavente
Blackmore
Bromfield
Burroughs
D'Annunzio
De la Roche
Dickinson
Doolittle
Dos Passos
Echegaray
Gjellerup
Goncharov
Hauptmann
Hawthorne
Hemingway
Karlfeldt
Lampedusa
Lermontov
Lovecraft
Mansfield
Marinetti
Masefield
Nietzsche
Pasternak
Priestley
Schreiner
Shimazaki
Sillanpää
Spitteler
Stapledon
Stevenson
Swinburne
Thackeray
Wodehouse

10
Baudelaire
Chesterton
Fitzgerald
Galsworthy
Lagerkvist
Longfellow
MacDiarmid
Mandelstam
Maupassant
Mayakovsky
McGonagall
Montgomery
Pirandello
Strindberg
Tarkington
Washington

11 ***and over***
Apollinaire (11)
Dostoyevsky (11)
García Lorca (11)
Kazantzakis (11)
Machado de Assis (14)
Maeterlinck (11)
Martin du Gard (12)
Sackville-West (13)
Sienkiewicz (11)
Sully-Prudmomme (14)
Wittgenstein (12)

MODERN

2
Ba
Oe
Oz

3
Abe
Eco
Fry
Lee
Lem
Nin
Paz
Roy
Tan

4
Agee
Amis
Beti
Boll
Cela
Dahl
Dick
Diop
Dove
Fine
Grau
Gunn
Head
Inge
Jong
Kerr
King
Laye
Levi
Nash
Neto
Ogot
Okri
Page
Puzo
Rand
Reed
Rice
Rich
Roth
Seth
Uris
West
Wolf
Wouk

5
Adams
Aidoo
Aiken
Albee
Allen
Auden

Banks
Barth
Bates
Behan
Blish
Block
Blume
Brink
Burke
Byatt
Camus
Carey
Carle
Chase
Clark
Cohen
Cunne
Desai
Doyle
Drury
Dugan
Duras
Evans
Farah
Foote
Frank
Genet
Gluck
Grass
Green
Haley
Havel
Heath
Himes
Hulme
James
Jones
Kesey
Kizer
Kumin
Lorde
Lowry
Lurie
Mamet
Munro
Nixon
Nwapa
O'Hara
Oates
Odets
Olsen
Oppen
Orton
Oyono
Paley
Paton
Percy
Petry
Plath
Potok
Queen
Ribas
Rulfo
Sagan
Scott
Seuss
Silko
Simak
Simic
Simon
Smith
Spark
Stead
Tlali
Tyler
Ulasi
Vidal
Waugh
Weiss
Welty
White
Wolfe

6

Achebe
Aldiss
Algren
Ambler
Asimov
Atwood
Baraka
Barker
Barnes
Bellow
Birney
Bishop
Brooks
Brutus
Butler
Capote
Carter
Carver
Clancy
Clarke
Cooper
Cullen
Delany
Dhlomo
Didion
Duncan
Ellroy
Elytis
Erdich
Farmer
Faulks
Fowles
Fugard
Fuller
Gaines
George
Gibson
Harris
Hayden
Heaney
Heller
Henley
Hersey
Hinton
Howard
Hughes
Irving
Jordan
Junitz
Kantor
Kelman
Kogawa
Koontz
L'Amour
Larkin
Le Fanu
Le Guin
Leiber
Levine
Lively
Lowell
Ludlum
Mailer
McBain
McEwan
Merwin
Miller
Milosz
Mosley
Naylor
Neruda
Norman
O'Brian
O'Brien
Okigbo
Oliver
Onetti
Orwell
Parker
P'Bitek
Piercy
Pilger
Pinter
Powell
Proust
Robert
Rylant
Sarton
Sartre
Scarry
Sendak
Sexton
Shange
Singer
Smiley
Snyder
Sofala
Sontag
Styron
Susann
Taylor
Thomas
Updike
Walker
Warren
Weldon
Wilbur
Wilson
Wright
Zindel

7

Ackroyd
Aickman
Aksenov
Alegria
Allende
Amichai
Andrews
Angelou
Anouilh
Ashbery
Awoonor
Baldwin
Ballard
Bambara
Beckett
Bennett
Brodsky
Buckler
Buckley
Bullins
Burgess
Calvino
Canetti
Cheever
Clavell
Clifton
Coetzee
Cookson
Cormier
Cozzens
DeLillo
Drabble
Durrell
Dworkin
Ekwensi
Ellison
Farrell
Fleming
Forsyth
Francis
Friedan
Fuentes
Gallant
Gardner
Golding
Gordone
Grafton
Grisham
Guthrie
Hayashi
Hazzard
Hellman
Herbert
Herriot

Hurston
Ionesco
Jackson
Jarrell
Johnson
Justice
Kennedy
Kerouac
Kincaid
Kinnell
Kundera
Kushner
La Farge
Laxness
Le Carré
Leonard
Lessing
Maclean
Mahfous
Malamud
Malraux
Merrill
Mishima
Mitford
Momaday
Moravia
Murdoch
Naipaul
Narayan
Nemerov
Ngugi wa
Nichols
O'Connor
Osborne
Pynchon
Renault
Rendell
Richler
Rodgers
Roethke
Rossner
Rowling
Rushdie
Saadawi
Sanchez
Saroyan
Seferis
Seghers
Seifert
Sembene
Senghor
Serling
Shapiro
Sheldon
Shepard
Shields
Sholomo
Simenon
Simpson
Soyinka
Spender
Stegner
Theroux
Thiong'o
Tutuola
Van Duyn
Van Vogt
Walcott
Wyndham
Zelazny

8

Abrahams
Anderson
Atkinson
Berryman
Betjeman
Bontemps
Bowering
Bradbury
Brookner
Caldwell
Cardenal
Clampitt
Cornwell
Cortázar
Crichton
Day-Lewis
Deighton
Ding Ling
Doctorow
Eberhart
Emecheta
Esquivel
Freeling
Gellhorn
Ginsberg
Giovanni
Gordimer
Hardwick
Harrison
Heinlein
Hijuelos
Ishiguro
Jhabvala
Keneally
Kingston
Kinsella
Kosinski
Laurence
Levertov
Lindgren
MacNeice
Marshall
Matheson
McCarthy
McGinley
McMillan
McMurtry
Meredith
Michener
Mitchell
Moorcock
Morrison
O'Faolain
Ondaatje
Paretsky
Perelman
Rattigan
Ringgold
Rukeyser
Salinger
Saro-Wiwa
Schwartz
Sillitoe
Southern
Spillane
Stafford
Stoppard
Sturgeon
Sutcliff
Thompson
Tsushima
Unsworth
Vonnegut
Wambaugh
Williams

9

Allingham
Ayckbourn
Barthelme
Benedetti
Burroughs
Chayefsky
Childress
Cristofer
Du Maurier
Hansberry
Highsmith
Hillerman
Isherwood
Lispector
Llewellyn
MacDonald
Macdonald
McCaffrey
McCullers
McPherson
Mphahlele
Pratchett
Prelutsky
Quasimodo
Reid Banks
Roa Bastos
Sholokhov
Snodgrass
Steinbeck
Vittorini

10

Bainbridge
Carpentier
de Beauvoir
Durrenmatt
MacLachlan
Silverberg
Sutherland

11

Auchincloss
Breytenbach
Matthiessen
Rabearivelo
Vargas Llosa
Voznesensky
Wasserstein
Yevtushenko

12 *and over*

Ashton-Warner (12)
Cabrera Infante (14)
Clarke-Bekederemo (16)
Ferlinghetti (12)
García Márquez (13)
Ratushinskaya (13)
Saint-Exupery (12)
Solzhenitsyn (12)

Section 3

5

abler	baler
abode	adobe
abort	tabor
about	U-boat
adder	dared
adder	dread
addle	laded
adept	pated
adept	taped
adobe	abode
adore	oared
adorn	radon
aglee	eagle
agree	eager
aimed	media
alert	alter
alert	later
algae	galea
alien	aline
alien	anile
aline	alien
allot	atoll
alloy	loyal
aloft	float
aloft	flota
alter	alert
alter	later
amber	bream
amble	blame
ambry	barmy
amend	maned
amend	named
amigo	imago
among	mango
ample	maple
amply	palmy
angel	angle
angel	glean
anger	range
angle	angel
angle	glean
angry	rangy
anile	alien
argon	groan
argon	nagor
argon	orang
argon	organ
argot	groat
argue	auger
argus	sugar
armed	derma
armed	dream
arson	sonar
askew	wakes
aspic	spica
aster	stare
astir	sitar
astir	stair
aswim	swami
atoll	allot
atone	oaten
atria	tiara
atrip	parti
atrip	tapir
attar	tatar
attic	tacit
auger	argue
bacon	banco
badge	debag
bagel	gable
bairn	brain
baker	brake
baker	break
baler	abler
baler	blare
baler	blear
balsa	basal
banco	bacon
barmy	ambry
basal	balsa
baste	beast
baste	tabes
beard	bread
beard	debar
beast	baste
bedim	imbed
begin	being
begin	binge
being	begin
below	bowel
below	elbow
bidet	debit
binge	begin
biter	tribe
blame	amble
blare	baler
blasé	sable
blear	baler
bleat	table
board	broad
boast	sabot
bogle	globe
boner	borne
bonus	bosun
borne	boner
bosun	bonus
bowel	below
bowel	elbow
brace	caber
braid	rabid
brain	bairn
brake	baker
brake	break
braze	zebra
bread	beard
break	baker
break	brake
bream	amber
bride	rebid
brief	fibre
broad	board
brose	sober
broth	throb
brume	umber
brunt	burnt
brush	shrub
brute	rebut
brute	tuber
budge	debug
bugle	bulge
bulge	bugle
burnt	brunt
burse	rebus
caber	brace
cadge	caged
cadre	cedar
caged	cadge
calve	clave
camel	macle
canoe	ocean
caper	crape
caper	pacer
caper	recap
carat	carta
caret	carte
caret	cater
caret	react
carob	cobra
carol	coral
carse	scare
carta	carat
carte	caret
carve	crave
cater	caret
cause	sauce
cedar	cadre
cense	scene
chain	china
charm	march
chart	ratch
cheap	peach
chert	retch
chief	fiche
china	chain
chine	niche
chore	ochre
churl	lurch
cider	cried
cider	dicer
cigar	craig
civet	evict
clasp	scalp
clave	calve
clean	lance
cloud	could
coast	costa
cobra	carob
combo	coomb
comer	crome
coomb	combo
copse	scope
coral	carol
cored	credo
cored	décor
corky	rocky
corns	scorn
corny	crony
costa	coast
could	cloud
craig	cigar
crake	creak
crane	nacre
crape	caper
crave	carve
creak	crake
cream	macer
credo	cored
creep	crepe
crepe	creep

cried	cider
crisp	scrip
crone	oncer
crony	corny
cruel	lucre
cruel	ulcer
cruet	eruct
cruet	truce
cruse	curse
crust	curst
curer	recur
curst	crust
dairy	diary
dared	adder
dared	dread
dater	rated
dater	trade
dater	tread
dealt	delta
debag	badge
debar	beard
debit	bidet
debug	budge
debut	tubed
decal	laced
décor	cored
defer	freed
deify	edify
delay	leady
delta	dealt
dense	needs
derma	armed
deuce	educe
devil	lived
diary	dairy
dicer	cider
dinar	drain
dinar	nadir
dingo	doing
dingy	dying
dirge	ridge
divan	viand
diver	drive
diver	rived
doing	dingo
donor	rondo
dorée	erode
dowry	rowdy
dowry	wordy
dowse	sowed
dozen	zoned
drain	dinar
drain	nadir
drake	raked
drape	padre
dread	adder
dread	dared
dream	armed
dried	redid
drier	rider
drive	diver
drone	ronde
drupe	duper
drupe	perdu
drupe	prude
duper	drupe
duper	perdu
dusty	study
dying	dingy
eager	agree
eagle	aglee
eagre	agree
early	layer
early	leary
early	relay
earth	hater
earth	heart
earth	rathe
easel	lease
eaten	enate
edify	deify
educe	deuce
egret	greet
eland	laden
elbow	below
elbow	bowel
elver	lever
elver	revel
embus	sebum
enate	eaten
enrol	loner
enter	treen
envoi	ovine
eosin	noise
equip	pique
erase	saree
erect	terce
erode	dorée
eruct	cruet
eruct	truce
ester	reset
ester	steer
ester	terse
estop	stope
ether	there
ether	three
ethos	those
evens	seven
evert	revet
every	veery
evict	civet
exalt	latex
extra	taxer
facer	farce
faker	freak
farce	facer
farle	feral
farle	flare
feast	festa
feral	farle
ferry	fryer
festa	feast
fetor	forte
fibre	brief
fiche	chief
field	filed
fiery	reify
filar	flair
filar	frail
filed	field
filer	flier
filer	lifer
filer	rifle
finer	infer
fired	fried
firer	frier
fires	fries
fires	serif
flair	filar
flame	fleam
flare	farle
fleam	flame
flesh	shelf
flier	filer
float	aloft
float	flota
flota	aloft
flota	float
flour	fluor
fluor	flour
forge	gofer
forte	fetor
forth	froth
fount	futon
frail	filar
freak	faker
freed	defer
freer	refer
fried	fired
frier	firer
fries	fires
froth	forth
fryer	ferry
futon	fount
gable	bagel
galea	algae
gamic	magic
gamma	magma
gaper	grape
gaper	pager
garni	grain
gazer	graze
gelid	glide
genom	gnome
genre	green
genus	negus
geode	ogee'd
ghoul	lough
gilet	legit.
giron	groin
girth	grith
girth	right
glair	grail
glans	slang
glare	lager
glare	large
glare	regal
glean	angel
glean	angle
glide	gelid
globe	bogle
gluer	gruel
glues	gules
gnome	genom
godly	goldy
gofer	forge
goldy	godly
goner	Negro
gouty	guyot
gowan	wagon

grade raged
grail glair
grain garni
grape gaper
grape pager
grate great
grate targe
graze gazer
great grate
green genre
greet egret
gride dirge
gride ridge
grist grits
grith girth
grith right
grits grist
groan argon
groat argot
gruel gluer
gules glues
guyot gouty
Hades shade
hadji jihad
haply phyla
hards shard
hardy hydra
hater earth
hater heart
hater rathe
haves shave
heaps pesah
heaps phase
heaps shape
heart earth
heart hater
heart rathe
helot hotel
heron Rhone
hewer where
hight thigh
hinge neigh
hires shier
hires shire
hives shive
hoots shoot
hoots sooth
horns shorn
horse shoer
horse shore

hosed shoed
hotel helot
hotel thole
hydra hardy
imago amigo
imbed bedim
inapt paint
inapt pinta
incur runic
inept nepit
inert inter
inert nitre
inert trine
infer finer
ingot tigon
inkle liken
inner renin
input put in
inset stein
inter inert
inter nitre
inter trine
islet istle
islet stile
islet tiles
istle islet
jaunt junta
jihad hadji
junta jaunt
karst stark
knead naked
Koran krona
krona Koran
laced decal
laded addle
laden eland
lager glare
lager large
lager regal
lance clean
lapse salep
lapse sepal
large glare
large lager
later alert
latex exalt
laver ravel
layer early
layer leary
layer relay

leady delay
leapt petal
leapt plate
leapt pleat
learn renal
leary early
leary layer
leary relay
lease easel
leash shale
least slate
least stale
least steal
least tales
legit. gilet
lemon melon
leper repel
lever elver
lever revel
liane alien
lifer filer
lifer rifle
liken inkle
limes slime
limes smile
litre tiler
lived devil
liver livre
livre liver
loden olden
loner enrol
lough ghoul
louse ousel
lovat Volta
lower rowel
loyal alloy
lucre cruel
lucre ulcer
lumpy plumy
lunar ulnar
lurch churl
macer cream
macho mocha
macle camel
magic gamic
magma gamma
maned named
manes manse
manes means
mango among

manor Roman
manse manes
manse means
maple ample
march charm
maser smear
mater tamer
matey meaty
means manes
means manse
meaty matey
media aimed
melon lemon
merit mitre
merit remit
merit timer
mitre merit
mocha macho
molar moral
monad nomad
moral molar
mores Morse
Morse mores
motet motte
motet totem
motte motet
mount notum
mourn munro
munro mourn
mused sedum
muser serum
nacre crane
nadir dinar
nadir drain
nagor argon
naked knead
named maned
nares snare
nasty tansy
navel venal
neath thane
needs dense
Negro goner
negus genus
neigh hinge
neper preen
nepit inept
nerve never
never nerve
nexus unsex

niche chine
Niger reign
night thing
nisus sinus
nitre inert
nitre inter
nitre trine
nodus sound
noise eosin
nomad monad
nonet tenon
nonet tonne
Norse noser
Norse senor
Norse snore
north thorn
noser Norse
noted toned
noter tenor
notum mount
Notus snout
Notus tonus
oared adore
oared oread
oaten atone
ocean canoe
ochre chore
ogee'd geode
olden loden
olive voile
oncer crone
onset set on
onset stone
optic picot
optic topic
orach roach
orang argon
oread oared
organ argon
ornis rosin
other throe
ottar tarot
otter torte
ought tough
ousel louse
outer outré
outer route
outré outer
outré route
overt voter
ovine envoi
owlet towel
pacer caper
padre drape
padre pared
pagan panga
pager gaper
pager grape
paint inapt
palmy amply
palsy splay
panel penal
panel plane
panga pagan
panne penna
pared padre
parse spare
parse spear
parti atrip
paste spate
pasty patsy
pated adept
pater prate
pater taper
patsy pasty
pavid vapid
payer repay
peach cheap
pedal plead
peels sleep
pelts slept
pelts spelt
penal panel
penal plane
penna panne
perdu drupe
perdu duper
perdu prude
peril piler
peril plier
per se spree
Pesah heaps
Pesah phase
Pesah shape
petal leapt
phase heaps
phase Pesah
phase shape
phyla haply
picot optic
picot topic
piler peril
piler plier
pines snipe
pines spine
pinta inapt
pinto piton
pinto point
pique equip
piste spite
piste stipe
piton pinto
piton point
plane panel
plane penal
plate leapt
plead pedal
pleat leapt
plier peril
plier piler
plumy lumpy
poesy sepoy
point pinto
point piton
pools sloop
pools spool
popsy soppy
porer repro
porer roper
ports sport
ports strop
poser prose
poser spore
pouts spout
pouts stoup
prate pater
prate taper
preen neper
pride pried
pried pride
pries prise
pries speir
pries spire
prise pries
prose poser
prose spore
prude drupe
prude perdu
puree rupee
purse sprue
purse super
put in input
quiet quite
quite quiet
quote toque
rabid braid
radon adorn
raged grade
raked drake
range anger
rangy angry
raspy spray
ratch chart
rated dater
rated trade
rated tread
rathe earth
rathe hater
rathe heart
ratty tarty
ravel laver
rayed ready
react caret
ready rayed
rebid bride
rebus burse
rebut brute
rebut tuber
recap caper
recur curer
redid dried
refer freer
regal glare
regal lager
reify fiery
reign Niger
reins resin
reins rinse
reins risen
reins serin
relay early
relay layer
relay leary
remit merit
renal learn
renin inner
repay payer
repel leper
repot toper
repot trope

repro porer
repro roper
resay sayer
reset ester
resin reins
resit tries
retch chert
retry tryer
revel elver
revel lever
revet evert
Rhone heron
rider drier
ridge dirge
ridge gride
rifle filer
rifle lifer
right girth
right grith
rinse reins
risen reins
rival viral
rived diver
roach orach
rocky corky
rogue rouge
Roman manor
ronde drone
rondo donor
roost roots
roost torso
roots roost
roper porer
rosin ornis
rouge rogue
roust torus
route outer
route outré
rowdy dowry
rowdy wordy
rowel lower
ruing unrig
rumba umbra
runic incur
rupee puree
sable blasé
sabot boast
saint satin
saint stain
salep lapse

salep sepal
salve vales
salve valse
salve slave
saree erase
sated stead
satin saint
satin stain
satyr stray
sauce cause
sayer resay
scalp clasp
scape space
scare carse
scarp scrap
scene cense
scion sonic
scope copse
scorn corns
scrap scarp
scrip crisp
sebum embus
sedum mused
seism semis
semis seism
senor Norse
senor snore
sepal lapse
sepal salep
sepoy poesy
serif fires
serin reins
serow sower
serow swore
serow worse
serum muser
serve verse
set on onset
set on stone
set-up upset
seven evens
sever verse
sewed swede
sewin sinew
sewin swine
sewin wines
shade Hades
shale leash
shape heaps
shape Pesah

shape phase
shard hards
share shear
shave haves
shear share
sheet these
shelf flesh
sherd shred
shier hires
shier shire
shire hires
shire shier
shive hives
shoed hosed
shoer horse
shoot hoots
shoot sooth
shore horse
shorn horns
shout south
shred sherd
shrub brush
sidle slide
silly slily
silos soils
sinew sewin
sinew swine
sinew wines
sinus nisus
sitar astir
sitar stair
skate stake
skate steak
skean snake
skean sneak
skint stink
skirt stirk
slain snail
slang glans
slate least
slave salve
slave vales
slave valse
sleep peels
sleep speel
sleet steel
sleet stele
slept pelts
slide sidle
slily silly

slime limes
slime smile
sloop pools
sloop spool
smear maser
smile limes
smile slime
smite times
snail slain
snake skean
snake sneak
snare nares
sneak skean
sneak snake
snipe pines
snipe spine
snoop spoon
snore Norse
snore senor
snout Notus
snout tonus
sober brose
soils silos
sonar arson
sonic scion
sooth hoots
sooth shoot
soppy popsy
sound nodus
south shout
sowed dowse
sower serow
sower worse
space scape
spare parse
spare spear
spate paste
spear parse
spear spare
speir pries
speir spire
spelt pelts
spica aspic
spilt split
spine pines
spine snipe
spire pries
spire speir
spite piste
splay palsy

split spilt
spool pools
spool sloop
spoon snoop
spore poser
spore prose
sport ports
sport strop
spout pouts
spout stoup
sprat strap
spray raspy
spree per se
sprue purse
spurt turps
stain saint
stain satin
stair astir
stair sitar
stake skate
stake steak
stale least
stare aster
stark karst
state taste
stead sated
steak skate
steak stake
steal least
steel sleet
steer ester
stein inset
stele sleet
stile islet
stink skint
stipe piste
stirk skirt
stoat toast
stone onset
stone set on
stope estop
stoup pouts
strap sprat
straw swart
stray satyr
strew trews
strew wrest
strop ports
strop sport
strow worst

strut trust
study dusty
stupe set-up
stupe upset
sugar argus
super purse
swage wages
swami aswim
swart straw
sweat tawse
sweat waste
swede sewed
swine sewin
swine sinew
swine wines
swore serow
swore worse
tabes baste
table bleat
tabor abort
tacit attic
taint titan
tales least
talon tonal
tamer mater
tango Tonga
tansy nasty
taped adept
taper pater
taper prate
tapir atrip
targe grate
tarot ottar
tarot troat
tarty ratty
taste state
tatar attar
tawse sweat
tawse waste
taxer extra
tenon nonet
tenon tonne
tenor noter
terce erect
terse ester
thane neath
there ether
there three
these sheet
thigh hight

thing night
thole hotel
thorn north
those ethos
three ether
three there
throb broth
throe other
throw worth
tiara atria
tigon ingot
tilde tiled
tiled tilde
tiler litre
tiles islet
timer merit
times smite
titan taint
toast stoat
tonal talon
toned noted
Tonga tango
tonne nonet
tonne tenon
tonus Notus
tonus snout
toper repot
topic optic
topic picot
toque quote
torso roots
torte otter
torus roust
totem motet
tough ought
towel owlet
tower wrote
trade dater
trade rated
tread dater
tread rated
treen enter
trews strew
trews wrest
tribe biter
tries resit
trine inert
trine inter
trine nitre
troat ottar

trope repot
truce eruct
trust strut
tryer retry
tubed debut
tuber brute
tuber rebut
turps spurt
ulcer cruel
ulcer lucre
ulnar lunar
umber brume
umbra rumba
unbar urban
unite untie
unlit until
unrig ruing
unsex nexus
untie unite
until unlit
upset set-up
upset stupe
urban unbar
vales salve
vales slave
vales valse
valse salve
valse vales
vapid pavid
veery every
venal navel
verse serve
verse sever
viand divan
viral rival
voile olive
Volta lovat
voter overt
vowel wolve
wages swage
wagon gowan
waker wreak
wakes askew
waste sweat
waste tawse
weird wired
whale wheal
wheal whale
where hewer
white withe

wines sewin
wines sinew
wines swine
wired weird
withe white
wolve vowel
wordy dowry
wordy rowdy
worse serow
worse sower
worse swore
worst strow
worth throw
wreak waker
wrest strew
wrest trews
wrote tower
zebra braze
zoned dozen

6

abided baddie
abuser bursae
action atonic
adders dreads
adhere header
adhere hedera
adverb braved
aerial realia
affair raffia
afield failed
afters faster
afters strafe
agreed dragee
agreed geared
ahorse ashore
ahorse hoarse
airman marina
albeit albite
albino Albion
Albion albino
albite albeit
alcove coeval
alegar laager
alerce cereal
allude aludel
allure laurel
almond dolman
alpine pineal
Altair lariat
Altair latria
aludel allude
alumna manual
ambler marble
ambler ramble
amused Medusa
anadem maenad
anchor archon
anchor Charon
anchor rancho
angled dangle
angler regnal
animal lamina
animal manila
anoint nation
antler learnt
antler rental
Anubis unbias
append napped
archon anchor
arcing caring
arcing racing
argent garnet
armful fulmar
armpit impart
arnica crania
arpent entrap
arpent panter
arpent parent
arpent trepan
arrest starer
arrowy yarrow
arsine arisen
artist strait
ascent stance
ash bin banish
ashler lasher
ashore ahorse
ashore hoarse
asleep elapse
asleep please
asleep sapele
aspire praise
assist stasis
astart strata
astute statue
aswing sawing
atonic action
attire ratite
attune tauten
avocet octave
awning waning
baddie abided
baleen enable
banish ash bin
bantam batman
barbed dabber
barbel rabble
barely barley
barely bleary
barley barely
barney nearby
bather breath
batman bantam
battle tablet
bawler warble
beater berate
beater rebate
bedlam beldam
bedlam blamed
begird bridge
beldam bedlam
beldam blamed
belied edible
berate beater
betrod debtor
binary brainy
binder inbred
birdie bridie
blamed bedlam
blamed beldam
bleary barely
blouse boules
blower bowler
boiler reboil
boring robing
boules blouse
bowler blower
brainy binary
braise rabies
braved adverb
breath bather
bridal ribald
bridge begird
bridie birdie
brumal lumbar
buffer rebuff
bugler bulger
bugler burgle
bulger bugler
bulger burgle
burble lubber
burden burned
burgle bugler
burgle bulger
burned burden
bursae abuser
bustle sublet
bustle subtle
cadent decant
cadger graced
caller cellar
caller recall
candle lanced
cannot canton
canter Cretan
canter recant
canter trance
cantle lancet
canton cannot

cantor carton
cantor contra
caring arcing
caring racing
carpel parcel
carpel placer
cartel claret
carter crater
carter tracer
carton cantor
carver craver
caster recast
castor costar
casual causal
causal casual
causer saucer
caveat vacate
cavern craven
cellar caller
cellar recall
centre recent
cereal alerce
chapel pleach
Charon anchor
chaser search
chaste sachet
chaste scathe
chesty scythe
chicle cliché
choice echoic
choker hocker
chrism smirch
cinema iceman
circle cleric
citric critic
claret cartel
cleric circle
cliché chicle
coeval alcove
coheir heroic
cohere echoer
cohere re-echo
coming gnomic
condor cordon
conker reckon
contra cantor
cordon condor
corked docker
corker rocker
corona racoon
corset coster
corset escort
corset sector
costar castor
coster corset
course source
couthy touchy
covert vector
coyote oocyte
crania arnica
crater carter
craven cavern
craver carver
credit direct
Cretan canter
critic citric
crusty curtsy
curdle curled
curled curdle
curtsy crusty
cutlet cuttle
cuttle cutlet
dabber barbed
damned demand
damned madden
dancer darned
danger gander
danger garden
dangle angled
dapper rapped
dapple lapped
darken ranked
darned dancer
darner errand
dawdle waddle
dealer leader
dearth hatred
dearth thread
debase sea bed
debtor betrod
decant cadent
decree recede
deduce deuced
deform formed
dehorn horned
demand damned
demand madden
demark marked
denial lead-in
denial nailed
denied nailed
depart parted
depart petard
deport redtop
derail relaid
dermal marled
dermal medlar
desalt slated
design singed
desire reside
detail dilate
detail tailed
deuced deduce
devoid voided
dewily widely
dewily wieldy
dibber ribbed
diddle lidded
digger rigged
dilate detail
dilate tailed
dimmer rimmed
dingle engild
dipper ripped
direct credit
docker corked
dogleg logged
dolman almond
dottle lotted
downer wonder
dowser drowse
dragee agreed
dragee geared
draped padder
drawer redraw
drawer reward
drawer warder
drawer warred
dreads adders
driest stride
drowse dowser
duffer ruffed
during ungird
duster rusted
dynamo Monday
earful ferula
earner nearer
earthy hearty
Easter reseat
Easter teaser

echoer	re-echo
echoic	choice
edible	belied
editor	triode
eighth	height
elapse	asleep
emboil	mobile
émigré	regime
enable	baleen
encase	séance
endive	veined
enfire	refine
enfold	fondle
engild	dingle
enigma	gamine
enlist	listen
enlist	silent
enlist	tinsel
entrap	arpent
entrap	parent
entrap	trepan
enwrap	pawner
erased	seared
errand	darner
errant	ranter
erring	ringer
escarp	scrape
escarp	spacer
escort	corset
esprit	priest
esprit	sprite
esprit	stripe
estate	tea set
except	expect
expect	except
fag end	fanged
failed	afield
falcon	flacon
fanged	fag end
fangle	flange
farmer	framer
faster	afters
faster	strafe
feints	infest
ferula	earful
ferule	refuel
fester	freest
fidget	gifted
filler	refill
filter	lifter
filter	trifle
finder	friend
finger	fringe
fitter	titfer
flacon	falcon
flange	fangle
florae	loafer
floret	lofter
flower	fowler
flower	reflow
flower	wolfer
fluent	netful
fluent	unfelt
fondle	enfold
footer	refoot
forest	foster
formed	deform
former	reform
foster	forest
fowler	flower
framer	farmer
freest	fester
friend	finder
fringe	finger
fulmar	armful
gainer	regain
gainer	regina
gaiter	triage
galore	gaoler
gamine	enigma
gander	danger
gander	garden
gander	ranged
ganger	grange
ganger	nagger
gaoler	galore
gaping	paging
garden	danger
garden	gander
garden	ranged
gargle	lagger
gargle	raggle
garner	ranger
garnet	argent
garret	garter
garret	grater
garter	garret
geared	agreed
geared	dragee
gelder	ledger
gelder	red leg
genial	linage
gifted	fidget
gilder	girdle
gilder	glider
girded	ridged
girdle	gilder
glider	gilder
globin	goblin
gnomic	coming
goblin	globin
goring	gringo
graced	cadger
grange	ganger
grange	nagger
grater	garret
grater	garter
greats	stager
grieve	regive
gringo	goring
groans	sarong
grudge	rugged
gurgle	lugger
halter	lather
hander	harden
harden	hander
hard-up	purdah
hatred	dearth
hatred	thread
hatter	threat
hawser	washer
header	adhere
header	hedera
hearer	rehear
hearty	earthy
hedera	adhere
hedera	header
height	eighth
heroic	coheir
hewing	whinge
hitter	tither
hoarse	ahorse
hoarse	ashore
hocker	choker
horned	dehorn
hornet	throne
hustle	sleuth
ice cap	ipecac
iceman	cinema
ignore	region

impart armpit
impure umpire
inbred binder
infest feints
ingest signet
inmost nomist
inroad ordain
insane sienna
insole lesion
instep spinet
insult sunlit
intern tinner
ipecac ice cap
itself stifle
kilter kirtle
kirtle kilter
laager alegar
labile liable
ladder raddle
lagger gargle
lagger raggle
lament mantle
lament mental
lamina animal
lamina manila
lanced candle
lancet cantle
lapped dapple
lariat Altair
lascar rascal
lascar sacral
lasher ashler
laster salter
laster slater
latent talent
lather halter
latria Altair
latter rattle
laurel allure
leaden leaned
leader dealer
lead-in denial
lead-in nailed
leaned leaden
leaper repeal
learnt antler
learnt rental
leaser resale
leaser sealer
ledger gelder

ledger red leg
lenses lessen
lentil lintel
lesion insole
lessen lenses
levied veiled
liable labile
lidded diddle
lifter filter
lifter trifle
lights slight
limner merlin
linage genial
linear nailer
lintel lentil
listen enlist
litter tilter
lively vilely
livens snivel
livery verily
loader ordeal
loader reload
loafer florae
lofter floret
logged dogleg
loiter toiler
looped poodle
looter rootle
lotted dottle
louvre velour
lovely volley
lubber burble
lubber rubble
lugger gurgle
lumbar brumal
lumber rumble
lustre result
lustre rustle
lustre sutler
lutein untile
madden damned
maenad anadem
maiden median
manila animal
manila lamina
mantis matins
mantle lament
manual alumna
mapper pamper
marble ambler

marble ramble
marina airman
marine remain
marked demark
marker remark
marled dermal
masher shamer
master stream
matins mantis
meanly namely
median maiden
medlar dermal
Medusa amused
mental lament
merlin limner
meteor remote
midden minded
minded midden
minder remind
minuet minute
minute minuet
mister smiter
mobile emboil
Monday dynamo
monism nomism
monist inmost
mutual umlaut
myrtle termly
nagger ganger
nagger grange
nailed denial
nailed lead-in
nailer linear
namely meanly
napped append
narked ranked
nation anoint
nature tea urn
nearby barney
nearer earner
nebula unable
netful fluent
netful unfelt
netted tented
neural unreal
neuter tenure
neuter tureen
nomism monism
nomist inmost
nomist monist

nudity	untidy
octave	avocet
onager	orange
oocyte	coyote
opaled	pedalo
option	potion
orange	onager
ordain	inroad
ordeal	loader
ordeal	reload
ovular	valour
oyster	storey
packer	repack
padder	draped
paging	gaping
paired	repaid
pamper	mapper
panter	arpent
papery	prepay
papery	yapper
parcel	carpel
parcel	placer
parent	arpent
parent	entrap
Parian	pirana
parley	pearly
parley	player
parley	replay
parrot	raptor
Parsee	serape
parser	rasper
parser	sparer
parted	depart
parted	petard
parter	prater
parure	uprear
passer	repass
passer	sparse
pastel	staple
paster	repast
pastil	spital
patent	patten
pathos	potash
patina	taipan
patrol	portal
patten	patent
pawner	enwrap
pearly	parley
pebbly	plebby
pedalo	opaled
pelmet	temple
perish	reship
petard	depart
petard	parted
phased	shaped
phrase	seraph
phrase	shaper
phrase	sherpa
piecer	pierce
piecer	recipe
pierce	piecer
pierce	recipe
pineal	alpine
pirana	Parian
pistol	spoilt
placer	carpel
placer	parcel
plaint	pliant
planer	replan
planet	platen
platen	planet
player	parley
pleach	chapel
please	asleep
plebby	pebbly
pliant	plaint
polyps	sloppy
poodle	looped
portal	patrol
porter	report
poseur	uprose
poster	repost
potash	pathos
potion	option
pouter	troupe
praise	aspire
prater	parter
prepay	papery
primes	simper
primus	purism
puisne	supine
pulper	purple
pulper	repulp
punish	unship
purdah	hard-up
purism	primus
purple	pulper
purple	repulp
quoter	roquet
quoter	torque
rabies	braise
racing	arcing
racing	caring
racoon	corona
raddle	ladder
raffia	affair
raggle	gargle
raggle	lagger
raiser	sierra
ramble	ambler
ramble	marble
rancho	anchor
ranged	garden
ranger	garner
ranked	darken
ranked	narked
ranter	errant
rapier	repair
rapped	dapper
raptor	parrot
rascal	lascar
rasher	sharer
rasper	parser
rasper	sparer
ratite	attire
rattan	tartan
rattle	latter
reader	reread
realia	aerial
reason	senora
rebate	beater
reboil	boiler
rebuff	buffer
recall	caller
recall	cellar
recant	canter
recast	caster
recede	decree
recent	centre
recipe	piecer
recipe	pierce
recite	tierce
reckon	conker
red leg	gelder
red leg	ledger
redraw	drawer
redraw	reward
redraw	warder
redraw	warred
redtop	deport

re-echo	cohere
re-echo	echoer
refill	filler
refine	enfire
reflow	flower
refoot	footer
reform	former
refuel	ferule
regain	gainer
regime	émigré
regina	gainer
region	ignore
regive	grieve
regnal	angler
rehear	hearer
relaid	derail
relive	revile
reload	loader
reload	ordeal
remain	marine
remark	marker
remind	minder
remote	meteor
rennet	tenner
rental	antler
rental	learnt
repack	packer
repaid	paired
repair	rapier
repass	passer
repass	sparse
repast	paster
repeal	leaper
replan	planer
replay	parley
report	porter
repost	poster
repulp	pulper
repulp	purple
reread	reader
resale	leaser
resale	sealer
reseat	Easter
reseat	teaser
resell	seller
reship	perish
reside	desire
resign	signer
resign	singer
resist	sister
resort	roster
resort	storer
result	lustre
result	rustle
result	sutler
retain	retina
retina	retain
retort	rotter
return	turner
revile	relive
reward	drawer
reward	redraw
reward	warder
ribald	bridal
ribbed	dibber
rictus	rustic
ridged	girded
rigged	digger
rimmed	dimmer
ringer	erring
ripped	dipper
risqué	squire
robing	boring
rocker	corker
rootle	looter
roquet	quoter
roster	resort
rotter	retort
rotund	untrod
rubble	lubber
ruffed	duffer
rugged	grudge
rumble	lumber
runway	unwary
rusted	duster
rustic	rictus
rustle	lustre
rustle	result
sachet	chaste
sacral	lascar
saliva	salvia
salter	laster
salvia	saliva
sapele	asleep
sarong	groans
sateen	senate
satrap	Sparta
saucer	causer
sawing	aswing
scathe	chaste
scythe	chesty
sea bed	debase
sealer	leaser
sealer	resale
séance	encase
search	chaser
seared	erased
seated	sedate
sector	corset
seller	resell
senate	sateen
senora	reason
serape	Parsee
seraph	phrase
server	verser
sestet	tsetse
sewing	swinge
shamer	masher
shaped	phased
shaper	phrase
shaper	sherpa
sharer	rasher
sherpa	phrase
sherpa	shaper
sienna	insane
sierra	raiser
siesta	tassie
sifter	strife
signer	resign
signet	ingest
silent	enlist
simper	primes
singed	design
singer	resign
sister	resist
slated	desalt
slater	laster
sleuth	hustle
slight	lights
sloppy	polyps
smirch	chrism
smiter	mister
snivel	livens
source	course
spacer	escarp
sparer	parser
sparer	rasper
sparse	passer
sparse	repass
Sparta	satrap

spinet	instep
spital	pastil
spoilt	pistol
sprite	esprit
squire	risqué
stager	greats
stance	ascent
staple	pastel
starer	arrest
stasis	assist
statue	astute
stifle	itself
storer	resort
storey	oyster
strafe	afters
strafe	faster
strait	artist
strata	astart
stream	master
stride	driest
strife	sifter
stripe	esprit
sublet	bustle
subtle	bustle
sunlit	insult
supine	puisne
sutler	lustre
sutler	result
swinge	sewing
tablet	battle
tailed	detail
tailed	dilate
taipan	patina
talent	latent
tannic	tin can
tantra	tartan
tartan	rattan
tartan	tantra
tassie	siesta
tauten	attune
tea set	estate
tea urn	nature
teaser	Easter
teaser	reseat
temple	pelmet
tenner	rennet
tented	netted
tenure	neuter
tenure	tureen
termly	myrtle
thawer	wreath
thesis	tithes
thread	dearth
thread	hatred
threat	hatter
throne	hornet
tierce	recite
tilter	litter
tin can	tannic
tinner	intern
tinsel	enlist
titfer	fitter
tither	hitter
tithes	thesis
toiler	loiter
torque	quoter
touchy	couthy
tracer	carter
trance	canter
travel	varlet
trepan	arpent
trepan	entrap
triage	gaiter
trifle	filter
trifle	lifter
triode	editor
tripod	torpid
troupe	pouter
tsetse	sestet
tureen	neuter
tureen	tenure
umlaut	mutual
umpire	impure
unable	nebula
unbias	Anubis
unfelt	fluent
unfelt	netful
ungird	during
united	untied
unreal	neural
unship	punish
untidy	nudity
untied	united
untile	lutein
untrod	rotund
unwary	runway
uprear	parure
uprose	poseur
vacate	caveat
valour	ovular
varlet	travel
vector	covert
veiled	levied
veined	endive
velour	louvre
verily	livery
verser	server
vilely	lively
voided	devoid
volley	lovely
waddle	dawdle
wander	warden
waning	awning
warble	bawler
warden	wander
warder	drawer
warder	redraw
warder	reward
warred	drawer
warred	redraw
washer	hawser
welkin	winkle
whinge	hewing
widely	dewily
wieldy	dewily
winkle	welkin
wither	writhe
wolfer	flower
wonder	downer
wreath	thawer
writhe	wither
yapper	papery
yarrow	arrowy

7

abreact	bearcat
abreact	cabaret
abridge	brigade
accurse	accuser
accuser	accurse
actinon	contain
actress	recasts
actress	casters
adapter	readapt
admirer	married
aerosol	roseola
ageless	sea legs
ailment	aliment
aimless	seismal
aliment	ailment
allergy	gallery
allergy	largely
allergy	regally
all over	overall
alyssum	asylums
amender	meander
amender	reamend
amenity	anytime
amentia	animate
anapest	peasant
animate	amentia
annelid	lindane
annoyed	anodyne
anodyne	annoyed
antigen	gentian
antique	quinate
anytime	amenity
aplenty	penalty
apricot	parotic
aptness	patness
arbiter	rarebit
article	recital
artisan	tsarina
artiste	striate
assuage	sausage
astride	disrate
astride	staired
asylums	alyssum
athirst	rattish
atingle	gelatin
atlases	sea salt
auction	caution
avarice	caviare
avenger	engrave
babbler	blabber
back set	setback
banshee	has-been
basinet	bestain
battler	blatter
bearded	breaded
bedroom	boredom
beldame	bemedal
bemedal	beldame
berried	briered
bespake	bespeak
bespeak	bespake
bestain	basinet
biltong	bolting
bipedal	piebald
bipolar	parboil
bizarre	brazier
blabber	babbler
blaster	stabler
blather	halbert
blatter	battler
blinder	brindle
blister	bristle
bloomer	rebloom
blotted	bottled
blotter	bottler
blowfly	flyblow
bluster	bustler
bolster	lobster
bolting	biltong
bondage	dogbane
boredom	bedroom
bottled	blotted
bottler	blotter
boulder	doubler
bounder	rebound
brawler	warbler
brazier	bizarre
breaded	bearded
breathe	herb tea
briered	berried
brigade	abridge
brindle	blinder
bristle	blister
builder	rebuild
built-in	inbuilt
bustler	bluster
cabaret	abreact
cackler	clacker
cackler	crackle
calorie	cariole
calorie	loricae
cameral	caramel
capsule	lace-ups
caramel	cameral
cargoes	corsage
cariole	calorie
cariole	loricae
cartoon	coranto
carving	craving
cassock	Cossack
casters	actress
caterer	retrace
caterer	terrace
caution	auction
caviare	avarice
certify	rectify
chained	echidna
chanter	tranche
chapter	patcher
chariot	haricot
charmer	marcher
chatter	ratchet
cheater	hectare
cheater	teacher
checker	recheck
cholera	chorale
chorale	cholera
chowder	cowherd
citadel	deltaic
citadel	dialect
citrine	inciter
citrine	neritic
clacker	crackle
claimer	miracle
claimer	reclaim
clasper	scalper
claypit	typical
climber	reclimb
clinker	crinkle
clipper	cripple
clobber	cobbler
coal pit	optical
coal pit	topical
cobbler	clobber
cocaine	oceanic
compile	polemic
conical	laconic
contain	actinon
contour	crouton

coranto	cartoon
corsage	cargoes
counsel	unclose
counter	recount
counter	trounce
couplet	octuple
cowherd	chowder
crackle	clacker
craving	carving
cremate	meercat
crinkle	clinker
cripple	clipper
crouton	contour
cruelty	cutlery
cutlery	cruelty
dangler	gnarled
darting	trading
dashing	shading
dealing	leading
decimal	declaim
decimal	medical
declaim	decimal
declaim	medical
defiant	fainted
defiler	fielder
defrost	frosted
delight	lighted
delimit	limited
deltaic	citadel
deltaic	dialect
density	destiny
deposit	posited
deprave	pervade
dervish	shrived
destiny	density
deviser	diverse
dialect	citadel
dialect	deltaic
dignity	tidying
disease	seaside
dishing	shindig
disrate	astride
diverse	deviser
dogbane	bondage
donator	tornado
dormant	mordant
doubler	boulder
doubter	obtrude
dowager	wordage
dragoon	gadroon
dustpan	upstand
earnest	eastern
earning	grannie
earthen	hearten
eastern	earnest
echidna	chained
editors	steroid
elision	lionise
emanate	manatee
enclave	valence
engrave	avenger
enraged	grandee
enraged	grenade
entrail	reliant
faience	fiancée
fainted	defiant
fangled	flanged
farming	framing
fastens	fatness
fatness	fastens
feeding	feigned
feigned	feeding
fiancée	faience
fielder	defiler
fighter	freight
flanged	fangled
Flemish	himself
flesher	herself
flowing	fowling
flowing	wolfing
flyblow	blowfly
fowling	flowing
framing	farming
freesia	sea fire
freight	fighter
fresher	refresh
fretful	truffle
frosted	defrost
funfair	ruffian
gadroon	dragoon
gallery	allergy
gallery	largely
garnish	sharing
gateman	magenta
gateman	magnate
gateway	getaway
gelatin	atingle
gentian	antigen
genuine	ingénue
getaway	gateway
girdled	griddle
glisten	singlet
gnarled	dangler
grandee	enraged
grandee	grenade
granite	ingrate
grannie	earning
gremlin	mingler
grenade	enraged
grenade	grandee
griddle	girdled
gunship	pushing
gunshot	shotgun
halbert	blather
haricot	chariot
has-been	banshee
haunter	unearth
hearten	earthen
hectare	cheater
hectare	teacher
heinous	in-house
herb tea	breathe
heroism	moreish
herself	flesher
himself	Flemish
hitting	tithing
holiday	hyaloid
hormone	moorhen
however	whoever
humidor	rhodium
hyaloid	holiday
ill-used	sullied
imposer	promise
inbuilt	built-in
incised	indices
inciter	citrine
indices	incised
infidel	infield
infield	infidel
ingénue	genuine
ingrate	granite
in-house	heinous
innings	sinning
instead	sainted
instead	stained
interim	termini
intrude	untired
intrude	untried
irately	reality
kinship	pinkish

kitchen	thicken
knitter	trinket
lace-ups	capsule
laconic	conical
largely	allergy
largely	gallery
largely	regally
lasting	salting
lattice	tactile
leading	dealing
lighted	delight
lighter	relight
limited	delimit
lindane	annelid
lionise	elision
lobster	bolster
loricae	calorie
loricae	cariole
magenta	gateman
magenta	magnate
magnate	gateman
magnate	magenta
magneto	megaton
magneto	montage
manatee	emanate
mantrap	rampant
marcher	charmer
marital	martial
married	admirer
martial	marital
maunder	unarmed
meander	amender
medical	decimal
medical	declaim
meercat	cremate
meeting	teeming
megaton	magneto
migrate	ragtime
minaret	raiment
mingler	gremlin
miracle	claimer
miracle	reclaim
misdeal	mislead
mislead	misdeal
monacid	nomadic
monadic	nomadic
montage	magneto
moorhen	hormone
mordant	dormant
moreish	heroism
moronic	omicron
moulder	remould
mounter	remount
mundane	unnamed
nastily	saintly
neither	therein
nomadic	monacid
nomadic	monadic
nor'east	senator
nor'east	treason
nowhere	whereon
nuclear	unclear
nuptial	unplait
observe	obverse
observe	verbose
obtrude	doubter
obtrude	redoubt
obverse	observe
obverse	verbose
oceanic	cocaine
octuple	couplet
oeuvres	overuse
omicron	moronic
opposer	propose
optical	coal pit
optical	topical
outbred	redoubt
outside	tedious
overall	all over
overuse	oeuvres
parboil	bipolar
parodic	picador
parotic	apricot
parsing	rasping
parsing	sparing
parsley	sparely
patcher	chapter
patness	aptness
peasant	anapest
penalty	aplenty
percept	precept
perlite	reptile
persist	stripes
pertain	repaint
pervade	deprave
phraser	sharper
picador	parodic
pickler	prickle
piebald	bipedal
pinkish	kinship
planter	replant
plaster	psalter
plaster	stapler
platter	prattle
pleaser	relapse
pointer	protein
polemic	compile
posited	deposit
posited	topside
prattle	platter
precept	percept
predate	red tape
predate	tapered
prelims	simpler
premier	reprime
prepare	repaper
present	serpent
presume	supreme
prickle	pickler
printer	reprint
promise	imposer
propose	opposer
protein	pointer
psalter	plaster
puritan	uptrain
pursuer	usurper
pushing	gunship
quester	request
quinate	antique
ragtime	migrate
raiment	minaret
rampant	mantrap
rarebit	arbiter
rasping	parsing
rasping	sparing
ratchet	chatter
rattish	athirst
realist	saltier
realist	saltire
reality	irately
reamend	amender
rebloom	bloomer
rebound	bounder
rebuild	builder
recasts	actress
recheck	checker
recital	article
reclaim	claimer
reclaim	miracle
reclimb	climber

recount	trounce
rectify	certify
redoubt	obtrude
redoubt	outbred
red tape	predate
red tape	tapered
refresh	fresher
regally	allergy
regally	largely
relapse	pleaser
related	treadle
reliant	entrail
reliant	retinal
relight	lighter
remains	seminar
remould	moulder
remount	mounter
repaper	prepare
replant	planter
reprime	premier
reprint	printer
reprise	respire
reptile	perlite
request	quester
reredos	rose-red
rescued	seducer
rescuer	securer
reserve	reverse
resound	sounder
respect	spectre
respire	reprise
respray	sprayer
restart	starter
rest day	strayed
resting	stinger
restive	veriest
restyle	tersely
rethink	thinker
retinal	reliant
retinue	reunite
retiral	retrial
retiral	trailer
retired	retried
retrace	terrace
retrain	terrain
retrain	trainer
retread	treader
retrial	retiral
retrial	trailer
retried	retired
retsina	stainer
reunite	retinue
reverse	reserve
rhodium	humidor
rickets	sticker
roseate	tea rose
roseola	aerosol
rose-red	reredos
rousing	souring
routing	touring
rowdily	wordily
ruffian	funfair
sainted	instead
sainted	stained
saintly	nastily
saltier	saltire
salting	lasting
salting	slating
saltire	realist
saltire	saltier
Samoyed	someday
sausage	assuage
saviour	various
scalper	clasper
scarper	scraper
scraper	scarper
sea-blue	sueable
sea fire	freesia
sea fowl	sea-wolf
sea legs	ageless
sea salt	atlases
seaside	disease
seating	teasing
sea-wolf	sea fowl
securer	rescuer
seducer	rescued
seethed	sheeted
seismal	aimless
selenic	silence
seminar	remains
senator	nor'east
senator	treason
serpent	present
servant	versant
setback	backset
setline	tensile
setting	testing
settler	trestle
sharing	garnish
sharper	phraser
sheeted	seethed
shindig	dishing
shooter	soother
shotgun	gunshot
shrived	dervish
signora	soaring
silence	selenic
simpler	prelims
singlet	glisten
sinning	innings
skating	tasking
slander	snarled
slating	salting
smother	Thermos
snarled	slander
soaring	signora
someday	Samoyed
soother	shooter
sounder	resound
souring	rousing
sparely	parsley
sparing	parsing
sparing	rasping
spatter	tapster
spectre	respect
spitter	tipster
sprayer	respray
stabler	blaster
stained	instead
stained	sainted
stainer	retsina
staired	astride
stapler	plaster
stardom	tsardom
starlet	startle
starter	restart
startle	starlet
staying	Stygian
steriod	editors
steroid	storied
stewpot	two-step
sticker	rickets
stinger	resting
stirpes	stripes
strayed	rest day
striate	artiste
stripes	persist
stripes	stirpes
strowed	worsted
student	stunted

stunted student
Stygian staying
stylite testily
sueable sea-blue
sullied ill-used
suntrap unstrap
supreme presume
swelter wrestle
swither withers
tableau tabulae
tabulae tableau
tactile lattice
tapered predate
tapered red tape
tap shoe teashop
tartlet tattler
tasking skating
tattler tartlet
teacher cheater
teacher hectare
tea rose roseate
teashop tap shoe
teasing seating
tedious outside
teeming meeting
Templar trample
tensile setline
termini interim
terrace caterer
terrace retrace
terrain retrain
tersely restyle
testily stylite
testing setting
theatre thereat
thereat theatre
therein neither
Thermos smother
thicken kitchen
thinker rethink
thorned throned
throned thorned
tickler trickle
tidying dignity
tipster spitter
tithing hitting
topical coal pit
topical optical
topside posited
tornado donator
tortile triolet
touring routing
towline two-line
trade-in trained
trailer retiral
trailer retrial
trained trade-in
trainer retrain
trample Templar
tranche chanter
treader retread
treadle related
treason nor'east
treason senator
trestle settler
trestle sterlet
triblet brittle
tribune turbine
trickle tickler
trinket knitter
triolet tortile
trounce counter
trounce recount
truffle fretful
tsardom stardom
tsarina artisan
tumbler tumbrel
tumbrel tumbler
turbine tribune
two-line towline
two-step stewpot
typical claypit
unarmed maunder
unclear nuclear
unclose counsel
undergo ungored
unearth haunter
ungored undergo
unmated untamed
unnamed mundane
unnoted untoned
unplait nuptial
unstrap suntrap
untamed unmated
untired intrude
untired untried
untoned unnoted
untried intrude
untried untired
upstand dustpan
uptrain puritan
usurper pursuer
valence enclave
varices viscera
various saviour
verbose observe
verbose obverse
veriest restive
versant servant
viscera varices
wangler wrangle
warbler brawler
weather whate'er
weather whereat
weather wreathe
whate'er weather
whate'er whereat
whate'er wreathe
wheedle wheeled
wheeled wheedle
whereat weather
whereat whate'er
whereon nowhere
whoever however
wiggler wriggle
withers swither
wolfing flowing
wordage dowager
wordily rowdily
worsted strowed
wrangle wangler
wreathe weather
wreathe whate'er
wrestle swelter
wriggle wiggler

8

ablution	abutilon
absorber	reabsorb
abutilon	ablution
acaridan	Arcadian
acrostic	Socratic
actinide	indicate
actinoid	diatonic
actuator	autocrat
adjuster	readjust
adroitly	dilatory
adroitly	idolatry
affirmer	reaffirm
agnostic	coasting
agonised	diagnose
alarming	marginal
alienist	Latinise
alighted	gilthead
allotted	totalled
Alpinist	tailspin
altitude	latitude
amenable	nameable
amortise	atomiser
aneurism	Sumerian
animated	diamanté
antimony	antinomy
antinomy	antimony
appearer	reappear
arborist	rib roast
Arcadian	acaridan
arcading	cardigan
archaism	charisma
arrester	rearrest
arrogant	tarragon
arsenate	serenata
arsenide	nearside
arsenite	resinate
artesian	Erastian
ascender	reascend
asperate	separate
aspirant	partisan
aspirate	parasite
aspiring	praising
assenter	sarsenet
assertor	assorter
assorter	assertor
atomiser	amortise
atrocity	citatory
attender	nattered
attestor	testator
autocrat	actuator
babbling	blabbing
backfire	fireback
backward	drawback
balancer	barnacle
Balinese	baseline
balsamic	cabalism
baritone	obtainer
barnacle	balancer
baseline	Balinese
beam-ends	bedesman
beanpole	openable
beavered	bereaved
bedesman	beam-ends
bedmaker	embarked
beetroot	boot tree
bereaved	beavered
biocidal	diabolic
blabbing	babbling
blasting	stabling
bleating	tangible
blessing	glibness
bogeyman	money bag
boneless	noblesse
bookcase	casebook
bookwork	workbook
bootjack	jackboot
boot tree	beetroot
bordello	doorbell
botanies	obeisant
brawling	warbling
breadnut	turbaned
cabalism	balsamic
canonist	sanction
capstone	opencast
capsular	scapular
cardigan	arcading
carolled	collared
casebook	bookcase
casually	causally
cat's tail	statical
causally	casually
cavitied	vaticide
cedar nut	underact
centroid	doctrine
ceramist	matrices
chainlet	ethnical
charisma	archaism
chenille	Hellenic
chlorate	trochlea
choirman	harmonic
citatory	atrocity
clanging	glancing
clerkess	reckless
coasting	agnostic
coiffeur	coiffure
coiffure	coiffeur
collapse	escallop
collared	carolled
colonise	eclosion
comedian	daemonic
comedian	mid-ocean
compiler	complier
complier	compiler
conflate	falconet
conveyer	reconvey
corselet	selector
costumed	customed
costumer	customer
coursing	scouring
creation	reaction
creative	reactive
creditor	director
Croatian	raincoat
customed	costumed
daemonic	comedian
daemonic	mid-ocean
dairyman	main yard
danseuse	Sudanese
date palm	palmated
deadener	endeared
deadlock	deckload
deceiver	received
decimate	medicate
deckload	deadlock
decrepit	depicter
deferrer	referred
deflower	flowered
deforest	forested
deformer	reformed
deifying	edifying
denarius	unraised
depicter	decrepit
depilate	pileated
designer	redesign
designer	resigned
despiser	disperse
dethrone	threnode
dewiness	wideness
diabolic	biocidal

diagnose agonised
diamanté animated
diatonic actinoid
dilatory adroitly
dilatory idolatry
director creditor
discreet discrete
discrete discreet
dishevel she-devil
disperse despiser
disunite nudities
doctrine centroid
dog's nose goodness
doorbell bordello
dormancy mordancy
downturn turn down
drawback backward
drugging grudging
dungaree underage
dungaree ungeared
duodenal unloaded
eclosion colonise
edifying deifying
eelgrass largesse
embarked bedmaker
empathic emphatic
emphasis misshape
emphatic empathic
endeared deadener
enduring unringed
enervate venerate
entirety eternity
entrepot tent rope
Erastian artesian
escallop collapse
espalier pearlies
eternity entirety
ethicist theistic
ethnical chainlet
ethology theology
Etruscan recusant
evilness vileness
expander re-expand
exporter re-export
fairness sanserif
falconet conflate
felinity finitely
fiendish finished
finished fiendish
finitely felinity

fireback backfire
flatiron inflator
flirting trifling
flounder unfolder
flowered deflower
flushing lungfish
forested deforest
forester fosterer
foretell toll-free
formalin informal
formulae fumarole
fosterer forester
fumarole formulae
fundable unfabled
galenite gelatine
galenite legatine
gamester gas meter
gas meter gamester
gatherer regather
gelatine galenite
gelation legation
germinal maligner
germinal malinger
gilthead alighted
glancing clanging
glibness blessing
gnomonic oncoming
goodness dog's nose
gradient treading
grayling ragingly
grounded underdog
grudging drugging
half-note halftone
halftone half-note
handover overhand
hangover overhang
harmonic choirman
harp seal pearl ash
hassling slashing
hatchery thearchy
headrail railhead
hectorer torchère
Hellenic chenille
heptagon pathogen
hogmanay mahogany
horseman shoreman
housetop pothouse
hustling sunlight
hypnotic pythonic
hypnotic typhonic

idolatry adroitly
idolatry dilatory
importer reimport
indented intended
indenter intender
indicate actinide
inflamer rifleman
inflator flatiron
informal formalin
informer reinform
infringe refining
ingrowth throwing
insecure sinecure
inserted resident
inserter reinsert
integral triangle
intended indented
intender indenter
intercut tincture
intimacy minacity
isocline silicone
isotropy porosity
jackboot bootjack
labrador larboard
lameness maleness
lameness nameless
larboard Labrador
largesse eelgrass
laterite literate
Latinise alienist
latitude altitude
layering yearling
legatine galenite
legation gelation
licensed silenced
listener re-enlist
literate laterite
littoral tortilla
lungfish flushing
mahogany hogmanay
main yard dairyman
maleness lameness
maligner germinal
malinger germinal
manorial morainal
marbling rambling
marginal alarming
mateless meatless
material real-time
matrices ceramist

meatless	mateless
medicate	decimate
mid-ocean	comedian
mid-ocean	daemonic
minacity	intimacy
minutely	untimely
misshape	emphasis
money bag	bogeyman
morainal	manorial
mordancy	dormancy
mutilate	ultimate
nameable	amenable
name-drop	pomander
nameless	lameness
natively	venality
nattered	attender
nearside	arsenide
nepotist	stone pit
neurosis	resinous
nightcap	patching
noblesse	boneless
nonesuch	unchosen
noseless	soleness
notarial	rational
notarise	senorita
nudities	disunite
nuthatch	unthatch
obeisant	botanies
obtainer	baritone
Olympian	palimony
oncoming	gnomonic
opencast	capstone
organist	roasting
oriental	relation
ornately	Tyrolean
overhand	handover
overhang	hangover
pack mule	plum cake
palimony	Olympian
palleted	petalled
palmated	date palm
palmette	template
parasite	aspirate
parental	paternal
parmesan	spearman
parroted	predator
parroted	teardrop
particle	prelatic
partisan	aspirant
patching	nightcap
paternal	parental
paternal	prenatal
pathogen	heptagon
pearl ash	harp seal
pearlies	espalier
pear tree	repeater
perverse	preserve
pervious	previous
pervious	viperous
petalled	palleted
pileated	depilate
pomander	name-drop
porosity	isotropy
posingly	spongily
postural	pulsator
pothouse	housetop
praising	aspiring
precious	rice soup
predator	parroted
predator	teardrop
prelatic	particle
prenatal	paternal
preserve	perverse
previous	pervious
previous	viperous
priestly	spritely
primrose	promiser
promiser	primrose
pulsator	postural
pursuing	usurping
pythonic	hypnotic
pythonic	typhonic
quartile	requital
ragingly	grayling
railhead	headrail
raincoat	Croatian
rambling	marbling
rational	notarial
reabsorb	absorber
reaction	creation
reactive	creative
readiest	steadier
readjust	adjuster
reaffirm	affirmer
real-time	material
reappear	appearer
rearrest	arrester
reascend	ascender
reascent	sarcenet
recanter	recreant
received	deceiver
reckless	clerkess
reconvey	conveyer
recourse	resource
recreant	recanter
recusant	Etruscan
redesign	designer
redesign	resigned
re-enlist	listener
re-expand	expander
re-export	exporter
referent	rent-free
referent	tree fern
referred	deferrer
refining	infringe
reformed	deformer
regather	gatherer
reimport	importer
reinform	informer
reinform	reniform
reinsert	inserter
relation	oriental
reinform	informer
reniform	reinform
rent-free	referent
repartee	repeater
repeater	pear tree
repeater	repartee
requital	quartile
research	searcher
reserved	reversed
resident	inserted
resigned	designer
resigned	redesign
resinate	arsenite
resinous	neurosis
resistor	sorriest
resorter	restorer
resource	recourse
restorer	resorter
restrain	strainer
restring	stringer
retrench	trencher
reversal	slaverer
reversed	reserved
revolute	true love
rib roast	arborist
rice soup	precious
rifleman	inflamer
roadside	side road

roasting	organist
royalist	solitary
sainfoin	sinfonia
sallying	signally
sallying	slangily
samphire	seraphim
sanction	canonist
sandworm	swordman
sanserif	fairness
sarcenet	reascent
sarsenet	assenter
sauciest	suitcase
scapular	capsular
scouring	coursing
sea horse	seashore
searcher	research
seashore	sea horse
seconder	seed corn
seed corn	seconder
seething	sheeting
seizable	sizeable
selector	corselet
senorita	notarise
separate	asperate
seraphim	samphire
serenata	arsenate
she-devil	dishevel
sheeting	seething
shoreman	horseman
side road	roadside
signally	sallying
silenced	licensed
silently	tinselly
silicone	isocline
sinecure	insecure
sinfonia	sainfoin
sizeable	seizable
skirting	striking
slangily	sallying
slashing	hassling
slaverer	reversal
slowness	snowless
snowless	slowness
Socratic	acrostic
solecist	solstice
soleness	noseless
solitary	royalist
solstice	solecist
sorriest	resistor
sortable	storable

spawning	wingspan
spearman	parmesan
spongily	posingly
spritely	priestly
stabling	blasting
staminal	talisman
statable	tastable
statical	cat's tail
steadier	readiest
stickler	strickle
stilbene	tensible
stingray	straying
stone pit	nepotist
storable	sortable
strainer	restrain
straying	stingray
strickle	stickler
striking	skirting
stringer	restring
Sudanese	danseuse
suitcase	sauciest
Sumerian	aneurism
sunlight	hustling
sunshade	unsashed
swordman	sandworm
tailspin	Alpinist
talisman	staminal
tangible	bleating
tangoist	toasting
Tantrism	transmit
tarragon	arrogant
tastable	statable
teamwork	workmate
teardrop	parroted
teardrop	predator
tearless	tesseral
template	palmette
tensible	stilbene
tent rope	entrepot
terminal	tramline
tesseral	tearless
testator	attestor
thearchy	hatchery
theistic	ethicist
theology	ethology
thoracic	trochaic
threnode	dethrone
throwing	ingrowth
tincture	intercut
tinselly	silently

toasting	tangoist
toll-free	foretell
tonsured	unsorted
torchère	hectorer
totalled	allotted
tramline	terminal
transmit	Tantrism
treading	gradient
tree fern	referent
trencher	retrench
triangle	integral
tribunal	turbinal
trifling	flirting
trochaic	thoracic
trochlea	chlorate
true love	revolute
turbaned	breadnut
turbinal	tribunal
turn down	downturn
typhonic	hypnotic
typhonic	pythonic
Tyrolean	ornately
ultimate	mutilate
unburden	unburned
unburned	unburden
unchosen	nonesuch
undashed	unshaded
underact	cedar nut
underact	untraced
underage	dungaree
underage	ungeared
underarm	unmarred
underdog	grounded
unfabled	fundable
unfolder	flounder
ungeared	dungaree
ungeared	underage
unleased	unsealed
unloaded	duodenal
unmarred	underarm
unnetted	untented
unpaired	unrepaid
unraised	denarius
unrepaid	unpaired
unringed	enduring
unsashed	sunshade
unsealed	unleased
unshaded	undashed
unsorted	tonsured
unstated	untasted

untasted	**unstated**	**vaticide**	**cavitied**	**warbling**	**brawling**
untented	**unnetted**	**venality**	**natively**	**wideness**	**dewiness**
unthatch	**nuthatch**	**venerate**	**enervate**	**wingspan**	**spawning**
untimely	**minutely**	**vileness**	**evilness**	**workbook**	**bookwork**
untraced	**underact**	**viperous**	**pervious**	**workmate**	**teamwork**
usurping	**pursuing**	**viperous**	**previous**	**yearling**	**layering**

9

abhorrent	earthborn
aborigine	baignoire
about-turn	turnabout
accretion	anorectic
acetamide	emaciated
addresser	readdress
admissive	misadvise
admonitor	dominator
adulation	laudation
adulatory	laudatory
alienator	rationale
alignment	lamenting
alinement	lineament
allotting	totalling
anarchist	cantharis
anchorite	antechoir
angelical	galenical
angerless	largeness
angleworm	lawmonger
angriness	ranginess
anorectic	accretion
antechoir	anchorite
antenatal	Atlantean
antitrade	attainder
apartheid	hit parade
apivorous	oviparous
appointor	apportion
apportion	appointor
Argentine	tangerine
argentite	integrate
ascertain	Cartesian
ascertain	sectarian
ashlaring	Shangri-la
aspectual	capsulate
assaulter	saleratus
asyndetic	syndicate
asynergia	gainsayer
Atlantean	antenatal
attainder	antitrade
attention	tentation
attentive	tentative
autoclave	vacuolate
back green	greenback
baignoire	Aborigine
Balkanise	lake basin
banderole	bandoleer
bandoleer	banderole
bargepole	porbeagle
beech fern	free bench
board foot	footboard
boathouse	houseboat
bottle gas	gas bottle
brasserie	brassiere
brassiere	brasserie
breathily	heritably
briefless	fibreless
broadleaf	loaf bread
broadtail	tailboard
brush fire	furbisher
butternut	nut butter
bystander	stander-by
callosity	stoically
cane sugar	sugar cane
canopying	poignancy
cantharis	anarchist
cantilena	lancinate
capsulate	aspectual
carcinoma	macaronic
card punch	punch card
Cartesian	ascertain
Cartesian	sectarian
casebound	subdeacon
Castalian	satanical
catalogue	coagulate
catechism	schematic
cautioner	Cointreau
ceilinged	diligence
celandine	decennial
centurion	continuer
certified	rectified
certitude	rectitude
chartered	three-card
chest note	chest tone
chest tone	chest note
chondrite	threnodic
coagulate	catalogue
coastline	sectional
coat dress	dress coat
coeternal	tolerance
cognation	contagion
cognition	incognito
Cointreau	cautioner
colcothar	ochlocrat
colourman	monocular
comforter	recomfort
concavely	covalency
concentre	connecter
concentre	reconnect
confirmer	reconfirm

congested decongest
connecter concentre
contagion cognation
container crenation
continuer centurion
copartner procreant
corkiness rockiness
covalency concavely
creatable traceable
crenation container
crimeless merciless
curtilage graticule
damnatory mandatory
decennial celandine
decimally medically
decollate ocellated
decongest congested
deer fence deference
deference deer fence
deferment fermented
deliriant drain tile
deliverer redeliver
demanding maddening
demeanour enamoured
descender redescend
developer redevelop
diametric matricide
diligence ceilinged
dissenter tiredness
dominator admonitor
doomwatch matchwood
drain tile deliriant
dress coat coat dress
earthborn abhorrent
eglantine inelegant
emaciated ecetamide
enamoured demeanour
endearing engrained
endearing grenadine
engrained endearing
epidermal impleader
epistoler pistoleer
eroticism isometric
Esperanto personate
excepting expecting
expecting excepting
fashioner refashion
fermented deferment
fibreless briefless
firestorm reformist
firestorm restiform
flowering reflowing
footboard board foot
foundling unfolding
free bench beech fern
furbisher brush fire
furbisher refurbish
furnisher refurnish
gainsayer asynergia
ganglions sing-along
gas bottle bottle gas
gathering night-gear
gnostical nostalgic
grandiose organised
graticule curtilage
greenback back green
grenadine endearing
gustiness gutsiness
gutsiness gustiness
hawk-nosed shakedown
heartfree hereafter
heartsome horsemeat
hereafter heartfree
heritably breathily
hibernate inbreathe
horseless shoreless
horsemeat heartsome
horsetail isotheral
houseboat boathouse
housework workhouse
howsoever whosoever
hurtfully ruthfully
ichnolite Neolithic
ill-nature tellurian
impartial primatial
impleader epidermal
inbreathe hibernate
inclosure reclusion
incognito cognition
inelastic sciential
inelegant eglantine
instanter transient
insurable sublinear
insurgent unresting
integrate argentite
interlace reclinate
interplay painterly
interplay party line
intestate satinette
introduce reduction

inveigler	relieving
ironstone	serotonin
isometric	eroticism
isotheral	horsetail
itinerant	nitration
lake basin	Balkanise
lancinate	cantilena
larvicide	veridical
laudation	adulation
laudatory	adulatory
Levantine	valentine
limestone	milestone
lineament	alinement
lion-tamer	mentorial
loaf bread	broadleaf
loaminess	melanosis
lucrative	revictual
macaronic	carcinoma
macintosh	monachist
maddening	demanding
magnesite	magnetise
magnetise	magnesite
mandatory	damnatory
maritally	martially
martially	maritally
mastering	streaming
matchwood	doomwatch
matricide	diametric
mechanics	mischance
medically	decimally
melanosis	loaminess
mentorial	lion-tamer
merciless	crimeless
metronome	monometer
metronome	monotreme
milestone	limestone
misadvise	admissive
mischance	mechanics
miscredit	misdirect
misdirect	miscredit
missioner	remission
monachist	macintosh
monocracy	nomocracy
monocular	colourman
monograph	nomograph
monometer	metronome
monometer	monotreme
monotreme	metronome
monotreme	monometer
monotypic	toponymic

neogothic	theogonic
Neolithic	ichnolite
nephology	phenology
nephritic	phrenitic
nephritis	phrenitis
night-gear	gathering
nomocracy	monocracy
nomograph	monograph
nomograph	phonogram
nostalgic	gnostical
nut butter	butternut
obversely	verbosely
ocellated	decollate
ochlocrat	colcothar
open-armed	promenade
operating	orange-tip
optically	topically
optometer	potometer
orange-tip	operating
organised	grandiose
oviparous	apivorous
painterly	interplay
painterly	party line
palm sugar	sugar plum
paramedic	preadamic
party line	interplay
party line	painterly
patroness	transpose
penetrant	repentant
peptonise	pipestone
percaline	Periclean
Periclean	percaline
peristome	temporise
personate	Esperanto
phaseless	shapeless
phenology	nephology
phonogram	nomograph
photogram	tomograph
phrenitic	nephritic
phrenitis	nephritis
piecework	workpiece
pipestone	peptonise
pistoleer	epistoler
platinous	pulsation
poignancy	canopying
polyester	proselyte
polythene	telephony
porbeagle	bargepole
porterage	reportage
posterior	repositor

potometer	optometer
pottering	repotting
preadamic	paramedic
prelusion	repulsion
prelusive	pulverise
prelusive	repulsive
prescient	reinspect
primatial	impartial
procedure	reproduce
procreant	copartner
promenade	open-armed
proselyte	polyester
Proustian	supinator
publisher	republish
pulsation	platinous
pulverise	prelusive
pulverise	repulsive
punch card	card punch
punctilio	unpolitic
quickener	requicken
racialist	satirical
rain cloud	uncordial
rascality	satyrical
raspingly	sparingly
reclinate	interlace
reclusion	inclosure
recomfort	comforter
reconfirm	confirmer
reconnect	concentre
rectified	certified
rectitude	certitude
redeliver	deliverer
redescend	descender
redevelop	developer
reduction	introduce
refashion	fashioner
reflowing	flowering
reformist	firestorm
refurbish	furbisher
refurnish	furnisher
reinspect	prescient
relieving	inveigler
remission	missioner
repentant	penetrant
reportage	porterage
repositor	posterior
repotting	pottering
reproduce	procedure
republish	publisher
repulsion	prelusion
repulsive	prelusive
repulsive	pulverise
requicken	quickener
rescuable	securable
resection	secretion
restiform	firestorm
revictual	lucrative
revisable	verbalise
rockiness	corkiness
roisterer	terrorise
rowdiness	wordiness
runcinate	uncertain
ruthfully	hurtfully
saltiness	slatiness
saltiness	stainless
saltpetre	steel trap
Samaritan	Sarmatian
Sarmatian	Samaritan
satanical	Castalian
satinette	intestate
satirical	racialist
satyrical	rascality
scatterer	streetcar
schematic	catechism
sciential	inelastic
secretion	resection
sectarian	ascertain
sectarian	Cartesian
sectional	coastline
securable	rescuable
semilunar	unrealism
serotonin	ironstone
shakedown	hawk-nosed
Shangri-la	ashlaring
shapeless	phaseless
shoreless	horseless
sing-along	ganglions
slatiness	saltiness
slatiness	stainless
sparingly	raspingly
stainless	saltiness
stainless	slatiness
stander-by	bystander
stateless	tasteless
statement	testament
stateside	steadiest
steadiest	stateside
steel trap	saltpetre
stoically	callosity
strapping	trappings

streaming	mastering
streetcar	scatterer
subdeacon	casebound
sublinear	insurable
sugar cane	cane sugar
sugar plum	palm sugar
sundering	undersign
supinator	Proustian
syndicate	asyndetic
tailboard	broadtail
tasteless	stateless
telephony	polythene
tellurian	ill-nature
temporise	peristome
tentation	attention
tentative	attentive
terminals	tramlines
terrorise	roisterer
testament	statement
theogonic	neogothic
three card	chartered
threnodic	chondrite
tiredness	dissenter
tolerance	coeternal
tomograph	photogram
tonsorial	torsional
top drawer	water drop
topically	optically
toponymic	monotypic
torsional	tonsorial
tow-headed	two-headed
traceable	creatable
tramlines	terminals
transient	instanter
transpose	patroness
trappings	strapping
two-headed	tow-headed
unaltered	unrelated
unbrushed	underbush
uncertain	runcinate
uncordial	rain cloud
underbush	unbrushed
undernote	undertone
underside	undesired
undersign	sundering
undertime	unmerited
undertone	undernote
undesired	underside
unfolding	foundling
unmerited	undertime
unpolitic	punctilio
unrealism	semilunar
unrelated	unaltered
unresting	insurgent
vacuolate	autoclave
valentine	Levantine
verbalise	revisable
verbosely	obversely
veridical	larvicide
water drop	top drawer
water flea	water leaf
water flow	waterfowl
waterfowl	water flow
water leaf	water flea
whosoever	howsoever
wordiness	rowdiness
workhouse	housework
workpiece	piecework

10

activation	cavitation
admonition	domination
admonitive	dominative
aerography	areography
alarmingly	marginally
allegorist	legislator
amphoteric	metaphoric
anaglyptic	play-acting
anapaestic	sea captain
anemograph	phanerogam
antagonist	stagnation
antimonial	lamination
antisepsis	inspissate
antiseptic	psittacine
arctophile	cartophile
areography	aerography
ascription	crispation
aspiringly	praisingly
Australian	saturnalia
cantilever	trivalence
carotenoid	coordinate
carotenoid	decoration
cartophile	arctophile
categories	categorise
categorise	categories
cavitation	activation
centesimal	lemniscate
certifying	rectifying
coal porter	percolator
cognominal	gnomonical
columnated	documental
compressed	decompress
concertino	concretion
conclusive	vice-consul
concretion	concertino
contravene	covenanter
coordinate	carotenoid
coordinate	decoration
cormophyte	ectomorphy
covenanter	contravene
creatively	reactively
creativity	reactivity
credential	interlaced
crescented	decrescent
crispation	ascription
crispbread	spider-crab
dealership	leadership
decompress	compressed
decoration	carotenoid
decoration	coordinate
decrescent	crescented
denominate	emendation
denotation	detonation
deposition	positioned
deprecator	tape-record
detonation	denotation
diamantine	inanimated
discoverer	rediscover
discreetly	discretely
discretely	discreetly
dominative	admonitive
earthiness	heartiness
ectomorphy	cormophyte
egocentric	geocentric
emendation	denominate
enduringly	underlying
enervation	veneration
ethologist	theologist
eviscerate	tea service
excitation	intoxicate
filtration	flirtation
fimicolous	music folio
fingerless	fringeless
first night	first thing
first thing	first night
flirtation	filtration
fringeless	fingerless
gadolinite	gelatinoid
gelatinoid	gadolinite
generation	renegation
geocentric	egocentric
glycosuria	graciously
gnomonical	cognominal
graciously	glycosuria
graveolent	lovat green
headmaster	headstream
headstream	headmaster
heartiness	earthiness
houseplant	sulphonate
iconolater	relocation
impenitent	pentimenti
impression	permission
impressive	permissive
inactivate	vaticinate
inanimated	diamantine
indiscreet	indiscrete
indiscreet	iridescent
indiscrete	indiscreet
indiscrete	iridescent

infarction	infraction
infraction	infarction
inspissate	antisepsis
interlaced	credential
intoxicate	excitation
iridectomy	mediocrity
iridescent	indiscreet
iridescent	indiscrete
iridosmium	osmiridium
lamination	antimonial
leadership	dealership
legislator	allegorist
lemniscate	centesimal
lentamente	tenemental
lovat green	graveolent
lustreless	resultless
marginally	alarmingly
mastership	shipmaster
masterwork	workmaster
maturation	natatorium
maundering	undreaming
mediocrity	iridectomy
metaphoric	amphoteric
monography	nomography
music folio	fimicolous
mythologer	thermology
natatorium	maturation
nectareous	raconteuse
negativism	time-saving
neoplastic	pleonastic
nephrology	phrenology
nomography	monography
nostologic	oncologist
notarially	rationally
olivaceous	violaceous
oncologist	nostologic
open stitch	pitch stone
osmiridium	iridosmium
parentally	paternally
paternally	parentally
peculation	unpoetical
penetrance	repentance
pentimenti	impenitent
perceptive	preceptive
percolator	coal porter
percussion	supersonic
permission	impression
permissive	impressive
persistent	prettiness
perviously	previously

perviously	viperously
pesticidal	septicidal
petitioner	repetition
phanerogam	anemograph
phrenology	nephrology
pitch stone	open stitch
plasticise	specialist
play-acting	anaglyptic
pleonastic	neoplastic
positional	spoliation
positioned	deposition
praetorian	reparation
praisingly	aspiringly
preceptive	perceptive
prettiness	persistent
previously	perviously
psittacine	antiseptic
raconteuse	nectareous
reactively	creatively
reactivity	creativity
rectifying	certifying
rediscover	discoverer
regelation	relegation
relativise	revitalise
relegation	regelation
relocation	iconolater
renegation	generation
reparation	praetorian
repentance	penetrance
repetition	petitioner
reservedly	reversedly
resultless	lustreless
reversedly	reservedly
sarmentose	sea monster
saturnalia	Australian
sea captain	anapaestic
sea monster	sarmentose
septicidal	pesticidal
shipmaster	mastership
sleetiness	steeliness
specialist	plasticise
spider-crab	crispbread
spirometer	temporiser
spoliation	positional
stagnation	antagonist
steeliness	sleetiness
sulphonate	houseplant
supersonic	percussion
tape-record	deprecator
tea service	eviscerate

technocrat	trench coat
temporiser	spirometer
tenemental	lentamente
theologist	ethologist
thermology	mythologer
time-saving	negativism
trench coat	technocrat
trichinous	unhistoric
trivalence	cantilever
underbrush	undershrub
underlying	enduringly
undernoted	undertoned
undershrub	underbrush
undertoned	undernoted
undreaming	maundering
unforested	unfostered
unfostered	unforested
unhistoric	trichinous
unmastered	unstreamed
unpoetical	peculation
unreserved	unreversed
unreversed	unreserved
unstreamed	unmastered
vaticinate	inactivate
veneration	enervation
vice-consul	conclusive
violaceous	olivaceous
viperously	perviously
workmaster	masterwork

11

antipyretic	pertinacity
armour plate	plate armour
attentively	tentatively
board school	school board
bottle glass	glass bottle
bottle green	greenbottle
broadcaster	rebroadcast
catechismal	schematical
certifiable	rectifiable
colonialist	oscillation
conditioner	recondition
conservable	conversable
conservancy	conversancy
considerate	desecration
constructer	reconstruct
consumerist	misconstrue
conversable	conservable
conversancy	conservancy
cosmetician	encomiastic
creationism	miscreation
creationism	romanticise
creationist	reactionist
deification	edification
desecration	considerate
determinant	detrainment
detrainment	determinant
edification	deification
encomiastic	cosmetician
entablature	untreatable
enumeration	mountaineer
establisher	re-establish
ethological	theological
examination	exanimation
exanimation	examination
festination	infestation
festination	sinfonietta
glass bottle	bottle glass
graphologic	logographic
greenbottle	bottle green
haptotropic	protopathic
histrionics	trichinosis
immortalise	memorialist
importunate	permutation
impressible	permissible
infestation	festination
inoculatory	locutionary
insectology	Scientology
inseminator	nitrosamine
internality	itinerantly
interpreter	reinterpret
itinerantly	internality
locutionary	inoculatory
logographic	graphologic
memorialist	immortalise
misconstrue	consumerist
miscreation	creationism
misrelation	orientalism
monological	nomological
mountaineer	enumeration
necessarian	renaissance
neotropical	percolation
nephologist	phenologist
nerve ending	never-ending
never-ending	nerve ending
nitrosamine	inseminator
nomological	monological
orchestrate	sacher torte
orientalism	misrelation
oscillation	colonialist
paramedical	preadamical
partitioner	repartition
partnership	transhipper
percolation	neotropical
peripatetic	precipitate
permissible	impressible
pertinacity	antipyretic
petrography	typographer
phenologist	nephologist
plate armour	armour plate
poenologist	stool pigeon
polarimetry	temporarily
preadamical	paramedical
precipitate	peripatetic
probationer	reprobation
protopathic	haptotropic
reactionist	creationist
rebroadcast	broadcaster
recondition	conditioner
reconstruct	constructer
rectifiable	certificable
re-establish	establisher
reinterpret	interpreter
renaissance	necessarian
repartition	partitioner
respectless	sceptreless
romanticise	creationism
sacher torte	orchestrate
sceptreless	respectless
schematical	catechismal

school board	board school
Scientology	insectology
serpiginous	spinigerous
sinfonietta	festination
spinigerous	serpiginous
springhouse	surgeonship
stalagmitic	stigmatical
stigmatical	stalagmitic
stool pigeon	poenologist
surgeonship	springhouse
temporarily	polarimetry
tentatively	attentively
tetrasporic	triceratops
theological	ethological
transhipper	partnership
triceratops	tetrasporic
trichinosis	histrionics
typographer	petrography
uncertified	unrectified
undiscerned	unrescinded
unrectified	uncertified
unrescinded	undiscerned
untreatable	entablature

12

abolitionism	mobilisation
assimilation	Islamisation
behaviourism	misbehaviour
Cartesianism	sectarianism
commissioner	recommission
conservation	conversation
conversation	conservation
countercharm	countermarch
countermarch	countercharm
court-martial	matriculator
creativeness	reactiveness
delicateness	delicatessen
delicatessen	delicateness
demagnetiser	disagreement
disagreement	demagnetiser
discreetness	discreteness
discreteness	discreetness
indiscreetly	indiscretely
indiscreetly	iridescently
indiscretely	indiscreetly
iridescently	indiscreetly
Islamisation	assimilation
manslaughter	slaughterman
matriculator	court-martial
microcephaly	pyrochemical
misbehaviour	behaviourism
mobilisation	abolitionism
performative	preformative
perviousness	previousness
preformative	performative
previousness	perviousness
pyrochemical	microcephaly
recommission	commissioner
sectarianism	Cartesianism
slaughterman	manslaughter
spermatozoic	zoospermatic
visitational	vitalisation
vitalisation	visitational
zoospermatic	spermatozoic